Z1

MYSTICISM
SACRED AND PROFANE

IN MEMORIAM

H. F. BISHOP

MYSTICISM

SACRED AND PROFANE

An Inquiry into some Varieties of Praeternatural Experience

R. C. ZAEHNER

OXFORD UNIVERSITY PRESS
LONDON OXFORD NEW YORK

OXFORD UNIVERSITY PRESS

Oxford London New York
Glasgow Toronto Melbourne Wellington
Cape Town Salisbury Ibadan Nairobi Lusaka Addis Ababa
Bombay Calcutta Madras Karachi Lahore Dacca
Kuala Lumpur Hong Kong Tokyo

First published by the Clarendon Press, 1957

First issued as an Oxford University Press paperback, 1961

This reprint, 1969

PRINTED IN THE UNITED STATES OF AMERICA

PREFACE

'Now from my own unforgettable experience I know well that there is a state in which the bonds of the personal nature of life seem to have fallen away from us and we experience an undivided unity. But I do not know—what the soul willingly imagines and indeed is bound to imagine (mine too once did it)—that in this I had attained to a union with the primal being or the godhead. . . . Nevertheless, in the honest and sober account of the responsible understanding this unity is nothing but the unity of this soul of mine, whose "ground" I have reached, so much so, . . . that my spirit has no choice but to understand it as the groundless. But the basic unity of my own soul is certainly beyond the reach of all the multiplicity it has hitherto received from life, though not in the least beyond individuation, or the multiplicity of all the souls in the world of which it is one—existing but once, single, unique, irreducible, this creaturely one: one of the human souls and not the "soul of the All"; a defined and particular being and not "Being"; the creaturely basic unity of a creature, bound to God as in the instant before release the creature is to the *creator spiritus*, not bound to God as the creature to the *creator spiritus* in the moment of release.'[1]

In these few words Martin Buber presents the problem which this book, presumptuously perhaps, attempts to solve—the proper relationship between the monist's felt conviction that soul and God are one thing on the one hand and what Buber calls the direct confrontation of 'I' and 'Thou' on the other.

Throughout this work I have tried, so far as is possible in any investigation the subject-matter of which lies beyond reason, to adhere to the maxim of the great Muslim mystic, Ghazālī,—a maxim, indeed, which he himself is forever violating,—that 'reason is God's scale on earth'. I have attempted to distinguish between what seem to be radically different types of mystical experience and to relate them to one another. If, in the process, I have been forced to disagree violently with the conclusions of eminent writers, it is only because the over-simplification of the very complex problem of praeternatural and mystical experience seems to me to destroy, rather than to broaden, the basis of religion.

Because I disagree so profoundly with the conclusions reached by Mr. Aldous Huxley in his *Doors of Perception*, my thanks to him for giving me

[1] Martin Buber, *Between Man and Man* (E.T.), Routledge and Kegan Paul, 1947, pp. 24–25.

CONTENTS

INTRODUCTION

It should be said at the outset that this book owes its genesis to Mr. Aldous Huxley. Had *The Doors of Perception* never been published, it is extremely doubtful whether the present author would have been rash enough to enter the field of comparative mysticism. Mr. Huxley left us no choice. For however much we may be disposed to make allowances for enthusiastic exaggeration in Mr. Huxley's account of his experiences when under the influence of mescalin, we cannot escape the fact that there underlies Mr. Huxley's attitude to praeternatural experiences a conviction that they must all be basically the same and that what he experienced under mescalin can therefore be related to the highest concepts of religion which the mystic claims to realize at least in part. The Beatific Vision, *Sac-cid-ānanda*, the Dharma-Body of the Buddha, these tremendous words all became 'as evident as Euclid'[1] to Mr. Huxley when under the influence of the drug.

In *The Doors of Perception* Mr. Huxley seemed to assume that praeternatural experiences, conveniently described by the all-embracing term 'mysticism', must all be the same in essence, no matter whether they be the result of intensive ascetic training, of a prolonged course of Yoga techniques, or simply of the taking of drugs. In making these assumptions, of course, Mr. Huxley was doing nothing new. We have been told *ad nauseam* that mysticism is the highest expression of religion and that it appears in all ages and in all places in a more or less identical form, often in a religious milieu that would seem to be the reverse of propitious. This view has recently been reaffirmed by Professor A. J. Arberry who writes: 'It has become a platitude to observe that mysticism is essentially one and the same, whatever may be the religion professed by the individual mystic: a constant and unvarying phenomenon of the universal yearning of the human spirit for personal communion with God.'[2] Similarly Dr. Enid Starkie, in discussing Rimbaud's ecstasies, writes: 'In his experience of God Rimbaud reached, without orthodox beliefs, the stage which mystics seek to attain, where there is no longer possibility for belief or disbelief, for doubt or for reflection, but only pure sensation, ecstasy and union with the Almighty.'[3] And again we are told: 'In *Les Illuminations* is found expressed, as nowhere else—except perhaps in the poems of Saint John of the Cross—man's

[1] *The Doors of Perception*, London, Chatto and Windus, 1954, p. 13.

[2] A. J. Arberry, *Sūfism, An Account of the Mystics of Islam*, London, George Allen and Unwin, 1950, p. 11.

[3] Enid Starkie, *Arthur Rimbaud*, revised ed., London, Hamish Hamilton, 1947, p. 422.

eternal longing for spiritual satisfaction and beauty.'[1] In actual fact there would appear to be nothing in Rimbaud to show that the poet ever considered that he had attained to union with God or that his ecstasies had any direct connexion with Him: nor does Dr. Starkie see fit to develop the interesting comparison with St. John of the Cross, nor is any attempt made to establish its validity. This is only too typical of the great majority of writers on mysticism. It will suffice to quote only one more example, for, as Professor Arberry has rightly remarked, 'it has become a platitude'.

The platitude was earlier enunciated by Professor Arberry's eminent predecessor in the Chair of Arabic at the University of Cambridge, E. G. Browne, the great Orientalist who did so much to familiarize the English-speaking world with Persian civilization. On the subject of mysticism he wrote: 'There is hardly any soil, be it ever so barren, where it [mysticism] will not strike root; hardly any creed, however stern, however formal, round which it will not twine itself. It is, indeed, the eternal cry of the human soul for rest; the insatiable longing of a being wherein infinite ideals are fettered and cramped by a miserable actuality; and so long as man is less than an angel and more than a beast, this cry will not for a moment fail to make itself heard. Wonderfully uniform, too, is its tenor: in all ages, in all countries, in all creeds, whether it come from the Brahmin sage, the Greek philosopher, the Persian poet, or the Christian quietist, it is in essence an enunciation more or less clear, more or less eloquent, of the aspiration of the soul to cease altogether from self, and to be at one with God.'[2]

Always it is *assumed* that mysticism is 'essentially one and the same': rarely is any attempt made to substantiate the assumption, and rarely are the equally significant differences analysed. We are greatly indebted to Mr. Huxley in that, in *The Doors of Perception*, he has carried the popular view to its logical conclusion: for since he has proved that praeternatural experience of the most vivid kind can be acquired by the taking of drugs and since the state of the drug-taker's consciousness bears at least a superficial resemblance to that of the religious mystic in that time and space appear to be transcended, must it not follow that this experience is 'one and the same' as that of the generally accredited mystics?

Huxley could, and should, have gone farther. Mescalin is clinically used to produce artificially a state akin to schizophrenia, more specifically the manic phase of the manic-depressive psychosis. It must therefore follow, if we accept the fatal 'platitude', that not only can 'mystical' experience be

[1] Enid Starkie, *Arthur Rimbaud*, p. 423.

[2] E. G. Browne, *A Year amongst the Persians*, London, Adam and Charles Black, 3rd ed., 1950, p. 136. Quoted by Margaret Smith, *An Introduction to the History of Mysticism*, London, Macmillan, 1930, p. 2.

obtained artificially by the taking of drugs, it is also naturally present in the manic.[1] It must then follow that the vision of God of the mystical saint is 'one and the same' as the hallucination of the lunatic. There would appear to be no way out, unless the original 'platitudinous' premiss is unsound; and it is into the validity of this premiss that this book will enquire. The book, however, makes no claim to be anything more than a preliminary investigation into what is believed to be a fairly typical cross-section of mystical writing selected from both European and Asiatic sources. In dealing with a category of experience where words have little meaning, it would be hopeless to expect to make out a watertight case to which we could affix that most satisfying of all formulae, 'Q.E.D.' We can, however, compare the various mystical traditions and show, without allowing ourselves to draw unwarrantable conclusions from seemingly similar phenomena in parallel traditions, what is the distinctive characteristic of each. Further we should be able to decide how far these different experiences are classifiable into types. Since *The Doors of Perception* is the occasion of this book, we must also draw on the experience of people who have taken drugs, of manic-depressives, and of those people,—not so rare as is sometimes thought,—who have been visited by similar experiences without any outside stimulus being applied and independently of any religious belief. In the present work we shall have occasion to consider the 'mystical' experiences of Richard Jefferies, Proust, and Rimbaud, all of whom help to throw light upon this vexatious problem. In addition we shall have to consider the all-important mystical tradition developed in India, as well as that of the Christians and of the Muslim mystics or Ṣūfīs. Relying on what the mystics say themselves we will try to ascertain what each different 'school' of mysticism considered to be its goal and to see whether they do, in fact, agree either with each other or with the 'free-lance' mystics of the type of Jefferies and Rimbaud.

I am aware that it may not be considered legitimate to compare the experiences or the theories of specifically religious mystics with the experiences of Mr. Huxley while under the influence of mescalin on the ground that Mr. Huxley's experiences do not tally with those of other mescalin-takers. It will be pointed out that while the incredible heightening and deepening of the sense of colour seems to be experienced by a large majority of those who take the drug, the sense of rising superior to the 'ego' and of what Huxley calls being a 'not-self', is not typical. To avoid the impression that I suppose Huxley's experience to be typical of what occurs to all who have taken mescalin, it has seemed worthwhile to attach as an appendix two separate accounts written by independent 'patients', both of which have

[1] For some details of an actual case of mania see Chapter V.

appeared in the British press;[1] and for the sake of further comparison I have also appended an account of my own experiences with the drug.[2]

My interest, however, has been not so much in the drug itself, for, as a producer of what is usually called a 'natural mystical experience' it seems to be less effective than nitrous oxide or even hashish; it has been rather in what Mr. Huxley experienced himself and in his assumption that his experience had religious significance. Baudelaire, of course, made similar experiments with hashish and has recorded them, with very different conclusions, in his *Le Poème du Haschisch*. William James, too, took nitrous oxide and, like Huxley, was so shattered by his experience that he found that, in his assessment of reality, he could not possibly disregard the profound transformation of consciousness which it produced. Thus, though Huxley's experiences may not be typical of the effects of mescalin, they are sufficiently similar to those of James with nitrous oxide and Baudelaire's with hashish to be of considerable interest. Moreover, they are so strikingly similar to the experience of nature mystics as to be of value in any general discussion of the subject.

It may seem surprising that the present author who has hitherto specialized on Zoroastrianism, the one major religion that never developed mysticism of any kind, should think fit to enter the field of comparative mysticism, —a field into which angels might well fear to tread. There are three reasons which have decided the present writer to take this step. First it seemed to him that in *The Doors of Perception* Mr. Huxley had thrown down a challenge which no one with any religious convictions at all could afford to neglect, for Huxley did not seem to be merely advocating yet another variety of religious 'indifferentism'; he was, simply by equating his own drug-induced experiences with the experiences of those who approach their goal by more conventional means, striking at the roots of all religion that makes any claim to be taken seriously. Such a challenge, when thrown down by an author of Mr. Huxley's standing and popularity, could not, with decency, be allowed to remain unanswered.

Thanks to the good offices of mescalin Mr. Huxley claims to have known 'contemplation at its height' though, he is modest enough to add, 'not yet in its fullness'.[3] On reading these prodigious syllables it occurred to me that I too must have known 'contemplation at its height' and that I was, on these grounds alone, qualified to offer some mild criticism of Mr. Huxley's more extravagant conclusions. At the impressionable age of twenty I was in fact the subject of a 'mystical' experience which combined all the principal

[1] See Appendix A.
[2] See Appendix B.
[3] *The Doors of Perception*, p. 31.

traits described in *The Doors of Perception*. When Mr. Huxley speaks of being a 'Not-self in the Not-self which was a chair',[1] I know that, as far as the normal, rational consciousness is concerned, he is talking horrid gibberish, but I equally know that I have myself experienced precisely this and the joy experienced as a result of this uncontrollable and inexplicable expansion of the personality is not to be brushed aside as mere illusion. On the contrary: beside it the ordinary world of sense experience seems pathetically unreal. This occurred to me when I was still an undergraduate and *before* I became interested in Oriental languages: it came wholly unheralded and no stimulants of any kind were involved. I know now that it was a case of what is usually called a 'natural mystical experience' which may occur to anyone, whatever his religious faith or lack of it and whatever moral, immoral, or amoral life he may be leading at the time. It is perhaps not without relevance to mention that at the time of this unsolicited experience, apart from a profound dislike of conventional Christianity, I had no religious beliefs of any kind, nor did it occur to me that the experience was in any sense religious. The experience was there in its own right, and I had no desire to explain it.

The wheel has now turned full circle, and I find myself once again a Christian, having entered the Roman Catholic Church in 1946. This is a fact that the reader should know since it would be disingenuous to pretend that, however painstakingly an author may strive after complete objectivity, he will actually achieve it if he has any views of his own at all. It is then only fair to the reader to inform him in advance what the author's religious views actually are although, in at least nine cases out of ten, the intelligent reader should be able to detect the bias (for bias there is bound to be) at an early stage. Thus the experience I had at the age of twenty which was so very similar to that of Mr. Huxley after he had taken mescalin, presents a very real problem to me since it has to be set beside an experience of what I can only assure Mr. Huxley is of another order,—the attempt, however bungling and inept, to make contact with God through what Catholics call the normal channels of grace. Thus whereas I think a cursory reading of the Christian mystics has given me some idea of what is meant by the Beatific Vision, namely, the direct experience of God in His unutterable holiness, I find myself unable to agree with Mr. Huxley that the natural mystical experience has any connexion with that Vision; for in my experience at least,—and, to judge from *The Doors of Perception*, in Mr. Huxley's too,—the adjective 'holy' would appear to be singularly out of place in that context. Thus it seemed to me that on grounds of experience alone I might

[1] Ibid., p. 16.

be able to make some slight contribution to this knotty problem of comparative mysticism which has received a certain unwelcome notoriety since Mr. Huxley published his findings.

The third reason which has impelled me to write on this subject is the fact that as an orientalist I am equipped, to some extent, to deal with the oriental sources in some of the original languages. With Persian I can claim complete familiarity, though in Arabic and Sanskrit I am very much less at home. Of Pali, Tibetan, and Chinese I am most unfortunately innocent; and it is for this reason that, if we have made only passing references to Buddhism, it is not because we underrate the enormous importance of that religion, but simply that we lack the linguistic equipment to do it justice.

The reader may, perhaps, wonder why so much space has been devoted to Rimbaud in this book. There are two reasons for this: first Rimbaud's experiences and his later reactions to them are of prime importance to any study of the varieties of mysticism. Secondly Rimbaud was, in fact, the innocent cause of the experience I have mentioned above and which seems to have been evoked by perhaps the third reading of his *Saison en Enfer*. More precisely it occurred when I reached the stupendous poem 'O saisons, ô châteaux' which, as Dr. Starkie rightly points out, 'is an almost hysterical expression of superhuman ecstasy'.[1] In this she is absolutely right; and in one case at least it gave rise to an answering ecstasy in the reader. Thus to return to Rimbaud after twenty-two years, but this time to call him as principal witness for the prosecution against the thesis that all praeternatural experience is 'essentially' and always 'one and the same', is for me an unmixed pleasure. I can only regret that I have fallen so far short of doing him the justice he deserves. For me he still remains an incomparably great poet; but now he seems even more remarkable for his unflinching honesty in denouncing his own praeternatural experiences as nothing but a lie. I have not followed him in this, but have tried, most inadequately I know, to offer some explanation for an experience which, as Rimbaud himself saw, is akin to madness. That it is quite distinct from the transports of Christian saints as well as from the 'self-realization' and 'self-isolation' of the Hindus, seems to have been sensed by Rimbaud and is one of the things which I hope to show.

In the analysis we have attempted of the various types of mysticism we have necessarily had to draw on Indian religion, and particularly on the Vedānta, as well as on the Christian and Muslim mystics. Here again we have been forced to the conclusion that the extreme non-dualist Vedānta of Śankara and his followers represents something different from the main

[1] *Arthur Rimbaud*, p. 203.

stream of Christian mysticism as well as from the 'orthodox' Muslim mysticism as formulated by Abū'l-Qāsim al-Junayd and Ghazālī. The realization of this difference (if difference it be) is, from the academic point of view, of considerable interest; for until we are tolerably clear in our own minds what the varieties of mystical experience actually are, it would be futile to attempt to sift out the various strands which meet in Ṣūfism and which make it so puzzling a phenomenon. In the course of reading the oriental sources of the latter half of this book I at least have become convinced that purely monistic ideas in Ṣūfism can be traced back to Abū Yazīd of Bisṭām who appears to have been directly influenced by the Vedānta.[1] From this it follows that purely monistic ideas in Abū Yazīd or in his successors cannot be treated as independent evidence for the ubiquity of the monist philosophy which is sometimes held to underlie all the manifestations of mysticism.

In this book I have attempted, with what success only the reader can judge, to separate out the varying phenomena that appear in praeternatural and 'mystical' experiences. In order to do this I have drawn widely on the ideas of Professor C. G. Jung which seem to illumine much in Oriental religion that had previously been obscure. If I have anywhere seriously misrepresented him,—and this is very possible owing to the 'fluid' nature of his subject-matter,—I must ask forgiveness and would be grateful for correction.

In seeking to draw what seems to me to be a valid as well as an obvious distinction between monism on the one hand and theistic mysticism on the other, it should not be thought that I am in any way seeking to belittle the enormous Indian contribution to religious thought. It is true that absolute monism is characteristic of much in Indian thought though it is by no means peculiar to it. It is, however, only one of many streams that go to make up the complex mosaic that is Hinduism. It is moreover a doctrine that has been vigorously disputed in India itself from the time of Rāmānuja onwards; and though it may, with plausibility, claim to represent the authentic teaching of the Upaniṣads, it is plainly at variance with the main teachings of the Bhagavad-Gītā; for both monism and monotheism are strongly represented in Indian religion. Thus when I argue that the monist completely misunderstands the position of the theistic mystic rather than vice versa, so far from arguing against Hinduism as such, I am arguing against a trend in *all* religions which is in most cases an aberration from the doctrine generally held by the main body of mystical thought within a given religious tradition. That it is actually impossible to hold monistic and

[1] See below, pp. 161 ff.

theistic opinions as both being *absolutely* true at one and the same time, seems obvious. In this book I have sought to show how the monists fit theism into their scheme of things, and I have also expounded the opposite point of view. I admit to having stressed the latter because I happen to believe that it is true. The reader must judge for himself on the evidence presented.

CHAPTER I

MESCALIN

IN our first two chapters we will be primarily considering the experiences described by Mr. Huxley in *The Doors of Perception* together with the morals he draws from them and the practical steps he considers might be taken for humanity to avail itself of the 'religion surrogate' which, he thinks, mescalin might supply.

It is, of course, a well-known fact that certain drugs,—and among them one may include alcohol,—modify the normal human consciousness and produce what can literally be called ec-static states,—states in which the human ego has the impression that it escapes from itself and 'stands outside' itself. Indian hemp and hashish have long been used in the East to produce precisely such a result. In the West, however, it has never been taken for granted that such states are necessarily associated with religion, while in the East there have always been sober spirits who regarded such 'religion surrogates' with the gravest suspicion. Mr. Huxley appears to have no such scruples, for he implies unmistakably that what he experienced after taking mescalin was explicable in terms of 'contemplation at its height'.[1] Herein lies the importance of Mr. Huxley's thesis; praeternatural experience, whether produced by drugs or not, is equated with specifically religious experience.

It is essential that we should pause for a moment here in order to consider what Mr. Huxley and his friends understand by religion since, obviously, it is not what Protestant Christians normally understand by the word. Since the Reformation we have drifted more and more into a position of identifying religion with an ethical code; and despite the regrettable fact that the vast majority of those who call themselves Christians make no noticeable effort to follow the more difficult and paradoxical commandments of Our Lord, we like to think that the Christian ethic is the most perfect that has ever been propounded and that therefore Christianity is the best and for that reason the true religion. On turning to the Oriental religions, however, we will see that in India and in those parts of Asia which have come under Indian influence, such views are far from finding universal acceptance. Religion for the Hindu or Buddhist, we are repeatedly told by the modern advocates of those two religions, is primarily a matter of experience: it is not so much something to be believed as something to be

[1] Cf. *The Doors of Perception*, p. 31.

lived. By belief or faith, too, they do not understand a series of propositions to which assent is given, they mean not only faith in, but contact with, a supra-sensory world. Religion, for them, is not so much something to be professed as something to be experienced; and such experience, in its higher forms, is usually called mystical experience. In the West the reverse is true: we have lost contact with the supra-sensory world to such an extent that many of us have come to deny it altogether. This is no place to discuss the effects of such an attitude on society at large; here we must be content to note that it leaves many people profoundly dissatisfied, and of these Mr. Huxley would seem to be a notable example.

Huxley's life would appear to have been one consistent revolt against the values of the nineteenth century, purely material values to which an air of respectability was lent by a decadent Christianity. Later in life he came into contact with the religious classics of the East which obviously attracted him strongly. Moreover, the fact that the Eastern religions had a far cleaner record than had Christianity in the matter of persecution, was one more point in their favour; and in the life of reflection, concentration, and contemplation which they stressed far more exclusively than did the Christian Church Huxley thought that at last he had found a sure anchor and lasting resting-place. Struck by the similarity of thought and expression he found in all the mystics, whether Hindu, Buddhist, Taoist, Muslim, or Christian, he reached the comforting conclusion that behind the great religions of the world there could be discerned a *philosophia perennis*, an ultimate truth of which all religions were only partial expressions. It was, however, the great religious systems of India which principally attracted him, particularly the Vedānta and those forms of Buddhism which are most akin to it. Just why this should have been it is difficult to say. Prima facie one might have supposed that his attraction was based on some profound religious experience and that this experience was felt to be in accordance with what the Vedānta taught rather than with what the Christian mystics described. Huxley himself, however, gives the lie to this in *The Doors of Perception*, for he there admits that until, thanks to mescalin, he came to know 'contemplation at its height', he had not in fact had any experience to which the word 'mystical' could possibly be applied. We can only conclude that Huxley's 'conversion' to a Vedāntin way of life was due to little more than a total rejection of everything that modern civilization stands for and to a deep-seated aversion to historical Christianity which, though it may not have directly given birth to the modern world, at least condoned it when it was born.

So it was that when Huxley came to take mescalin, his mind was permeated through and through with Vedāntin and Mahāyāna Buddhist ideas, and these ideas seem actually to have affected his vision; for as Baudelaire has rightly observed, drugs can add nothing new to a man, but can only raise to a higher power what is already within him.[1]

Despite its diminutive compass *The Doors of Perception* is an important book, for it presents a challenge to all who are interested in religious experience; and the mere fact that mescalin does not always produce such satisfactory results does not invalidate the argument that even if there is only a 5 per cent. chance of beholding something that seems to approach the Beatific Vision, surely such a chance is worth taking. Further, Huxley's experiences under the influence of mescalin as recorded by himself are interesting from the point of view of what we may call 'clinical' religion. They provide a case-history parallel to those collected by William James in his *The Varieties of Religious Experience*, and as such they are of value. Secondly the book is important in that Huxley draws definite conclusions from his experience. Coming from so eminent an author these conclusions cannot decently be simply brushed aside. In our next chapter we will have occasion to examine some of these conclusions and to test the validity of the premisses on which they are based. In the present chapter we will do no more than give an account of Huxley's experiences while bearing in mind that other people have taken the drug and that their experiences, although they mainly agree in this, that normal sensation is enormously heightened and transformed, are by no means identical with Mr. Huxley's.[2]

About the drug itself, Mr. Huxley informs us that it is the active principle in a root called peyotl which West Indians of Mexico and the American South venerate as a deity much as the ancient Indians and Iranians worshipped the plant *soma* or *haoma* which appears to have grown in the Himalayas and which, to judge from the hymns addressed to it in the Rig-Veda, must have produced results not unlike those described by Mr. Huxley in *The Doors of Perception*. The advantage of mescalin over other intoxicants such as alcohol, hashish, and opium is that when 'administered in suitable doses, it changes the quality of consciousness more profoundly' than they, 'yet is less toxic than any other substance in the pharmacologist's repertory'.[3] In other words it equals or excels the most potent of the oriental drugs and has the additional advantage of having no disagreeable aftermath. Further, we are told, unlike tobacco, opium, and hashish, it does

[1] *Le Poème du Haschisch*, iii, in *Œuvres*, Bibliothèque de la Pléiade, Paris, Gallimard, 1954, p. 445.

[2] Cf. Appendix A, but contrast Appendix B.

[3] *The Doors of Perception*, p. 5.

not develop a craving, though if the experiences are as satisfying as they appear to be to the Mexican Indians, it is difficult to see why not.

In summarizing Mr. Huxley's experiences we will constantly be coming across technical terms borrowed from Oriental religion which will no doubt be familiar to Mr. Huxley's habitual readers but which may seem strange to those who have not followed his spiritual odyssey. These I shall endeavour to explain as they turn up or wherever seems appropriate. Even apart from the terminology, however, *The Doors of Perception* leaves one with a sense of confusion; for unless one happens to have had an experience similar to that described by Mr. Huxley, it is very difficult to understand what the intense excitement is due to. We shall have more to say about this later. For the moment we must confine ourselves to summarizing the evidence as presented by Huxley.

Huxley took his mescalin pill at eleven o'clock in the morning. It took half an hour to work, and continued to work for a total of about eight hours. Throughout the period normal perception was greatly heightened.

The patient was sitting in his study. In the room was a small glass vase containing three flowers, 'a full-blown Belle of Portugal rose, shell pink with a hint at every petal's base of a hotter, flamier hue; a large magenta and cream-coloured carnation; and, pale purple at the end of its broken stalk, the bold heraldic blossom of an iris'.[1] Earlier in the day he had been struck by the dissonance of the colours. However, half an hour after taking the drug such purely aesthetic criteria no longer held good. 'That was no longer the point. I was not looking now at an unusual flower arrangement. I was seeing what Adam had seen on the morning of his creation—the miracle, moment by moment, of naked existence.'

Obviously, then, Huxley was experiencing something very unusual indeed. 'Is it agreeable?' somebody asked. 'Neither agreeable nor disagreeable', he replied, 'it just *is*.'

We must now allow Huxley to speak for himself. Whether or not he would have used these words or words at all similar to them, had he not spent so much of his time reading in Hindu and Buddhist works, it is impossible to say with certainty; but when we compare the account of his experiences with those reproduced in the appendices, it seems unlikely. For the moment, however, let us confine ourselves to quoting Huxley verbatim:

'*Istigheit*—wasn't that the word Meister Eckhart liked to use? "Is-ness". The Being of Platonic philosophy—except that Plato seems to have made the enormous, the grotesque mistake of separating Being from becoming, and identifying

[1] *The Doors of Perception*, p. 11.

it with the mathematical abstraction of the Idea. He could never, poor fellow, have seen a bunch of flowers shining with their own inner light and all but quivering under the pressure of the significance with which they were charged; could never have perceived that what rose and iris and carnation so intensely signified was nothing more, and nothing less, than what they were—a transience that was yet eternal life, a perpetual perishing that was at the same time pure Being, a bundle of minute, unique particulars in which, by some unspeakable and yet self-evident paradox, was to be seen the divine source of all existence.

'I continued to look at the flowers, and in their living light I seemed to detect the qualitative equivalent of breathing—but of a breathing without returns to a starting-point, with no recurrent ebbs but only a repeated flow from beauty to heightened beauty, from deeper to ever deeper meaning. Words like Grace and Transfiguration came to my mind, and this of course was what, among other things, they stood for. My eyes travelled from the rose to the carnation, and from that feathery incandescence to the smooth scrolls of sentient amethyst which were the iris. The Beatific Vision, *Sat Chit Ananda*, Being-Awareness-Bliss—for the first time I understood, not on the verbal level, not by inchoate hints or at a distance, but precisely and completely what those prodigious syllables referred to. And then I remembered a passage I had read in one of Suzuki's essays. "What is the Dharma-Body of the Buddha?" [The Dharma-Body of the Buddha, Huxley is good enough to explain, "is another way of saying Mind, Suchness, the Void, the Godhead".] The question is asked in a Zen monastery by an earnest and bewildered novice. And with the prompt irrelevance of one of the Marx Brothers, the Master answers, "The hedge at the bottom of the garden." "And the man who realizes this truth," the novice dubiously enquires, "what, may I ask, is he?" [To which he receives the disconcerting reply,] "A golden-haired lion."

'It had been', Huxley goes on, 'when I read it, only a vaguely pregnant piece of nonsense. Now it was as clear as day, as evident as Euclid. Of course the Dharma-Body of the Buddha was the hedge at the bottom of the garden. At the same time, and no less obviously, it was these flowers, it was anything that I—or rather the blessed Not-I released for a moment from my throttling embrace—cared to look at. The books, for example, with which my study walls were lined. Like the flowers, they glowed, when I looked at them, with brighter colours, a profounder significance. Red books, like rubies; emerald books; books bound in white jade; books of agate, of aquamarine, of yellow topaz; lapis lazuli books whose colour was so intense, so intrinsically meaningful, that they seemed to be on the point of leaving the shelves to thrust themselves more insistently on my attention.'[1]

Leaving aside the theological issues involved in this vivid and surprising piece of descriptive writing, little more can be said of this particular experience except that, as is usual with mescalin-takers, Huxley's sense of colour was immensely heightened and natural objects seemed to be endowed with

[1] Ibid., pp. 12–13.

a reality and meaning they did not normally possess. All this seemed to correspond to the experiences of the Zen Buddhists (whose cryptic remarks thereby became 'as evident as Euclid') and therefore, as both Huxley and the investigator appear to have supposed, to mystical experiences in general. Now one of the commonplaces of practically every type of mystical experience is that time and space appear to be transcended: the mystic lives, as Meister Eckhart is particularly fond of pointing out, in an 'eternal now'. With this experience the investigator seems to have been familiar, for he goes on to ask, 'What about spatial relationships?'

This Huxley had some difficulty in answering. It was true that the perspective looked rather odd, and that the walls of the room no longer seemed to meet at right angles. But this wasn't the point. The point, we are told, was that 'spatial relationships had ceased to matter very much' and that the 'mind was perceiving the world in terms of other than spatial categories.' The mind was not perceiving in terms of space at all: it was perceiving in terms of intensity, 'of intensity of existence, profundity of significance, relationships within a pattern'. *Where* they were with relationship to Huxley or to each other was beside the point. This did not mean that the category of space had, in some miraculous way, been abolished, since Huxley was able to get up, walk quite normally, and judge distances correctly in the usual way. 'Space was still there' all right; 'but it had lost its predominance. The mind was primarily concerned, not with measures and locations, but with being and meaning.'

And so with time. On being asked what he thought about time Huxley disarmingly replied that there was plenty of it! This answer too was intended to convey the impression that time, as well as space, had become entirely irrelevant. 'My actual experience', he says, 'had been, was still, of an indefinite duration or alternatively of a perpetual present made up of one continually changing apocalypse.'

From the concepts of time and space Huxley's attention was diverted by the investigator to the furniture. At first he saw it as 'an intricate pattern of horizontals, uprights and diagonals—a pattern all the more interesting for not being interpreted in terms of spatial relationships'. In fact he saw it as a Cubist picture. This experience was, however, shortly to give way to something much more exciting. 'This purely aesthetic Cubist's-eye view gave place to what I can only describe as the sacramental vision of reality.' He was back to where he had been when he had been contemplating the flowers. 'Everything shone with the Inner Light, and was infinite in its significance. The legs, for example of that chair—how miraculous their tubularity, how supernatural their polished smoothness! I spent several minutes—or was it several centuries?—not merely gazing at those bamboo legs, but actually *being* them—or rather being myself in them; or, to be still more accurate (for "I" was not involved in the case, nor in a certain sense were "they") being my Not-self in the Not-self which was the chair.'[1]

The vocabulary used by Huxley in this astonishing passage is largely borrowed from the Vedānta and from Mahāyāna Buddhism. To the normal, rational mind his remarks make no sense whatever, and might therefore be dismissed as the illusions of a lunatic. But to anyone who has actually had a similar experience they mean a great deal; for these experiences which sound so ridiculous when transferred to the printed page, always leave one with an impression of greater reality than anything supplied by ordinary sense perception. Part of the difficulty is, I suppose, that language has no words with which to describe these prodigies. It has in fact no words with which to describe mystical experiences of any kind. Despite this fact the nature of the particular experience is at least *indicated* by the words used, and in order to distinguish one type of experience from another it will be necessary to distinguish between the types of vocabulary used. We shall have more to say on this subject in a later chapter.

At this point Huxley interrupts the narrative of his experiences to embark on a dissertation on what he calls Mind at Large. We shall return to this later, but for the moment it would seem more logical to confine ourselves to his actual experiences. Four or five hours later when, he alleges, the effects of the drug were beginning to wear off, he was taken to a drug-store. Here he picked up an art book and opened it at an illustration of Van Gogh's 'the Chair'. Oddly enough, this did not produce on him the same devastating effect that the furniture in his study had done, for, as he puts it, 'though incomparably more real than the chair of ordinary perception, the chair in this picture remained no more than an unusually expressive symbol of the fact'.[2] It was no more than a symbol though, as Huxley says, the chair Van Gogh had seen was obviously the same in essence as the chair he had himself so intimately experienced earlier in the morning. Seen in this perspective art was merely imitation (more or less successful) of reality apprehended in a state of heightened awareness similar to that artificially produced by mescalin and similar drugs.

The picture, therefore, was a disappointment, and Huxley's attention was distracted from Van Gogh's poor symbol to, of all things, the trousers draping his own crossed legs! 'Those folds in the trousers—what a labyrinth of endlessly significant complexity! And the texture of the grey flannel—how rich, how deeply, mysteriously sumptuous! And here they

[1] *The Doors of Perception*, pp. 15–16. [2] Ibid., p. 21.

were again in Botticelli's picture.' For, bored with the Van Gogh, he had turned to a 'Judith' of Botticelli and had once again experienced in her 'pleated bodice and long wind-blown skirts' what he had previously experienced in the flowers and in the furniture in his own study. Why his grey flannel trousers or indeed Judith's bodice should have had this miraculous effect on him while the Van Gogh left him cold, Huxley was at a loss to explain. Yet so it was:

'more even than the chair, though less perhaps than those wholly supernatural flowers, the folds of my grey flannel trousers were charged with "is-ness".... Poring over Judith's skirts, . . . I knew that Botticelli—and not Botticelli alone, but many others too—had looked at draperies with the same transfigured and transfiguring eyes as had been mine that morning. They had seen the *Istigkeit*, the Allness and Infinity of folded cloth and had done their best to render it in paint or stone. Necessarily, of course, without success. For the glory and the wonder of pure existence belong to another order, beyond the power of even the highest art to express. But in Judith's skirt I could clearly see what, if I had been a painter of genius, I might have made of my old grey flannels. Not much, heaven knows, in comparison with the reality, but enough to delight generation after generation of beholders, enough to make them understand at least a little of the true significance of what, in our pathetic imbecility, we call "mere things" and disregard in favour of television.'[1]

While Huxley was still contemplating these ineffable realities, the investigator intervened and asked him about human relations. And here we come to a crucial and most important part of the experiment, as Huxley himself clearly saw. 'One ought to be able', he said, 'to see these trousers as infinitely important and human beings as still more infinitely important.' Unfortunately this was far from being the case: 'in practice it seemed impossible'. For as Huxley (somewhat obscurely) observes, 'Persons are selves and, in one respect at least, I was now a Not-self, simultaneously perceiving and being the Not-self of the things around me. To this newborn Not-self, the behaviour, the appearance, the very thought of the self it had momentarily ceased to be, and of other selves, its one-time fellows, seemed not indeed distasteful . . . but enormously irrelevant.'[2] So much so indeed that he deliberately avoided the eyes of those who were with him in the room. One of these was his wife, another a man whom he greatly respected and liked; but for Huxley at the time 'both belonged to the world from which, for the moment, mescalin had delivered me—the world of selves, of time, of moral judgments and utilitarian considerations, . . . of cocksureness, of over-valued words and idolatrously worshipped notions'.

[1] *The Doors of Perception*, pp. 25–26. [2] Ibid., pp. 26–27.

To this world which Huxley is not alone in disliking belonged both his wife and a great friend.

And this world seemed to be epitomized by a portrait by Cézanne which was now handed to Huxley. Presumably because it was a good portrait and therefore brought out what was most 'personal' in the sitter, Huxley could only laugh derisively. 'Who on earth does he think he is?', he indignantly exclaimed. How much better to return to the magical grey flannel of his trousers which were at least without pretensions, content to be themselves, 'sufficient', as he puts it, 'in their suchness, not acting a part, not trying, insanely, to go it alone, in isolation from the Dharma-Body, in Luciferian defiance of the grace of God'.[1]

Once again the investigator intervened, for it was plain that the patient had little or no use for his human companions. He was requested to shut his eyes, but the result was disappointing in the extreme; for all he saw was 'brightly coloured, constantly changing structures that seemed to be made of plastic or enamelled tin'.[2] It was cheap, and it was shoddy. 'It became very clear that this five-and-ten-cent ship . . . this suffocating interior of a dime-store ship was my own personal self; these gimcrack mobiles of tin and plastic were my personal contributions to the universe.' This, apparently, was abnormal; for usually the mescalin-taker sees not only the outside world transformed, but his own inner world as well. Whether Huxley was right in identifying his banal vision with a banal 'ego' is plainly not a matter on which anyone but himself can venture an opinion.

His experiences in listening to music are of little interest. Mozart's C-minor piano concerto left him cold and Alban Berg sounded 'rather funny'. ' "Isn't he sorry for himself!" I commented with derisive lack of sympathy. . . . "Who cares what his feelings are? Why can't he pay attention to something else?" ' 'I cite it for what it is worth,' Huxley goes on, 'and because that is how, in a state of pure contemplation, I reacted to the *Lyric Suite*.'[3]

'Pure contemplation.' Elsewhere he speaks of 'contemplation at its height', though 'not yet in its fullness'[4] apparently oblivious to the absurd arrogance that this reveals and which is, in fact, not uncommon in manic cases. This is the key mood of the whole book, for although on a later page Huxley's claims for his experience are less outrageous, he nevertheless seems to see nothing incongruous in claiming to have reached a state of 'pure contemplation' from which, by the grace of mescalin alone, he was in a position to pronounce Olympian judgements on works of art, seeing

[1] Ibid., p. 29.
[2] Ibid., p. 34.
[3] Ibid., p. 40.
[4] Ibid., p. 31.

them, presumably, from the higher standpoint of what he is pleased to call Mind at Large. This and similar unpleasing abnormalities, however, we will have to leave to a later chapter. We must once again return to the experiences themselves.

Huxley was next taken for a walk in the garden. Though he now felt that his experiencing faculty was somehow divorced from his body, he was nevertheless able to get up and walk in the ordinary way. 'It was odd', he says, 'to feel that "I" was not the same as these arms and legs "out there", as this wholly objective trunk and neck and even head.' In using the word 'I', it should be noted, Huxley seems to be reverting to a more normal use of language which is scarcely consonant with his previous remarks about being his 'Not-self in the Not-self that was the chair'. This momentary lapse, however, he corrects a few lines lower down where he says that in his present state 'awareness was not referred to an ego; it was, so to speak, on its own'.[1] In this respect Huxley seems to be following, rather unnecessarily, the irritating ambiguity of the Hindu classics in which the pronoun *ātman-* has to do duty both for the 'ego' and for what Huxley calls the 'Not-self'.

However that may be, Huxley's body managed to make its way into the garden. There it came upon a kind of pergola covered partly by a climbing rose-tree and partly by laths. 'The sun was shining and the shadows of the laths made a zebra-like pattern on the ground and across the seat and back of a garden chair, which was standing at this end of the pergola.' All this seems ordinary enough. Very far from it to the mescalin-taker.

'That chair,' exclaims Huxley in ecstasy, 'shall I ever forget it? Where the shadows fell on the canvas upholstery, stripes of a deep but glowing indigo alternated with stripes of an incandescence so intensely bright that it was hard to believe that they could be made of anything but blue fire. For what seemed an immensely long time I gazed without knowing, even wishing to know, what it was that confronted me. At any other time I would have seen a chair barred with alternate light and shade. To-day the percept had swallowed up the concept I was so completely absorbed in looking, so thunderstruck by what I actually saw, that I could not be aware of anything else. Garden furniture, laths, sunlight, shadow—these were no more than names and notions, mere verbalizations, for utilitarian or scientific purposes, after the event. The event was this succession of azure furnace-doors separated by gulfs of unfathomable gentian. It was inexpressibly wonderful, wonderful to the point, almost, of being terrifying. And suddenly I had an inkling of what it must feel like to be mad.'

This is the climax of Huxley's experiences with mescalin, as he himself

[1] *The Doors of Perception*, p. 41.

realized. Something had gone wrong: things were getting out of hand, and it seems natural that at this point of the book Huxley should suddenly remember that the clinical use of mescalin is to produce a modification of the consciousness akin to schizophrenia, a condition which he had referred to a few pages earlier as 'pure contemplation'. 'Confronted by a chair which looked like the Last Judgment', he goes on, 'or, to be more accurate, by a Last Judgment which, after a long time and with considerable difficulty, I recognized as a chair—I found myself all at once on the brink of panic. This, I suddenly felt, was going too far. Too far, even though the going was into intenser beauty, deeper significance.'[1] The fear, as he analysed it in retrospect, was of disintegrating under the pressure of a reality greater than the finite mind, as normally conditioned by its association with the body, could possibly bear. He compares it, not inappositely, to the shrinking of the soul from what the Tibetan *Book of the Dead* calls the 'Clear Light of the Void'. The symbol of the Last Judgment is also aptly chosen, for this too is a scene of panic:

> Quid sum miser tunc dicturus?
> Quem patronum rogaturus,
> Cum vix justus sit securus?[2]

There seems to be no escape, for 'once embarked upon the downward, the infernal road, one would never be able to stop. That,' says Huxley, 'now, was only too obvious'; and he thought he understood only too well what it must be like to be mad.

None too soon, as he says, was he steered away from the 'disquieting splendour' of the garden chair. The crisis, however, had passed, for he seems to have been able to contemplate with equanimity a group of red-hot pokers, flowers, one would have thought, which might almost have been created to play a sinister part in the Judgment scene.

This really closes the cycle of Mr. Huxley's experiences after taking mescalin. What he records after this is of little interest since the effects of the drug were already beginning to wear off. We have reproduced what seems to us to be the most characteristic and the most important parts of Mr. Huxley's experiences. Before proceeding to analyse their significance, if any, it will be useful to sum it all up in Mr. Huxley's own words.

'What happens to the majority of the few who have taken mescalin under supervision can be summarized as follows.

(1) The ability to remember and to "think straight" is little if at all reduced.

[1] Ibid., p. 43.

[2] 'What shall I, poor wretch, have to say for myself then? Whose help shall I ask when even the righteous will hardly be secure?' From the *Dies Irae* (Mass for All Souls Day).

(Listening to the recordings of my conversation under the influence of the drug, I cannot discover that I was then any stupider than I am at ordinary times.)

(2) Visual impressions are greatly intensified and the eye recovers some of the perceptual innocence of childhood, when the sensum was not immediately and automatically subordinated to the concept. Interest in space is diminished and interest in time falls almost to zero.

(3) Though the intellect remains unimpaired and though perception is enormously improved, the will suffers a profound change for the worse. The mescalin taker sees no reason for doing anything in particular and finds most of the causes for which, at ordinary times, he was prepared to act and suffer, profoundly uninteresting. He can't be bothered with them, for the good reason that he has better things to think about.

(4) These better things may be experienced (as I experienced them) "out there", or "in here", or in both worlds, the inner and the outer, simultaneously or successively. That they *are* better seems to be self-evident to all mescalin takers who come to the drug with a sound liver and an untroubled mind.'[1]

These characteristic reactions were all experienced by Huxley. One reaction, however, seems to have been peculiar to himself, and that is his experience not only of perceiving external objects, but also of *being* them. This phenomenon is common to many nature mystics and is not necessarily to be attributed to Huxley's familiarity with Hinduism, a religion which delights in emphasizing the identity of subject and object. We shall see the phenomenon occurring again and again in persons who had no knowledge of Eastern religions.

The real importance of Huxley's book, however, is that in it the author clearly makes the claim that what he experienced under the influence of mescalin is closely comparable to a genuine mystical experience. If he is right, then it can only be said that the conclusions to be drawn from this are alarming. One thing seems certain; and that is that both the mescalin-taker who does not happen to be of a sceptical turn of mind and the mystic seem utterly convinced that their respective experiences are incomparably more real than their ordinary sense experiences. Moral problems, it is clear, have no meaning once one obtains this 'higher' vision, and personal relationships too cease to have any importance. The mundane world is transcended, and therefore what goes on there, or should we say, what appears to be going on there, can have no possible interest.

For the moment we are not concerned with the truth or falseness of these theories. In the past mystics, even in India, have been few and far between, and praeternatural experiences of any sort have been well out of the reach

[1] *The Doors of Perception*, pp. 18–19, but see Appendices A and B. In actual fact it does not seem possible to make *any* generalization about the effects of mescalin on different subjects.

of the average man; and no visible harm has been done by the small band of ecstatics who had, or thought they had, transcended good and evil. The advent of mescalin in commercial quantities could change all that as Huxley sees, to my mind, all too clearly. The second part of his book treats with this question and draws the conclusion that mescalin is potentially a cure for the egocentricity of modern man just as religion was the recognized cure in the past. Obviously, if mescalin can produce the Beatific Vision here on earth,—a state that we had hitherto believed to have been the reward for much earnest striving after good,—the Christian emphasis on morality is not only all wrong but also a little naïve. Mescalin presents us not only with a social problem,—for how on earth could a society composed exclusively of ecstatics possibly be run?—but also with a theological problem of great magnitude. Mr. Huxley is to be thanked for having set the problem.

CHAPTER II

MESCALIN INTERPRETED

In our last chapter we did little more than summarize Mr. Huxley's experiences under the influence of mescalin. It now remains for us to summarize the conclusions he draws from his experiences.

One thing is certain; and that is that Huxley was taken off his guard by his experiment and almost overwhelmed by it: and the reason for this appears to be that it was the first time he had had an experience of this kind. This is somewhat surprising: for it seemed natural to suppose that an author who has gone through all the outward manifestations of a religious conversion and who, ever since he published *Time Must Have a Stop*, has written about little except his new philosophy of life, must have gone through some supremely meaningful experience which occasioned his conversion and which led him to adopt the esoteric philosophy he has since favoured. This philosophy, which he calls the *philosophia perennis*, claims to be based on the experience of religious mystics of all nations and all faiths. It seemed, then, fair to assume that Huxley had had some praeternatural experience which, by enabling him to discern in all mystics an absolute unity of idea behind a considerable diversity of expression, had convinced him that what the mystics were trying to describe was essentially the same experience, however different the expression of it might be. It came, then, as something of a shock to the present author at least when he read that 'until this morning I had known contemplation only in its humbler, its more ordinary forms—as discursive thinking; as a rapt absorption in poetry or painting or music; as a patient waiting upon those inspirations, without which even the prosiest writer cannot hope to accomplish anything; as occasional glimpses, in nature, of Wordsworth's "something far more deeply interfused"; as systematic silence leading, sometimes, to hints of an "obscure knowledge"'.[1]

Huxley's concept of 'contemplation' seems to have been extremely wide, extending indeed to all the activities of normally educated and cultivated persons. It would never have occurred to the great majority of these to refer to their appreciation, rapt or otherwise, of poetry, painting, or music as 'contemplation', a term which has come to have religious overtones. Nor does the word naturally occur to one in connexion with discursive think-

[1] *The Doors of Perception*, p. 31.

ing,—a process which is generally regarded as being the reverse of contemplation. It seems, then, fairly clear that, before taking mescalin, Huxley had only the haziest notion of what 'contemplation', used in a religious sense, meant. On taking mescalin, he was pitchforked into a realm of experience about which he had written volumes, but which he appears never to have lived. He would, then, appear to have been converted to the *philosophia perennis* on purely intellectual grounds. Because there were certain common characteristics between the mystics of all religions, Huxley came to the conclusion that these common characteristics must represent one metaphysical truth. He does not seem to have realized that even in the writings of the mystics there are divergences not only of approach, which can be attributed to the different religious backgrounds on which they are grafted, but of substance; and that any arbitrary selection from their writings can demonstrate nothing except the subjective views of an individual. What attracted him in the mystics,—using this word in a wide sense for the moment,—was that one and all they claimed to have transcended the empirical 'self' and broken into a new and larger sphere of perception. Mysticism, so interpreted, could include not only the classical monistic mysticism of India, but the strictly pantheistic and 'pamphysistic' outpourings of, for instance, Walt Whitman: it could include not only those solipsistic Muslim mystics who identified themselves with God, but also pure visionaries who did no such thing, but lived in a different private universe of their own in the manner of William Blake. The only common factor between these different types of mysticism is that, one and all, they provide release from the everyday, humdrum existence of subject-object relationship and of what, for lack of a better word, we must continue to call the individual 'ego'. That it was precisely such release from the 'ego' that Huxley was in search of, emerges clearly from the epilogue of *The Doors of Perception*.

'That humanity at large will ever be able to dispense with Artificial Paradises seems very unlikely. Most men and women lead lives at the worst so painful, at the best so monotonous, poor and limited that the urge to escape, the longing to transcend themselves if only for a few moments, is and has always been one of the principal appetities of the soul.'[1] This is rather a bold generalization; but it is a generalization that is typical of the intellectual and particularly of the intellectual who has been born and bred in an industrial civilization. The 'urge to escape' is, of course, the mainspring of Gnosticism, and particularly of Manichaeanism which described the body as a 'carrion and a prison', a satanic substance in which the

[1] Ibid., p. 49.

heavenly soul was unnaturally confined.[1] Mānī, like the founders of practically all heresies, as opposed to the founders of religions that last, was an intellectual; and his religion, in common with the other Gnostic sects, made an immediate appeal to the intelligentsia. His was a religion, exclusively, of escape and release: and in this he was catering for that 'urge to escape' which, according to Huxley, is and always has been one of the principal appetities of the human soul.

This is one point of view. Another has been expressed as follows: 'It is no good telling people that life is "pain" if they persist in regarding it as "fun", just as it is no good asking them if they are saved if they have not the slightest idea of what on earth they are supposed to be saved from, and would not in any case want to be saved from "it" even if they knew what "it" was supposed to be.'[2] This is a view which I expressed three years ago; and I still believe that it is more true than that expressed by Huxley, at least as far as this country is concerned, and that Huxley greatly exaggerates this urge to escape and longing to transcend ourselves. Fundamentally this is only true of the neurotic: it is not true of what William James called the 'healthy-minded', a class to which even now, I am optimistic enough to believe, the great majority of the human race still belongs.

Huxley's outlook is preconditioned by his intellectualism. In the best tradition of intellectuals he started off as a rebel. His rebellion seems to have gone through two stages: first he revolted against the established form of society and its conventions, and when this revolt only involved him in new and deeper bondages, he rose in revolt against and from himself. The second rebellion really developed out of the first; for, as Huxley himself says in *Ends and Means*,[3] although the revolt against the 'political and economic system' may have been justified on the ground that it was unjust, he and his friends had nothing to put in its place. It was a revolt into meaninglessness; and it is not in the nature of persons so markedly cerebral as Huxley to live in a vacuum for long. His revolt against sexual morality was equally unrewarding, as, in the long run, it always is. It is easy to become impatient with the Evangelical Counsel of chastity, and it is even easier to flout it and tread it under foot. Huxley, however, found that by so doing he enmeshed and entangled himself further in the material world which nauseated him and from which even then he longed to escape. He slowly came to realize, what all the great religions have always taught, that

[1] See H-C. Puech, *Le Manichéisme, Son Fondateur, Sa Doctrine*, Publications du Musée Guimet, Paris, 1949, pp. 82–83: cf. R. C. Zaehner, *Zurvan, A Zoroastrian Dilemma*, Oxford, 1955, p. 169.

[2] Id., *Foolishness to the Greeks*, Oxford, 1953, p. 14.

[3] In Collected Edition, London, Chatto and Windus, 1948, pp. 275 ff.

bondage to the passions is as harsh a slavery as that imposed by any political system. Or, to put it in a more practical way, in the long run it is less trouble to be chaste. Huxley's whole career then predisposed him to conversion to a type of religion that would provide him with a way of escape from a world into which he had found it so extraordinarily difficult to fit himself. He had, it seems, not been a happy man; and because he was both unhappy and introspective, he needed a philosophy or religion that would deliver him from both his unhappiness and himself. Being a highly intelligent man he realized that the unhappiness and the self were in some way connected; and this is the beginning of religion. What Huxley calls the 'poisonous fruits' of the philosophy of meaninglessness forced him to look beyond himself for something a little more satisfactory. Realizing that preoccupation with self is the source of all unhappiness, he turned towards the two religions which made this connexion most clear,—Hinduism and Buddhism. He was right to do this: for though the Gospels teach that one must die to oneself in order to live, this is only one of many Christian teachings, whereas both Hinduism and Buddhism regard the elimination of the ego as the *sine qua non* of 'liberation' or 'enlightenment' and never tire of saying so. Moreover, a return to Christianity would have been difficult for Huxley since he remembered it only as something dry, moralistic, and pharisaical, as part and parcel of an inhuman and mechanistic society against which he, like Kierkegaard before him, had revolted. There would have been no sense in returning to a religion that seemed to have become ossified into a not very indispensable adjunct of a questionable social system. There was the further point too that Christianity was far less clear in teaching that unhappiness and the ego are one and the same thing than was either Buddhism or Hinduism. There are, of course, texts in the Gospels which say very nearly this; but modern Christianity has not been at great pains to emphasize them. Buddhism, on the other hand, emphasizes and constantly reiterates that since all phenomenal things are impermanent and in perpetual flux, there can be no real happiness in them, and that impermanence is therefore identical with pain. The cause of pain is 'craving', and release from pain can only be obtained by stamping out all craving, that is, by suppressing all desire. It is against this background that Huxley can write of the urge to escape and the longing to transcend oneself as being one of the principal appetites of the soul. That mescalin provided Huxley with such an escape is absolutely obvious from what he writes. And because it did so for him, he assumes that it will do so for everyone else, provided they have not had a recent attack of jaundice, that their livers are in order, and that they are not a prey to constant worry.

It does not appear to have occurred to Mr. Huxley that even in our modern civilization there are still people whose 'selves' are uncomplicated and tolerably decent. These persons may be irreligious in Huxley's sense of the word 'religious', in that they feel no need to escape from themselves into another less personal world. I am not referring to what the late Mr. Coomeraswamy, an eminent exponent of the *philosophia perennis*, used to call the 'spiritual proletariat' who have been brutalized by industrialism and its attendant materialism into complete forgetfulness of all spiritual values. These present a very real problem, but we must not digress to consider their plight, for, though they probably do not know it, plight it is. I am thinking rather of those genuinely carefree, generous persons whom everyone likes and who do good to others, not by any conscious effort, but by simply being what they are. Speaking in accordance with Christian theology this would mean such people from whom the sacrament of Baptism really does seem to have washed away the stain of original sin. Such people are saved, *salvi facti sunt*, they have been made whole. These do not feel any need for escape, nor can they be attracted by any religion which offers them only this (though I do not suggest for a moment that Hinduism and Buddhism have nothing further to offer, for obviously they have): for they have been made whole, and it is only what is partial or maimed that can feel the need for completion. Thus for them the word 'escape' has very little meaning.

In the order of Nature Man alone is endowed with reason; he alone is a 'rational animal' as Aristotle long ago observed; and it is because he has the power to reason that he is both puzzled and frightened by the prospect of death which seems to make nonsense of all human endeavour. The fear of death lies at the root of religion. Yet there are many people who are quite conscious of the fact that they must die and are nevertheless quite content that a lifetime should be granted them in which to develop into what they potentially are. This process has been described by Jung as 'becoming what one is',[1] and it has been beautifully put by Oscar Wilde (of all people) in the following passage:

'It will be a marvellous thing—the true personality of man—when we see it. It will grow naturally and simply, flowerlike, or as a tree grows. It will not be at discord. It will never argue or dispute. It will not prove things. It will know everything. And yet it will not busy itself about knowledge. It will have wisdom. Its value will not be measured by material things. It will have nothing. And yet it will have everything, and whatever one takes from it, it will still have, so rich will it be. It will not be always meddling with others, or asking them to be like

[1] C. G. Jung, *Principles of Practical Psychotherapy*, in Collected Works, vol. xvi, London, Routledge and Kegan Paul, 1954, p. 10.

itself. It will love them because they will be different. And yet while it will not meddle with others, it will help all, as a beautiful thing helps us, by being what it is. The personality of man will be very wonderful. It will be as wonderful as the personality of a child.'[1]

Here we have the obverse of Huxley's 'urge to escape'. Huxley sees salvation as an escape from self, as the annihilation of the ego and merging into a greater entity which he calls Mind at Large. Wilde sees it as a natural growth of the whole individual personality to its full stature in which soul, mind, and body all develop along their own lines, not encroaching on one another but balancing one another. In such a description as Wilde has given of the 'true personality of man' Christians can, without irreverence, recognize Adam as he emerged from the hand of God, Adam as we still see him painted on the ceiling of the Sistine Chapel. When we come to consider the Hindu mystics with their use of the word 'self' (*ātman-*) both for what Huxley calls the 'Not-self' and for the individual soul, the relevance of this passage will become apparent.

Before proceeding to the discussion of Huxley's experiences after taking mescalin and before seeking to explain it by similar experiences which others have had, and before we attempt to fit it into a general pattern, it would be as well to summarize the conclusions that Huxley has himself drawn from his excursion into the extra-temporal world and to study his recommendations for the greater use of drugs in the furtherance of the happiness of the human race. These recommendations and conclusions will be found in the epilogue to *The Doors of Perception*. They are remarkable. But nowhere does Huxley seem to face up to the main problem: what is the relationship between the ecstasies of persons of heroic sanctity and those of the mescalin-taker?

In the concluding section of his book Huxley implies that the taking of drugs is, or should be, part and parcel of all religion; and on this basis he criticizes Christianity for not 'baptizing' mescalin or similar drugs and incorporating them into Christian worship. This sounds outrageous: but it is not really so if we continue to bear in mind his major premiss that 'the urge to escape from selfhood and the environment is in almost everyone almost all the time'.[2] The premiss seems false, for it does not correspond to observed fact; and it would be only side-stepping the issue to say that this 'urge' is more often than not unconscious, since until the urge has been brought up into consciousness, it cannot be stated that it is there at all. The premiss should be emended to some such formula as this: 'the urge

[1] From *The Soul of Man under Socialism*, New Collected Edition, London, Collins, 1948, p. 1023.

[2] *The Doors of Perception*, p. 50.

to escape selfhood and the environment (which are two very different things) is in almost every introspective introvert who is naturally retiring, over-cerebral, and over-sensitive, and who has been brought up in a materialist and industrialized environment, almost all the time'. If we are prepared to 'emend' the premiss in this way, Huxley's panacea for society becomes intelligible,—except, of course, that we can no longer speak of society as such, but only of a limited number of hyper-civilized persons in search of their soul. In lumping together 'the urge to escape from selfhood' and 'the urge to escape from the environment' Huxley is confusing two quite separate things. It is what William James calls the 'sick soul' which longs to escape from itself, and it is what Coomaraswamy calls the 'spiritual proletariat' that aspires to escape from its environment. This 'proletariat' now forms a large part of any industrial society. Its members are occupied in doing intrinsically boring jobs, and if they seek relief in the cinema, television, and the 'comics', they do so not in order to escape from themselves, but in order to project themselves into what seems to them a more meaningful existence. Their plight is the exact opposite of that of the neurotic intellectual; for the latter lives by and on introspection and is bound, sooner or later, to long to escape from a subject that has become a monomania, whereas the former has not yet got as far as finding a 'self' from which he could wish to escape. He feels no urge to escape from himself, only an urge to escape from the dullness of everyday life in which no 'self' of any sort has any chance to develop.

On the subject of how mescalin could be utilized for the good of humanity, Huxley's ideas appear to be extraordinarily confused. He oscillates in the most alarming manner between identifying the mescalin experience with the Beatific Vision on the one hand and regarding it as a safe substitute for alcohol on the other. The baffled reader finds himself wondering whether he regards the highest states of the mystics as being not only comparable to, but identical with, the effects of alcohol and drugs, or not. 'The Beatific Vision, *Sat Chit Ananda*, Being-Awareness-Bliss—for the first time I understood, not on the verbal level, not by inchoate hints or at a distance, but precisely and completely what those prodigious syllables referred to.' This is what he says on pages 12–13. If this means anything, then surely it must mean that what he was experiencing at the time was a near approximation to what Christians call the Beatific Vision and what the Hindus mean by *Sat Chit Ananda*. Yet when he comes to describe his own experience in detail, he describes it as follows:

'I continued to look at the flowers, and in their living light I seemed to detect the qualitative equivalent of breathing—but of a breathing without returns to a starting-point, with no recurrent ebbs but only a repeated flow from beauty to heightened beauty, from deeper to ever deeper meaning. Words like Grace and Transfiguration came to my mind, and this of course was what, among other things, they stood for. My eyes travelled from the rose to the carnation, and from that feathery incandescence to the smooth scrolls of sentient amethyst which were the iris.'

Possibly I am wrong, but I had always understood that the Beatific Vision means a direct apperception of God, not through a glass, darkly, but face to face, with all the veils of sense stripped aside, as the Muslim mystics would say. Unless Huxley's descriptive powers have failed him altogether, I am afraid that I cannot discern any likeness between what he experienced and what is generally understood by the Beatific Vision. Why should we be asked to believe that a vision of nature transfigured in any way corresponds to the vision of God Himself? Though Zen Buddhists may speak of the Dharma-Body of the Buddha *being* the hedge at the bottom of the garden, Christian mystics use no such terminology to describe the unitive state. The only way to emphasize how great the difference is between Huxley's mescalin-induced visions and the experiences of Christian mystics is to quote the texts side by side. Let us then turn to Blessed Henry Suso who, as being a pupil of Meister Eckhart, a near-monist, on the one hand, and a *beatus* of the Catholic Church on the other, should meet the requirements of most religious tastes. The quotation is from *The Little Book of Truth*, and can be regarded as being fairly typical of Christian mysticism. We shall have occasion to quote further passages from theistic mystics, both Christian and Muslim, in our later chapters. This is what Suso says:

'It happens, no doubt, that, when the good and faithful servant enters into the joy of his Lord, he becomes intoxicated with the immeasurable abundance of the Divine house. For in an ineffable manner, it happens to him as to a drunk man, who forgets himself, is no longer himself. He is quite dead to himself, and is entirely lost in God, has passed into Him, and has become one spirit with Him in all respects, just as a little drop of water that is poured into a large quantity of wine. For, as this is lost to itself, and draws to itself and into itself the taste and colour of the wine, similarly it happens to those who are in the full possession of blessedness. In an inexpressible manner all human desires fall away from them, they melt away into themselves, and sink away completely into the will of God. If anything remained in man, and was not entirely poured out of him, then the Scripture could not be true that says: God is to become all things to all things. Nevertheless, his being remains, though in a different form, in a different glory, and in a different power. And all this comes to a man through his utter abandonment of self.'[1]

[1] Henry Suso, *Little Book of Eternal Wisdom* and *Little Book of Truth*, tr. J. M. Clark, London, Faber and Faber, 1953 p. 185.

Literally hundreds of passages from Christian and Muslim mystics could be quoted which depict the union of the soul with God and which are closely parallel to the passage we have just quoted from Suso. But where is the likeness to Huxley's experience under the influence of mescalin? True, Suso speaks of 'utter abandonment of self', and Huxley describes himself as a 'Not-self, simultaneously perceiving and being the Not-self of the things around me'.[1] Even allowing for the Buddhist convention of using the word 'Not-self' to mean something other than the ego which has direct experience of both the subjective self and of objective phenomena, there still seems to be no parallel, unless one accept the proposition that God, as understood by Suso, means the same as the Dharma-Body of the Buddha which in turn is the hedge at the bottom of the garden. Yet even if we make this enormous concession, there is still no real parallel. In the case of Huxley, as in that of the manic, the personality seems to be dissipated into the objective world, while in the case of Suso, as of other theistic mystics, the human personality is wholly absorbed into the Deity Who is felt and experienced as being something totally distinct and other than the objective world. Suso is describing a state in which both the subject, 'I', and the object, 'the world', are momentarily excluded from consciousness, and in which the soul is literally 'filled' through and through 'with the Holy Ghost': in such a state, however we choose to interpret the 'Dharma-Body of the Buddha', one thing at least is certain, and that is that 'the hedge at the bottom of the garden' and, with it, all hedges and all gardens have ceased to exist for the soul rapt in God. How is it possible for a sane man seriously to maintain that such an experience which excludes all sensation of the objective world is the same as 'not merely gazing at those bamboo legs, but actually *being* them—or rather being myself in them; or, to be still more accurate . . . being my Not-self in the Not-self which was the chair'?[2] In the first case we have the 'deification' of a human soul in God, the loss of consciousness of all things except God; in the second we have the identification of the self *via* the 'Not-self' (which we shall be able to define a little more exactly later) with the external world to the exclusion, it would appear, of God; for, significantly enough, even Huxley under the influence of mescalin fails to identify his Not-self with God though he does not feel this to be incongruous in the case of the 'Dharma-Body of the Buddha'. The sensation that the individual human being and his external surroundings are not really distinct is not so uncommon as is normally supposed, as we shall shortly have occasion to see. It is, however, unusual

[1] *The Doors of Perception*, p. 27.
[2] Ibid., pp. 15–16.

to find a serious author identifying this experience, sometimes called the 'natural' mystical experience, with the Beatific Vision.

The confusion of thought that mescalin seems to have induced in Mr. Huxley is best illustrated in the epilogue. For here he says: 'I am not so foolish as to equate what happens under the influence of mescalin or of any other drug, prepared or in the future preparable, with the realization of the end and ultimate purpose of human life: Enlightenment, the Beatific Vision.'[1] It should merely be regarded, he says, as 'what Catholic theologians call "a gratuitous grace", not necessary to salvation but potentially helpful and to be accepted thankfully, if made available'. This is indeed a serious modification of his former position; and it is a modification by which he seems to stand. Yet from this it follows that intoxication of any sort must also be a 'gratuitous grace', and in so far as the Church teaches that the fruit of the vine and the beverages that derive from it are a gift of God and to be enjoyed in moderation, this view does not seem to be objectionable. His position, however, becomes much more shaky when he assails the Church for not enlivening her ceremonies with a little sacramental mescalin as the 'Native American Church' apparently does.

Huxley's impatience with the tedium and dullness of the average Christian service is comprehensible enough; and the dullness of our services and of our priests and pastors has done perhaps more than anything to empty the churches in this country. As Huxley's plea for sacramental mescalin, quixotic though it may be, all too clearly shows, the Churches in England are leaving unsatisfied a human religious need more genuinely felt, albeit often unconsciously, than the urge simply to escape from self, I mean the need to get into contact with the Divine Reality or what is felt to be such. How deep this need is has been sufficiently illustrated by the astonishing success that Dr. Billy Graham enjoyed in this country. Dr. Graham was able to attract record crowds of people not normally interested in religion simply because he had found a way of cutting through the fog of dullness with which modern Christianity has succeeded in obfuscating the most moving and prodigious 'myth' of all time.

Bearing in mind, then, how disgracefully Christianity has been whittled away in modern times, I confess that my approach to the practices of the Native American Church is not unsympathetic. Their principal rite, it appears, 'is a kind of Early Christian Agape, or Love-Feast, where slices of peyote (from which mescalin is derived) take the place of the sacramental bread and wine'. They 'regard the cactus as God's special gift to the Indians, and equate its effects with the workings of the divine Spirit'.[2]

[1] Ibid., p. 58. [2] Ibid., p 55.

Their rites, it appears, are decorous; and there is none of the extravagance that characterized the rites of many of the dervish orders among some of which drugs were also used. In the performance of these rites they were neither stupefied nor drunk: they did not get out of rhythm nor fumble their words. They were quiet, courteous, and considerate. A Professor Slotkin who has lived among them is quoted as saying that he had never been in a white man's house of worship where there was either so much religious feeling or so much decorum. And what is the result of the drug on these pious Indians? 'Sometimes (according to the reports collected by Dr. Slotkin) they see visions, which may be of Christ Himself. Sometimes they hear the voice of the Great Spirit. Sometimes they become aware of the presence of God and of those personal short-comings which must be corrected if they are to do His will.' 'A tree', Huxley adds, 'with such satisfactory fruits cannot be condemned out of hand as evil.' No more it can: but is it necessary, as Huxley seems to think, to introduce mescalin or, for that matter, alcohol into our churches? Is communion with God in fact facilitated by the use of drugs and alcohol? or is this merely a vulgar error shared by many primitive communities and certain ecstatic sects? All sorts of fundamental issues are raised here which Huxley quietly ignores. Men must be enabled to get out of themselves, he argues. This is an absolute necessity; and the means and the purpose of the escape matter little. 'Ideally', he writes, 'everyone should be able to find self-transcendence in some form of pure or applied religion. In practice it seems very unlikely that this hoped for consummation will ever be realized.'[1] The mistake of Christianity was, he considers, that it failed to sacramentalize the use of alcohol. In this case it was a very ancient mistake, and one which may have caused St. Paul the gravest concern; for surely it is precisely such 'sacramentally alcoholic' *agapes* that he has in mind in 1 Corinthians xi: 'And when you assemble together, there is no opportunity to eat a supper of the Lord; each comer hastens to eat the supper he has brought for himself, so that one man goes hungry, while another has drunk deep. Have you no homes to eat and drink in, that you should show contempt to God's church, and shame the poor?'[2]

In this passage St. Paul roundly condemns persons who turn up to the eucharistic sacrifice drunk. It is not said whether they did so in order to heighten their perception for the actual Communion. If this was their motive, then we can imagine St. Paul debating the question: Was it legitimate to use alcohol to stimulate the senses at the time of the sacrificial meal? Was it legitimate to employ physical means in order to produce

[1] *The Doors of Perception*, p. 54. [2] vv. 20–22 (Mgr. Knox's translation).

an artificial ecstasy and to enable the senses of sensual man to partake of the spiritual union between man and God which the Christian *agape* was held to symbolize, or rather actually to be? St. Paul, we may suppose, felt strongly that the two were totally distinct and should by no means be confused. Huxley adopts precisely the opposite view, for he says: 'Even the most tolerant [of Christians] have made no attempt to convert the drug to Christianity, or to sacramentalize its use. The pious drinker is forced to take his religion in one compartment, his religion-surrogate in another. And perhaps this is inevitable. Drinking cannot be sacramentalized except in religions which set no store on decorum. The worship of Dionysos or the Celtic god of beer was a loud and disorderly affair. The rites of Christianity are incompatible with even religious drunkenness. This does no harm to the distillers, but it is very bad for Christianity. Countless persons desire self-transcendence and would be glad to find it in church. But, alas, "the hungry sheep look up and are not fed". They take part in rites, they listen to sermons, they repeat prayers; but their thirst remains unassuaged. Disappointed, they turn to the bottle.' Therefore, the argument goes on, now that a greater than the bottle is with us, let us make use of it, sacramentalize it, and be grateful.

Huxley is admittedly both incoherent and self-contradictory. Nevertheless, if I understand him correctly, what he seems to be arguing is this. Religion means principally escape from the ego. What have all the great mystics of all time done? They have shaken off their egos, they have become gods, Not-selfs, or what you will. What do alcohol and mescalin do for you? They do precisely this: they enable you to shake off the ego and give you a glorious feeling of release. Therefore they must be of the same nature as religion: therefore they are good. St. Paul, if we interpret the passage at all correctly, took a different view. For what was he trying to say to those ever back-sliding Corinthians?

We are at liberty to imagine him addressing them somewhat as follows: 'You Corinthians have come over to Christ because the story of the life, death, and resurrection of Jesus of Nazareth which has taken place in Judaea in our own times, seems so striking a confirmation and actualization in history and in time of what your mystery religions have always taught. In your Bacchic orgies you thought that, by devouring the quivering flesh of beasts, you were entering into direct contact with the divine. This you did in a state of frenzy, even madness. You may have thought that this was what I offered you in the sacrificial meal we call the *agape*. If you did, you were wrong: for whereas your own sacrificial meals may well have prefigured the Christian sacrament, they were essentially different in kind.

They provided you certainly with a temporary release from your egos; and that is why they satisfied you, and will probably satisfy others like you till the end of time. Strong drink, you found, contributed to the attainment of ecstasy, and for that reason you used it in your ceremonies. This is not, however, what I preach. I preach to you redemption through Christ. When you come to take part in the sacrificial meal, I would prefer that you came without having taken any stimulants. Christ came to make you whole: he did not come to make you ecstatics. He came to make you sane: he did not come to make you mad. Therefore it is wrong to approach his table when you are half-drunk, because, if you do so, you are confusing this new mystery with your own more ancient ones. By the Christian mystery you enter into the life of Christ which is the life of God transmitted by grace to this imperfect world. In your ancient mysteries you sought to escape out of yourselves: you wanted ecstasy. The Christian mystery is not primarily designed for this purpose. Its purpose is that Christ should live in you, and you should live in Christ. Our Lord said that each and all of us should make full use of the talents that are his; each person must complete and fulfil his natural self. Only then will he be ripe for the life of grace which elevates him above nature on to a supernatural plane. During this process it may be that you will have praeternatural experiences: you may have ecstasies; you may see visions and dream dreams. All this means nothing, for the same effects can be produced by the use of wine or drugs. Do not be led astray into thinking that what happens in the Eucharist is the same as, or even comparable to, what happens to you in a Bacchic orgy. In the Christian Eucharist you will probably have no sensible impression at all. It is not exciting: you will feel nothing; you will *experience* nothing. But something is in fact going on in your soul which in the fullness of time will become apparent in your life. Above all do not mistake elation for grace. Elation or exaltation is a state that is common to saints and sinners alike: it can be produced by alcohol or drugs, but do not confuse that with the grace that is infused into you at our *agape*. For in this *agape* which we call a "rational oblation", there is no room for ecstasy. It is a receiving of Christ quietly into the inmost essence of your soul. You must realize that there is a total difference between the two.'

I probably have no right to put such words into the mouth of St. Paul personally; but I do think that the sentiments expressed in these words are in harmony with what the Church at large thinks and has always thought on these matters. It would, however, be a grave mistake to underrate the challenge thrown down by Mr. Huxley and by many who think like him. What, then, is this challenge? It is this: that religion is a matter of experience, almost of sensation; that religious experience means 'mystical' experience; and that mystical experiences are everywhere and always the same. Acting on this assumption Huxley first became interested in the Vedānta philosophy of the Hindus since only in that philosophy is praeternatural experience, deduced from the contents of the Upaniṣads, made the basis of all speculation. This teaching, in its extreme form, is the philosophy, not so much of the oneness of all things, but of the actual identity of the individual soul with the *Brahman* which can best be translated as 'the Absolute'. All mystical experience, according to this school of thought, ultimately leads to this identity,—a conclusion that Westerners may find surprising. By a mystical experience Huxley seems to understand not only the experiences of all the recognized mystics, but experiences such as his own under the influence of mescalin; and, since he is honest, he would be forced to add, the experiences of madness. In Chapter V we will be dealing with the experiences of a manic-depressive; and these show the clearest possible resemblance to Huxley's own experiences. It is not for nothing that Huxley said that he thought he knew what it felt like to be mad.

It is not easy to see what Huxley's intention was when he wrote *The Doors of Perception*: for hitherto he had been one of the most stubborn defenders of what he calls the *philosophia perennis*, that philosophy which maintains that the ultimate truths about God and the universe cannot be directly expressed in words, that these truths are necessarily everywhere and always the same, and that, therefore, the revealed religions which so obviously differ on so many major points from one another, can only be relatively true, each revelation being accommodated to the needs of the time and the place in which it was made and adapted to the degree of spiritual enlightenment of its recipients. Thus, as Coomaraswamy, another exponent of the *philosophia perennis*, has said,[1] the only real heresy is to maintain that one religion only is in exclusive possession of the truth. All are rather facets of the same truth, this truth being presented in a different manner at different times in accordance with the spiritual development of the society to which it is directed. The truth itself is that experienced by the mystics whose unity of thought and language is said to speak for itself.

There seem to be two very strong objections to such a theory. The first is that few of these authors can or will define what precisely constitutes a mystical experience, and that until that is done, we do not really know what we are talking about. The second is that to assert that all mystics speak the same language and convey the same message does not seem to be true even within one particular religious tradition. For our present purposes

[1] A. K. Coomaraswamy, *The Bugbear of Literacy*, London, Dobson, 1949, p. 49.

we may as well follow Mr. Huxley in including his own experiences under the influence of mescalin in the category of 'mysticism'. If we do this, however, we must also include the experiences of manic-depressives since mescalin is clinically used to reproduce artificially the state of mind typical of that distressing psychosis, and because, in fact, the experiences of manic-depressives show a marked resemblance not only to Huxley's experience, but also to that of some more conventional mystics. We will, then, first be dealing with those experiences which are usually termed pantheistic, the experience which tells you that you are all and that all is you, 'when I am inseparably this and that and this and that are I; when I experience the other person as myself and the other, as myself, experiences me'.[1] This experience is described clearly and with admirable concision in the *Kauṣītakī Upaniṣad*[2] in the memorable formula, 'Thou art this all'. This is the experience of the 'nature mystic': it is the experience of all as one and one as all. It is common in the later Ṣūfī writers and can also be found in the works of modern authors who are not otherwise known as mystics. To call it 'pantheistic' is wrong, for in the proposition 'Thou art this all', neither term represents or can be construed as 'God', and 'pantheism', when translated into English, of course, means 'all-God-ism'. It would be far more accurate to describe this experience as 'pan-en-hen-ism', 'all-in-one-ism', for that is what in fact the experience tells us. It is, of course, the experience of Huxley not only perceiving his chair legs transformed, but actually being them, 'being his Not-self in their Not-self', as he accurately puts it.

Is this experience the same as that described by the so-called *mahāvākyāni* or 'great sayings' which are the key texts of the Vedānta? These are four in number, and together they may be said to sum up the whole of Vedāntin monism. They read as follows: (1) 'Thou art that':[3] (2) 'This *ātman* is *Brahman*', 'This individual soul is the Absolute':[4] (3) 'I am *Brahman*':[5] and (4) 'Consciousness is *Brahman*'.[6] What is meant by this? *Brahman* is the word used to represent the Absolute: it is the sole truly existing and eternal reality, beyond time and space and causation and utterly unaffected by these which, from its own standpoint, have no existence whatever. *Ātman* means 'self', the individual soul. The proposition, then, that '*Ātman* is *Brahman*' means that the individual soul is substantially and essentially identical with the unqualifiable Absolute. From this it follows that the

[1] John Custance, *Adventure into the Unconscious*, London, Christopher Johnson, 1954, p. 4 (quoting Jung).

[2] *Kauṣ. Up.* 1. 6 (idaṁ sarvam asi).

[3] *Chāndogya Upaniṣad* 6. 9. ff. (tat tvam asi).

[4] *Māṇḍūkya Up.* 2 (ayam ātmā brahma).

[5] *Bṛhadāraṇyaka Up.* 1. 4. 10 (ahaṁ brahmāsmi).

[6] *Aitareya Up.* 5. 3 (prajñānaṁ brahma).

phenomenal world has no true existence in itself: from the point of view of the Absolute it is absolutely non-existent. Therefore, the soul which realizes itself as the Absolute, must also realize the phenomenal world as non-existent. This, then, is to experience one's own soul as being the Absolute, and not to experience the phenomenal world at all. To say that this is identical with the pan-en-henic experience, is to say something that is patently and blatantly untrue. For what sort of sense does it make to say that to experience oneself as actually being three chair legs which represent a minute proportion of the phenomenal world, is the same as to experience oneself as the Absolute for which the phenomenal world is simply not-being? Here, then, we already have two wholly distinct forms of 'mystical experience'.

Thirdly there is the normal type of Christian mystical experience in which the soul feels itself to be united with God by love. The theological premiss from which this experience starts is that the individual soul is created by God in His own image and likeness from nothing and that it has the capacity of being united to God, of being 'oned' to Him as the mediaeval English mystics put it. Here again we have a third type, distinct, it would appear, from the other two. For whereas both the Christian and the Vedāntin experiences are wholly different from the pan-en-henic, so do they differ from each other. No orthodox Christian mystic, unless he is speaking figuratively or in poetry as Angelus Silesius does, can well go farther than to say that his individual ego is melted away in God by love: something of the soul must clearly remain if only to experience the mystical experience. The individual is not annihilated, though transformed and 'deified' as St. John of the Cross says: it remains a distinct entity though permeated through and through with the divine substance. For the non-dualist Vedāntin this is not so: the human soul IS God; there is no duality anywhere. Superficially, at least, there is an enormous difference between the two. Whether in fact the gulf can be bridged and, if so, how, will occupy us in the later parts of this book. For the moment we must consider the experiences of the nature mystics who will be seen to have enjoyed similar transports to those of Mr. Huxley without, however, having recourse to any artificial stimulant.

CHAPTER III

SOME NATURE MYSTICS

WE have seen that, so far as we can judge from the evidence, there are three types of praeternatural experience. These can be pin-pointed by studying the terminology used. If we are then told that the experiences are such that they cannot be described and that all descriptions are only approximations to the ineffable experience,—the variety of these approximations being explicable by the supposed fact that the One Truth is viewed from different angles,—then plainly there is no point in discussing the matter further. Unless, however, we are prepared to concede that the descriptions are utterly meaningless and therefore not approximations at all, we are surely entitled to study the evidence and to draw what conclusions we can. When the *Cloud of Unknowing*, for example, speaks of being 'oned' with God, does it mean the same as the Vedāntin assertion that the individual soul *is* Brahman or as Ḥallāj's ecstatic pronouncement *Anā'l-Ḥaqq*, 'I am the Truth' (that is, 'I am God') or as Huxley's experience of being a Not-self in the Not-self of a chair?

Any enquiry which aims at an unbiassed approach to the phenomenology of mysticism is liable to be met with opposition not so much from the orthodox of the various creeds as from the advocates of a *philosophia perennis* which would set itself above creed and which therefore interprets all creeds from its own *a priori* notions. This tendency has been associated with the names of the late Ananda Coomaraswamy and René Guénon, the first an unusually well-equipped Oriental scholar, the second a self-appointed interpreter of the Vedānta with a pronounced animus against orientalists. Their mantle now seems to have fallen on M. Frithjof Schuon who has developed this 'metaphysic' at some length in his *Transcendent Unity of Religions*.[1] The distinction he makes between a higher 'metaphysical' and a lower 'religious' knowledge is reminiscent of the 'higher' and 'lower' knowledge of Brahman adopted by Śankara, the ninth-century Indian philosopher, and the ways of 'truth' and 'opinion' of Parmenides. According to this scheme of things the 'higher' metaphysical view is alone absolutely true, though the 'lower' or 'religious' one is also true, but only relatively so and in its proper time and place. Hence we are asked to believe that Islam, for instance, is true wherever Islam is practised, and Christianity (by which M. Schuon understands Roman Catholicism and

[1] English translation by Peter Townsend, London, Faber and Faber, 1953.

Greek Orthodoxy only) is equally true throughout Christendom. Conversely, we are left to believe, Christianity is false in Arabia, and Islam in Italy. From the absolute standpoint alone are these conflicting and often warring 'truths' seen to be one; and, it would appear, only M. Schuon and those initiated into his own peculiar form of gnosis have authority to enunciate metaphysical truth from the absolute point of view. Thus M. Schuon seems to set himself up as the sole arbiter of what the various individual religions really mean; he establishes himself as a kind of super-Pope who alone can interpret both the exoteric and esoteric meanings of all 'true' and 'orthodox' religions. Such a procedure may be permissible in Śankara when he assesses the various trends in Hinduism; for Śankara was himself a Hindu and in Hinduism the widest divergences of belief are tolerated and admitted because Hindus believe that all worship, all meditation, and all contemplation are ways leading to the same experience of Brahman. When this method is extended to all the great religions, however, it is bound either to break down or to lead to self-deception. It is quite absurd, for example, to quote the late philosophic mystic, Ibn al-ʿArabī, as an authentic exponent of the Muslim 'tradition' since he has been rejected by the majority of the orthodox as being heretical. This M. Schuon repeatedly does in defiance of the main stream of Muslim orthodoxy. Such a 'method' has nothing to commend it. It merely serves to irritate those who are genuinely puzzled by the diversity of the world's great religions and who are not prepared to succumb to this higher mystification.

In this book, fortunately, we are not concerned with comparative theology; we are concerned only with the comparative study of mysticism and of mystical experience, and whether all such experiences are reducible to one pattern. Before proceeding to discuss this theme in detail, however, it would be just as well to have a fairly clear idea of what we mean by mysticism. In Christianity the word is usually held to mean a direct apprehension of the Deity. Sanctifying grace, according to orthodox doctrine, does in fact establish a direct relationship between the soul and God: God is said actually to dwell in the soul that is in a state of grace. It is, however, obvious that the average soul in this state has no sensible experience of the presence of God. Persons technically in a state of grace do not look different or behave in a noticeably different manner from their fellows who may be in a state of mortal sin. Again orthodox doctrine holds that on receiving Holy Communion the soul is united to God. The recipient is only very rarely indeed actually aware of this ineffable union, whereas the onlooker may be permitted to doubt it. In a mystical experience, on the other hand, there is a direct apperception of the Deity; the mystic *knows* that God is in him and with him; his body has literally become a 'temple of the Holy Ghost'. This is no longer a dogma accepted on faith, but, the mystic would allege, an experienced fact. The experience has nothing to do with visions, auditions, locutions, telepathy, telekinesis, or any other praeternatural phenomenon which may be experienced by saint and sinner alike and which are usually connected with an hysterical temperament.[1] It is true that some advanced (and canonized) mystics have been subject to these disturbances, but they have no essential connexion with the mystical experience itself, the essence and key-note of which is union. Praeternatural phenomena that may or may not accompany it are subsidiary, accidental, parasitic.

In Christian terminology mysticism means union with God: in non-theistical contexts it also means union with some principle or other. It is, then, a unitive experience with someone or something other than oneself. In Huxley's case it was union with and direct experience of three chair legs, grey flannel trousers, and, by extension, with all natural objects within his vision. If, then, we define a mystical experience as a sense of union or even identity with something other than oneself, Huxley can claim to have had a mystical experience, and this experience can be, and was, induced by mescalin. According to this definition are we entitled to class the experience of the *advaita*, that is, the strictly non-dualist, Vedāntins as mystical? The difficulty is that in this case it is not strictly proper to speak of union at all; for according to the proposition 'I am Brahman', which means that I am the sole unqualifiable Absolute, One without a second, I cannot logically speak of being united to Brahman, since I am already He (or It). Just as, according to Christian doctrine, the Christian in a state of grace is a temple of the Holy Ghost, so, according to Vedāntin doctrine, is man, whether in a state of grace or not, identical with the Absolute. In both cases, in the ordinary course of events, they are unaware of it; and in both cases mystical experience brings to light an already existing state of affairs. There is, of course, a difference between the two. The Christian mystic, if he is orthodox, will not go so far as to say that he actually *is* God in any absolute and unqualified sense. It is possible that Suso did actually feel in ecstasy that this would have been a true description of what he felt, but that he was prevented from saying so because this happened to have been one of the propositions of his master, Eckhart, which had been condemned by the Pope. However that may be, this is a manner of expressing the ineffable experience which Christians normally avoid. Sticking strictly to the letter,

[1] On this subject the reader may consult Herbert Thurston, S.J., *The Physical Phenomena of Mysticism*, London, Burns Oates, 1952, and id., *Surprising Mystics*, London, Burns Oates, 1955.

then, for the moment, a distinction must be drawn between the Christian experience in which the individual soul is united or 'oned' with God, to use the expression of the *Cloud of Unknowing*, and the Vedāntin experience which is one of absolute identity with Brahman,—'I am Brahman' and 'What thou art, that am I'.[1] In any case, for the purposes of this work we propose to extend the meaning of 'union' to include actual 'unity', for no treatment of mysticism that claims to be serious can afford to ignore the all-important Indian contribution.

Though there is a difference, and a real difference, between the Vedāntin and Christian ways of defining the unitive experience, the difference may well be only one of terminology. There is however a radical difference between both of them and Huxley's experience under the influence of mescalin. For in strictly religious mysticism, whether it be Hindu, Christian, or Muslim, the whole purpose of the exercise is to concentrate on an ultimate reality to the complete exclusion of all else; and by 'all else' is meant the phenomenal world or, as the theists put it, all that is not God. This means a total and absolute detachment from Nature, an isolation of the soul within itself either to realize itself as 'God', or to enter into communion with God. The exclusion of all that we normally call Nature is the *sine qua non* of this type of mystical experience: it is the necessary prelude to the further experience of union with God in the Christian and Muslim sense, or the realization of oneself as Brahman in the Vedāntin sense. To state, then, or to imply, as Huxley does, that his own experience is either identical with, or comparable to, either the Christian Beatific Vision or to what the Hindus call *Sac-cid-ānanda* (*Sat Chit Ananda*), 'Being-Awareness-Bliss', is to state or to imply an obvious untruth. If we take the extreme Vedāntin position that the individual soul *is* Brahman, and that the realization of oneself as Brahman means the destruction of what the Vedāntins call *upādhis* or 'illusory adjuncts', then there can be no participation in the illusory or transient life of those adjuncts; there is only the realization of oneself as the only true One without a second. This is the exact opposite of being a 'Not-self in the Not-self of three chair legs'. The experiences are not comparable and need to be explained in different ways. Thus when I read in a recent book on English mysticism[2] that we can call the mystical experience which the author assumes to be identical in all cases 'cosmic emotion' or 'the love of God' according to taste, I can only conclude that he is not investigating the recorded facts, but assuming, before investigation, that the recorded facts, however great the divergence in their expression, must

[1] *Kauṣītakī Upaniṣad*, I. 6 (yas tvam asi so 'ham asmi).

[2] Gerald Bullett, *The English Mystics*, London, Michael Joseph, 1950.

represent one and the same experience. He is as much the slave of his own preconceptions as is the average writer on this elusive subject.

The author of the book I refer to, Mr. Gerald Bullett, writes as one who has himself had a praeternatural experience. That this experience (if it took place) was similar to the experience of Richard Jefferies and other nature mystics seems clear from the fact that the author is quite prepared to treat all mystical experiences as one. If you have lain in the grass on a warm summer's day, he seems to assume, and felt yourself transfused and penetrated by Nature; if you have felt this mysterious and (to you) very actual identity with Nature, then what the theistic mystics say about a similar transfusion and penetration by God must be the same thing. Having experienced Nature as being one with himself, the nature mystic is all too prone to identify Nature with God: he accepts without question the *Deus sive Natura*, 'God or Nature', of Spinoza. God and Nature, for him, must be interchangeable terms. The bliss he encounters in his mysterious union with Nature is so totally different from anything he has experienced before that he feels it must be identical with the bliss described by all other mystics, however different the expression of it in words may be. It is not simply that it is a far greater pleasure than all else he had ever perceived: it is altogether of a different order, and beside it all other pleasures are as nothing.

'Is it agreeable?' Huxley was asked when under the influence of mescalin. 'Neither agreeable nor disagreeable,' he answered, 'it just *is*.' This is, perhaps, not very illuminating, but it does at least indicate that the normal ways of referring to emotional experiences are not applicable to this kind of thing. The natural mystical experience is different in *kind* from ordinary sense experience. As the Muslim mystics would put it, you cannot describe a praeternatural experience, you can only give indications (*ishārat*) which may or may not make sense to the enquirer. This too is the attitude of the Zen Buddhist masters who wilfully make *their* 'indications' as obscure and outrageous as possible.

It is interesting and instructive to see what persons Mr. Bullett selects as being typical English mystics. Among them are the following: Richard Jefferies, Tennyson, John Scotus Erigena, the author of the *Cloud of Unknowing*, Richard Rolle, Julian of Norwich, George Fox, John Donne, George Herbert, Henry Vaughan, Thomas Traherne, the Cambridge Platonists, William Law, William Blake, and Wordsworth. It will be seen that he draws his net pretty wide and includes many who, according to the definition of mysticism we have adopted, would not be eligible at all. Nothing that Mr. Bullett quotes from Wordsworth, for instance, would indicate that he had actually had a mystical experience at least in the sense that we have defined. In Wordsworth there seems to be no intuitive realization of the identity or union of the individual with something else, either with Nature, or with God, or with that unidentifiable entity which Huxley calls the 'Not-self' and which may be distinct from both. The experience may be difficult or impossible to describe, but though you may not understand it when described and may consider it blatant nonsense, the condition described is none the less unmistakable. The following passage from *Tintern Abbey* is perhaps the most commonly quoted of all in this context:[1]

> 'And I have felt
> A presence that disturbs me with the joy
> Of elevated thoughts; a sense sublime
> Of something far more deeply interfused,
> Whose dwelling is the light of setting suns,
> And the round ocean and the living air,
> And the blue sky, and in the mind of man:
> A motion and a spirit, that impels
> All thinking things, all objects of all thought,
> And rolls through all things.'

In these lines there is an intimation, if you like, of something which transcends and informs transient Nature, but it is no more than an intimation. It amounts to little more than that there is a Spirit somewhere which pervades all Nature. There is no trace of an actual experience at all, either of union with Nature or communion with God. There is a dim perception only that there is a unifying principle in the universe. On these grounds Wordsworth can scarcely be classed as a mystic since, to judge from his writings, he does not seem to have had a 'unitive' experience of any of the types we have discussed. Nor does he conform to Mr. Bullett's own definition as being one who 'has enjoyed a sense of communion or "at-one-ment" with a reality infinitely transcending himself'.[2] Similarly, according to this definition, it is difficult to see how Blake fits in. Blake was rather a seer in the literal sense of the word: he lived in a world in which angels, prophets, patriarchs, demons, and even fairies were more real that the world of everyday life around him with which alone most of us are familiar. Though superb both as a poet and as a painter, he cannot be strictly classed as a mystic. Mysticism has no necessary connexion with the arts any more than it has with such praeternatural phenomena as clairvoyance and the

[1] Cf. G. Bullett, op. cit., p. 213. [2] Ibid., p. 16.

like. It is true that music or painting or poetry *may* induce a natural mystical experience. In most cases, however, this will be *per accidens* and will depend on a variety of psychological causes that elude us.

Mystics of all schools insist that their experiences are not reducible to words, and few of them have had any interest in art or poetry or music as such. Their own artistic productions may be good, bad, or indifferent, though at the time of composition they doubtless think they are an 'indication' of the highest truth. There is precious little beauty in the prose Upaniṣads, yet as mystical treatises their value is unique. The fact that Persian mysticism is largely expressed in poetry,—and frequently in poetry of a very high order,—proves nothing. The fact remains that the essence of it is expressed with much more accuracy and force in the very bald aphorisms of the early Ṣūfīs on which their more sophisticated successors built. Ṣūfism, in its extreme form, which was almost to become a rival orthodoxy in later times, is expressed quite as adequately and much more directly in such 'shocking' aphorisms as the 'I am the Truth' of Ḥallāj, and the 'Glory be to me, how great is my glory', of Abū Yazīd of Bisṭām, than it is in the whole enormous poetical output of Jalāl-al-Dīn Rūmī. Huxley, it will be remembered,[1] speaks of the 'more ordinary' forms of 'contemplation': 'For until this morning I had known contemplation only in its humbler, its more ordinary forms—as discursive thinking; as a rapt absorption in poetry or painting or music; as a patient waiting upon inspirations, without which even the prosiest writer cannot hope to accomplish anything; as occasional glimpses, in nature, of Wordsworth's "something far more deeply interfused"; as systematic silence leading, sometimes, to hints of an "obscure knowledge".' After taking mescalin he too realized that these humble 'forms of contemplation' bore no real relation to the 'natural' mystical experience which mescalin gave him: this, according to his own showing, was totally and entirely beyond anything he had experienced before: it took him into a different world.

Perhaps the only way to illustrate what we mean by a 'natural mystical experience' is to quote a number of examples. Let us first look at some passages in William James's *Varieties of Religious Experience*. The first is from a letter of Tennyson and reads as follows:

'I have never had any revelations through anaesthetics, but a kind of waking trance—this for lack of a better word—I have frequently had, quite up from boyhood, when I have been all alone. This has come upon me through repeating my own name to myself silently, till all at once, as it were out of the intensity of the consciousness of individuality, individuality itself seemed to dissolve and

[1] See above, p. 14.

fade away into boundless being, and this not a confused state but the clearest, the surest of the surest, utterly beyond words—where death was an almost laughable impossibility—the loss of personality (if so it were) seeming no extinction, but the only true life. I am ashamed of my feeble description. Have I not said the state is utterly beyond words?'[1]

About the reality of the experience Tennyson had no doubts whatever. Speaking of the same condition he is recorded as saying: 'By God Almighty! there is no delusion in the matter! It is no nebulous ecstasy, but a state of transcendent wonder, associated with absolute clearness of mind.'[2] It is surely significant that it never occurred to Tennyson to connect this experience with God. That he should have had no such idea would mean either that he had no knowledge of the classics of Christian mysticism and therefore had nothing with which he might compare his own vision of immortality, or that his religion meant so little to him that, although he must have known about the doctrine of the Beatific Vision, it in fact meant nothing to him, or finally, what is more likely, that the experience, praeternatural though it undoubtedly was, did not suggest the presence of God at all.

The case of John Addington Symonds quoted on the next page of James's book is even more remarkable, but cannot be regarded as typical since it is obviously influenced by Hindu ideas which are used to explain, or explain away, the actual experience. In James's chapter on mysticism example crowds on example, and the piled up evidence leaves us in no doubt of the felt truth, if we may so express it, of the experience. We must be content with two examples only, one from Amiel's *Journal Intime* and the other from the German idealist, Malwida von Meysenbug. The first runs as follows:

'Shall I ever again have any of those prodigious reveries which sometimes came to me in former days? One day, in youth, at sunrise, sitting in the ruins of the castle of Faucigny; and again in the mountains, under the noonday sun, above Lavey, lying at the foot of a tree and visited by three butterflies; once more at night upon the shingly shore of the Northern Ocean, my back upon the sand and my vision ranging through the milky way;—such grand and spacious, immortal, cosmogonic reveries, when one reaches to the stars, when one owns the infinite! Moments divine, ecstatic hours; in which our thought flies from world to world, pierces the great enigma, breathes with a respiration broad, tranquil, and deep as the respiration of the ocean, serene and limitless as the blue firmament; . . . instants of irresistible intuition in which one feels one's self great as the universe, and calm as a god. . . . What hours, what memories!

[1] W. James, *The Varieties of Religious Experience*, London, Longmans, Green and Co., revised edition, 1902, p. 384.

[2] Ibid.

The vestiges they leave behind are enough to fill us with belief and enthusiasm, as if they were visits of the Holy Ghost.'[1]

Notice the phrase: 'breathes with a respiration, broad, tranquil, and deep'; and compare it with Huxley's vision of the flowers: 'I continued to look at the flowers, and in their living light I seemed to detect the qualitative equivalent of breathing.' The sea, the earth, trees, and breathing,—these are figures that continually occur in descriptions of this experience. Or perhaps it would be more accurate to say that they are the symbols which most naturally evoke the experience and abolish the consciousness of the personal ego. That the Holy Ghost (*Spiritus Sanctus* = 'Holy Breath') is mentioned in this context is, perhaps, no accident.

Our second and last example drawn from James is equally typical:

'I was alone upon the seashore as all these thoughts flowed over me, liberating and reconciling; and now again, as once before in distant days in the Alps of Dauphiné, I was impelled to kneel down, this time before the illimitable ocean, symbol of the Infinite. I felt that I prayed as I had never prayed before, and knew now what prayer really is: to return from the solitude of individuation into the consciousness of unity with all that is, to kneel down as one that passes away, and to rise up as one imperishable. Earth, heaven, and sea resounded as in one vast world-encircling harmony. It was as if the chorus of all the great who had ever lived were about me. I felt myself one with them, and it appeared as if I heard their greeting: "Thou too belongest to the company of those who have overcome." '[2]

Again we have the same symbols,—earth, heaven, and sea, and the same sense of the unity of all things, the same certainty of immortality.

To cap this series of quotations we may now turn to Jung's *Psychology of the Unconscious* where Karl Joel, a German philosopher who flourished in the early decades of this century, is quoted as saying:

'I lay on the seashore, the shining waters glittering in my dreamy eyes; at a great distance fluttered the soft breeze; throbbing, shimmering, stirring, lulling to sleep comes the wave beat to the shore—or to the ear? I know not. Distance and nearness become blurred into one; without and within glide into each other. Nearer and nearer, dearer and more homelike sounds the beating of the waves; now like a thundering pulse in my head it strikes, and now it beats over my soul, devours it, embraces it, while it itself at the same time floats out like the blue waste of waters. Yes, without and within are one. Glistening and foaming, flowing and fanning and roaring, the entire symphony of the stimuli experienced sounds in one tone, all thought becomes one thought, which becomes one with feeling; the world exhales in the soul and the soul dissolves in the world. Our small life is encircled by a great sleep—the sleep of our cradle, the sleep of our

[1] *The Varieties of Religious Experience*, pp. 394–5.

[2] Ibid., p. 395.

grave, the sleep of our home, from which we go forth in the morning, to which we again return in the evening; our life but the short journey, the interval between the emergence from the original oneness and the sinking back into it! Blue shimmers the infinite sea, wherein dreams the jelly fish of the primitive life, toward which without ceasing our thoughts hark back dimly through eons of existence. For every happening entails a change and a guarantee of the unity of life. At that moment when they are no longer blended together, in that instant man lifts his head, blind and dripping, from the depths of the stream of experience, from the oneness with the experience; at that moment of parting when the unity of life in startled surprise detaches the Change and holds it away from itself as something alien, at this moment of alienation the aspects of the experience have been substantialized into subject and object, and in that moment consciousness is born.'[1]

This passage again is strikingly similar to the two last we quoted from James's *Varieties*. The symbols of ocean and breath are there again, and the overriding sense of the oneness of being. Yet the purpose of Jung's quotation of it is very different from what we might have been expecting. Unlike Mr. Huxley and Mr. Bullett, Jung is not compiling an anthology to show that mysticism is a *philosophia perennis* that permeates and transcends all creeds. He quotes this as a final and (to him) convincing example in a chain of evidence drawn from mythology and literature which is held to show, as Jung puts it, 'in unmistakable symbolism, the confluence of subject and object as the reunion of mother and child'. It is true that when Jung wrote *Psychology of the Unconscious* he was still very much under the influence of Freud, and that he tended to interpret everything in the light of a mother 'fixation'. He had not yet come to distinguish what he was later to call 'individuation' or 'integration of the personality' which is a psychological advance beyond mere ego-dominated consciousness, from the subconscious longing, characteristic of psychologically immature persons, for the security of the infantile state and the pre-natal condition in which there is real identity of subject and object in the shape of the embryo enclosed in the mother's womb. This seemingly noble instinct which Huxley describes as a longing for self-transcendence and which he considers to be one of the principal appetites of the soul, this instinct which William James found equally unsympathetic in saint and madman, but the importance and wide prevalence of which he was quite unable to deny, was reduced by Jung, as well as by Freud, to a dim memory of childhood, that state of consciousness not yet born in which the infant is still unable to distinguish itself from the mother who gave it life and who continues to maintain it

[1] C. G. Jung, *Psychology of the Unconscious*, London, Routledge and Kegan Paul, 1919, pp. 198–9.

alive. 'The blessed state of sleep' referred to by Joel, the state called *suṣupti* in the Upaniṣads, that deep dreamless sleep in which all becomes one and which is the nearest approximation to ultimate bliss, this blessed state which Joel identified with the soul's condition before birth and after death, is, according to Jung, simply the 'thoughtless state of early childhood, where as yet no opposition disturbed the peaceful flow of dawning life, to which the inner longing always draws us back again and again, and from which the active life must free itself anew with struggle and death, so that it may not be doomed to destruction'. This nature mysticism, then, according to this school of psychology, is nothing more than an attempt to realize a pre-natal and prehistoric state. The commonest symbols of mysticism,—the sea, the air, trees, water,—are nothing more than symbols of the eternal feminine both in mythology and psychology; and the mystical experience, figured in practically all mystical traditions as a drop of water or a river dissolving into the sea, is simply a sign of infantilism in the adult, the desire to be unconscious once again in the security of the womb, a desire that the adult must overcome if he is ever to grow up at all.

Since Jung wrote *Psychology of the Unconscious* he has very greatly modified his views. He has given up much of the cruder sexual symbolism of Freud and has evolved the more fruitful ideas of the collective unconscious and the integration of the personality to which we shall have to return again and again. It does not seem, however, that nature mysticism can be wholly explained by the 'back to the womb' theory, attractive though it may be. Jung's later theory that every human being is psychologically androgynous, that is to say that every male has within his own psyche a female principle which Jung calls the *anima* and, conversely, every female has a male principle within herself, the *animus*, seems to be more sound and may be of help in elucidating some of the phenomena of nature mysticism, though not, I think, of theistic mysticism proper. Yet none of these theories fully explains all the phenomena of the natural mystical experience,—and in the case of Tennyson cited above they scarcely seem applicable,—for in this experience the subject is not only swallowed up in the greater whole; the greater whole, by an inconceivable paradox, actually seems to be part of oneself. This is very forcibly illustrated in the following quotation from the Irish novelist, Forrest Reid:

'It was as if I had never realized before how lovely the world was. I lay down on my back in the warm, dry moss and listened to the skylark singing as it mounted up from the fields near the sea into the dark clear sky. No other music ever gave me the same pleasure as that passionately joyous singing. It was a kind of leaping, exultant ecstasy, a bright, flame-like sound, rejoicing in itself. And then a curious experience befell me. It was as if everything that had seemed to be external and around me were suddenly within me. The whole world seemed to be within me. It was within me that the trees waved their green branches, it was within me that the skylark was singing, it was within me that the hot sun shone, and that the shade was cool. A cloud rose in the sky, and passed in a light shower that pattered on the leaves, and I felt its freshness dropping into my soul, and I felt in all my being the delicious fragrance of the earth and the grass and the plants and the rich brown soil. I could have sobbed with joy.'[1]

It is a little difficult to see just how this experience can be interpreted simply as a longing for the security of the womb. Here, it would appear, the roles have been reversed; for, in this case, the human subject appears in the role of the 'mother' and 'Mother Nature' has herself become the child! The symbolism has been reversed: son has become mother, and mother son!

The interpretation of this we must, for the present, leave to the psychologists. Here we only wish to emphasize the overwhelming nature of the evidence for the universality of this natural mystical experience. The nature of the experience can best be summed up in two phrases drawn from the passages we have quoted above: (i) 'without and within are one', and (ii) 'death was an almost laughable impossibility'. In other words nature mysticism means to transcend space and time.

The experience does not seem to be confined to any particular type of person; certainly it is not confined to neurotics, nor does it appear to be the result of any *conscious* desire to transcend oneself. I know that in my own case no such desire had ever entered my head; and the same was probably true of both Tennyson and Forrest Reid. It must be admitted that Forrest Reid had a marked interest in the praeternatural, and if we are to take his novels as reflecting his own interior life, he must have felt himself in communion with kindly powers in Nature which he liked to identify with the antique gods. But, as we have already seen, a visionary is not a mystic. It is one thing to feel that one is in contact with localized spirits, with gnomes and elves and the like; it is quite another to lie in the grass and to feel that you and Nature are mysteriously but literally one; 'without and within are one'.

William James, whose book is so valuable because his approach is so very detached and because it does succeed in being a model of objective scholarship, was obviously much puzzled by the whole phenomenon; and it is significant that he does not attempt to brush it aside as 'mere' illusion. His sympathies were plainly all on the side of the 'healthy-minded' as

[1] Forrest Reid, *Following Darkness*, London, Arnold, 1902, p. 42.

against the 'sick soul' who must be born again. Unlike Huxley he had no case to argue, no animosities to work off; but like Huxley he was struck by the similarity of the experiences of certain mystics and the effects produced by alcohol and drugs. This is a commonplace in the terminology of Islamic and particularly Persian mysticism in which 'drunkenness' is used figuratively for that type of ecstasy in which all sense of self seems to vanish away. Urged on by his curiosity to get to the bottom of the mystery, James decided himself to take nitrous oxide in order to see what its effects might be.

'One conclusion', he writes, 'was forced upon my mind at that time, and my impression of its truth has ever since remained unshaken. It is that our normal waking consciousness, rational consciousness as we call it, is but one special type of consciousness, whilst all about it, parted from it by the filmiest of screens, there lie potential forms of consciousness entirely different. We may go through life without suspecting their existence; but apply the requisite stimulus, and at a touch they are there in all their completeness, definite types of mentality which probably somewhere have their field of application and adaptation. No account of the universe in its totality can be final which leaves these other forms of consciousness quite disregarded. How to regard them is the question,—for they are so discontinuous with ordinary consciousness. Yet they may determine attitudes though they cannot furnish formulas, and open a region though they fail to give a map. At any rate, they forbid a premature closing of our accounts with reality. Looking back on my own experiences, they all converge towards a kind of insight to which I cannot help ascribing some metaphysical significance. The keynote of it is invariably a reconciliation. It is as if the opposites of the world, whose contradictoriness and conflict make all our difficulties and troubles, were melted into unity. Not only do they, as contrasted species, belong to one and the same genus, but *one of the species*, the nobler and better one, *is itself the genus, and so soaks up and absorbs its opposite into itself*. This is a dark saying, I know, when thus expressed in terms of common logic, but I cannot wholly escape from its authority. I feel as if it must mean something, something like what the hegelian philosophy means, if one could only lay hold of it more clearly. Those who have ears to hear, let them hear; to me the living sense of its reality only comes in the artificial mystic state of mind.'[1]

This, from James, is a startling confession, for his whole book shows that instinctively he is at home only with the 'healthy-minded', and not with the searchers for deliverance. He is with the Oscar Wildes against the Huxleys; he regards salvation as being a development and enlargement of the self, not as an annihilation in something higher and other. For, he says, 'if we are peevish and jealous, destruction of the self must be an element of

[1] *Varieties of Religious Experience*, pp. 388–9.

our religion; why need it be one if we are good and sympathetic from the outset? If we are sick souls, we require a religion of deliverance; but why think so much of deliverance, if we are healthy-minded? Unquestionably, some men have the completer experience and the higher vocation, here just as in the social world; but for each man to stay in his own experience, whate'er it be, and for others to tolerate him there, is surely best.'[1]

Great as is my sympathy with, and admiration for, William James, it seems to me that the last sentence, if literally interpreted, is open to criticism, since it does not wholly square with what he says elsewhere on the interesting subject of 'diabolic mysticism'. Both the Catholic Church and the Ṣūfīs have always believed and still believe in the Devil and his ability to counterfeit mystical states. Such a belief may sound old-fashioned, quixotic, or merely idiotic today; yet many Christian mystics, including St. Teresa of Avila, claim to have experienced such diabolical visitations. If, like James, we are prepared to accept the evidence of the mystics as genuine and to believe that they are doing their best to describe their experiences as they themselves felt them, then we must accept the distinction they draw between divine and diabolic visitations. James himself was not so foolishly sceptical as to discount the possibility of a diabolical mysticism, and he rightly saw that it manifested itself in insanity.

'In delusional insanity,' he writes, 'paranoia, as they sometimes call it, we may have a *diabolical* mysticism, a sort of religious mysticism turned upside down. The same sense of ineffable importance in the smallest events, the same texts and words coming with new meanings, the same voices and visions and leadings and missions, the same controlling by extraneous powers; only this time the emotion is pessimistic: instead of consolations we have desolations; the meanings are dreadful; and the powers are enemies to life. It is evident that from the point of view of their psychological mechanism, the classic mysticism and these lower mysticisms spring from the same mental level, from that great subliminal or transmarginal region of which science is beginning to admit the existence, but of which so little is really known.'[2]

This 'subliminal or transmarginal region' from which James here seems to derive all mystical experience seems to be an adumbration of what Jung now calls the 'collective unconscious': it is what Bucke preferred to call 'cosmic consciousness', and Huxley prefers to call 'Mind at Large'. If I understand Jung rightly, the collective unconscious might be compared to a vast sea of common race experience from which the individual consciousness sticks up like the top of an iceberg. Following up this metaphor we may say that the submerged and much larger portion of the iceberg would

[1] Ibid., pp. 487–8. [2] Ibid., p. 426.

be the personal unconscious. To achieve equilibrium between the three is to achieve sanity, integration, wholeness, salvation. To live in total disregard of the unconscious, as modern man tries to do, is to court disaster; for the unconscious which is irrational and 'bestial' in the sense that it recognizes neither good nor evil, the unconscious which represents the vegetable and animal souls of Aristotle and the schoolmen, the triad of imagination, anger, and lust of Avicenna and Ghazālī, cannot be disregarded, but must be acknowledged and controlled. The wild dicrepancies that exist between 'natural' and 'diabolical' mystical experiences, between the 'manic' and the 'depressive' states of the manic-depressive psychosis, between the glory and the terror experienced by Huxley under the influence of mescalin, are not explicable in terms of union with the Deity or unity in the Absolute or even of union with Nature. With the first two they have nothing to do at all. They are only explicable if we assume that beyond the individual soul there is a 'cosmic consciousness' or 'collective unconscious', a *vijñānālaya* or 'reservoir of consciousness' as the Mahāyāna Buddhists call it, which could be described as the totality of what Jung calls *anima* and what the Hindus call *prāṇa*,—a term that means both 'breath' and, by a natural philological extension, 'spirit' (*spiritus*, πνεῦμα), the non-rational animating principle of the universe. To judge by its operation in those who claim to have made contact with it, it is neither good nor evil. To judge from the experience of manic-depressives, it would seem to be good in so far as you are in harmony with it, and evil in so far as you are out of harmony. In it, according to Huxley, you will find not only original sin, but also 'original virtue'.[1] In this case Huxley would seem to have hit on a good idea, and it is a pity that he should have forgotten all about it in *The Doors of Perception.* Put briefly the idea is approximately this: the experience of manic-depressives, the manic side of which is almost identical with the 'natural' mystical experience, is not explicable in terms of pantheism or monism, since the 'depressive' experience illustrates all too clearly that though the manic may assert and vividly feel the unity of all things, the depressive feels precisely the opposite. The one is the dream of perfect harmony, the other the nightmare of senseless and malevolent discord. Both are experienced as equally real. Thus if you argue, with James and all serious students of the 'natural' mystical phenomenon, that you must accept the fact that, to the experiencer, this mystical state has transcendent reality other than, more valuable and more real than, all sense experience and discursive thought, and that this state is one of harmony, reconciliation, and oneness, by the same token you cannot deny an equal reality to the

[1] *The Devils of Loudun*, London, Chatto and Windus, 1952, p. 104.

depressive experience. If God is present in the first, then the Devil is equally present in the second. Alternatively, and more probably, both are manifestations of the 'collective unconscious', that mysterious psychic underworld that partakes equally of good and evil. One explanation of this phenomenon can be found in the ancient doctrine of the Fall and Original Sin: and this is a topic to which we shall have to return.

Before closing this chapter reference will have to be made to an outstanding English 'natural' mystic of the nineteenth century, Richard Jefferies, not so much because of the admirable word-pictures in which he expresses his sense of communion with Nature as because he is one of the few nature mystics who advances a theory which seeks to reconcile his praeternatural experiences with the hard world of 'fact'. In *The Story of my Heart* Jefferies attempts to put into words his spiritual development from the day when, at the age of eighteen, he first sensed his 'kinship' with all things, until his middle age.

Jefferies had broken with all organized religion which he invariably refers to as 'superstition'; and in particular he rejected the idea of a personal God Who deals out rewards and punishments. However, his 'pantheistic' experiences and the joy he derived from them did not in any way blind him to the wretchedness of human existence, nor did they produce in him any vision of a divine purpose. Julian of Norwich, a theistic mystic who believed herself to be in close union with God, was convinced that, despite appearances to the contrary, all was and would be 'very well'.[1] Jefferies would have none of this, for his experience taught him no such thing: this was not the message of Nature. Quite the contrary: to Jefferies the mere suggestion that there might be a wise disposer of the universe was a wicked insult to the human intelligence. 'How can I adequately express', he writes, 'my contempt for the assertion that all things occur for the best, for a wise and beneficent end, and are ordered by a humane intelligence! It is the most utter falsehood and a crime against the human race.'[2] Jefferies was, then, in the conventional sense, an atheist, and the fact that his ecstasies leave God strictly out of account is therefore not surprising. But his attitude to Nature is no less harsh. Nature is totally indifferent to the lot of man, and the rapture Jefferies derives from the contemplation of it, he derives, as he believes, from quite another source. The earth, the sea, the sun, and the trees, all of which are the 'matter' of his raptures, are, as objective entities, not only indifferent but hostile. For a 'nature mystic', the occasion for

[1] Julian of Norwich, *Revelations of Divine Love*, London, Burns Oates, 2nd ed., 1952, pp. 48 ff.

[2] *The Story of my Heart*, London, Duckworth, new ed., 1912, p. 104.

whose ecstasies were precisely the sun, the sea, and the earth, Jefferies has refreshingly few illusions.

'There is nothing human in nature', he roundly asserts. 'The earth, though loved so dearly, would let me perish on the ground, and neither bring forth food nor water. Burning in the sky the great sun, of whose company I have been so fond, would merely burn on and make no motion to assist me. Those who have been in an open boat at sea without water have proved the mercies of the sun, and of the deity who did not give them one drop of rain, dying in misery under the same rays that smile so beautifully on the flowers. In the south the sun is the enemy; night and coolness and rain are the friends of man. As for the sea, it offers us salt water which we cannot drink. The trees care nothing for us; the hill I visited so often in days gone by has not missed me. . . . All nature, all the universe that we can see, is absolutely indifferent to us, and except to us human life is of no more value than grass. If the entire human race perished at this hour, what difference would it make to the earth? What would the earth care? As much as for the extinct dodo, or for the fate of the elephant now going.

'On the contrary, a great part, perhaps the whole, of nature and of the universe is distinctly anti-human. The term inhuman does not express my meaning, anti-human is better; outre-human, in the sense of beyond, outside, almost grotesque in its attitude towards, would nearly convey it. Everything is anti-human.'[1]

Yet this is the same Jefferies who could almost identify himself with sun, earth, and sea; for these things, these anti-human and 'grotesque' objects were capable of stirring him to his depths and of evoking in him a sense of timelessness. This is how he describes his first experience of nature mysticism at the age of eighteen:

'I was utterly alone with the sun and the earth. Lying down on the grass, I spoke in my soul to the earth, the sun, the air, and the distant sea far beyond sight. I thought of the earth's firmness—I felt it bear me up; through the grassy couch there came an influence as if I could feel the great earth speaking to me. I thought of the wandering air—its pureness, which is its beauty; the air touched me and gave me something of itself. I spoke to the sea: though so far, in my mind I saw it, green at the rim of the earth and blue in deeper ocean; I desired to have its strength, its mystery and glory. Then I addressed the sun, desiring the soul equivalent of his light and brilliance, his endurance and unwearied race. I turned to the blue heaven over, gazing into its depth, inhaling its exquisite colour and sweetness. The rich blue of the unattainable flower of the sky drew my soul towards it, and there it rested, for pure colour is rest of heart. By all these I prayed; I felt an emotion of the soul beyond all definition; prayer is a puny thing to it, and the word is a rude sign to the feeling, but I know no other.

'. . . Touching the crumble of earth, the blade of grass, the thyme flower, breathing the earth-encircling air, thinking of the sea and the sky, holding out

[1] *The Story of my Heart*, pp. 43–45.

my hand for the sunbeams to touch it, prone on the sward in token of deep reverence, thus I prayed that I might touch to the unutterable existence infinitely higher than deity.'[1]

How then was it possible for Jefferies to describe the sun, the earth, and the sea as 'anti-human' and 'grotesque' after such an experience of 'intense communion'[2] as this, particularly as this communion was to lead to the further stage, so common to the nature mystics, in which he envisaged his own immortality? Before giving the answer (his own answer), however, we must, I fear, quote this later experience in which he feels himself as having transcended Time:

'Mystery gleaming in the stars, pouring down in the sunshine, speaking in the night, the wonder of the sun and of far space, for twenty centuries round about this low and green-grown dome. Yet all that mystery and wonder is as nothing to the Thought that lies therein, to the spirit that I feel so close.

'Realizing that spirit, recognizing my own inner consciousness, the psyche, so clearly, I cannot understand time. It is eternity now. I am in the midst of it. It is about me in the sunshine; I am in it, as the butterfly floats in the light-laden air. Nothing has to come: it is now. Now is eternity; now is the immortal life. Here this moment, by this tumulus, on earth, now; I exist in it.'[3]

These rhapsodies, described by Jefferies, in which time has no place, are occasioned by the sun, the air, the earth, and the sea, or, more specifically, by the 'idea' that underlies them: and yet, perhaps, not even that, for it is man who gives meaning to these objective symbols. It is true that 'they gave me inexpressible delight, *as if*[4] they embraced and poured out their love upon me'; but '*it was I*[4] who loved them, for my heart was broader than the earth. . . . After the sensuous enjoyment always came the thought, the desire: That I might be like this; that I might have the inner meaning of the sun, the light, the earth, the trees and grass, translated into some growth of excellence in myself, both of body and of mind'.[5]

In this passage we begin to realize how it is that Jefferies can at the same time condemn the whole of Nature, the whole of the universe, as being 'anti-human' and 'grotesque', and yet derive spiritual nourishment from it. It is not the physical object with which he communes, but its 'inner meaning', the idea or essence that man projects into it, or which he draws out of it. 'Feeling this by the sea, under the sun, my life enlarges and quickens,

[1] Ibid., pp. 3–4.

[2] Ibid., p. 4.

[3] Ibid., p. 30: cf. the classic formula of Parmenides (C. J. de Vogel, *Greek Philosophy*, i, Leyden, Brill, 1950, p. 38: cf. J. Burnet, *Early Greek Philosophy*, London, Adam and Charles Black, 4th ed., 1930, p. 174): *οὐδέ ποτ' ἦν οὐδ' ἔσται, ἐπεὶ νῦν ἔστιν ὁμοῦ πᾶν, | ἕν, ξυνεχές*—'It never was, nor shall it be ever; for it is now, together, all, one, continuous.'

[4] Author's italics.

[5] *The Story of my Heart*, p. 56.

striving to take to itself the largeness of the heaven. The frame cannot expand, but the soul is able to stand before it. No giant's body could be in proportion to the earth, but a little spirit is equal to the entire cosmos, the earth and ocean, sun and star-hollow.'[1]

So, according to Jefferies, the human soul is able to contain the entire universe within itself; but it only becomes conscious of this when it contemplates natural objects which are themselves soulless. Yet Nature itself, though 'anti-human' and much less than human, *is* animated. True,

'there is no god in nature, nor in any matter anywhere, either in the clods on the earth or in the composition of the stars. For what we understand by the deity is the purest form of Idea, of Mind, and no mind is exhibited in these. That which controls them is distinct altogether from deity. It is not force in the sense of electricity, nor a deity as god, nor a spirit, not even an intelligence, but a power quite different to anything yet imagined. I cease, therefore, to look for deity in nature or the cosmos at large, or to trace any marks of divine handiwork. I search for traces of this force which is not god, and is certainly not the higher than deity of whom I have written. It is a force without a mind. I wish to indicate something more subtle than electricity, but absolutely devoid of consciousness, and with no more feeling than the force which lifts the tides.'[2]

If this is so, then how are Jefferies's intense acts of communion with sun, earth, and sea to be explained? It would seem that he supposes all Nature to be pervaded by a force 'more subtle than electricity' which nevertheless has the power of producing a powerful sympathetic reaction in the human mind. The Indians long ago recognized the existence of such a force: they called it *prāṇa* which means 'breath' and can be translated as 'vital force' or simply 'wind', the spirit which animates the universe and which breathes in man. It is extremely interesting that Jefferies should have reached a similar idea independently, and particularly that he should draw so clear a distinction between it and what he calls 'deity' by which he means 'the purest form of Idea, of Mind', an intellectual substance distinct from the world and in no way responsible for it. 'Deity', again, in Jefferies's terminology, does not mean what Christians call 'God'. The idea of God (in Whom Jefferies professed not to believe) he expresses by the phrase 'higher than deity'. This is the supreme goal of all human endeavour and as such identical with 'God' as understood by St. Thomas Aquinas.

Jefferies, then, who thought that he had rejected Christianity as an outworn superstition, appears in fact as an unwilling witness on Christianity's behalf, for not only does he draw a clear distinction between the animating power in Nature which is capable of producing such surprising effects on the

[1] *The Story of my Heart*, pp. 81–82.

[2] Ibid., pp. 49–50.

sensitive subject, and the 'higher than deity' to which his soul constantly aspires and which it can never attain;[1] he also propounds what he thinks is a novel and interesting theory, namely that man's body is by nature immortal, but what is in fact a refreshing and original restatement of the doctrine of Original Sin and its deadly fruit. 'Our bodies are full of unsuspected flaws', he writes, 'handed down it may be for thousands of years, and it is of these that we die, and not of natural decay.'[2] Death, then, appears on earth not as a natural phenomenon, but as a hereditary flaw which we inherit from defective parents; and it is within man's power to remove this flaw and thereby to become immortal in body as well as in soul. This is almost exactly the Christian doctrine of Original Sin; for, according to the Christian legend, death came upon the human race as a result of Adam's sin. Man was created immortal in body and soul, and were it not for the hereditary 'defect' that has passed on to us from our first parent, our bodies would to this day be immortal. To Christians the guarantee that this 'original innocence' will one day be restored in its totality, is the Resurrection of Jesus Christ and his bodily Ascension into heaven. Jefferies differs from the orthodox Christian only in that he thinks that bodily immortality can be restored here and now. That he can seriously propound so preposterous a view only shows how profoundly his whole thought and life was imbued with what Huxley brilliantly calls 'original virtue'.

Jefferies is a rare case among mystics, whether 'natural' or otherwise. He is totally opposed to any form of mysticism that is based on asceticism: this he roundly condemns as 'the vilest blasphemy'.[3] His is a mysticism of soul *and* body, a mysticism as yet unsatisfied because he could never reach the 'higher than deity' to which he so fervently aspired. By his emphasis on the worthiness of the body as well as the soul, Jefferies stands nearer to orthodox Christian tradition than do many of the Christian mystics themselves whose excessive mortification of the body stems rather from that hidden residue of Manichaeanism which has been the curse of post-Augustinian Christianity, rather than from the risen Christ. Jefferies, like Rimbaud whom we will discuss in our next chapter, envisaged, however dimly, matter ennobled and sanctified by spirit. He might well have concluded his work, as Rimbaud concluded *Une Saison en Enfer*, with the words: 'et il me sera loisible de *posséder la vérité dans une âme et un corps*'.[4]

[1] Ibid., p. 82: 'No thought which I have ever had has satisfied my soul.' p. 146: 'All, all the cosmos is feeble; it is not strong enough to utter my prayer-desire. My soul cannot reach to its full desire of prayer.'

[2] Ibid., p. 108.

[3] Ibid., p. 88.

[4] Arthur Rimbaud, *Œuvres Complètes*, Paris, Bibliothèque de la Pléiade, Gallimard, 1954 (2nd imp.), p. 244: 'and it will be permitted me to possess the truth in a soul and a body.'

CHAPTER IV

GOD OR NATURE? (PROUST AND RIMBAUD)

We saw in the last chapter that the 'natural mystical experience' is a widely authenticated fact. It is frequently termed 'pantheistic'. This is a misnomer as will have appeared from the examples we have quoted in which there is no mention of God. It would, therefore, be more accurate to describe it either as a 'pamphysistic' or 'pan-en-henic' experience, an experience of Nature in all things or of all things as being one. In all cases the person who has the experience seems to be convinced that what he experiences, so far from being illusory, is on the contrary something far more real than what he experiences normally through his five senses or what he thinks with his finite mind. It is, at its highest, a transcending of time and space in which an infinite mode of existence is actually experienced. No wonder, then, that such an experience should appear to the subject to partake of a far greater degree of reality than our normal experiences, all of which are necessarily limited by the twin factors of space and time. Generalize this experience into a philosophy for which you claim universal validity, and you get the Vedānta ('that which is the finest essence this whole world has as its self. That is the real. That is the Self. That art thou'),[1] you get Parmenides (*νῦν ἔστιν ὁμοῦ πᾶν*).[2] Prima facie, then, it would appear that the Vedānta is a rationalization and systematization of the pan-en-henic experience; and this is something that we shall have to consider carefully later.

In this and the following chapter we shall be discussing three other cases of nature mysticism,—Proust, Rimbaud, and John Custance. This may seem an odd and arbitrary selection, but each of them has something important to say and helps to throw light on this curious phenomenon. Of the three Proust is perhaps the most important, first because the plan for his whole enormous novel seems to owe its origin to precisely the sort of experience which we have been describing, and secondly because he had an acutely analytical mind and by that token should, if anyone, be able to offer a rational explanation for this very irrational fact. His case is further interesting in that though he had an intimate knowledge of Catholic theology and Catholic practice, it never occurred to him to explain his own experience as an apprehension of God.

[1] *Chāndogya Upaniṣad*, 6. 9. 4 (sa ya eṣo 'ṇimā etad-ātmyam idaṁ sarvaṁ, tat satyaṁ, sa ātmā, tat tvam asi).

[2] See p. 47, n. 3.

Rimbaud is interesting from another point of view; for in him the 'natural' and the 'supernatural' seem to meet. Rimbaud was born and bred a Catholic and although he revolted against the Church with all the violence of which he was capable, he never wholly shook himself free from the formative influences of his childhood. On the other hand his actual praeternatural experiences which he describes in *Une Saison en Enfer* are akin to the cases of nature mysticism which we tried to analyse in the last chapter. Jefferies, Forrest Reid, and most of the persons we have discussed hitherto, were sane men: many of them might have been classed by William James among the 'healthy-minded'. Nobody could possibly put Rimbaud in such a category. During the years in which he was writing the *Illuminations* Rimbaud was mad in the sense that Blake was mad. His everyday world was not only the world of objective fact, it was a world in which the creatures of his fancy claimed equal reality with sense data; but over and above all this Rimbaud was haunted with a passionate longing for a personal relationship with God, and this, like Jefferies, he never found. The interest of Rimbaud's case is that though he attained his first objective which was to transcend the ego and to enter into an eternal mode of existence beyond space and time and beyond good and evil, he never attained to what he knew must be the final goal of the mystic, communion with God.

The last case we shall be studying is that of John Custance, a man who has on several occasions suffered for prolonged periods from acute mania and who has, at the same time, the ability to put the experiences of madness into words. His case is interesting first because his experiences are so strikingly similar to those of Mr. Huxley when under the influence of mescalin and to those of the nature mystic who is sane, and secondly because there is no doubt that these experiences were solely due to his insanity. This establishes the awkward fact that, as Huxley clearly realized, there is a definite connexion between nature mysticism and lunacy. It is not, then, surprising to find the Ṣūfīs continually employing the metaphor of 'madness' to describe their ecstasies and to read that one of their number at least, Shiblī, was in fact put under restraint in a lunatic asylum.[1] Thus though we may be prepared to concede for the time being that this experience, this blissful realization of the unity of all things in oneself, may be what the Zen Buddhists understand by 'enlightenment', and though it may lead to an integration of the personality as it appears to have done in the case of Proust, it may equally result in a complete breakdown of all accepted

[1] Abū Naṣr al-Sarrāj, *Kitābu'l-Luma'*, ed. R. A. Nicholson, Leyden, E. J. Brill, 1914, p. 50 of the Arabic text (*udkhila'l-māristāna wa-quyyida*,—'he was shut up in a lunatic asylum and fettered').

values, in a total indifference to good and evil, in madness and schizophrenia.

Proust's case is, in some ways, the most interesting, for the experience, with him, was productive of much good. It may, perhaps, be thought fanciful to attribute a 'mystical' significance to Proust's great novel. None the less this mystical element is the key to the whole book as anyone who reads the work carefully must realize. *A la Recherche du Temps perdu* has for its theme the transience of all things human and the folly of attaching one's affections to what, of its nature, is corrupt and must pass away. The theme is thoroughly oriental, more specifically Buddhistic; for Buddhism, by emphasizing the instability of all created things, preaches a disillusion and disgust with the world of which Proust's novel is a monumental illustration. Buddhism, however, also teaches that the transience and instability of the world can be overcome by the attainment of the state of *nirvāṇa.* Though it is certainly true that there is nothing in our mortal existence which is free from birth and death, coming to be and passing away, there is nevertheless 'an unborn, not become, not made, uncompounded, and were it not . . . for this unborn, not become, not made, uncompounded, no escape could be shown here for what is born, has become, is made, is compounded'.[1] The mere fact of transience is said to imply its opposite, the permanent, the unborn, *nirvāṇa,* immortality.

It is very doubtful whether Proust had any knowledge of the Buddhist classics; and it is therefore all the more interesting that his novel should in fact be one vast illustration of the Buddhist thesis. Everything in Proust is contrived: nothing is fortuitous. Hence when one first reads him, one is again and again held up by passages which seem unconnected with the main narrative and which are without any doubt descriptions of natural mystical experiences.

The theme first appears in the first part of the gigantic work, *Du Côté de chez Swann,* which both serves as an introduction to the whole and is also the whole work in miniature. The author has returned tired and dispirited from an afternoon walk, and his mother offers him a cup of tea and 'un de ces gâteaux courts et dodus appelés Petites Madeleines'. Depressed and mortally bored the author dips the bun into his tea and raises it to his lips.

'Mais à l'instant même où la gorgée mêlée des miettes du gâteau toucha mon palais, je tressaillis, attentif à ce qui se passait d'extraordinaire en moi. Un plaisir délicieux m'avait envahi, isolé, sans la notion de sa cause. Il m'avait

[1] *Udāna,* 81: cf. Edward Conze, *Buddhist Texts through the Ages,* Oxford, Bruno Cassirer, 1954, p. 95.

aussitôt rendu les vicissitudes de la vie indifférentes, ses désastres inoffensifs, *sa brièveté illusoire*,[1] de la même façon qu'opère l'amour, en me remplissant d'une essence précieuse: ou plutôt cette essence n'était pas en moi; *elle était moi*.[1] J'avais cessé de me sentir médiocre, *contingent*, *mortel*.[1] D'où avait pu me venir cette puissante joie? Je sentais qu'elle était liée au goût du thé et du gâteau, mais qu'elle le dépassait infiniment, ne devait pas être de même nature. D'où venait-elle? Que signifiait-elle? Où l'appréhender?'[2]

To anyone who has even dimly experienced the ecstasies described in the last chapter, this passage is arresting and at the same time tantalizing. Yet the evidence seems clear enough: the mere taste of a bun soaked in tea had, for no reason at all, suggested to Proust unmistakably that the shortness of life is illusory, that the 'precious essence' which filled him was at the same time himself, and that his being was therefore eternal and immortal. Like the supreme artist he is, Proust leaves the astonishing episode to speak for itself and resumes the main thread of his narrative with little further comment. The reader is left wondering whether he was not mistaken and whether he was in fact reading into the episode of the 'petite madeleine' a content that it could not bear.

Patience is, however, rewarded: for,—again in *Du Côté de chez Swann*,—we soon stumble upon a similar passage, a similar mood, this time evoked by the sight of the spires of Martinville. On this occasion Proust, with the exquisite artistry we expect from him, is far less explicit. He says nothing of the felt certainty of immortality which comes as such a shock to the reader of the first passage. This time he is content, like the Ṣūfī poets, to throw out a hint only,—a hint which will be avidly seized upon by the initiate but which will pass the casual reader by unnoticed. All that actually happens is that he looks at the spires a second time and is, again for no reason, intoxicated by the mere sight of them. 'Bientôt leurs lignes et leurs surfaces ensoleillées, comme si elles avaient été une sorte d'écorce, se déchirèrent, un peu de ce qui m'était caché en elles m'apparut, j'eus une pensée qui n'existait pas pour moi l'instant avant, qui se formule en mots dans ma

[1] Author's italics.

[2] *A la Recherche du Temps perdu*, Paris, Bibliothèque de la Pléiade, Gallimard, 1954, vol. i, p. 45: 'But at the very moment when the mouthful mixed with the crumbs of the cake touched my palate, I shuddered, as I took note of the strange things that were going on inside me. An exquisite pleasure had invaded me,—isolated, with no idea of what its cause might be. Immediately it had made the vicissitudes of life indifferent, its disasters inoffensive, its brevity illusory,—in much the same way as love operates, filling me with a precious essence: or rather this essence was not *in* me, it *was* me. I had ceased to feel mediocre, contingent, or mortal. Whence should this strong joy have come to me? I felt that it was connected with the taste of the tea and the cake, but that it transcended it infinitely and could not be of the same nature. Whence did it come? What did it mean? How to lay hold of it?'

tête, et le plaisir que m'avait fait tout à l'heure éprouver leur vue s'en trouva tellement accru que, pris d'une sorte d'ivresse, je ne pus plus penser à autre chose.'[1] And that is all. Once again the reader rubs his eyes and wonders even more (so vague are the indications) whether he had not been mistaken the first time.

Once again, half-way through *A l'Ombre des jeunes Filles en Fleur*, Proust throws out another hint. This time the mysterious joy is caused by the sight of three trees which seemed to claim a reality denied to all the rest of the landscape, to friends and acquaintances, and to the very life that Proust was living. 'Tout d'un coup', he writes, 'je fus rempli de ce bonheur profond que je n'avais pas souvent ressenti depuis Combray, un bonheur analogue à celui que m'avaient donné, entre autres, les clochers de Martinville.'[2]

And this appears to be the sum-total of Proust's mystical experience, for the reader reads on and on through what appears to be the main theme of the novel, the author's penetration into, and analysis of, a dying aristocratic society, the 'grandeurs et misères' of M. de Charlus, the author's own tragically egotistical love affair, his self-torture, and final disillusionment with all things. What has become of the 'petite madeleine' and the spires of Martinville, the little things that held the keys of immortality?

The reader will have been bleakly impressed by this magnificent display of the natural corruption of all things, this vanity of vanities from which there appears to be no escape. 'Were it not . . . for this unborn, not become, not made, uncompounded, no escape could be shown here from what is born, has become, is made, is compounded.' What, then, has become of the unborn which seemed to show itself in a little bun dipped in a cup of tea?

Patience, however, is once again rewarded, for on reaching the second half of *Le Temps retrouvé* we find the author weary and dejected approaching yet another tiresome reception at the town house of the new Princesse de Guermantes,—and once again the miracle happens. As he is about to enter the house he stumbles over some paving-stones. On regaining his balance he puts one foot on a stone situated a little higher than the one on which his other foot is resting. On doing this 'tout mon découragement

[1] *A la Recherche du Temps perdu*, vol. i, pp. 180–1: 'Soon their sun-drenched lines and surfaces split open just as if they had been a kind of bark, and a little of what had been hidden from me in them, appeared to me; I had a thought which, a moment ago, had not existed for me and which took on verbal form in my head. The pleasure which the sight of them had just awakened in me, was so greatly enlarged that, seized with a sort of drunkenness, I could think of nothing else.'

[2] Ibid., p. 717: 'All of a sudden I was filled with that profound happiness which I had not often felt since Combray,—a happiness analogous to that which the spires of Martinville, among other things, had given me.'

s'évanouit devant la même félicité qu'à diverses époques de ma vie m'avaient donnée la vue d'arbres que j'avais cru reconnaître dans une promenade en voiture autour de Balbec, la vue des clochers de Martinville, la saveur d'une madeleine trempée dans une infusion, tant d'autres sensations dont j'ai parlé et que les dernières œuvres de Vinteuil m'avaient paru synthétiser'.[1]

Earlier in this book we compared Huxley's experience under the influence of mescalin to what the Zen Buddhists describe as *satori*. For the achievement of this state normally two things are necessary; first the mind should be emptied of all conceptual thought, and images should be allowed to pass freely through it. Secondly, in order that the actual state of *satori* which seems to be identical with the natural mystical experience, should be produced, some slight external shock is necessary. This may be anything: it might be the sight of a flower in spring, or the unexpected dropping of a solid object: it might be simply the sensation of a slight lack of balance produced by having the feet unexpectedly placed at different levels, or the sight of a church spire, or the re-reading of a poem that one had thought was familiar.

So too for Proust, these glimpses of eternity were produced by events which, in themselves, were not at all extraordinary,—little things that nevertheless gave him an insight into a timeless world. That this insight was overpowering and quite extraordinary is plain from Proust's own words. 'De nouveau la vision éblouissante et indistincte me frôlait comme si elle m'avait dit: "Saisis-moi au passage si tu en as la force, et tâche à résoudre l'énigme de bonheur que je te propose."'[2] Yet what had happened? In what did the vision actually consist? 'Et presque tout de suite', he goes on, 'je la reconnus, c'était Venise.'[3] The two paving-stones on different levels had brought to mind, or perhaps it would be more accurate to say, had brought to life two similar paving-stones in the baptistery of St. Mark's and, with the paving-stones, the complete and total memory, the relived experience of a time long past. Yet how should this account for the sudden joy, the sudden and total disappearance of anxiety and doubt? 'Pourquoi', Proust asks, 'les images de Combray et de Venise m'avaient-elles, à l'un

[1] Ibid., vol. iii, p. 866: 'All my depression vanished away before the same blissfulness which I had experienced at different periods of my life,—in the sight of trees I had thought I recognized in a drive around Balbec, in the sight of the spires of Martinville, in the taste of a bun dipped in a cup of tea, in so many other feelings of which I have spoken and which the last works of Vinteuil had seemed to sum up.'

[2] Ibid., p. 867: 'Once again the blinding yet indistinct vision lightly touched me as if it had said to me, "Grasp me as I flit by you, if you have strength enough, and try to solve the riddle of happiness that I put before you."'

[3] 'And almost at once I recognized it, it was Venice.'

et à l'autre moment, donné une joie pareille à une certitude, et suffisante, sans autres preuves, à me rendre la mort indifférente?'[1] What had a mere memory, however perfectly re-created, to do with an experience that seemed to transcend time? Both the uneven paving-stones and the relived memory were only symptoms; they did not by any means constitute the actual experience. For what had the baptistery at St. Mark's meant to Proust at the time? Nothing at all. It was the reliving of a past moment that was significant, not that moment itself: for in this experience the past met the present, and both were felt with a totally new intensity. It was a 'renewal' and a liberation. Past and present met with such a sense of actuality that Proust had difficulty in knowing which he was living in. Moreover, it was not at all clear whether it was Proust himself who was experiencing those blessed moments or another being which had temporarily displaced him.

'Au vrai,' he writes, 'l'être qui alors goûtait en moi cette impression la goûtait en ce qu'elle avait de commun dans un jour ancien et maintenant, dans ce qu'elle avait d'extra-temporel, un être qui n'apparaissait que quand, par une de ces identités entre le présent et le passé, il pouvait se trouver dans le seul milieu où il pût vivre, jouir de l'essence des choses, c'est à dire en dehors du temps. Cela expliquait que mes inquiétudes au sujet de ma mort eussent cessé au moment où j'avais reconnu inconsciemment le goût de la petite madeleine, puisqu'à ce moment-là l'être que j'avais été était un être extra-temporel, par conséquent insoucieux des vicissitudes de l'avenir. Cet être-là n'était jamais venu à moi, ne s'était jamais manifesté, qu'en dehors de l'action, de la jouissance immédiate, chaque fois que le miracle d'une analogie m'avait fait échapper au présent.'[2]

Who was this being that has so suddenly and disconcertingly come to life in Marcel Proust?

'L'être', he goes on to say, 'qui etait rené en moi quand, avec un tel frémissement de bonheur, j'avais entendu le bruit commun à la fois à la cuiller qui touche l'assiette et au marteau qui frappe sur la roue, à l'inégalité pour les pas

[1] 'Why had the images of Combray and of Venice, at each separate moment, given me a joy which amounted to a certitude and was sufficient, without further proof, to make death a matter of indifference to me?'

[2] *A la Recherche du Temps perdu*, vol. iii, p. 871: 'In truth the being which was then tasting this impression in me tasted it in what was common between a day long past and now, in what was outside time: and this being would only appear at a time when, through one of these identities between the present and the past, it could exist in the only atmosphere in which it could live and enjoy the essence of things, that is to say outside time. That explained why my preoccupation with death should have ceased at the moment when, unconsciously, I recognized the taste of the little bun; for at that moment the being that I had been was an extra-temporal being and therefore careless of the vicissitudes of the future. This being had never come to me, had never revealed itself except as outside action and immediate sensations of enjoyment, every time that the miracle of an analogy had enabled me to escape from the present.'

des pavés de la cour Guermantes et du baptistère de Saint-Marc, etc., cet être-là ne se nourrit que de l'essence des choses, en elle seulement il trouve sa subsistance, ses délices.... Mais qu'un bruit, qu'une odeur, déjà entendu ou respirée jadis, le soient de nouveau, à la fois dans le présent et dans le passé, réels sans être actuels, idéaux sans être abstraits, aussitôt l'essence permanente et habituellement cachée des choses se trouve libérée, et notre vrai moi qui, parfois depuis longtemps, semblait mort, mais ne l'était pas entièrement, s'éveille, s'anime en recevant la céleste nourriture qui lui est apportée. Une minute affranchie de l'ordre du temps a recréé en nous, pour la sentir, l'homme affranchi de l'ordre du temps. Et celui-là, on comprend qu'il soit confiant dans sa joie, même si le simple goût d'une madeleine ne semble pas contenir logiquement les raisons de cette joie, on comprend que le mot de "mort" n'ait pas de sens pour lui; situé hors du temps, que pourrait-il craindre de l'avenir?'[1]

It is extremely interesting that in this passage Proust should distinguish two 'selves',—one the ordinary, everyday self which somehow is thrust aside during these brief moments of ecstasy, and the other, the 'self' which he refers to as 'cet être', this being, the real self which normally seems dead, but which is brought to life in these unaccountable visitations of the infinite. Yet it plainly did not mean for him any expansion of the everyday ego; it was rather a suppression of that tiresome entity. For 'au lieu de me faire une idée plus flatteuse de mon moi, j'avais, au contraire, presque douté de la réalité actuelle de ce moi'.[2]

In trying to explain the actual mechanics of the experience Proust distinguishes two things. First there is the immediate occasion for the experience, —the uneven steps, the sound of a spoon on a plate, or whatever it may be that brings to life, out of the unconscious, a whole scene from the past.

[1] Ibid., pp. 872–3: 'The being that had been reborn in me when, with so great a quiver of happiness, I heard a noise that was common both to a spoon touching a plate and to a hammer striking against a wheel, to the unevenness, perceptible to the feet, both of the Guermantes quadrangle and the baptistery of St. Mark's etc., —that being feeds on nothing but the essence of things, in them alone it finds its subsistence and its delight. . . . It suffices that a sound once heard before, or a scent once breathed in, should be heard and breathed again, simultaneously in the present and the past, real without being actual, ideal without being abstract; then, immediately, the permanent essence of things which is usually hidden, is set free, and our real self, which often had seemed dead for a long time, yet was not dead altogether, awakes and comes to life as it receives the heavenly food now proffered to it. One minute delivered from the order of time creates in us, that we may enjoy it, the man delivered from the order of time. How easy to understand that this man should be confident in his joy, even if the mere taste of a bun may not seem, logically, to contain within itself the reasons for that joy. It is understandable that the word "death" can have no meaning for him: situated, as he is, outside time, what could he fear from the future?'

[2] 'Instead of taking a more flattering view of my ego, I had, on the contrary, almost doubted the actual reality of the ego.'

This scene is experienced so vividly,—in its essence, as he puts it,—that it is impossible to say whether the past or the present is the more actual and real. The common elements in the past and the present experience fuse together in an identity which seems to be outside time and which participates in the nature of eternity. The past combines with the present, but only for a moment, for the present must always prove the stronger in the end.

'Toujours, dans ces résurrections-là, le lieu lointain engendré autour de la sensation commune s'était accouplé un instant, comme un lutteur, au lieu actuel. Toujours le lieu actuel avait été vainqueur; toujours c'était le vaincu qui m'avait paru le plus beau. . . . Et si le lieu actuel n'avait pas été aussitôt vainqueur, je crois que j'aurais perdu connaissance; car ces résurrections du passé, dans la seconde qu'elles durent, sont si totales qu'elles n'obligent pas seulement nos yeux à cesser de voir la chambre qui est près d'eux pour regarder la voie bordée d'arbres ou la marée montante; elles forcent nos narines à respirer l'air de lieux pourtant lointains, notre volonté à choisir entre les divers projets qu'ils nous proposent, notre personne tout entière à se croire entourée par eux, ou du moins à trébucher entre eux et les lieux présents, dans l'étourdissement d'une incertitude pareille à celle qu'on éprouve parfois devant une vision ineffable, au moment de s'endormir.'[1]

Thus though the vision is composed of elements detached from time, the contemplation, though it is of eternity, lasts only for the twinkling of an eye. This vision, or rather this series of visions, seems to have constituted a turning-point in Proust's life; for out of it sprang the whole theory that was to be brought to its triumphant conclusion in *Le Temps retrouvé*, 'Time rediscovered', or the finding of eternity within the human self. 'La seule manière de les goûter davantage, c'etait de tâcher de les connaître plus complètement, là ou elles se trouvaient, c'est à dire en moi-même, de les rendre claires jusque dans leurs profondeurs.'[2] Proust had perhaps at last

[1] *A la Recherche du Temps perdu*, vol. iii, pp. 874–5: 'In these resuscitations the far-off place brought to life around a common sensation had always, like a wrestler, come to grips with the place in which one actually was. It was the present that always proved the victor, yet always did the vanquished seem to me the more beautiful. . . . Had the present place not straightway proved the victor, I think I should have lost consciousness: for these resuscitations of the past are, for the moment that they last, so total that they force not only our eyes to stop seeing the room in their immediate vicinity in order to look at a tree-lined road or the rising tide; they force our nostrils to breathe the air of places which are yet far distant, our will to choose between the different plans they offer us, and our whole person to believe that it is surrounded by them, or at least to stumble between them and the present location, in a stupefied uncertainty similar to what we sometimes experience before an ineffable vision as we are about to fall asleep.'

[2] Ibid., p. 877: 'The only way to savour them more intensely was to try to know them more completely where they really were, that is to say, in myself, and to make them luminous right down to their depths.'

discovered the meaning of that deceptively simple phrase, 'The kingdom of God is within you'; for the kingdom of God is necessarily eternity, but the kingdom and the King are two different things.

To regard Proust as a pessimist is equivalent to regarding the Buddha in this light, and both views are widely maintained. Yet the greatness and point of Proust's work consists in his ability to see the permanent beneath the merely transitory and frivolous. It is true that all purely human relationships in his novel go sour, and that superficially it is the story of one long decline from grace and of accumulated disillusion. But to see only this is to miss the point entirely; for the pathetic decline and Proust's merciless exposure of it must be seen against the background of what is to Proust the profounder reality,—the reality revealed by such apparently insignificant experiences as the dipping of a bun into a cup of tea or the tinkle of a spoon against a plate. These are the little things that suggested correspondences with events and emotions in time past, and through these correspondences and analogies produced a vision of a harmonious reality, the sum-total of which adds up to the fulfilled personality of Marcel Proust himself. Thus when Proust speaks of the other being who is at the same time himself and a stranger to himself and too often seemingly dead, he speaks not, I think, of an indwelling God, but of a human personality finally realized in an environment which is neither identical with space and time nor with eternity, but which partakes of both. This environment is the mode in which the Angels live, according to St. Thomas; it is *aevum* or 'aeveternity'.

Proust makes no claim that this second 'self' which experiences these visions is the God dwelling within him. He sees them rather as the sum-total of his life in time and space, not one moment of which is permanently lost. Because of all men who have left records of their 'natural mystical' experiences he had by far the most acute and remorselessly analytical mind, his writing on this matter is worthy of the most respectful attention. He too was unable to describe his experience as accurately as he wished, yet it is true to say that he drew no pantheistic or monistic conclusions from it, and that he was content to note that another 'self', a self that usually seems to be dead, was discovered below the ordinary experiencing ego, and that this self was concerned with experiences that transcended time and space, but did not, for all that, transcend the personality of Marcel Proust and the life which formed the sum-total of that personality. Thus Proust differs from the 'nature mystics' we have discussed hitherto in that he experiences no enlargement of the personality beyond its natural bounds. In his experience there is no merging into Nature, there is only a complete realization of self.

It is not what Jung calls a case of inflation, but a genuine case of 'integration'. It brings to mind Wilde's description of the 'true personality of man':

'It will be a marvellous thing—the true personality of man—when we see it. . . . It will know everything. And yet it will not busy itself about knowledge. It will have wisdom. Its value will not be measured by material things. It will have nothing. And yet it will have everything, and whatever one takes from it, it will still have, so rich will it be.'[1] Or again, to quote the same author, '"Know thyself!" was written over the portal of the antique world. Over the portal of the new world, "Be thyself" shall be written. And the message of Christ to man was simply "Be thyself". That is the secret of Christ.'[2]

Christians will no doubt dispute this particularistic interpretation of the teaching of their Founder; but as an enunciation of what Proust was later to achieve,—the realization of his true self through a praeternatural experience,—it is singularly apt. To be oneself, in this sense, means to realize oneself not as a person limited to a mortal body and therefore essentially dependent on space and time, but as 'the real self set free from the order of time' which, for Proust, seemed to have very little to do with his transient ego which, though it had achieved most of what it had set out to achieve, remained, nevertheless, eternally unsatisfied.

Proust, then, saw this experience as the occasion for the integration of his personality: it was the psychological cure of his neurosis. He neither saw it nor felt it as an absorption into a larger entity, an experience which the psychologists would explain as a yearning for the state of security that the embryo enjoys in its mother's womb or as the overwhelming of the ego by the contents of the unconscious. His experience, though superficially it may have much in common with the ecstasies of the Richard Jefferies type in that there is the same feeling of joyous release and of union with something that is normally imperceptible to the everyday ego, is really quite different; for whereas the nature mystics we dealt with in the last chapter all seem to experience a kind of union with Nature or oneness with all things, Proust, on the contrary, experiences his whole individual life as being integrated outside time. In the one case,—and I am thinking particularly of the passage I quoted from Forrest Reid,—it is the impression that the human being in some sense comprises all Nature or is dissolved into Nature; in the other it is the certainty that one has realized one's own soul as it is in eternity. The one would appear to be the fusion of the human psyche with Nature, the other is rather the realization of one's true nature

[1] See above, p. 18.

[2] From *The Soul of Man under Socialism*; *The Works of Oscar Wilde*, London, Collins, 1948, p. 1024.

in itself. Or, if we prefer the Aristotelian phraseology, Proust became his final cause; or, to use the Jungian jargon, he achieved the integration of his personality or 'individuation'. He became 'what he is and always was'.[1]

Proust achieved this not by any conscious effort, for it was not by self-analysis that he crossed the threshold of eternity, but in spite of and against that self-analysis which, so far from integrating his personality, had done much, it would seem, to dissociate it from its unconscious roots. The magic moments he describes came to him unsolicited; they were a 'gratuitous grace' which revealed a 'second self' within him whose operation was outside time and which therefore was unquestionably immortal. Proust's experience, unlike the experiences of Huxley, Jefferies, and the other cases we have discussed, is neither the absorption of the natural order into the experiencing self nor the dissolution of the latter in the spirit that pervades all Nature; it is the rounding off of an individual personality in both past and present, and in eternity. It is the realization of the individual soul as something other than the ego, something of which the 'other self', as he calls it, is the imperishable centre. This is quite distinct from the 'pan-en-henic' experience; it is simply the felt realization of one's soul as immortal.

The case of Arthur Rimbaud is quite different and far more complicated. Proust was a neurotic and an introvert of the most extreme type. He had never sought out praeternatural experiences, but when they came unasked, he did his best to analyse them and to profit by them. His upbringing had been theistic and his knowledge of the Catholic religion was considerable, and it would be surprising if he had not at least a nodding acquaintance with the Catholic mystics. Yet it never seems to have occurred to him that his tasting of immortality and the seeming liberation of his 'second' and immortal self could be attributed to any direct action of God. Proust's case is not comparable either to the pan-en-henic experience, or to the theistical mystic's experience of being united to God: it is simply the realization of the wholeness of his own personality in independence,—separate both from God (if we concede His existence) and from the world. Proust's experience is in accordance with the Sāṁkhya-Yoga 'philosophy' (a better term would be 'psychology') the aim of which is precisely to liberate the immortal soul from all its purely mortal trappings.[2]

With Rimbaud we pass to the other extreme. He seems to be a case of self-induced psychosis, of praeternatural experience deliberately and

[1] From *Principles of Practical Psychotherapy*, in *Collected Works*, London, Routledge and Kegan Paul, vol. xvi, 1954, p. 10.

[2] See below, pp. 98–99 and 107–9.

recklessly sought. His is not a case of 'grace' gratuitously given or appearing unsolicited and one knows not whence. Rather, he seeks to take heaven by storm, and to capture it not by the regular warfare prescribed by the Church but by a surprise attack which was to seize upon the holy place from the quarter in which it would be least prepared, from the approaches of Hell.

Rimbaud, like many of the best and most generous spirits of his generation, was in revolt against the contemporary 'bourgeois' morality, what he calls his 'sale éducation d'enfance'.[1] He was, therefore, in revolt against the Church too which, like Marx and Engels, he saw as a staunch ally of the bourgeois order, the order, for him, of middle-class respectability and cant. It is certainly true of the case of Rimbaud that he was driven on by the urge 'to escape selfhood and the environment', and it is precisely in this that he differed so sharply from the great majority of his fellow-men. There was, however, more to it than this. Whatever the methods he employed, he was not merely in search of an experience which would break down the walls between himself and the objective world, he was consciously in search of God Himself. Despite the blasphemies[2] and despite the condition of temporary madness that he deliberately induced, Rimbaud knew that he could never be satisfied with a praeternatural experience as such; he could not be satisfied unless and until he felt himself to be in the presence of God.

In this chapter we shall analyse, to the best of our ability, his experiences as presented in *Une Saison en Enfer* which was certainly based on his actual experience. According to Dr. Enid Starkie, the *Saison* was planned from the beginning on the lines of the finished product,[3] and it represents Rimbaud's final judgement on his excursion into the realms beyond space and time.

Dr. Starkie has rightly pointed out that Rimbaud's experiment is conditioned by two warring and irreconcilable doctrines, Christianity and an amoral alchemical theory presumably derived from his reading in the public library. We should, I think, accept Dr. Starkie's thesis that Rimbaud had absorbed a certain amount of alchemical theory though the evidence of how and when he did so seems to be a trifle thin.[4] That he based his 'aesthetic doctrine' on an advanced type of pantheistic theory akin to the Kabbala on the one hand and to certain types of Hindu mysticism on the other, seems proved by the letters to Izambard of 13 May 1871 and to

[1] Arthur Rimbaud, *Œuvres Complètes*, Paris, Bibliothèque de la Pléiade, 1954, p. 241.

[2] As Rimbaud's younger sister, Isabelle, sensibly remarks, 'Pour le côté irréligieux, je vous dirai seulement: le blasphème implique nécessairement la foi'. (Ibid., p. 604.)

[3] Enid Starkie, *Arthur Rimbaud*, revised ed., London, Hamish Hamilton, 1947, p. 253.

[4] See ibid., pp. 124–37.

Démeny of 15 May of the same year. This doctrine has much in common with the theory of Mind at Large put forward by Mr. Huxley in *The Doors of Perception*. Its purpose is to dissolve the ego in what Rimbaud calls 'the universal mind', an entity that seems to correspond fairly exactly to the 'collective unconscious' of Jung.

The poet is no longer himself: this is the *leitmotif* of Rimbaud's theory of poetry as developed in the two letters mentioned above. 'Car JE est un autre',—'I is another', he disconcertingly declares in the letter to Démeny. 'Si le cuivre s'éveille clairon, il n'y a rien de sa faute. Cela m'est évident: j'assiste à l'éclosion de ma pensée: je la regarde, je l'écoute: je lance un coup d'archet: la symphonie fait son remuement dans les profondeurs, ou vient d'un bond sur la scène.'[1]

'I is another.' This is precisely what Proust had found on the steps of the town house of the Princesse de Guermantes. Behind and beyond the ego is another ego, another self, 'un autre moi', which lives in eternity, beyond time and space, the immortality of which, when once it has been found, cannot be doubted. 'Les vieux imbéciles n'avaient pas trouvé du Moi que la signification fausse';[2] the 'I' or 'self' had previously been misinterpreted, for the real 'I' is another: 'JE est un autre.' The function of the poet who, for Rimbaud, is identical with the seer ('Je dis qu'il faut être *voyant*, se faire *voyant*'),[3] is to discover himself, the real self dormant below the busy ego. This is the classic doctrine of alchemy, the search of the *lapis*; as it is also the central doctrine of Hindusim, the search of the *ātman* or transcendental self. This 'self' Rimbaud appears to identify with 'universal mind (l'intelligence universelle)' which throws out its ideas 'naturally', that is in accordance with Nature with which it seems to be identical. These ideas have never been collected in their entirety. It is true that certain elect spirits had worked through this 'universal mind' and written at its dictation, but no one had been awakened fully to the 'great dream'. 'On agissait par, on en écrivait des livres: telle allait la marche, l'homme ne se travaillant pas, n'étant pas encore éveillé, ou pas encore dans la plénitude du grand songe. Des fonctionnaires, des écrivains: auteur, créateur, poëte, cet homme n'a jamais existé.'[4]

[1] *Œuvres Complètes*, p. 270: 'If the brass wakes up as a bugle, it is through no fault of its own. That is plain enough to me: I am a spectator at the burgeoning of my thought: I look at it and listen to it: I play one stroke of the bow. The symphony stirs in the depths, or with one bound leaps on to the stage.'

[2] Ibid.: 'The old idiots only succeeded in finding the wrong meaning of the ego.'

[3] Ibid.: 'I say that we must be *seers*, we must make ourselves *seers*.'

[4] Ibid.: 'People acted by it, wrote books from it: that is how things went on, man not working upon himself, not having yet woken up, or not being yet in the fullness of

Whatever Rimbaud's reading at Charleville may have been, it is quite clear that he had in fact struck something that was very like the classical Vedānta of the Hindus.[1] The 'universal mind' would correspond to Brahman, the 'great dream' to the concept of *māyā*, the phenomenal world seen as a dream or an illusion imposed by Brahman on himself, whereas the 'other self' corresponds to the *ātman*, the individual soul which, according to the orthodox Vedānta, is fully identical with Brahman, the Absolute. Hence in order to participate in the 'great dream' it is first necessary to know oneself through and through, for basically one is identical with the 'universal mind' or Brahman.

Thus it seems quite natural to Rimbaud to pass without any apparent connecting link from the consideration of the operations of the universal mind in individual men to the necessity of knowing oneself. 'La première étude de l'homme qui veut être poëte est sa propre connaissance, entière; il cherche son âme, il l'inspecte, il la tente, l'apprend. Dès qu'il la sait, il doit la cultiver! Cela semble simple: en tout cerveau s'accomplit un développement naturel.'[2] Each soul develops 'naturally' back to Nature; but for Rimbaud this is not enough. He rejects the method of concentration (the Yoga techniques of the East, had he been familiar with them) and insists on a technique the aim of which is not to control the senses but to throw them into the maximum disorder.

'Le Poëte se fait *voyant* par un long, immense et raisonné *dérèglement* de *tous les sens*. Toutes les formes d'amour, de souffrance, de folie; il cherche lui-même, il épuise en lui tous les poisons, pour n'en garder que les quintessences. Ineffable torture où il a besoin de toute la foi, de toute la force surhumaine, où il devient entre tous le grand malade, le grand criminel, le grand maudit,—et le suprême Savant!—Car il arrive à l'*inconnu*! Puisqu'il a cultivé son âme, déjà riche, plus qu'aucun! Il arrive à l'inconnu, et quand, affolé, il finirait par perdre l'intelligence de ses visions, il les a vues!'[3]

the great dream. Civil servants, writers! Author, creator, poet,—such a man has never existed.'

[1] That Rimbaud must have had a slight acquaintance with Hinduism is proved by his reference to the Apsaras (*Œuvres Complètes*, p. 246), a class of female Hindu deity.

[2] Ibid., p. 270: 'The first task for the man who wants to be a poet is to know himself, entirely: he searches out his soul, inspects it, tests it, learns it. Once he knows it, he must cultivate it. That sounds simple: in every brain a natural development is fulfilled.'

[3] Ibid.: 'The Poet makes himself a *seer* by a long, immense, and reasoned *derangement* of *all the senses*. Every possible form of love, suffering, and madness; he searches for himself, exhausts all the poisons within himself, keeping only their quintessences. Indescribable torture in which he needs all faith, all superhuman strength, in which he becomes, above all others, the great invalid, the great criminal, the greatest among the damned,—and the highest Sage! —For he reaches the *unknown*! Because he has cultivated his soul, already rich, more than anyone! He reaches the unknown and even though, in his madness, he should lose the understanding of his visions, he will have seen them!'

Rimbaud knows full well that getting to know the unknown is no easy matter even if he takes the short cut of drugs and debauchery. Far from being a pleasure to him this course is a necessary martyrdom, a crucifixion[1] that must be undergone if he is to become a seer, the 'other', the greater than he, who 'thinks him' and controls him. 'C'est faux de dire: Je pense. On devrait dire: On me pense.'[2] This 'other', once found, must be obeyed, for the seer *becomes* the other. You must ask it no questions but let it take control completely, for 'il est chargé de l'humanité, des *animaux* même; il devra faire sentir, palper, écouter ses inventions; si ce qu'il rapporte de *là-bas* a forme, il donne forme; si c'est informe, il donne l'informe'.[3] The poet, when controlled by the 'other', is powerless, he merely produces what the 'other' inspires; and this may have form, or it may be formless. It may produce poetry of the highest order or pure gibberish: it is utterly incalculable, it is irrational and, as we shall see, it is beyond or below good and evil. Hence, as Rimbaud insists, it is in charge even of the animals. It is in fact nothing other than the 'collective unconscious' of Jung which, in its turn, seems to be identical with the Mind at Large of Huxley: it is Rimbaud's 'universal mind' or 'universal soul'. By identifying himself with this entity the poet-seer becomes all-powerful. 'Le poëte définirait la quantité d'inconnu s'éveillant en son temps dans l'âme universelle: . . . Enormité devenant norme, absorbée par tous, il serait vraiment *un multiplicateur de progrès!*'[4]

That Rimbaud conceives his 'universal mind' and 'universal soul' as distinct from the God of Christianity, is made clear by the statement that the future he envisages will be *materialist*. His universal mind or soul are, then, the substratum of the *material* universe, and his absolute is a material absolute just as it is in the earliest Indian speculation where the Absolute, Brahman, is alternately identified with 'food',[5] with breath,[6] or with a trinity consisting of heat, water, and food.[7] To achieve union with this was only possible by the *dérèglement de tous les sens*, the dissolution of the conscious personality and the flight into the unconscious, or, in the terminology

[1] 'Stat mater dolorosa, dum pendet filius', he writes to Izambard (*Œuvres Complètes*, p. 268—'The mother stands grieving while her son hangs').

[2] Ibid.: 'It's wrong to say "I think". You should say "Someone thinks me".'

[3] Ibid., p. 271: 'He (the poet or his controller) is put in charge of humanity, even of the *animals*: he will have to make his inventions heard, touched, listened to; if what he brings back from the *beyond* has form, he gives form; if it is formless, he gives what is formless.'

[4] Ibid.: 'The poet would define the quantity of the unknown, waking up in his own time in the universal soul: . . . Enormity becoming the norm, absorbed by all, he would be indeed a *multiplier of progress!*'

[5] The main theme of the *Taittirīya Upaniṣad*.

[6] Main theme of the *Kauṣītakī Up.* Common also elsewhere.

[7] *Chāndogya Up.* 6. 1–6.

of the alchemist, by the flight into Mother Nature (Ô Nature! ô ma mère!).[1] 'Nature obeys them' (the thaumaturges), writes Dr. Starkie, on the authority of Eliphas Lévi, the well-known nineteenth-century writer on magic, 'because what they wish is the law of Nature, they are Nature itself, and they have reached the real Kingdom of God, the *Sanctum Regnum* of the Cabala. They have, on their own, attained, in a certain measure, the omnipotence of a God.'[2]

This, of course, is the crux. Is it true that by 'being Nature itself' the magician or ecstatic attains to oneness with God? Dr. Starkie is at one with Mr. Huxley and Spinoza in assuming that the terms 'Nature' and 'God' are interchangeable. 'In his experience of God', Dr. Starkie proceeds, 'Rimbaud reached, without orthodox beliefs, the stage which mystics seek to attain, where there is no longer possibility for belief or disbelief, for doubt or for reflection, but only pure sensation, ecstasy and union with the Almighty.'[3] From such passages as these we can only assume that to identify Nature with God seems wholly natural and self-evident to Dr. Starkie. Very many nature mystics have thought the same because they have been deceived by the mere sensation of union or of unity into the belief that the object of such a union must always be the same. Theistic (and dualistic) mystics have always abhorred this doctrine, as we shall see in the latter part of this book. For Ghazālī, the great mystical doctor of Islam, love of the world and love of God were mutually exclusive; and he quotes the Prophet as saying, 'God, may He be glorified and exalted, created nothing more inimical to Himself than the world. When He created the world He would not even look at it.'[4]

Here we are brought face to face with the dilemma as seen by the mystics themselves. The theistic mystics, with only a few exceptions, when faced with other persons who themselves claim to be mystics yet whose conduct is the reverse of holy, are horrified not because they doubt the good faith of their rivals, but because they had been brought up to believe that God

[1] In a letter to Delahaye (*Œuvres Complètes*, pp. 287 and 288): so too in *Une Saison en Enfer* Rimbaud says, 'et je vécus, étincelle d'or de la lumière *nature*'. ('And I lived, a golden spark of the light of nature.')

[2] Op. cit., pp. 168–9.

[3] Op. cit., p. 422. Elsewhere (p. 294) she speaks of Rimbaud seeing God 'face to face' without attempting to substantiate this from his writings.

[4] Ghazālī, *Kīmiyā-yi Sa'ādat*, Tehran, 1319 A.H. (solar), vol. ii, p. 617: 'Ḥaqq subḥāna-hu va ta'ālā hīch chīz nay-āfurīd bar rūy-i zamīn dushman-tar bar vay az dunyā, va tā dunyā āfurīd hargiz ba-vay na-nigarīst.' The *Kīmiyā-yi Sa'ādat* or 'Alchemy of Happiness' is an abridgement in Persian by Ghazālī himself of his huge work in Arabic, *Iḥyā 'Ulūmi'l-Dīn* or 'The Revival of the Religious Sciences'. A useful abridgement of this, in French, is now available as: G.-H. Bousquet, *Ghazālī, Ih'ya 'Oloûm ed-Dîn ou Vivification des Sciences de la Foi*, Paris, Max Besson, 1955. This quotation does not appear there.

is good, and that an evil fruit or a fruit that 'transcends' good and evil, that is, which does not recognize any validity in these two terms, cannot possibly proceed from God. Hence they will usually ascribe it to the Devil. Few Christian mystics have failed to warn their flock against the raptures which the Evil One may cause, 'for I tell thee truly, that the devil hath his contemplatives as God hath his'.[1]

Rimbaud's *dérèglement de tous les sens* would seem to belong precisely to what the mediaeval mystics believed to be 'the devil's contemplation', for the true mystic 'desireth not to un-be: for that were devil's madness and despite unto God'.[2] Rimbaud's aim was precisely this, to obliterate all sense of personality and to abandon himself to 'the other', the irrational spirit from which madness proceeds. When he wrote his famous letter to Démeny he knew that madness might result from the course he had chosen, but in the interests of learning to know the unknown, he thought this a small price to pay. 'Qu'il crève dans son bondissement par les choses inouïes et innommables',[3] he defiantly says: though he should die in his quest, others will take up the torch. The vision itself is its own reward.

This was one side of Rimbaud's mysticism. The other which derives from his Catholic upbringing was no less strong; and the proof of this is in *Une Saison en Enfer*, that astonishing work in which he dramatically reviews the period of his raptures and his madness and in which he rejects it all as a lie. That this is in fact the message of the *Saison* seems certain from the agreement of two such contrasted interpreters of the work as Isabelle Rimbaud, the poet's very devout younger sister, and Dr. Starkie herself.

It is clear from the *Saison* that, despite the *Credo* he enunciates in the letters to Izambard and Démeny, Rimbaud was in search not only of a 'universal mind' or a 'universal soul' into which he could ecstatically disintegrate, he was also in search of God Himself for Whom he 'gluttonously hungered':[4] and by 'God', we must deduce from the *Saison* itself, he meant not 'Nature' which he nowhere identifies with God, but the God of his first Communion,[5] the:

' "Dieu d'Abraham, Dieu d'Isaac, Dieu de Jacob," non des philosophes et des savants.

[1] *The Cloud of Unknowing*, London, Burns Oates, revised ed., 1952, p. 63.

[2] Ibid., p. 61.

[3] *Œuvres Complètes*, p. 271.

[4] See below, p. 69.

[5] Cf. Starkie, op. cit., p. 36: 'At the time of his First Communion he was possessed by a burning faith, a passionate piety, that made him eager and ready to become a martyr. One day he attacked a group of boys bigger than himself whom he had seen playing with the holy water in the font outside the church, and splashing one another with it; but they set on him all at once and trounced him soundly, calling him "sale cagot", a dirty hypocrite.'

Certitude. Certitude. Sentiment. Joie. Paix.
Dieu de Jésus-Christ.
Deum meum et Deum vestrum.
"Ton Dieu sera mon Dieu."
Oubli du monde et de tout, hormis Dieu.'[1]

It seems strange indeed that these words of Pascal should be quoted as being comparable to Rimbaud's ecstasies.[2] The latter were achieved by the *dérèglement de tous les sens* and were afterwards rejected with contempt and disgust,[3] whereas Pascal achieved certainty, peace, and joy in his total surrender to God in Whom the world and all things were forgotten.

As we shall see, Rimbaud tried to find a short cut to God through what could be described as the way of perversion, through the *putrefactio* of the alchemists[4] as interpreted by himself. According to Dr. Starkie the way was paved with absinthe, drugs, and homosexuality, though the evidence produced for the consistent use of drugs and for actual homosexual practice is somewhat thin. Ecstasy he certainly achieved, but he neither achieved union with God, nor did he claim to have done so,—he was far too honest for that,—nor yet did he achieve peace which, as Pascal saw, was one sure sign of the union of the soul with God. And it is precisely this that makes the case of Rimbaud so illuminating. He himself saw that the ecstasy reached through the way of perversion in which the 'ego' is 'oned' with all natural things and dissolved in them, and through which the expanded personality,—the 'other' who is mysteriously present in all of us,—plunges beyond good and evil, was no vision of God, but what Rimbaud had the courage to denounce as a lie, what we are now encouraged to call an overwhelming unconscious content and a psychological reality. Rimbaud had been seeking the 'God of Abraham, Isaac, and Jacob': what he found was a wildly irrational joy that dissolved his ego in a flash of lunatic exultation in which God had no part. 'De joie, je prenais une expression bouffonne et égarée au possible.'[5] It took much courage and an extraordinary understanding of the realities of mystical experience to reject these ecstasies as

[1] Preface to the *Pensées*. '"God of Abraham, God of Isaac, God of Jacob," not of the philosophers and the wise.
Certainty. Certainty. Feeling. Joy. Peace.
God of Jesus Christ.
My God and your God.
"Thy God will be my God."
Forgetfulness of the world and of all things, except God.'

[2] Starkie, op. cit., p. 202.

[3] In the first draft of *Une Saison en Enfer* he writes: 'Je hais maintenant les élans mystiques et les bizarreries de style. / Maintenant je puis dire que l'art est une sottise.'—'Now I hate mystical transports and stylistic quirks. / I can now say that art is a form of foolishness.' (*Œuvres Complètes*, p. 251.)

[4] See Jung, *Psychology of the Transference*, chapter vi: *Collected Works*, vol. xvi, pp. 256 ff.

[5] *Œuvres Complètes*, p. 236: 'Joy,—to express it I resorted to all that was most clownish and wild.'

a lie, and to return right back to where he had started, to the irksome and, for him, well-nigh impossible task of adapting himself to an ununderstanding world. We must now try to follow this amazing young man in his spiritual odyssey which was to go so tragically astray.

'J'attends Dieu avec gourmandise',[1]—'I wait on God like a glutton', we might almost translate. And later this 'gluttony' seems to be satisfied: 'Dieu fait ma force, et je loue Dieu';[2] and as if to make his theological position absolutely clear he adds: 'Je ne suis pas prisonnier de ma raison. J'ai dit: Dieu. Je veux la liberté dans le salut.'[3] In his consciousness of God, as we have already seen, Rimbaud differs from all the cases we have discussed hitherto in that he remains basically a theist and, subconsciously at least, dogmatically a Catholic. It is true that he had rejected with violence and contumely the externals of Catholicism: he had not,—or so it would appear from the *Saison* with which we are principally concerned,—abandoned the Church's basic teachings on God, Christ, and salvation. Despite the pantheistic theories he had earlier elaborated to Démeny, Rimbaud was not primarily interested in praeternatural experiences as such, though he had these in plenty: 'J'ai dit: Dieu',—'I have said, "God"', and with nothing short of God would this 'gluttonous' young man be satisfied. 'J'ai songé à rechercher la clef du festin ancien, où je reprendrais peut-être appétit. La charité est cette clef.'[4] This phrase occurs in the introductory section of the *Saison*, a section that is otherwise devoted to Rimbaud's plunge into the abyss, when he did his best to stifle all hope and took upon himself all the torments of the damned. The introduction of the idea of 'charity' or divine love would be wholly out of place were Rimbaud still adhering to his earlier theories. He is, however, as always, torn in two: on the one side he senses the grace of God,—charity,—which he still knows to be the golden key that opens the way to God Himself: on the other he is dragged away by the conviction that the unknown must be sought by extracting the quintessence of his being from all the poisons that he had himself distilled within himself. He is the victim of conflicting dogmas. And so the recollection of the 'key of charity' which opens up the way to the 'ancient feast',—possibly a reference to the Eucharist,—is immediately suppressed as being a counter-inspiration which 'proves he had been dreaming'. Charity is not a virtue that can be practised by one who is deliberately courting damnation,—'Gagne la mort avec tous tes appétits, et ton egoïsme et tous les péchés

[1] Ibid., p. 221.

[2] Ibid., p. 224: 'God constitutes my force, and I praise God.'

[3] Ibid., p. 225: 'I am not the prisoner of my reason. I have said, "God". I desire freedom in salvation.'

[4] Ibid., p. 219: 'I thought of seeking out again the key to the ancient feast at which, perhaps, I might recover my appetite. Charity is that key.'

capitaux.'[1] If eternal life was to be gained, death had to be sought out first; for had not Christ Himself taught that life can only be won through death, and that 'he that findeth his life shall lose it; and he that loseth his life for my sake shall find it'?[2]

Rimbaud might be described as a moral schizophrene. In the *Saison* he lives his Hell and his Heaven (and also, it may be said, his Limbo) and knows the key to them all. Deliberately he rejects charity as a dream and embraces what have always been the ingredients of Hell,—a living death made intolerable by 'the carnal appetites, selfishness, and all the deadly sins'. It is true that genuine schizophrenes often see their depression as the fruit of their sins and see in it a merited damnation from which there is no escape. Rimbaud, on the other hand, deliberately courts his Hell out of what appears to be sheer perversity, and he sees clearly what the ingredients are that make it what it is. He knows the key which will open the gates of the prison-house, but he will not use it since this would conflict with the 'aesthetic theory'. He does this on purpose because he is determined to know what despair really means. 'Je parvins à faire s'évanouir dans mon esprit toute l'espérance humaine. Sur toute joie pour l'étrangler j'ai fait le bond sourd de la bête féroce.'[3] Claudel described Rimbaud as 'un mystique à l'état sauvage'.[4] Rather it might be said that Rimbaud's behaviour was inevitable, for he had rejected the normal channels of grace offered by the Church, yet none the less hungered 'gluttonously' for God. Given his rejection of the Church and his passionate longing for the divine presence, he had no alternative. It is almost as if Rimbaud were trying to force God to reveal Himself by offending Him to the utmost. It is the reaction of a child against the apparent indifference of his father.

For Rimbaud orthodox Christianity had failed to produce what he expected of it,—the immediate vision of God. Yet despite his dabbling in alchemy the *Saison* proves that he had never quite abandoned Christianity itself: beyond the 'visions' of the 'unknown' it still obstinately remained his ideal. Thus he sees himself as a Crusader. 'Je me rappelle l'histoire de la France fille aînée de l'Église. J'aurais fait, manant, le voyage de terre sainte; j'ai dans la tête des routes dans les plaines souabes, des vues de Byzance, des ramparts de Solyme; le culte de Marie, l'attendrissement sur le crucifié s'éveillent en moi parmi mille féeries profanes.'[5] 'Féeries profanes' he was

[1] *Œuvres Complètes*, p. 219: 'Win through to death with all your appetites, and your selfishness, and all the capital sins.'

[2] Matt. x. 39.

[3] *Œuvres Complètes*, p. 219: 'I succeeded in extinguishing all human hope in my spirit. Like a wild beast I pounced blindly upon every joy that I might throttle it.'

[4] *Œuvres de Arthur Rimbaud*, Paris, Mercure de France, 1929, p. 3.

[5] *Œuvres Complètes*, pp. 220–1: 'I remember the history of France, eldest

to have in plenty since he deliberately sought them out,—and this for the simple and pathetic reason that he felt that the divine grace was withheld from him, and that, for any reason that he could see, through no fault of his own. 'Je ne me vois jamais dans les conseils du Christ; ni dans les conseils des Seigneurs,—représentants de Christ.'[1] Shut out from heaven, shut out from the Church, shut out from all the normal channels of grace because, understandably and more than pardonably, he fails to recognize the Church of God in the Catholic Church of his day and particularly in the austere and unbending piety of his mother, he nevertheless continues to hunger for God and for the 'counsels' of Christ.

But Rimbaud, despite the 'weakness' of which he so frequently and so unnecessarily accuses himself, was not the sort of person to be put off by the indifference of either Church, Christ, or God. 'J'ai de mes ancêtres gaulois l'œil bleu blanc, la cervelle étroite, et la maladresse dans la lutte. . . . D'eux, j'ai: l'idolâtrie et l'amour du sacrilège;—oh! tous les vices, colère, luxure,—magnifique, la luxure;—surtout mensonge et paresse.'[2] With so impressive an equipment how could he fail to react to what he must have considered a divine snub?

'Le sang païen revient! L'Esprit est proche, pourquoi Christ ne m'aide-t-il pas, en donnant à mon âme noblesse et liberté. Hélas! l'Évangile a passé! l'Évangile! l'Évangile!'[3] This is the parting of the ways. Rimbaud, like an unhappy child (and who isn't an unhappy child at the age of eighteen?), is hopelessly perplexed. How can it be that the Son of God will not help him in his search for the Father? What sort of charity is this? Why is he outcast and rejected though he longs for nothing except God Himself? Why can he no longer draw spiritual sustenance from the Gospel? 'Hélas, l'Évangile a passé! l'Évangile! l'Évangile!'—'My God, my God, why hast Thou forsaken Me?'

And it is at this point that he angrily cries: 'J'attends Dieu avec gourmandise. Je suis de race inférieure de toute éternité.'[4] And the implication

daughter of the Church. As a serf I would have made the journey to the Holy Land; I have in my head roads in the Suabian plains, views of Byzantium, ramparts of Solyma; the cult of Mary, compassion for the Crucified awaken in me among a thousand profane enchantments.'

[1] Ibid., p. 221: 'I never see myself in the counsels of Christ; nor in the counsels of their lordships,—the representatives of Christ.'

[2] Ibid., p. 220: 'From my Gaulish ancestors I have pale blue eyes, a narrow brain, and clumsiness in fighting. . . . From them, I have,—idolatry and the love of sacrilege;—Oh! all the vices, anger, lust,—magnificent, lust;—above all lying and sloth.'

[3] Ibid., p. 221: 'My pagan blood comes back! The Spirit is near; why does Christ not help me, by giving my soul nobility and liberty? Alas! the Gospel has passed! the Gospel! the Gospel!'

[4] Ibid., p. 221: 'I wait gluttonously upon God. I am of an inferior race for all eternity.'

seems clear. God will not have him because he is inferior. All right, then, let his pagan blood return. He will set out for the hot South where 'les climats perdus me tanneront. Nager, broyer l'herbe, chasser, fumer surtout; boire des liqueurs fortes comme du métal bouillant,—comme faisaient ces chers ancêtres autour des feux.

'Je reviendrai, avec des membres de fer, la peau sombre, l'œil furieux: sur mon masque, on me jugera d'une race forte. J'aurai de l'or: je serai oisif et brutal. Les femmes soignent ces féroces infirmes retour des pays chauds. Je serai mêlé aux affaires politiques. Sauvé.'[1] Saved! and what a salvation, for he knows that the whole silly dream is a stupid lie and a more than derisory substitute for the real object of his quest. It is simply an idle and pathetic gesture of defiance to the God Who will not hear him. If the father will not take him in, then at least he will make good in the world, vulgarly and alone.

This is, however, a passing (and prophetic) fancy; for he has his real and present Hell to contend with. He is burdened with what he calls his vice, his inability to come to terms with God. What can he do? For though he has rejected God, he still needs someone or something to worship, someone whom he can serve.

'A qui me louer? Quelle bête faut-il adorer? Quelle sainte image attaque-t-on? Quels cœurs briserai-je? Quel mensonge dois-je tenir?—Dans quel sang marcher?'[2] There is no answer, only 'l'abrutissement pur', only a bestial stupor. '*De profundis, Domine*, suis-je bête!' How stupid, bestial, and degrading it all is!

The next section follows naturally on what has gone before. He calls to mind the years when he had admired only force; he was, he says, an amoralist, below good and evil, a beast. 'Je n'ai jamais été chrétien; je suis de la race qui chantait dans le supplice; je ne comprends pas les lois; je n'ai pas le sens moral, je suis une brute.'[3] But brute though he may be, he still believes that he can be saved,—'Je puis être sauvé.'

Then something very strange happens.

[1] *Œuvres Complètes*, pp. 221–2: 'Lost climates will tan me. Let me swim, crush the grass, hunt, smoke especially; drink strong liqueurs like molten metal,—as those dear ancestors used to do around their fires. / I will return with limbs of iron, a dark skin, and a savage look: with such a mask I shall be thought to belong to a hardy race. I shall have gold: I shall be idle and brutal. Women look after such savage invalids on their return from the hot lands. I shall be mixed up in politics. Saved!'

[2] Ibid., p. 222: 'To whom shall I hire myself? What beast shall I adore? What holy image shall I attack? What hearts shall I break? What lie must I live? In what blood walk?'

[3] Ibid., p. 223: 'I have never been a Christian; I belong to a race that used to sing in the midst of torment; I do not understand the laws; I have no moral sense, I am a brute.'

'Les blancs débarquent. Le canon! Il faut se soumettre au baptême, s'habiller, travailler.

'J'ai reçu au cœur le coup de la grâce. Ah! je ne l'avais pas prévu!'[1]

The whole mood of the work suddenly changes. From despair Rimbaud leaps to a wild and apparently unmotivated jubilation. 'The whites disembark.' This phrase seems to make no sense unless we remember that Rimbaud had referred in a letter[2] to the *Saison* as a 'Livre *nègre*'. Rimbaud, then, identifies himself with the negro natives of his imaginary southern land, the 'race inférieure' to which he claims to belong. The coming of the whites must symbolize the long-resisted re-emergence of the Christian as opposed to the alchemical idea. This is to be a conversion by force; 'il *faut* se soumettre au baptême'. And because the conversion is forced, it very soon becomes apparent that it is also false.[3] From revolt he passes to the other extreme, to a state which he elsewhere refers to as innocence,[4] a state in which he has the conviction not that his sins are forgiven, but that he is miraculously preserved from sin.

'Je n'ai point fait le mal. Les jours vont m'être légers, le repentir me sera épargné. Je n'aurai pas eu les tourments de l'âme presque morte au bien, où remonte la lumière sévère comme les cierges funéraires. . . . Sans doute la débauche est bête, le vice est bête; il faut jeter la pourriture à l'écart. . . . L'amour divin seul octroie les clefs de la science. Je vois que la nature n'est qu'un spectacle de bonté. Adieu chimères, idéals, erreurs.'[5]

It would be facile and comforting to think that Rimbaud had really been answered by God, and lifted out of the slough of his despond into the pure air of his native innocence and of fellowship with God for Whom he had hungered so long in vain. Unfortunately his feeling of a complete freedom from sin ('je n'ai point fait le mal' etc.) is so characteristic of the manic phase of the manic-depressive psychosis[6] that it would be rash to assume that anything of the sort has happened unless, of course, we are prepared to admit that acute mania and mescalin experiences are also direct divine interventions.

[1] Ibid., p. 224: 'The whites disembark. The canon! We must submit to being baptized, to wearing clothes, and to working. / I have been struck in the heart by the blow of grace. Ah! I had not foreseen it.'

[2] Letter to Delahaye, ibid., p. 288.

[3] Cf. the title 'Fausse Conversion' in the first draft of the *Saison*: ibid., p. 246.

[4] See particularly the letter to Delahaye, l.c.

[5] Ibid., p. 224: 'I have done no wrong. My days will not weigh on me and repentance will be spared me. I shall not have had the torments of a soul almost dead to the good in which a sombre light rises up like candles at a funeral. . . . Without doubt debauchery is stupid, vice is stupid; the rottenness must be thrown aside. . . . Divine love alone disposes of the keys of knowledge. I see that nature is one great vision of goodness. Farewell, chimaeras, ideals, errors.'

[6] See below, p. 93.

The remainder of this section is in the same exalted tone: 'Le chant raisonnable des anges s'élève du navire sauveur: c'est l'amour divin.— Deux amours! je puis mourir de l'amour terrestre, mourir de dévouement. J'ai laissé des âmes dont la peine s'accroîtra de mon départ! Vous me choisissez parmi les naufragés; ceux qui restent sont-ils pas mes amis?

'Sauvez-les!'[1]

As so much else in *Une Saison en Enfer* it is difficult to decide whether this is simply exaltation due to mania or whether it should be interpreted as a religious conversion. In this delicate matter the last word must surely rest with Rimbaud. It is a 'false conversion', and the whole thing is an elaborate fancy. The poet does not mean a word of it. He sees himself as alone chosen from among his ship-wrecked companions, and in his new-found 'charity' he asks God that they too may be saved. What, however, is entirely lacking is any direct apperception of the divine presence; and from the theistic point of view, whether Christian, Muslim, or Hindu, this is what marks off that form of mysticism which results or is alleged to result in union of the human soul with God, from all others. For Rimbaud 'divine love' is still an abstraction, something suggested by 'le chant raisonnable des anges': it is not an intense personal relationship.

Rather, Rimbaud has an intuition only of what the divine love might be: he does not experience it, for it neither brings him peace, nor is it akin to prayer. That this should be so he himself recognizes, for almost immediately he goes on to say: 'Si Dieu m'accordait le calme céleste, aérien, la prière,—comme les anciens saints.'[2] Despite the 'coup de la grâce' which seemed to have revealed to him that he had never done wrong and was free from sin, Rimbaud remains unsatisfied. None of his experiences had the quality of peace ('le calme céleste') or of prayer. It was not what the saints had tasted of old; it was neither the 'prayer of quiet' nor the 'mental prayer' of which St. Teresa had written. Instinctively Rimbaud realized that because all his praeternatural experiences lacked the qualities of prayer and peace, they could not be directly of God.

'The two loves!' he exclaims; but of the two it is only the earthly one that touches him. Of this he could die, heartless though he claimed to be:[3] the other he is content to mention as an abstract ideal which leaves him cold.

[1] *Œuvres Complètes*, p. 224: 'The rational song of the angels arises from the ship of rescue: it is divine love.—Two loves! I can die of earthly love, die of devotion. I have left behind souls whose pain will increase when I am gone. You choose me out from among the ship-wrecked; are not they who remain my friends? / Save them.'

[2] Ibid., p. 225: 'If only God would grant me that heavenly, aerial calm, prayer,—like the saints of old.'

[3] 'Ce qui fait ma supériorité, c'est que je n'ai pas de cœur', he is alleged to have said to Delahaye (ibid., p. xxv).

Perhaps the point we are trying to make can best be illustrated by a comparison. The ninth-century Muslim mystic, Rābi'at al-'Adawiyya, in a well-known passage, also speaks of 'the two loves'. Between hers and Rimbaud's there is all the difference in the world. Unlike Rimbaud, Rābi'a addresses herself directly to God:

'I have loved Thee with two loves, a selfish love and a love that is worthy of Thee.
As for the love which is selfish, therein I occupy myself with Thee, to the exclusion of all others.
But in the love which is worthy of Thee, Thou dost raise the veil that I may see Thee.
Yet is the praise not mine in this or that,
But the praise is to Thee in both that and this.'[1]

Rābi'a's *lower* love is to love God to the exclusion of all else, the 'oubli du monde et de tout, hormis Dieu' of Pascal. Rimbaud's is pity only for the fellow-men he imagines he must leave behind. The first has all the marks of the 'genuine' mystic's utter self-abandonment to God, the second is pure hallucination, a 'false conversion' and a 'lie'. Rābi'a's goal is absolutely clear: Rimbaud is hopelessly confused, and contradicts himself in an alarming way. His is the sudden passage from the Hell of depression to the Heaven of mania in which all seems magically to right itself.

'La raison m'est née. Le monde est bon. Je bénirai la vie. J'aimerai mes frères. Ce ne sont plus des promesses d'enfance. Ni l'espoir d'échapper à la vieillesse et à la mort. Dieu fait ma force, et je loue Dieu.'[2]

This sounds sincere enough, but it is strangely naïve; for it is—what he says it is not—'des promesses d'enfance', the seeping through of his lost innocence into the quagmire of his madness, what he elsewhere calls his 'sale éducation d'enfance'. He is like an incorrigible little boy who, after making a 'good' act of contrition, emerges from the confessional and, bathed in pious emotion, fondly imagines that he will never sin again, oblivious of the seven devils that are already taking up their quarters in his house so nicely swept and garnished.

So does Rimbaud, in his madness, think that his torments are at an end, and that in his recovered innocence he can enter into the possession of the celestial calm he has surely deserved.

'L'ennui n'est plus mon amour. Les rages, les débauches, la folie, dont

[1] Quoted in Margaret Smith, *Studies in Early Mysticism in the Near and Middle East*, London, The Sheldon Press, 1931, p. 223.

[2] Rimbaud, op. cit., p. 224: 'Reason is born in me. The world is good. I will bless life. I will love my brothers. These are no longer childhood promises. Nor the hope of escaping from old age and death. God constitutes my strength, and I praise God.'

je sais tous les élans et les désastres, — tout mon fardeau est déposé. Apprécions sans vertige l'étendue de mon innocence.'[1] One wonders what has become of his 'gourmandise de Dieu': what has induced this sudden complacency, this quiet contemplation of his famous 'innocence', this sudden conviction that God constitutes his force which he now takes so lightly for granted. One had hardly expected this almost quietist dénouement.

Characteristically it is not the dénouement at all, for once again the mood changes abruptly. The poet no longer speaks of the birth of 'reason' in him, nor of the divine love. He has passed beyond all this, for he has said 'God'.

'Je ne suis pas prisonnier de ma raison. J'ai dit: Dieu. Je veux la liberté dans le salut: comment la poursuivre? Les goûts frivoles m'ont quitté. Plus besoin de dévouement ni d'amour divin. Je ne regrette pas le siècle des cœurs sensibles. Chacun a sa raison, mépris et charité: je retiens ma place au sommet de cette angélique échelle de bon sens.'[2]

If this means anything at all, it means that Rimbaud has reached a stage in which he can dispense with God's love (which in any case he had not yet known); for he is now at the top of the heavenly ladder,—a position normally occupied by the Almighty. Rimbaud can now say with the Upaniṣad, '*ahaṁ brahmāsmi*', 'I am Brahman', 'I am God'. Prior to receiving his 'coup de la grâce' he admitted to the necessity of submitting to Baptism and to work. 'La vie fleurit par le travail',[3] he is still prepared to admit as a rule that holds good for the generality of men. As for himself: 'moi, ma vie n'est pas assez pesante, elle s'envole et flotte loin au-dessus de l'action, ce cher point du monde.'[4] This is the apotheosis of his 'paresse'. His hunger for God has in fact reduced itself to an Olympian detachment from which God has been dethroned. Yet even this sublime detachment he knows to be a 'lie' for it is at this point that he begs God to grant him the 'celestial calm' of the saints which is 'prayer'.

Thus the significance of Rimbaud's case lies in the fact that, despite his exaltation, he realizes that his place at the top of the angelic ladder which is 'above action' is not the place he had been looking for. He is not interested in the 'sainte indifférence' of the Quietists, the *vairāgya* of the

[1] *Œuvres Complètes*, pp. 224–5: 'Ennui is no longer what I love. Rages, debauches, madness, all the transports and disasters of which I know,—my whole burden has been laid down. Let us appreciate, without becoming giddy, the extent of my innocence.'

[2] Ibid., p. 225: 'I am not a prisoner of my reason. I have said, "God". I desire freedom in salvation: how should I set about getting it? Frivolous tastes have left me. No longer any need for devotion or divine love. I do not regret the days when hearts were sensitive. Each man has his own reason, disdain, and charity: I keep my place at the top of this angelic ladder of good sense.'

[3] Ibid.: 'Life bursts into flower by work.'

[4] Ibid.: 'As for me, my life is not heavy enough, it takes wing and floats far above action, that point so dear to the world.'

Hindu ascetics, or the ἀταραξία of the Stoics: he still wants God, and still he has not found Him. And his final comment on this episode? 'La vie est la farce à mener par tous.'[1]

The two following sections of the *Saison—Nuit d'Enfer* and *Délires I*—are of little interest to our study of mysticism. In both Rimbaud sees himself in Hell: this is the depressive phase of his self-induced psychosis, the dark side to the raptures he is later to experience. *Délires I* may well be a description of his life with Verlaine, but this is irrelevant to our purpose, and we will therefore proceed directly to *Délires II* which leads up to the climax when Rimbaud captures his 'artificial paradise' by storm.

We need not allow ourselves to be detained by what Rimbaud calls his 'alchimie du verbe'. It is, however, a true alchemy, for Rimbaud, whether consciously or not, is seeking to transform his normal consciousness into something else, though he may well not have known what. He galvanizes his already perfervid imagination into yet more hectic life; and this, in turn, gives way to pure hallucination,—and here we are getting very close to the type of natural mystical experience with which we dealt in our first chapters. The distinction between the individual self and the outside world and between different objects of the outside world begins to disappear.

'Je m'habituai à l'hallucination simple: je voyais très franchement une mosquée à la place d'une usine, une école de tambours faite par des anges, des calèches sur les routes du ciel, un salon au fond d'un lac; . . .'[2]

And again as the excitement mounts:

'Je devins un opéra fabuleux: je vis que tous les êtres ont une fatalité de bonheur: l'action n'est pas la vie, mais une façon de gâcher quelque force, un énervement. La morale est la faiblesse de la cervelle.

'A chaque être, plusieurs *autres* vies me semblaient dues. Ce monsieur ne sait ce qu'il fait: il est un ange. Cette famille est une nichée de chiens. Devant plusieurs hommes, je causai tout haut avec un moment d'une de leurs autres vies.—Ainsi, j'ai aimé un porc.

'Aucun des sophismes de la folie,—la folie qu'on enferme,—n'a été oublié par moi: je pourrais les redire tous, je tiens le système.'[3]

[1] Ibid.: 'Life is a farce that all must go through.'

[2] Ibid., p. 234: 'I got used to simple hallucination: I saw quite clearly a mosque instead of a factory, a phalanx of drums made by angels, coaches on the roads of heaven, a drawing-room at the bottom of a lake.'

[3] Ibid., p. 237: 'I became a fabulous opera: I saw that all beings are destined for happiness: action is not life, but a way of spoiling some kind of force, an enervation. Morality is feeble-mindedness. / It seemed to me that several *other* lives were due to every being. This gentleman does not know what he is doing: he is an angel. This family is a litter of dogs. In the presence of many men I talked aloud to a moment of one of their other lives. So, I fell in love with a pig. / None of the sophistries of madness,—the madness that is put away,—was forgotten by me: I could repeat them all, I own the system.'

There is a basic honesty about Rimbaud rarely found among 'ecstatics'. Whatever symbolism he may introduce to help to explain an experience which no words can directly describe, he has the kindness to warn us that, whatever else the mood may be or signify, it stems from sheer lunacy ('la folie qu'on enferme'). The fact that, before the climax is reached, Christian symbols are again used, signifies nothing. These are conditioned by Rimbaud's Catholic upbringing; they appear because subconsciously he wishes them to appear. In his previous utterances which we have just quoted, there is no trace of Christianity: they are pure pagan pantheism, the apotheosis of his famous 'paresse' which he opposes to the life of action, itself only a 'way of spoiling some kind of force'. He remains amoral,—'morality is feeble-mindedness'. In becoming a 'fabulous opera' he includes all things within himself, the distinction between subject and object becomes obliterated, he *is* the all.

'Sur la mer, que j'aimais comme si elle eût dû me laver d'une souillure, je voyais se lever la croix consolatrice. J'avais été damné par l'arc-en-ciel. Le Bonheur était ma fatalité, mon remords, mon ver: ma vie serait toujours trop immense pour être dévouée à la force et à la beauté.'[1]

As Rimbaud himself points out, this is madness; it is acute mania, what Jung calls a 'positive inflation' when 'the personality becomes so vastly enlarged that the normal ego-personality is almost extinguished. In other words, if the individual identifies himself with the contents awaiting integration, a positive or negative inflation results. Positive inflation comes very near to a more or less conscious megalomania; negative inflation is felt as an annihilation of the ego.'[2] In cases like Rimbaud's 'positive' and 'negative' inflation seem to overlap,—the extremes meet, and the result is an almost frenzied joy; for, to use Jung's terminology again, the ego is *both* infinitely expanded so as to comprise all things, *and* it is equally annihilated in 'Nature' or in what Jung calls the collective unconscious. This must mean that the consciousness is overwhelmed by the uprush of the contents of the collective unconscious. If this is so, then what is the significance of the Cross which we are told is the symbol of integration and wholeness?[3] The Cross emerging from the sea should mean integration proceeding from the depths of the collective unconscious. In that case 'inflation' which Jung regards as a grave danger on the way to 'individuation' or 'integration of the personality', is not necessarily incompatible with the process of

[1] *Œuvres Complètes*, pp. 237–8: 'On the sea which I loved as if it were to have cleansed me from a defilement, I saw the consoling Cross arise. I had been damned by the rainbow. Happiness was my fatality, my remorse, my worm: my life would always be too vast to be devoted to force and beauty.'

[2] *Psychology of the Transference*, ch. vi, in *Collected Works*, vol. xvi, p. 262.

[3] Ibid., p. 303.

individuation itself. Both are a 'bellica pax, vulnus dulce, suave malum'.[1] 'Le Bonheur était ma fatalité, mon remords, mon ver: . . . Le Bonheur! Sa dent, douce à la mort. . . .'

In the best alchemical and Tantric traditions the opposites are reconciled, as Rimbaud shows, in an ecstasy of acute mania:

'Enfin, ô bonheur, ô raison, j'écartais du ciel l'azur, qui est du noir, et je vécus, étincelle d'or de la lumière *nature*. De joie, je prenais une expression bouffonne et égarée au possible:

Elle est retrouvée!
Quoi? l'éternité.
C'est la mer mêlée
Au soleil.

Mon âme éternelle,
Observe ton vœu
Malgré la nuit seule
Et le jour en feu.'[2]

Although Rimbaud's experiences are of a different order from Proust's, one result is nevertheless the same, the consciousness and certainty of the immortality of the human soul. For Proust this meant genuine integration or realization of himself as an immortal being;[3] it left permanent effects and gave a purpose to his life. In Rimbaud's case it seems to have been an experience of the most baffling kind, *both* a return to the pre-natal state or what Jung's pupil, Erich Neumann, calls the 'Uroboros', symbolizing the undifferentiated state of the collective unconscious, *and* conscious integration (sun and sea representing the fusion of the male and female principles, and the 'golden spark' representing the integrated new life born from them,—the Divine Child of Jungian psychology). This state is, perhaps, the 'fourth state' of the Vedāntins which we shall have occasion to discuss later. Despite the sudden appearance of the consoling Cross, it would be wrong to regard Rimbaud's experience as being in any way comparable to those of the accredited Christian mystics, for it lacks entirely any sense of communion with God Who, at the height of Rimbaud's ecstasy, is not mentioned at all.

[1] Ibid., pp. 167 and 303: 'A warlike peace, a sweet wound, a gentle evil.'

[2] Rimbaud, ibid., p. 236: 'At last, O happiness, O reason, I stripped the sky of its blue which is black, and lived, a golden spark of natural light. Joy—to express it I resorted to all that was most clownish and wild. / It is found again! What? Eternity. It is the sea mingled with the sun. / My eternal soul, observe thy vow, despite the lonely night and the day aflame.'

[3] According to Jung, op. cit., p. 184, 'The self as such is timeless and existed before any birth.' In a footnote he adds: 'This is not a metaphysical statement but a psychological fact.' I fail to see what proof there can be of this.

The *Saison* reaches its climax with the words, 'Le Bonheur! Sa dent, douce à la mort, m'avertissait au chant du coq,—*ad matutinum*, au *Christus venit*,—dans les plus sombres villes.'[1] And then Rimbaud breaks into that wonderful paean of joy,—'O saisons, ô châteaux!'

'O saisons, ô châteaux!
Quelle âme est sans défauts?

J'ai fait la magique étude
Du bonheur, qu'aucun n'élude.

Salut à lui, chaque fois
Que chante le coq gaulois.

Ah! je n'aurai plus d'envie:
Il s'est chargé de ma vie.

Ce charme a pris âme et corps
Et dispersé les efforts.

O saisons, ô châteaux!

L'heure de la fuite, hélas!
Sera l'heure du trépas.

O saisons, ô châteaux!'[2]

This poem, as Dr. Starkie rightly points out, is the quintessence of Rimbaud's ecstatic experience. The words in themselves have little meaning. Like an Indian *mantram* they are designed to evoke a mood of intense joy. The virtue of the poem is not so much in the meaning as in the 'magical' power of the words themselves. Nevertheless the meaning seems clear enough, for it corresponds exactly to Rimbaud's mystical doctrine as elaborated in the letters to Izambard and Démeny,—'JE est un autre'. The 'other' has here completely taken over,—'On me pense'.

'Ah! je n'aurai plus d'envie:
Il s'est chargé de ma vie.

Ce charme a pris âme et corps
Et dispersé les efforts.'

This is the consummation: and this is the goal that Rimbaud, as *voyant*,

[1] *Œuvres Complètes*, p. 238: 'Happiness! Its tooth sweet even unto death, gave me warning at the crow of the cock,—*ad matutinum* (at dawn), at the *Christus venit* (Christ has come),—in the darkest of towns.'

[2] Ibid.: 'O seasons, O castles! What soul has no defect? / I have made the magic study of happiness which none escapes. / Hail to him, every time that the Gallic cock crows. / Ah! I have no more desire: he has taken charge of my life. / This charm has taken on soul and body and scattered all our efforts. / O seasons, O castles! / The hour of flight, alas! will be the hour of death./ O seasons, O castles!'

had set himself: the wood has been fashioned into a violin on which the 'other' plays ('tant pis pour le bois qui se trouve violon').[1] The poet has succeeded in depersonalizing himself, and the 'other' (the unconscious, if you will) *has* taken over, but still there is something lacking. Rimbaud, the alchemist, discovers that in finding the 'other self', he has not found God.

Whatever the source of the philosophy he develops in the two letters may be, in the *Saison* he symbolizes it as the wisdom of the East. 'Je retournais à l'Orient et à la sagesse première et éternelle.—Il paraît que c'est un rêve de paresse grossière!'[2] Ecstasy as such, the abandonment of the ego to the 'other' absolutely, has been tried and found wanting. What Rimbaud had understood by the 'eternal wisdom of the East' turns out to be only the ecstasy of acute mania.

'Les gens d'Église diront: C'est compris. Mais vous voulez parler de l'Éden. Rien pour vous dans l'histoire des peuples orientaux.—C'est vrai; c'est à l'Éden que je songeais!'[3] Rimbaud, always torn between his violence which would take the kingdom of heaven by storm and his longing for a return of the innocence and purity of his childhood, now realizes that the violent approach has failed, and that what he had subconsciously been wanting all along was 'Eden' or 'original innocence', the original relationship of man to God and the world as it is said to have been before sin confused his intellect.

Of this he had indeed had a vivid glimpse: for he had found both the 'Limbo' of mania and the 'Hell' of depression; and it is remarkable that Rimbaud should have regarded both experiences as being of 'Hell'. 'C'était bien l'enfer; l'ancien, celui dont le fils de l'homme ouvrit les portes.'[4] Now, speaking of the *Saison en Enfer*, Rimbaud is reported as having said, 'J'ai voulu dire ce que ça dit, littéralement et dans tous les sens',[5] 'I meant to say what it says, literally and in all its meanings'. If this is so, then the ancient Hell, the doors of which were opened by the Son of Man, can only refer to what is conventionally called the Limbo of the Patriarchs; and the characteristic of Limbo is that man is said there to enjoy the highest *natural* bliss without being able to attain to the Beatific Vision. Elsewhere in the *Saison*[6] Rimbaud speaks of 'l'innocence des limbes', 'the innocence of Limbo'; and it would therefore seem fair to conclude that in certain stages

[1] Ibid., p. 268: 'So much the worse for the wood which finds itself turned into a violin.'

[2] Ibid., p. 240: 'I went back to the East and its wisdom, primaeval and eternal.—It seems that it is a dream of gross laziness.'

[3] Ibid.: 'Church people will say, "We understand. But what you mean is Eden. There is nothing for you in the history of the Eastern peoples."—It's true; it was Eden that I was thinking of.'

[4] Ibid., p. 242: 'It was Hell all right; the ancient one, the one whose gates were opened by the Son of Man.'

[5] Recorded by Paterne Berrichon, ibid., p. xxvii.

[6] Ibid., p. 234.

of his career through 'Hell' he recovered or thought he recovered his lost innocence, the innocence of Limbo which is akin to Eden. This was at least his impression while he was actually undergoing the experience: 'Les rages, les débauches, la folie, dont je sais tous les élans et les désastres,—tout mon fardeau est déposé. Apprécions sans vertige l'étendue de mon innocence.'[1]

Thus while realizing that he had not come face to face with God, Rimbaud would seem to claim that he had tasted the 'innocence' of Limbo. 'Ô pureté! pureté!' he writes, 'C'est cette minute d'éveil qui m'a donné la vision de la pureté! —Par l'esprit on va à Dieu!'[2] What he understands by 'éveil' seems clear enough from the letter to Démeny: 'Le poëte définirait la quantité d'inconnu s'éveillant en son temps dans l'âme universelle.'[3] This must surely mean that the vision of, and participation in, Nature transformed which is the common experience of nature mystics is not necessarily evil in itself. Theologically it means a return to Eden, a return to the primitive condition when man had not tasted of the Tree of the Knowledge of Good and Evil, a return to the innocence of early childhood. This was for Rimbaud the 'vision of purity'. It is not the vision of God which can only be obtained by *Spirit*, for in the theory elaborated in the two letters to Izambard and Démeny the future era, which the new race of poets is to inaugurate, is specifically spoken of as being *materialist*.[4] Rimbaud thus draws the clearest distinction between Nature and Spirit, and he was well aware that though he communed with the first, he had failed even to approach God Who is worshipped 'in spirit and in truth'.

Rimbaud's experiment, then, had the salutary effect of revealing to him the vision of 'innocence' and 'purity', of 'Eden' and 'Limbo'. On the debit side it had also brought him to the confines of madness, to what Jung calls 'positive inflation', the megalomania characteristic of the manic and the drug-addict.

'Moi!' he exclaims, 'moi qui me suis dit mage ou ange, dispensé de toute morale, je suis rendu au sol, avec un devoir à chercher, et la réalité rugueuse à étreindre! Paysan!'[5] Other persons who have had experiences similar to his, as for instance William James after taking nitrous oxide, tend, even when they are fully restored to normal consciousness, to regard such experiences as being in some sense more real than the ordinary experiences of everyday life. Rimbaud, violent as always, rejects it all as a lie. 'Enfin, je

[1] *Œuvres Complètes*, pp. 224–5. See p. 76, n. 1.

[2] Ibid., pp. 240–1: 'O purity, purity! It was that minute of awakening that gave me the vision of purity!—By the spirit man goes to God!'

[3] Ibid., p. 271. Cf. p. 65, n. 4.

[4] Ibid., p. 272.

[5] Ibid., p. 243: 'I,—I who called myself Magus or Angel, exempt from all morality, I have been brought back to earth, with a duty to find and a gnarled reality to embrace! Peasant!'

demanderai pardon pour m'être nourri de mensonge.'[1] This is a return to a harsh reality, to duty, and to the Christian ethic from which he had sought to escape. There is no more 'gluttony for God', only a return to the humblest of beginnings, penitence and the hope of forgiveness.

This does not mean, of course, that Rimbaud had at this stage become reconciled to the Church. He had not, and his dislike of organized religion was to continue unabated for some time to come. His private spiritual struggle had exhausted him, and with the *Saison en Enfer* we have the last document of his spiritual development. 'Le combat spirituel est aussi brutal que la bataille d'hommes; mais la vision de la justice est le plaisir de Dieu seul.'[2] His own spiritual conflict had been enough and more than enough for him; henceforth he would make no more attempts to take heaven by storm but would abandon the 'vision of justice' to God to Whom it rightly belongs. Then, and only then, would it be lawful for him 'to possess the truth in a soul and a body'. This phrase, which is italicized in the original, has been much discussed. Rimbaud, however, insists that the *Saison* means exactly what it says, 'literally and in all its meanings'.[3] Now, his spiritual struggle over, he, who called himself 'a Magus or an Angel', will be content to live as a man 'in a soul and a body', not as a discarnate spirit or as a magician who, at one fell swoop, would take the supernatural by storm.[4]

We have tarried long enough over Rimbaud as it is, and we will not attempt to follow his career up to the death-bed reconciliation with the Catholic Church, for this would take us into a controversial field, and would, in any case, serve no useful purpose since there is no evidence at all which throws any light on Rimbaud's spiritual development between the time when he wrote *Une Saison en Enfer* and his death in 1891. His case, however, is of as great importance for our investigation as is that of Proust, for in Rimbaud 'natural' and 'theistical' mysticism meet, and the former is weighed in the balance by the latter, and found wanting. Perhaps alone among 'nature' mystics Rimbaud rejected the natural mystical experience as a 'lie'. Even William James, for all his elaborate objectivity and scepticism, had not been able to do that. That Rimbaud could do what James could not, was due to the fact that he had a standard against which natural mysticism could be judged. 'J'ai dit: Dieu', and against such a standard, it would seem, even the legitimate joys of a primal innocence were as nothing.

[1] Ibid., p. 243: 'At last I shall ask to be forgiven for having fed myself on lies.'

[2] Ibid., p. 244: 'The spiritual struggle is as tough as a battlefield; but the vision of justice is the pleasure of God alone.'

[3] See p. 81.

[4] Cf. Baudelaire, *Le Poème du Haschisch*, *Œuvres Complètes* (Bibliothèque de la Pléiade), p. 477: 'Ces infortunés . . . demandent à la noire magie les moyens de s'élever, d'un seul coup, à l'existence surnaturelle.'

CHAPTER V

MADNESS

By now it should be clear that Mr. Aldous Huxley, by bringing the use of drugs for the purpose of producing ecstasy into connexion with religious experience proper, has opened up wide and puzzling perspectives. By equating his experiences under the influence of mescalin both with the Beatific Vision and with the *Sac-cid-ānanda* or 'Being-Awareness-Bliss' of the Hindus, he is in fact denying any specific religious basis to either Hinduism or Christianity. In the previous chapters we have seen that the particular unitive experience which Huxley first identifies with the Beatific Vision and which he is subsequently content to call a 'gratuitous grace', is by no means uncommon, and that it was certainly present in Rimbaud's passage through Hell. We saw further that Rimbaud who, despite his extreme youth, speaks with a greater understanding of these matters than does Mr. Huxley, himself realized that his visions and the supremely joyous states that accompanied them belonged properly to the sphere of madness, —'la folie qu'on enferme',—as he puts it. On Huxley's premisses, then, we are forced to the uncomfortable conclusion that both mescalin and mania are capable of producing the Beatific Vision and of enabling us to realize ourselves as the threefold Absolute of Being-Awareness-Bliss. This is to reduce all meditative and contemplative religion to pure lunacy. Whether this was Huxley's intention or not, is not wholly clear. That, however, is the net result of his brave incursion into the field of contemplative religion.

Since it may be objected that Rimbaud was not mad in the accepted sense of the word and that he was much rather a genius who, for that reason, may have been in touch with a 'higher reality', we must, in this chapter, deal with the case of a certified manic-depressive whose symptoms will by now be familiar ground to the reader. Before, however, proceeding to the case of John Custance, it will not be irrelevant to quote a passage from a notable treatise on mysticism written by the Muslim mystic, Abu'l-Qāsim al-Qushayrī, who flourished in the second half of the eleventh century of the Christian era.

The Muslim mystics were perfectly aware that the human psyche is subject to more or less violent oscillations between extremes, especially when it lays itself open to both supernatural and praeternatural visitations by following a methodical ascetic training. In Islam these states are reflected in God Himself who is both *Al-Rahmān*, 'the Compassionate', and *Al-*

Qahhār, 'the Avenger'. The contrast between the two poles of the Deity is far more marked in Islam than it is in Christianity. The latter is at present content with the divine mercy and the divine justice, and prefers to draw a veil over the anger of God which figures so prominently in the Old Testament. God's mercy and justice are not themselves easily reconciled, but they are less violently contrasted than are the compassion and vengeance of Allah. The Muhammadan conception of God also colours the theory and practice of Muslim mysticism. The mystic's relation with God may be summed up in the two words 'hope' (*rajā*) and 'fear' (*khawf*); and in all Ṣūfī treatises on the mystical life these two virtues or 'states' play an important part.

Hope and fear, in this context, mean hope of the divine mercy and fear of the divine chastisement, hope of heaven and fear of hell: both are concerned with future states, with man's last end. Analogous to them are the states called by the Arabs *basṭ* and *qabḍ* which mean literally 'expansion' and 'contraction'. The term 'expansion' does in fact accurately describe what the nature mystics conceive happens to the soul. Contraction is the opposite condition, the phenomenon of extreme depression and sense of utter abandonment to oneself in oneself which William James describes in his chapter on the 'sick soul'. These states are now recognized as being the manic and depressive poles of what we now call a manic-depressive psychosis.

Let us now produce, in translation, what Qushayrī has to say on the subject of 'expansion' and 'contraction'.[1]

'These are two (emotional) states which supervene when the servant (of God) has passed through the states of fear and hope. Contraction in the adept (*'ārif*) corresponds to fear in the beginner, and expansion to hope. The difference between fear and hope on the one hand and expansion and contraction on the other is that fear is confined to something in the future, be it the loss of a beloved object or the onslaught of something perilous. So too, hope refers to the attainment of a desired object in the future, to the removal of an obstruction, or to the end of unpleasantness. All this refers to the future and is experienced by the beginner. Contraction, however, means something actually present at the time: so also expansion. The subject experiencing either fear or hope has his mind fixed on the future; whereas those who experience expansion and contraction are presently and actually the prisoner of an overwhelming obsession (inspiration or mood, —*wārid*). The experiences of persons affected by expansion and contraction will vary according to their respective (spiritual or emotional) states. One kind of obsession (or mood) brings on contraction, but even so the appetite for other

[1] Qushayrī, *Risāla*, ed. Z. Ansārī, Cairo, 1367/1948, pp. 32–33. For transliteration of the Arabic text see Appendix C, p. 227.

things remains; for the mood is not exhaustive. But there are also contracted men who have no appetite whatever for anything except their obsession, for they are entirely devoted to it to the exclusion of everything else. One of the Ṣūfīs has said (in this connexion), "I am shut up", meaning that he had no appetite for anything. Similarly the expanded man experiences an expansion great enough to contain (all) creation; and there is practically nothing that will cause him fear. Nothing affects him in whatever state he may be. . . . One of the proximate causes of contraction is that the mind is attacked by an obsession, the cause of which is the presentiment of damnation and a mysterious intuition that such punishment is deserved. Inevitably contraction will gain possession of the mind. The occasion for the (opposite) mood is a presentiment of drawing near to or approaching some sort of favour or welcome; then the mind will experience expansion. . . .

'There are cases of contraction the cause of which is not easily ascertainable by the subject; and he cannot make out the occasion for, or the cause of, it. The only remedy for this condition is complete submission (to the will of God) until the mood passes. For if the sufferer exerts his will in a wild effort to shake himself out of it, or anticipates the mood before it attacks him, the contraction will only increase, and this may be accounted boorishness in him. However, if he submits to the dictates of the mood, his contraction will soon pass. . . .

'Expansion (on the other hand) comes suddenly and strikes the subject unexpectedly, so that he can find no reason for it. It makes him quiver with joy, yet scares him. The way to deal with it is to keep quiet and to observe conventional good manners. There is the greatest danger in this mood, and those who are open to it should be on their guard against an insidious deception. One of the Ṣūfīs has said, "One of the doors of expansion opened out to me. I slipped; and the (spiritual) station (which I had at that time attained) was veiled from my sight." The Ṣūfīs therefore say, "Be chary of expansion and beware of it."

'Both conditions, that of expansion as well as that of contraction, have been considered by those who have investigated the truth of these matters to be things in the face of which one should take refuge in God, for both must be considered to be a poor thing and a harmful one if compared with the (spiritual) states which are above them, such as the (apparent) annihilation of the servant (of God) and his gradual upward progress (*indirāj*) in the Truth.'

This passage seems to be of the highest interest and importance since it was written by a theistic mystic who was plainly familiar with the psychological phenomena called 'mania' and 'depression', which the Ṣūfīs referred to, with rather more accuracy, as 'expansion' and 'contraction'. Although they claimed Qur'ānic authority for the use of these terms (as they did in all things), the authority in this case is so singularly poor[1] that we are forced to the conclusion that the terms were originally used to signify well-known

[1] Qur'ān, 2. 246: 'wa'llāhu yaqbiḍu wa-yabsuṭu',—'God holds tight, but is open-handed too'.

phenomena of elation and depression. What they mean by 'expansion' is plainly the 'natural mystical experience' which we have discussed at such length, whereas their 'contraction' refers to the depression which is its opposite, and which we have already observed, though not very closely, in Rimbaud. That we are dealing with the very same phenomenon seems to be sufficiently indicated by Qushayrī's description of it,—'the expanded man experiences an expansion great enough to contain (all) creation'. This is the genuine pantheistic or 'pan-en-henic' experience quite unmistakably, the 'Thou art this all' of the Upaniṣads, or the sensation that Forrest Reid describes of containing all Nature within oneself.[1] It is an experience which makes the subject both quiver with joy and which nevertheless scares him: it is then quite certainly what Huxley experienced under the influence of mescalin. That Qushayrī should see the 'greatest danger' in such a condition and speak of it as an 'insidious deception' is surely significant. For the early Muslim mystics of the *via media* instituted by Junayd of Baghdad, —and Qushayrī was one of them,—conceived mysticism, like their Christian counterparts, as an *askesis* leading to union with God in Whose personal and unique existence they firmly believed; and they knew that this expansive experience which appeared to embrace all Nature, though not evil in itself, was a snare in their path: it was an 'insidious deception' (*makran khafīyan*). Christian mystics may well be referring to this experience when they speak of the Devil's ability to counterfeit mystical states. In Islam *makr*, 'deception', 'guile', or 'craftiness', is a quality attributed to Allah Who, in one passage of the Qur'ān, is described as 'the best of the crafty ones',[2] 'for many a one does he catch unawares and change his aspirations to evil works'.[3] So too Qushayrī regards the state of 'expansion' as a trap set by God in the path of the aspirant Ṣūfī through which He can sift the wheat from the chaff.

The early Muslim mystics, then, unlike their successors, were wary of this state of 'expansion' and regarded it as being even more dangerous to the beginner than the opposite state of 'contraction' which could not be mistaken for a higher state because it brought nothing but misery. They considered it to be nothing more than a divine testing.

We have now seen how the more perspicacious of the early Muslim mystics regarded the natural mystical experience. It is now time to consider the case of Mr. John Custance who has so ably described his experiences when suffering from acute mania. From these we shall see that if

[1] See above, pp. 40–41.

[2] Qur'ān, 3. 47: 'wa'llāhu khayru'l-mākirīna'.

[3] Ghazālī, *Kīmiyā-yi Sa'ādat*, vol. ii, p. 724: 'kih bisyār khalq-rā ghāfil gardānd va dā'iyah i īshān ba-kārhā-yi bad ṣarf kard'. The idea of God's *makr* is a commonplace among the Ṣūfīs.

we adopt the thesis of Mr. Huxley and those who think like him and persist in regarding the experience of nature mystics as either the Beatific Vision, a surrogate Beatific Vision, or even as a 'gratuitous grace', then we must face the fact that what we are seeking is neither God, nor the Godhead, nor the *nirguṇa*[1] Brahman, nor the *saguṇa*[2] Brahman, nor the Dharma-Body of the Buddha, but simply an attack of acute mania.

The reader may recall this passage from *The Doors of Perception*:

' "So you think you know where madness lies?"
My answer was a convinced and heartfelt, "Yes."
"And you couldn't control it?"
"No, I couldn't control it. If one began with fear and hate as the major premiss, one would have to go on to the conclusion." '[3]

Oddly enough Huxley realized the connexion between the effects of mescalin and schizophrenia, yet he seems to have refused to face the fact that what he calls religion is simply another word for the manic-depressive psychosis. If religion does really boil down to this, then Huxley deserves much credit for having brought this important fact to the public notice. It remains now to be seen what a genuine manic-depressive has to say on the subject.

The case of Mr. Custance is interesting in that his bouts of mania and depression are sporadic. He has long periods of complete sanity, and is now set, I hope and believe, for final recovery. He does, however, have an uneasy conviction that during his manic periods he obtains a more profound insight into reality than he does when he is merely sane; and this is the common experience of all nature mystics. Deeply read in the psychology of Jung, he seems quite prepared to accept Jung's theory of the collective unconscious together with the archetypes that people it,—the anima, the shadow, the wise old man, the terrible mother, and all the rest of them. At the same time he has attempted to work out a philosophy of life which seeks to combine the sane with the manic. In his second book, *Adventure into the Unconscious*, he writes of how, during one of his manic periods, he attempted to put his theory into practice,—it would appear, with remarkable success. This theory which may be called a theory of opposites and their reconciliation to which parallels can be found in China and India as well as among the mediaeval alchemists, we cannot discuss now not because they are not intrinsically interesting (they are) but because they would seem to fall rather outside the scope of this book.

Of the cases of nature mysticism we have discussed so far none, I think,

[1] 'without quality'.
[2] 'having qualities'.
[3] *The Doors of Perception*, p. 45.

could be classed as one of madness. The only exception is Rimbaud who was, however, consciously seeking out madness ('dérèglement de tous les sens') as a way of escaping from himself and of transcending good and evil. None of the cases we have so far cited could be regarded as being one of certifiable madness. It will then be interesting to see in what, if anything, Mr. Custance differs from them.

The difference, it would appear, is only one of degree, not of kind. The reader will perhaps remember that Huxley classified his experiences under the influence of mescalin in four categories. First, he said, the ability to think straight was little, if at all, reduced; second, visual impressions were greatly intensified; third, the will was weakened, and moral values ceased to make much sense; fourth, what he calls 'the better things' were experienced as being both inside and outside oneself.

The difference between Huxley and Custance is that whereas the effects of mescalin can be relied on not to last more than eight hours, mania, when not produced by drugs, may last almost any length of time. In the case of Mr. Custance his manic states lasted for months. The list of periods in which he was more or less continuously in a manic state is as follows:

May 1936–November 1936: November 1938–April 1939: October 1944–March 1945: February 1947–April 1947: August 1947–October 1947: October 1949–April 1950.

Thus while it is unlikely that the mescalin-taker will run into trouble during his eight hours of bliss, the possibility that one may fall foul of the authorities during a continuous seven months of unreasoning ecstasy is very great indeed. The loosening of the moral sense, or rather, in this case, its diversion from its normal channels, is, of course, what is most liable to bring the manic into conflict with the authorities, or, as in Mr. Custance's case, with his own material interests and those of his family. Thus, when a man sees in every street-walker a consecrated hierodule and, out of reverence almost, gives her hundreds of pounds, there is every chance of trouble. There may be little harm in Raskolnikov kneeling at the feet of Sonya, the prostitute *malgré soi*, as before the symbol of the sufferings of the world, but when this gesture is accompanied by the disbursal of large sums of money by a family man, fact and fantasy are liable to come into serious conflict. This is not, however, how the manic sees it. For him fantasy *is* fact: indeed it is a great deal more real than the majority of things that pass for fact in everyday life. His devils and his angels, his pagan gods and familiar spirits are more real than his very furniture, because, so far from *their* being the symbol of anything, merely natural objects are rather the symbols of them. Thus it merely infuriates the manic to be told that his hallucinations and illusions are not there. For him they really are, and nothing can persuade him that they are not. Hallucinations, however, though they frequently accompany the manic state, are not essential to it. Conversely hallucinations of the most violent kind, which can be felt to be very real, occur to canonized saints. St. Teresa has much to say on the subject of the Devil's unwelcome importunities in physical form.[1] These visitations, however, whether they be of the Devil himself or of minor sprites, are 'accidental' only both to the 'natural' and to the specifically theistic experience, and do not therefore properly enter into our subject.

As we have seen, most of the nature mystics whom we have considered so far, have not connected their experiences with God. Custance, however, does speak of nearness to God; and in his first book 'God' is much in evidence, and we shall have to consider what he means by that term. Just as in the case of Rimbaud we could never be quite certain whether his return to Christian symbols was merely a reversion to his childhood or a genuine passage from what Qushayrī calls 'expansion' to a direct apprehension of the Deity, so in the case of Custance we do not know what exactly he means when he uses the term 'God'. Belief in God (not precisely defined) which he inherited, and belief in Jung's collective unconscious which was later to have a profound influence on his interpretation of his own experiences, seem to have become confused and identified in his mind. Thus St. John of the Cross and St. Teresa are called in as witnesses to the identity of all mystical experiences, as is Plotinus. 'I have come to realize', Custance says, 'that this experience was almost precisely the same as that of the mystics; Plotinus put it in classic words: "For everyone hath all things in himself, and again sees all things in another, so that all things are everywhere and all is all and each is all, the glory is infinite." '[2] This is an over-simplification; and it is the same over-simplification that we have met with in the case of Mr. Bullett. It is characteristic of the nature mystic. 'Good is that which makes for unity', Huxley says somewhere. 'Evil is that which makes for separateness.'[3] This is all very well so far as it goes, and it is implicit in the Christian doctrine of the Communion of Saints: but, obviously, if there is a supreme principle with which union is possible, that will be a higher union than any union with the natural universe. Custance, however, would claim to have experienced both. This is how he describes it:

[1] In *Life*, ch. 31. For a collection of well-attested para-normal phenomena connected with reputed religious mystics the reader may refer to Herbert Thurston, S.J., *Surprising Mystics*, London, Burns Oates, 1955.

[2] John Custance, *Adventure into the Unconscious*, London, Christopher Johnson, 1954, p. 3.

[3] Quoted by Victor Gollancz, *A Year of Grace*, London, Gollancz, 1950, p. 105.

'The experience partakes of the nature of good-fellowship produced by alcohol; it also constitutes in some degree a regression to a childish faith and confidence in the benevolence, the "akinness" of the surrounding world. . . . It is actually a sense of communion, in the first place with God, and in the second place with all mankind, indeed with all creation. It is obviously related to the mystic sense of unity with the All . . . in fact it is probably the same sense.

'A feeling of intimate personal relationship with God is perhaps its paramount feature. The sun is shining on the paper as I write, and it suggests to me at once that the *Sun* of Righteousness, which is also the Son of God, is watching and helping me. The sun suggests, as it has in fact often suggested to me before when I was in a manic phase, an intense sense of the immediate presence of God, in the person of Jesus.'[1]

Now all this symbolism is psychologically interesting, and has been treated by Jung in *Psychology of the Unconscious* and elsewhere. 'The attributes and symbols of the divinity', he writes, 'must belong in a consistent manner to the feeling (longing, love, libido, and so on). If one honours God, the sun or the fire, then one honours one's own vital force, the libido.'[2] That Christ was early named *Sol justitiae*, 'the Sun of Righteousness', merely shows that the early Church unconsciously adapted the figure of the Redeemer to the Sun as a source of energy. Custance, then, unconsciously confirms Jung's theories, and shows that by God he means that power which the Sun represents, 'energy', 'libido', 'life-force', 'élan vital', or what you will. It is what the devotees of the Rāja-yoga in India call *prāṇa*, a word which means breath, then spirit, and finally the power that underlies all physical phenomena and physical change. It is with this power that this type of Yogin seeks to identify himself, and through which he claims to obtain supernatural powers. 'To bear a God within one's self', Jung continues, 'signifies a great deal; it is a guarantee of happiness, of power, indeed even of omnipotence, as far as these attributes belong to the Deity. To bear a God within one's self signifies just as much as to be God one's self.'[3] Now this is precisely what the Yogin of the Rāja-yoga school claims, and it is just this that John Custance felt. 'I feel so close to God, so inspired by His Spirit that in a sense I am God. I see the future, plan the Universe, save mankind; I am utterly and completely immortal; I am even male and female. The whole Universe, animate and inanimate, past, present and future, is within me. All nature and life, all spirits, are co-operating and connected with me; all things are possible. I am in a sense identical with all spirits from God to Satan. I reconcile Good and Evil and create light, darkness, worlds, universes.'[4]

[1] Custance, *Wisdom, Madness and Folly: The Philosophy of a Lunatic*, London, Gollancz, 1951, p. 37.

[2] *Psychology of the Unconscious*, p. 52.

[3] Ibid.

[4] Custance, *Wisdom*, p. 51.

Custance, however, is sane enough to realize that this must really be nonsense; but, if so, why is it so similar to what, he claims, the mystics have experienced? Let us continue to quote from him, for his dilemma is real and there is no easy solution to it.

'Of course', he continues, 'it is all a dream, a vision, pure imagination if there is such a thing. I know perfectly well in fact that I have no power, that I am of no particular importance and have made rather a mess of my life. I am a very ordinary man and a miserable sinner; and I can truthfully say that never in the midst of the wildest flights of grandiose ideas have I ever allowed myself to forget that. Moreover, psychologically speaking, I know that my delusions of grandeur are merely compensations for the failures and frustrations of my real life. In particular, in my sane periods, the sense of identity with God seems to me an appalling blasphemy. Yet it is absolutely overwhelming, however much I struggle against it and endeavour to rationalize it on orthodox Christian lines as a vision vouchsafed by God. The fact that it is not only a common feature of insane conditions but also an experience of many of the mystics seems to show that the instinctive drive to power and the experience of the Immanent God are more closely related than is generally realized.'

This, I think, was written before the author became deeply interested in Jung; for had he studied him closely at the time, he would have found that both the drive to power and the Immanent God are identified by Jung with the libido, a term which seems to mean little more than psychic energy.

It is easy to sympathize with Custance, for many theistic mystics do from time to time express their relationship to God in terms of identity, Eckhart and Angelus Silesius certainly among the Christians, Abū Yazīd, Ḥallāj, Abū Sa'īd ibn Abī'l-Khayr, Ibn al-'Arabī, and Jīlī among the Muslims. Suso and Ghazālī came very near to doing this, and Ghazālī argued that this sense of identity could be explained by the fact that the senses are rapt away in God during the actual experience, and that when reason returns, the mystic realizes that the experience cannot be formulated in this way.[1] Ḥallāj, on the other hand, refused to retract and was maimed and crucified on that account. These, however, seem to fall within a different category, for in their cases there is no question of a sudden illumination; the experience is rather the result of a long search after God and it is God who almost always takes the initiative. In the case of Custance God seems to be simply a symbol for the Universe or the All, the totality with which he feels himself to be identified. This is, of course, real pantheism, if the premiss that God and Nature are identical is accepted as true. The examples we have cited hitherto, however, tend to show that the nature mystic does not intro-

[1] See below, p. 158.

duce the idea of God unless he already holds pantheistic or semi-pantheistic views. Jefferies, for instance, rejected the term 'god' as being incompatible with his experiences; and Proust, though his experience was different, does not even think of connecting it with a divine agency, while Rimbaud, that unique and incomparable genius, saw clearly that though he had drunk to the depths of the mysticism of Nature, he had not thereby drawn one step nearer to God.

Custance too seems to feel this in his second book, for there he scarcely introduces the idea of God in this connexion since this merely confuses the issue. He seems to find a more adequate symbol for what he felt in Jung's collective unconscious; for, although for ten years he had not experienced depression, he remembers this terrifying experience, the essence of which is to feel utterly alone and to have the certainty that one is irrevocably damned, and knows that this is the obverse pole of the manic state. In depression he felt complete isolation, whereas in mania he thought he experienced the unity of all things and, to judge from our other examples, may very well have done so. This at least is how it seemed to him.

'In its favourable aspect', he writes, 'it is a strange and lovely land beyond individuality, and incidentally also beyond good and evil, since the opposites are reconciled and the peace that passes all understanding rules supreme. In it there is no death, no final separation, no fundamental or absolute division or distinction, no time, for all that ever was still is, now and for evermore.'[1] 'Heaven and Hell wedded, the wonderful longing for the abyss; whatever strict logic and morality may have to say about the apprehension, there is no doubt that we are somehow touching the springs of the soul. It is the ultimate uniting, the final synthesis, the rebirth that makes all things new.'[2] Or again, in a more pantheistic strain: 'Probably I am mad enough at the moment to produce a precise theory, but I know from bitter experience that I should only scrap it later. All I will say is that in some way, once the opposites are bridged—and my state of elation is itself a bridging of or making contact between the opposites—the watertight compartments of individuality, the hard shells that surround our egos, tend to disappear. I am not I, but many: those I meet are not merely themselves but many others too.'[3] How reminiscent of Rimbaud! 'A chaque être, plusieurs *autres* vies me semblaient dues. . . . Devant plusieurs hommes, je causai tout haut avec un moment d'une de leurs autres vies.—Ainsi, j'ai aimé un porc!'[4]

'For', Custance continues, 'we are not ourselves; of that I am as certain

[1] *Adventure*, p. 4.
[2] Ibid., p. 62.
[3] Ibid., p. 112.
[4] See above, p. 77, n. 3.

as that I am sitting in my little hotel bedroom looking over the lovely roofs of Paris. We are our ancestors, right back to whatever form of life first emerged from primeval slime; we are in a sense the gods and goddesses they worshipped, the devils, gnomes and goblins they feared; we are our friends, characters we have admired in history, or even in novels or poems; indeed I think we are also our homes, or places we have loved. . . . I am also Paris, and perhaps Berlin and London, too.' Here we seem to have a very clear case of what Qushayrī called 'expansion' and what Jung calls 'positive inflation'. It is a case of the man who 'experiences an expansion great enough to contain (all) creation'.[1]

Qushayrī described the opposite state to 'expansion' as 'contraction': this was caused by an apprehension of damnation and the feeling that this damnation was deserved. St. Teresa too thought of herself as a most heinous sinner, but her case is wholly different; for her sins which, by ordinary standards, were the mildest of imperfections, must appear enormous when one is, or considers oneself to be, constantly in the presence of the Holy of Holies. Moreover, in Teresa's case the consciousness of sin brings on no fit of depression; it merely increases her grateful amazement at the infinite mercy of God. Custance's experiences of depression, however, follow the normal schizophrenic pattern, examples of which will be found in the chapter on the 'sick soul' in James's *Varieties of Religious Experience*. As Qushayrī rightly saw, the sufferer feels himself to be constricted and is oppressed by an overwhelming sense of sin. Lastly he conceives himself as being utterly alone, yet never really alone because sin always accompanies him. 'Bishop Berkeley was right;' says Custance, 'the whole universe of space and time, of my own senses, was really an illusion. Or it was so for me, at any rate. There I was, shut in my own private universe, as it were, with no contact with real people at all, only with phantasmagoria who could at any moment turn into devils. I and all around me were utterly unreal. There in the reflection lay proof positive. My soul was finally turned into nothingness—except unending pain.'[2]

Similarly on the actual experience of contraction he says:

'In the Kingdom of Hell which depression reveals, the ego is not merely cut off; it is also increasingly *restricted*,[3] until it seems to become an almost infinitesimal point of abject misery, disgust, pain and fear. It is very noticeable that the repulsion is not only felt for the outside world; it invades the personality in the form of intense disgust for oneself, horror of one's body, of seeing one's reflection in a mirror and so on. Clothes and personal property associated with oneself

[1] Above, p. 86.
[2] *Wisdom*, p. 73.
[3] Author's italics.

become objects of repulsion, whereas in the manic phase clothes and other property take on an extraordinarily attractive aspect; I have often felt them imbued with magical powers, filled with "mana" as it were. [One remembers Huxley's ecstasies on beholding the transformation that had taken place in the folds of his grey flannel trousers.] At the same time one takes a narcissistic delight in one's own body.'[1]

Here we meet with an essential difference between nature mysticism and what we must call the mysticism of the spirit. Mystics of the great religions, whether they be Hindu, Muslim, or Christian, are all trained in what we call the mortification of the flesh. This may either take the form of extreme asceticism as in the case of the desert fathers, St. Catherine of Genoa, Suso, and a host of others, or of the extremists among the Yogins; or it may take the form of simply preserving the mean in all that is connected with the body as recommended, for instance, by the Bhagavad-Gītā and the Buddha. 'Yoga', says the Gītā, is not for him who eats too much or for him who eats nothing at all; it is not for him who makes sleep a constant habit nor for him who stays awake too long. Yoga destroys all pain when practised by one who controls his food, recreation, exercise, sleep, and waking.'[2] Yet even for Yogins who follow this middle path the idea of rejoicing in one's own body as Whitman and Custance, in his manic phase, do, would not only be incomprehensible, but would be regarded as militating against the whole object of a technique which aims at the conquest of sense in order to concentrate on the reality that lies beyond sense.

Of all the cases of nature mysticism that we have studied so far and which the evidence of Custance proves to be so closely allied to mania, only Custance himself speaks of 'an intense sense of the presence of God'. Rimbaud alone seems to have an instinctive understanding of the nature of God and of His essential difference from the created all. Even Custance does not seem to use the word in the Christian sense: his is rather the God of the pantheists, symbolized in the sun and all created things. His actual experience would appear to be one of union with all Nature; and always when he returns to a normal form of perception, he has not only the sense of being an exile from paradise, but realizes that he must have been talking nonsense. 'After every bout of manic elation there comes in my experience an unpleasant awakening to hard facts, a morning after the night before. The bills have to be paid; the chickens sent out on flights of inflated imagination come home to roost.'[3] There comes the uncomfortable

[1] *Wisdom*, pp. 78–79.

[2] *BhagG.* 6. 16–17: 'nātyaśnatas tu yogo 'sti na caikāntam anaśnataḥ / na cāti-svapna-śīlasya jāgratō naiva cārjuna. yuktāhāra-vihārasya yukta-ceṣṭasya karmasu / yukta-svapnāvabodhasya yogo bhavati duḥka-hā.'

[3] *Adventure*, p. 148.

realization that perhaps after all good and evil are not so easily reconciled, that to identify oneself with God is blasphemous, and to have the sensation that one is omnipotent is not the same as actually to be omnipotent. Yet it cannot be denied that the manic and the natural mystical experience leave with all those who have had it an overwhelming sense that what they have experienced is not only real in a sense that ordinary sense experience is not, but also that it has profound metaphysical meaning.

The whole thing can, of course, be dismissed as mere imagination; and Custance's own case seems to be weakened by the fact that not only does he feel that his sense of expanded personality and of comprising all things within him is real, but also that his hallucinations, his familiar devils, and personal friends in the spirit world are equally real. Should we, then, attach more importance to his pan-en-henic experience simply because it is common to a large number of men, both sane and mad, than to his own visions which are personal to himself? His fellow lunatics also had their private delusions and private worlds, but into these Custance could not penetrate.

Yet I do not think that his case in any way invalidates the natural mystical experience any more than the physical phenomena which sometimes attach themselves to mysticism,—levitation, claivoyance, and the rest,—invalidate spiritual mysticism. Custance's evidence cannot be written off on the ground that he also had hallucinations any more than can St. Teresa's on the ground that she levitated and had visions of the Devil. In both cases the visions are parasitic to the main experience, and neither confirm nor invalidate it.

Before closing this chapter we must refer to a physical symptom of the manic state, since it corresponds so closely to similar symptoms provoked by the adepts of the Rāja-Yoga that it is difficult to dissociate the two. Attacks of mania, according to Mr. Custance, are not unheralded. 'At the onset of phases of manic excitement I have sometimes noticed the typical symptoms, the pleasurable tingling of the spinal chord and warm sense of well-being in the solar plexus, long before any reaction in the mental sphere occurred.'[1] Again he interprets this as a psycho-physical parallelism. 'It is almost as though it were evidence in favour of the old concept of psycho-physical parallelism, now virtually abandoned, which regarded the nervous system as a kind of telephone system with the nerves as lines and the ganglia as vast telephone exchanges, through which the whole process of thought as well as of reaction to environment was worked.'[2] Mr. Custance attaches considerable importance to this warning shiver, and quotes Le Bon as

[1] *Wisdom*, p. 16: cf. p. 45: 'I had the excited shivers in the spinal column and tingling of the nerves that always herald my manic phases.'

[2] Ibid., p. 54.

saying that crowd hysteria primarily reacts on, or is produced by, the marrow of the spine.[1]

Whether there is any scientific explanation for this phenomenon, I do not know. It does, however, bear a striking resemblance to the physical theory on which Yoga practices are based. These are described by Vivekānanda, the leading disciple of the Hindu saint, Rāmakrishna, in his little book on the Rāja-Yoga. The description is perhaps worth quoting in full since Vivekānanda had made a lifelong practice of Yoga and in his time achieved considerable notoriety in the West.

> 'According to the *Yogis*', he says, 'there are two nerve currents in the spinal column, called *Pingalâ* and *Idâ*, and a hollow canal called *Sushumnâ* running through the spinal cord. At the lower end of the hollow canal is what the *Yogis* call the "Lotus of the *Kundalini*". They describe it as triangular in form, in which, in the symbolical language of the *Yogis*, there is a power called *Kundalini* coiled up. When that *Kundalini* awakes, it tries to force a passage through this hollow canal, and as it rises step by step, as it were, layer after layer of the mind becomes open and all the different visions and wonderful powers come to the *Yogi*. When it reaches the brain, the *Yogi* becomes perfectly detached from the body and mind; the soul finds itself free.'[2]

Whether there is any medical explanation for these Yogic theories, I do not know. It is, however, interesting that Mr. Custance should also have experienced shivers at the base of his spine prior to the onset of his manic phases. *A priori*, then, it would appear that the technique described by Vivekānanda, which is a recognized Yoga technique, is simply an artificial means of inducing conditions akin to acute mania,—a condition which was thrust upon Mr. Custance against his will.

Moreover, the Rāja-Yoga, as expounded by Vivekānanda, seems not only to lead to the natural mystical experience, but also makes extravagant claims to supernatural powers. Sufferers from acute mania make similar claims, it would appear, for similar physiological and psychological reasons. Manics are usually shut up in a mental hospital, but this does not appear to cure them of their illusions of omnipotence. Vivekānanda and his successors are free to spread their doctrines in the West and have succeeded in making a number of distinguished converts among the intelligentsia, Romain Rolland and Aldous Huxley among them. There seems to be an anomaly here.

It is almost certainly true that Yogins are able to produce a condition which is indistinguishable from the natural mystical experience through a

[1] Ibid., p. 173.

[2] Swami Vivekananda, *Raja-Yoga or Conquering the Internal Nature*, 9th ed., Advaita Ashrama, Almora, 1951, p. 57.

series of exercises. Were this not so, it would be difficult to see why they should have persisted in these practices for perhaps as long as 3,000 years.

However, whatever the practices of these latter-day Yogins may be, the purpose of the classical Yoga was quite different. One must, I think, assume that the technique has remained more or less unchanged, and that the first object of the exercise has always been to bring about a release of what Freud called libido, or psychic energy, resulting in a state of 'expansion', which, as we have seen, is Qushayrī's description of the natural mystical experience we have been discussing.

It now becomes necessary to say something of the theory on which the Yoga practice is based. This theory is not the monistic Vedānta, but the dualistic Sāṁkhya; and the Sāṁkhya view of the universe can be briefly summarized as follows.

Every human being is basically a *puruṣa*, meaning literally a male person. *Puruṣa* has become enmeshed in *prakṛti*, 'Nature', which, in gender at least, is feminine. *Prakṛti* is a perpetually active principle compounded of what are called the three *guṇas*: these are known as *sattva*, *rajas*, and *tamas*. To find an adequate translation for these words is well-nigh impossible. *Rajas* means 'energy' or the active principle; *tamas* means 'darkness' and is associated with sloth and desire; *sattva* is the highest principle and is usually translated as 'goodness': it is the principle which helps the *puruṣa* or male soul to its proper end. Sāṁkhya psychology is in fact peculiarly like the psychology of Plato's *Republic* with its λογικόν or reasonable, θυμοειδές or passionate, and ἐπιθυμητικόν or lustful parts of the soul, or that of the Muslim philosophers who divided the psyche, as opposed to the governing intelligence, into a triad of imagination, anger, and lust.

Puruṣa, then, the male soul, is enmeshed in Nature which is composed of these three *guṇas* or qualities; and the soul's destiny is to return to its original state of isolation. In the Yoga system, as opposed to the Sāṁkhya proper, he is helped on to this goal by *Īśvara*, the Lord. By *Īśvara*, however, the ancient Yogins did not at all mean what we understand by God, and any comparison would be misleading. He is simply a special soul, all goodness, and free from all defilement, though he is defiled by proxy for as long as any merely human soul remains in bondage to Nature. He it is who helps the imprisoned souls to realize themselves in isolation; for the goal of the soul is not union with Īśvara, the Lord, but complete and utter isolation of itself in itself as an indivisible monad. In the Sāṁkhya the separation of soul from Nature is thus described:

'As a dancer, after showing herself to the audience, leaves off dancing, so does Nature reveal herself to the soul, and then disappear. Though she is possessed of qualities and he (the soul) possesses none, by manifold means she helps him on though he helps her not at all; she achieves his goal for him, though achieving nothing for herself. Nothing is more generous than Nature, or so I think. Content that she has been seen by the soul, she never again exposes herself to him.'[1]

It is at this point, it would seem, that the natural mystical experience would fit in. All the sources we have quoted (with the exception of Mr. Custance whose use of the term 'God' is confusing) would seem to agree that what they experienced was an enlargement of the ordinary field of consciousness in a vision that seemed to comprise all Nature; and Nature showed herself to be marvellously beautiful,—far more beautiful and with a far deeper unity than the normal consciousness could even suspect. But the soul realizes equally well that, according to this dualist system, this is not its end, and that having seen the beauty of Nature, it must pass on to its own proper state of original isolation, there to contemplate its own far greater beauty for ever and ever.

Now, it may be asked, if Nature in itself is so beautiful, then why should the soul wish to leave it? And here is precisely where we begin to touch on mysticism proper; for the 'Nature' of the Sāṁkhya seems to be what Jung means by the 'collective unconscious'. It is the sum-total of the phenomenal universe and the life-force that keeps it in being. It is the world of perpetual flux in which no form is permanent, and yet where nothing irrevocably passes away. It is the stuff of which both body and psyche are made, always changing and never at rest,—not staying for one moment the same, but in its quantitive totality remaining, presumably, always the same though perpetually passing through different forms. It is Aristotle's matter, and the three *guṇas* or qualities are what give it form. Thus the human psyche, normally restricted to a very narrow range, may, and obviously does, on unaccountable occasions, or through the use of a deliberate technique, or by the taking of drugs, catch a glimpse of the workings of Nature as a whole. This total vision, as Rimbaud instinctively understood, is what Catholics mean by Limbo. It is the highest happiness that man can attain to in isolation from God.

Now the natural mystical experience, whether it is expressed in pseudo-philosophical terms or whether it comes as an actual experience to human beings, can, of itself, *prove* nothing at all. It can only *indicate* clearly that

[1] *Sāṁkhya-Kārikā*, 59–61: 'rangasya darśayitvā nivartate nartakī yathā nṛtyāt / puruṣasya tathā 'tmānaṁ prakāśya vinivartate prakṛtiḥ. / nānā-vidhair upāyair upakāriṇy anupakāriṇaḥ puṁsaḥ / guṇavaty aguṇasya satas tasyārtham apārthakaṁ carati. / prakṛteḥ sukumārataraṁ na kiñcid astīti me matir bhavati / yā dṛṣṭāsmīti punar na darśanam upaiti puruṣasya.'

there is in Nature a deeper and more intimate unity than is normally perceptible, and that the barrier between the individual and his environment is possibly not as absolute as might be supposed. Yet I do not think that one need be unduly impressed by the consensus of opinion of the nature mystics: for what does this consensus amount to? It amounts to this, that they experience themselves as actually being something greater than themselves, they experience Nature as being mysteriously not only outside themselves but inside themselves, or like Proust (who made no claim to transcend *space*), they experience the past in the present. They fixedly and firmly believe that they have transcended time and space, and since this is precisely a permanent condition attributed to God, they tend to identify themselves with God. The problem is further complicated by the fact that all have the greatest difficulty in expressing what they actually feel, and since they are thereby forced to resort to metaphor, they become obscure and discredit their own case. Proust alone among them tried to pinpoint his experiences, and his novel is his justification. He interpreted his experience as being a more or less miraculous integration of his personality and his life; he realized himself at once as being outside time and being adjusted to the universe as a whole. This is self-realization in the true, Aristotelian sense, the individual realizes his final cause; and though one is bound to admit that Proust's experience, in so far as, for a moment, it dissolved the individual ego and revealed a timeless and eternal self, has much in common with the other experiences we have quoted, the difference is equally marked: for Proust does not allow himself to be carried away by a condition which has much in common with a heightened form of mania; he does not allow himself to succumb to what the Ṣūfīs call spiritual 'drunkenness', but remains firmly on the path of what they call 'sobriety',—according to the more orthodox among them, the higher state. The difference between Proust and the nature mystics, the manics, and the expanded personalities, is that the first experiences the eternal in himself as an integrating force appearing as a 'second self' which deposes the mere ego from its previous supremacy, whereas the manics exhibit a limitless expansion of the ego in which there is no directing, co-ordinating principle at all, and in which all sense of values is lost. Natural mystics proper, when they are sane, may fall anywhere between the two poles.

Qushayrī sensed the difference clearly when he drew a sharp distinction between the dangerous state of 'expansion' and the states of 'awe' (*hayba*) in the presence of God and 'fellowship' (*uns*) with God that immediately follow after it in the text. 'The expanded man', he says, 'experiences an expansion great enough to include (all) creation.' And although his whole treatise is on theistic mysticism and the steps that lead up to the union with God, there is no hint that this experience of 'expansion' necessarily contributes to this union which is the sole purpose of the whole Ṣūfī *askesis*.

Muslim mysticism was plagued practically from its beginnings both by this so-called pantheistic trend (that is the 'natural' or pan-en-henic experience) and the monistic which it probably derived directly from India.[1] Both Junayd (9th–10th century) and Ghazālī (11th–12th century) sensed the danger and tried to combat it, ultimately without success. Qushayrī seems to have felt that this state was, in a sense, independent of the direct action of God, and regarded it rather as a manifestation of His *makr*, His craftiness by which He 'leads astray whom He will',[2] an activity which Christians prefer to attribute to Satan. For the moment let us content ourselves with saying that it can be explained as being a descent (or ascent) into Jung's collective unconscious by which they are either overwhelmed or in which they miraculously discover the 'self' which then takes on the control of the whole psyche. It is true that it is difficult to attach any precise meaning to this term, but sure it is that it takes account of neither good nor evil. To translate Jung into Christian terms we could say that this represents the realizing of oneself as the first Adam; or in Hermetic terms, the microcosm realizes itself as the macrocosm. In this state we become as Adam was before he tasted of the Tree of the Knowledge of Good and Evil and before Eve was separated out from him, when he was, as so many of the primal gods of antiquity, androgynous. In this way it was possible for Mr. Custance to speak of himself as being both male and female. In *The Devils of Loudun* Huxley has hit upon a similar idea.[3] 'This personal subconscious', he says, 'is the haunt of our indwelling criminal lunatic, the *locus* of Original Sin. But the fact that the ego is associated with a maniac is not incompatible with the fact that it is also associated (all unconsciously) with the divine Ground.'

Here Huxley goes straight to the crux of the whole matter. The evidence we have analysed does seem to show that certain states usually referred to as mystical are also characteristic of lunacy, whether criminal or otherwise. There seem to be three principal modes of these states:

(1) an intense communion with Nature in which subject and object seem

[1] See below, pp. 161–3.

[2] Qur'ān, 6. 39, 125: 40. 74, &c.

[3] *Devils*, p. 104. I now learn that the idea of mystical knowledge being akin to Adam's state before he sinned was first put forward by Abbot Chapman in 1928. See further Herbert Thurston, S.J., *Surprising Mystics*, London, Burns Oates, 1955, p. 99, who refers back to the article on *Contemplation* in *Dictionnaire de Spiritualité* (cols. 1742–62) and *Downside Review*, 1928, pp. 1–24. This view occurred to the present author before he was acquainted with this literature.

identical. Of the examples quoted above Forrest Reid is perhaps the clearest:

(2) the abdication of the ego to another centre, the 'self' of Jungian psychology: 'JE est un autre', 'On me pense' (Rimbaud) etc.:

(3) a return to a state of innocence and the consequent sense that the subject of the experience has passed beyond good and evil (Rimbaud and Custance).

To these must be added (4) the complete certainty that the soul is immortal, and that death is therefore at least irrelevant and at most a ludicrous impossibility (Proust and Tennyson). This, possibly combined with (2), is clearly what Jung calls 'individuation' or 'integration'. It cannot be classed with the other categories because it represents not a diffusion or uncontrolled 'expansion' of the personality, but the organization of the completed psyche under the central control of the 'self' in which collective unconscious, personal unconscious, and the ego are brought into equilibrium.

The second of these phenomena again almost always combines with the first, and both are present in mania. This conquest of the ego by another unconscious 'centre' was formerly rightly called possession. Physically it can and does show itself in automatic writing and the like. Now, if we grant that this state is one of possession either by an external agency (angel, devil, etc.) or by an internal 'autonomous complex', there is no reason to believe that this agency must in all cases be the same. The agency may be either good, evil, or neutral; and the differing nature of the agency would account for the distressingly various 'fruits' of ecstatics. We shall later see that the early Muslim mystics also distinguished between 'inspirations' (*khawāṭir*) arising from God, an angel, a devil, or the 'lower self' (*nafs*): they considered that the identity of the agency behind these manifestations could only be discerned through the effects produced in the life of the patient. In the case of what Jung calls a successful transference, that is, of the transference of the control of the psyche from the ego to the 'self', the 'possessing factor' (the self) must be man's own immortal soul or spirit, that essential and fundamental centre which according to Judaeo-Christian (and Muslim) theology is made 'in the image and likeness of God'.

The superficially similar phenomenon which Custance experienced, the apparent reconciliation of the opposites, the conviction that one is a god and able to do all things, is, as the Ṣūfīs rightly saw, akin to intoxication; it is a not uncommon effect of alcohol and is very commonly produced by drugs. The ecstatic's conviction has no permanence and is always liable to give way to its opposite, depression or 'contraction'. Such a state will often be accompanied by the blissful feeling that somehow the external world is not really distinct from the percipient subject, that 'without and within are one'. These feelings often coincide with a blunting of the moral sense or in its distortion. The mediaevals attributed such states to the Devil (as did Baudelaire) because, though bringing with them absolute conviction, they were transitory and, like ordinary intoxication, were followed by depression. There is, however, no denying that the conviction of their reality remains, as William James himself has testified.

There is no rational solution to this mystery and it is easily written off as an illusion; but, if so, it is an illusion which all who have undergone it find almost impossible to shake off.

The age-old myth of microcosm and macrocosm which we find in one form or another all over the world, may be used to illustrate, though not to explain, the nature of this experience. Jung quotes Origen[1] as saying, 'Intellige te alium mundum esse in parvo et esse intra te Solem, esse Lunam, esse etiam stellas.'[2] The meaning of this would appear to be that to all outward objects there correspond psychological realities in the human soul (sun = psychic energy, sea = the collective unconscious, etc.), and that when Forrest Reid, for instance, feels the trees waving within him, this is merely a *rapport* suddenly established by what Jefferies calls the 'power more subtle than electricity' between the actual external trees and their 'image' within him. For if we are to believe Nicholas of Cusa, man is not only the *imago Dei*, but in his body and instincts he is also the *imago mundi*, and it is possible for him to feel his identity with either, for he is an analogy of both. 'Homo enim Deus est, sed non absolute, quoniam homo. Humane igitur est Deus. Homo etiam mundus est, sed non contracte omnia, quoniam homo. Est igitur homo μικρόκοσμος':[3] 'for man is God, though not absolutely, for he is man. He is therefore God in a human way. Man is the world too, not indeed all things compressed into a small compass, since he is man. He is therefore man as microcosm.'

According to Nicholas of Cusa, then, it is possible for man to feel his identity with Nature because his body is the world in miniature; and it is equally possible for him to 'be' God *humane*, so far as it is possible for man to participate in the divine essence. He can never *be* God absolutely as the Vedāntins would maintain because omnipotence, omniscience, and absolute sanctity belong to God alone and are demonstrably absent in man.

[1] *Hom. in Leviticum*, 126, 5, 2 *apud* Jung, *Collected Works*, vol. xvi, p. 196.

[2] 'Know that you are another world in miniature and that in you there is a sun, a moon, and stars too.'

[3] *De docta ignorantia*, 122, ii. 3 *apud* Jung, op. cit., p. 317.

He can, however, be God through the descent of the Holy Spirit Who transforms his nature, body and soul, and makes him wholly divine. But whereas communion with Nature is attainable without any effort and without any moral perfection, without charity and even self-denial, communion with God is impossible until sin is eradicated: for 'ces infortunés qui n'ont ni jeûné, ni prié, et qui ont refusé la rédemption par le travail, demandent à la noire magie les moyens de s'élever, d'un seul coup, à l'existence surnaturelle. La magie les dupe et elle allume pour eux un faux bonheur et une fausse lumière.'[1] In these words Baudelaire condemns the use of hashish and other drugs because the paradises they produce are artificial and superimpose illusions on a genuine praeternatural experience. The same is true of manic states. When, however, these pan-en-henic experiences supervene spontaneously, there would seem to be no valid reason why they should not be accepted with gratitude. The experience in itself is neither good nor evil: it is a revelation of the unity of man with the spirit that sustains all Nature, presumably the 'spirit that brooded over the face of the waters' at the beginning of time, and which gave form and beauty to the material world. If the experience has the additional effect of 'raising' the subject above good and evil, this can only mean that he is, even under normal circumstances, morally weak. The experience which, in its pan-en-henic aspect, is identical with that of manics and the takers of drugs, has, in itself, no moral value, either for good or for evil. Since, however, it enormously heightens the susceptibilities, it will make the good man better and the bad man worse. In one case the moral sense will entirely disappear, in another it will, if it is already strong, be immensely strengthened. 'L'oisif s'est ingénié pour introduire artificiellement le surnaturel dans sa vie et dans sa pensée; mais il n'est, après tout et malgré l'énergie accidentelle de ses sensations, que le même homme augmenté, le même nombre élevé à une très-haute puissance.'[2]

This is profoundly true: and it is this that, *pace* Mr. Custance, distinguishes St. Teresa both from himself and from all the nature mystics we have cited hitherto. I must confess that, try as I will, I cannot see in what the alleged resemblance between the experiences recorded by Mr. Custance and those of St. Teresa lies: but, even granting such resemblance,

[1] Baudelaire, *Œuvres Complètes*, p. 477: 'These unfortunates who have neither fasted nor prayed and who have refused redemption by work, ask from black magic the means of raising themselves, at one fell swoop, to a supernatural existence. Magic dupes them and kindles for them a false happiness and a false light.'

[2] Ibid., p. 445: 'The idle man has contrived to introduce the supernatural into his life and thought artificially; but he remains, after all and despite the accidental strength of his sensations, only the same man, though augmented, the same number raised to a very high power.'

St. Teresa's experience differs fundamentally in this, that it effected a total transformation and sanctification of character which no merely praeternatural agency could bring about. This, when all is said and done, is the only method we have of judging between divine and 'natural' mysticism. To say, as one of Jung's disciples does, that the two are identical on the grounds that 'the collective spiritual forces are as much parts of the uroboros as the collective instinctual forces pulling in the opposite direction',[1] may have meaning for the author. Others may be pardoned if they see in it only pseudo-scientific verbiage that does little credit to 'depth psychology'.

[1] Erich Neumann, *The Origins and History of Consciousness*, p. 187.

CHAPTER VI

INTEGRATION AND ISOLATION

In our study of nature mysticism we have been forced to the conclusion that this experience is, if not identical with the 'manic' state in the manic-depressive psychosis, then at least it is its second cousin. Jungian psychologists would say that the manic state represents an uprush from the collective unconscious in which the reason is temporarily submerged and in which irrational forces from the unconscious take charge. Now, however agreeable the manic state may be to the individual who undergoes it, it is obvious that it can be an intolerable nuisance to society at large. In the case of manic-depressives the unconscious has wholly submerged the conscious: the individuating, classifying, and thinking ego is overtaken by the irrational, abdicates, and hands over control to the unconscious which, of its nature, is chaotic and uncontrolled. Avicenna,[1] and following him most of the Muslim writers on psychology, distinguished two distinct parts in the human soul,—the higher or rational soul which naturally strives upward and whose goal is the acquisition of knowledge of God, and the lower soul usually called the *nafs* or 'self' which is tripartite, being composed of the imagination, anger, and lust. These three are indissolubly attached to the rational soul, and no escape from them is possible or even desirable during this life. 'Wretched man,' Avicenna says, 'you are bound to these evil companions and are so glued to them that you cannot escape unless you emigrate to a strange land where they cannot follow you.'[2] Unlike the mystics who do all they can to impose an iron discipline on the so-called lower soul, Avicenna holds that this lower soul has to be recognized for what it is, and has to be organized by reason. Thus anger and lust are regarded as opposites and each can be used to restrain and temper the other. To suppress them altogether, he considers, would be to invite disaster. Thus, for Avicenna as for Jung, integration of the personality was man's first aim on earth, and his lower soul does not seem to differ greatly from Jung's collective unconscious.

According to Jung[3] the collective unconscious is not only composed of

[1] e.g. in his *Hayy ibn Yaqẓān*. See H. Corbin, *Avicenne et le Récit visionnaire*, Teheran, 1952, p. 4 of the Persian text, p. 6 in Corbin's translation.

[2] Ibid., p. 16 (text): 'va turā, ay miskīn, bad-īn yārān i bad bāz basta and va bā īshān bar dūsānīda and chunānkih az īshān judā na-tavānī shudan magar kih ba-gharībī shavī ba-shahrhā-ī kih īshān ānjā na-tavānand āmadan'.

[3] *The Integration of the Personality*, E.T., London, Routledge and Kegan Paul, 1940, p. 147.

man's race memories, but stretches right back to the time when man was still an ape, to what he calls the 'animal level'. It is then curious and interesting that the Muslim mystics speak of Avicenna's faculties of anger and lust as the bestial soul and the animal soul, the difference between 'beast' (Ar. *sab'*, Pers. *dad* or *dada*) and 'animal' (Ar. *bahīma*, Pers. *sutūr*) being that between the carnivores and domestic animals. In India too we find much the same thing. We have already mentioned the concept of the three *guṇas* which are the basic constituents of all things, and we shall have to discuss them a little more fully now. The Sanskrit names are *sattva*, *rajas*, and *tamas*. Literally these mean 'goodness' or 'truth', 'energy', and 'darkness'. There is, however, no exact agreement on what the precise characteristics of these three inherent qualities are, for the earliest sources differ considerably among themselves. According to the *Mānava-dharma-śāstra*, 'The Law Book of Manu',[1] *tamas* is characterized by desire, *rajas* by ambition, and *sattva* by justice. The *Sāṁkhya-Kārikā* (§ 12), however, which should perhaps be regarded as authoritative, regards *sattva* as being of the nature of what is agreeable, *rajas* as that which is disagreeable, and *tamas* as being of the nature of depression (*viṣāda*). The function of the first is to illuminate, of the second to activate, and of the third to constrict. *Sattva* is light and illuminative, *rajas* is stimulating and mobile, while *tamas* is heavy and confining. In the Sāṁkhya system it is *sattva* that leads the imprisoned soul out of the amorous embrace of Nature; *rajas* is the creative, active, and at the same time destructive spirit, while *tamas* is of the nature of heaviness, sloth, and depression. Both Nature as a whole and each individual are composed of a mixture of these three modes of existence. The Bhagavad-Gītā describes the function of these *guṇas* in some detail and is worth quoting. '*Sattva*, being immaculate, illumines and gives health. It binds by attachment to what is pleasant and to knowledge. Know that *rajas* is of the nature of passion. It arises from craving and attachment. It binds the soul by attachment to works. Know that *tamas* is born of ignorance. All souls are deluded by it. It binds by sloth, lethargy, and sleepiness. *Sattva* attaches one to what is pleasant, *rajas* to action, while *tamas*, by smothering knowledge, attaches one to sloth. . . . When all the doors of the body are illumined by knowledge, it can be assumed that *sattva* has increased. When acquisitiveness, activity, the undertaking of works, impatience, and craving arise, that is due to an increase of *rajas*. When there is neither illumination nor activity, but only sloth and delusion, that is due to an increase of *tamas*.'[2]

[1] 12. 38.

[2] *BhagG.* 14. 6–13: 'tatra sattvaṁ nirmalatvāt prakāśakam anāmayam / sukha-saṅgena badhnāti jñāna-saṅgena cānagha. / rajo rāgātmakaṁ viddhi tṛṣṇā-saṅga-samudbhavam, / tan nibadhnāti, Kaunteya, karma-saṅgena dehinam. / tamas tv ajñāna-jaṁ viddhi mohanaṁ sarvadehinām, /

The parallel with the Muslim idea is not exact, but is close enough to be of some interest. In the Indian system it is not only the human soul that is compounded of the three qualities but also the whole of Nature. When the qualities are in equilibrium, Nature is at rest: there is neither consciousness nor activity: all is at rest and all is one. From time to time, however, the equilibrium breaks down, and the universe evolves through the interplay of the three inherent qualities. We will not here go into the Sāṁkhya theory concerning the evolution of the world which is involved and none too coherent. One point, however, needs stressing, and that is that both the material world and the mind of man are believed to evolve from an original disharmony. The first and highest evolute of Nature is called *buddhi*, a word derived from the root √*budh-* meaning 'to be awake'. This may be translated as 'mind' though *buddhi* would also include the will. Its functions are mental effort (*adhyavasāya*), virtue (*dharma*), knowledge, absence of passion, and lordship.[1] This is the first evolute of *prakṛti* or Nature, and it precedes the appearance of the *ahaṁkāra* or ego-principle. Huxley, it will be remembered, in *The Doors of Perception*, speaks of Mind at Large. Whether or not such an entity actually exists, the term does in fact accurately describe what the Sāṁkhya means by *buddhi*. It is the mind or consciousness of Nature.

As we have seen, in the Sāṁkhya system Nature is totally distinct from soul. Souls exist in infinite number; each is a monad and totally distinct from all other individual souls with which it has no connexion or communication whatever. For reasons which are left wholly unexplained, when Nature begins to evolve owing to the equilibrium of the inherent qualities being upset, the *puruṣas* or souls are drawn into Nature and imprisoned there. Thus the Sāṁkhya makes the sharpest possible distinction between body and 'psyche' on the one hand and the *puruṣa* or independent spiritual entity on the other. Just as in the Manichaean system man has a dual personality, belonging by his body to Matter or Concupiscence which is the principle of evil, and by his soul to the Father of Greatness or King of Light, so, in the Sāṁkhya system, is man compounded of the *puruṣa* (meaning literally 'a male person'), an independent spiritual monad on the one hand, and a psycho-physical body and mind on the other, which are an

pramādālasya-nidrābhis tan nibadhnāti, Bhārata. / sattvaṁ sukhe sañjayati, rajaḥ karmaṇi, Bhārata; / jñānam āvṛtya tu tamaḥ pramāde sañjayaty uta. / . . . sarva-dvāreṣu dehe'smin prakāśa upajāyate / jñānaṁ yadā, tadā vidyād vivṛddhaṁ sattvam ity uta. / lobhaḥ, pravṛttir, ārambhaḥ karmaṇām, aśamaḥ, spṛhā, / rajasy etāni jāyante vivṛddhe, Bharatarṣabha. / aprakāśo'pravṛttiś ca pramādo moha eva ca / tamasy etāni jāyante vivṛddhe, Kurunandana.'

[1] *Sāṁkhya-Kārikā*, § 23.

evolute of Nature and which therefore do not strictly belong to him at all. The Sāṁkhya did not make the mistake that Mānī made and identify Nature and the body with evil. Quite the contrary,—Nature is regarded as a kindly and purposeful, though not intelligent, agency which entangles the *puruṣa* within itself, but works, through the quality of *sattva*, for the ultimate release of the *puruṣa*.

Nature mysticism is explicable in terms of the Sāṁkhya system only if *puruṣa* is eliminated altogether. The nature mystic identifies himself with the whole of Nature, and in his exalted moments sees himself as being one with Nature and as having passed beyond good and evil. This feeling of being beyond good and evil, which has always shocked Christians, is characteristic of the nature mystic; and were he not concerned with something quite other than the theistic mystic, his experience would indeed point to a non-moral God who would thus be, like Nature itself, neither good nor evil, but beyond and indifferent to both. This appears to have been the position of the Beghards and Brethren of the Holy Spirit in the Middle Ages, and they were attacked for precisely this by Ruysbroeck. It is also the position of Huxley when under the influence of mescalin and of Custance when under the influence of mania. Jung, too, in *The Integration of the Personality* and elsewhere, takes the view that the 'shadow' or evil and generally suppressed side of the ego is a psychological fact which must be accepted as such and brought into harmony with the wholly integrated personality; and by an integrated personality he means a reconciliation between the collective unconscious which is chaotic and impersonal, the personal unconscious, and the conscious mind. One might be tempted to see in this a reconcilation of *puruṣa* and *prakṛti*; but in actual fact this does not appear to be so. It is much rather a reconciliation of the various elements which go to make up *prakṛti*; and this was only to be expected, for modern psychology is the science of the sick psyche, not of the immortal spirit which the nature mystic experiences beneath it. It is the science of the 'lower soul' of the Muslims, and does not, and presumably cannot, touch the 'higher soul' or spirit which all religions affirm to be immortal. When the Jungians attempt to penetrate into this region, they understandably become more than usually obscure.

Thus, though Jung borrows his concept of the 'self' from Indian psychology, his self is something quite different from the *ātman*, at least as understood by Śankara and his school of extreme monists. Jung's 'self' is the centre of the psyche, and it 'is meant to include the totality of the psyche in so far as this manifests itself in an individual. The self is not only the centre, but also the circumference that encloses consciousness and the unconscious'.[1] In other words the self would appear to be the totality of any given personality; it is the ego plus the personal unconscious plus the collective unconscious, all meeting in a perfect balance. As Jung himself puts it, 'In a certain sense, the thing we are trying to express is the feeling of having been "replaced", but without the connotation of having been "deposed". It is as if the leadership of the affairs of life had gone over to an invisible centre.'[2]

'In this remarkable experience', Jung continues, 'I see a phenomenon resulting from the detachment of consciousness, through which the subjective "I live", becomes the objective "It lives me".[3] This condition is felt to be higher than the earlier one; it is really as if it were a sort of release from compulsion and impossible responsibility which are the inevitable results of *participation mystique*. This feeling of release filled Paul completely. It is the consciousness of being a child of God which then frees one from the spell of the blood. Also, it is a feeling of reconciliation with what is happening, and that is the reason that the glance of "one who has attained fulfilment", according to the *Hui Ming Ching*, returns to the beauty of nature.'

It is interesting to compare Jung's views as expressed in this passage with the following which we have already quoted.

'Looking back on my own experiences, they all converge towards a kind of insight to which I cannot help ascribing some metaphysical significance. The keynote of it is invariably a reconciliation. It is as if the opposites of the world, whose contradictoriness and conflict make all our difficulties and troubles, were melted into unity. Not only do they, as contrasted species, belong to one and the same genus, but *one of the species*, the nobler and better one, *is itself the genus, and so soaks up and absorbs its opposite into itself*.'[4]

The quotation, it will be remembered, is from William James, and he is describing his own feelings after taking nitrous oxide.

Now, this is very strange; for if Jung is right, and a complete personality centred round what he calls the 'self' in which consciousness and the unconscious live in harmony, is the *summum bonum* that psychology has to offer, then, it would appear, such a state can be attained, at least momentarily, by the use of drugs. This does indeed seem to be true; but it must be remembered that the integration of the personality which many of Jung's patients have achieved and which Proust plainly achieved in his vision on the steps of the town house of the Princesse de Guermantes, is

[1] *The Integration of the Personality*, p. 96.

[2] *The Secret of the Golden Flower*, Richard Wilhelm and C. G. Jung, E.T., London, Kegan Paul, Trench and Trubner, 1938, p. 132.

[3] Cf. Rimbaud: 'C'est faux de dire: Je pense. On devrait dire: On me pense.' (*Œuvres Complètes*, p. 268.)

[4] William James, *The Varieties of Religious Experience*, p. 388.

a radical reorganization of the psyche which produces permanent results. The same result can be achieved in more violent form by the taking of drugs, or indeed in mania, but such states are only temporary, and for that reason can only in the long run lead to further disorder.

Contact with Eastern thought influenced Jung profoundly; but it is characteristic of him as an empirical psychologist that although he found in *The Secret of the Golden Flower* all the psychological mythology that he had already met with in the dreams of his patients, he should refuse to pursue the matter to the end; for the end of all Yoga disciplines,—so far as I know Chinese as well as Indian,—is the liberation of the eternal self (in the Indian sense of that word) from all that is not eternal, that is from the whole sphere of the unconscious as well as the conscious mind. The aim of Yoga is the isolation of the *puruṣa* from all that *prakṛti* or Nature can produce, the final separation of the eternal monad from all that is dependent on time, space, and causation. Jung's integrated personality may be a beautiful thing, but it is still only on the psychological level; it does not touch that highest point of the spirit of which the Christian mystics speak. The integrated personality of Jung is what Oscar Wilde envisaged when he described the true personality of man:

> 'It will be a marvellous thing—the true personality of man—when we see it. It will grow naturally and simply, flowerlike, or as a tree grows. It will not be at discord. It will never argue or dispute. It will not prove things. It will know everything. And yet it will not busy itself about knowledge. It will have wisdom. Its value will not be measured by material things. It will have nothing. And yet it will have everything, and whatever one takes from it, it will still have, so rich will it be. It will not be always meddling with others, or asking them to be like itself. It will love them because they will be different. And yet while it will not meddle with others, it will help all, as a beautiful thing helps us, by being what it is. The personality of man will be very wonderful. It will be as wonderful as the personality of a child.'

The secret of the integrated personality is one of passivity, of 'allowing things to happen to one',—a technique developed by one school of Zen Buddhists in Japan. It is to allow the 'feminine' or instinctive principle of the unconscious to emerge into daylight without allowing it to swamp the 'masculine', rational and individuating principle of consciousness; and since this 'feminine' element is, according to Jung, the common property of all mankind, its emergence will necessarily blur the line that separates the thinking and feeling subject from what is thought and felt. One of Jung's patients who had achieved such an integration, wrote to him as follows:

'Out of evil, much good has come to me. By keeping quiet, repressing nothing, remaining attentive, and hand in hand with that, by accepting reality—taking things as they are, and not as I wanted them to be—by doing all this, rare knowledge has come to me, and rare powers as well, such as I could never have imagined before. I always thought that, when we accept things, they overpower us in one way or another. Now this is not true at all, and it is only by accepting them that one can define an attitude toward them. So now I intend playing the game of life, being receptive to whatever comes to me, good and bad, sun and shadow that are for ever shifting, and, in this way, also accepting my own nature with its positive and negative sides. Thus everything becomes more alive to me. What a fool I was! How I tried to force everything to go according to my idea!'[1]

Now all this is related to the natural mystical experience in so far as unity with Nature is felt to be a constituent element in it. However, this integration of the personality goes farther than the natural mystical experience. Jung, of course, accepts the Chinese division of all Nature into male and female, positive and negative constituents. The Chinese call these *yang* and *yin*, and readers of Huxley will already be familiar with the idea. Thus the human psyche itself is androgynous, the consciousness corresponding to the male element and the unconscious to the female. The war of the sexes is a very real one in the psyche, and it is only when the struggle is resolved in what could be called a psychic marriage that integration takes place, and harmony and peace ensue. In the case of Mr. Custance his fits of mania and depression represent the alternate 'possession' of the ego by the 'female' unconscious and the 'male' consciousness. In the first case, since the psyche is entirely dominated by the collective unconscious, the fluid element which, if I understand Jung rightly, may be said to pervade all life, there is a feeling of unity or even identity with all Nature: in the second, on the other hand, all Nature is perceived as pure illusion, and the ego is shut up in its private universe which alone seems real. In Custance's case the private universe was one of sheer horror. Between the two poles, according to Jung, lies sanity and integration.

It is odd that Jung should have used this particular Taoist text to illustrate the integration process, for here the way of integration lies wholly through the male principle or *yang*. The English translator of *The Secret of the Golden Flower* summarizes the theory as follows:

'*Tao* the undivided, Great *One*, gives rise to two opposite reality principles, Darkness and Light, *yin* and *yang*. These are at first thought of only as forces of nature apart from man. Later, the sexual polarities and others as well, are derived from them. From *yin* comes *K'un*, the receptive feminine principle;

[1] *The Secret of the Golden Flower*, p. 126.

from *yang* comes *Ch'ien*, the creative masculine principle; from *yin* comes *ming*, life; from *yang*, *hsing* or essence.

'Each individual contains a central monad which, at the moment of conception, splits into life and essence, *ming* and *hsing*. These two are super-individual principles, and so can be related to *eros* and *logos*.

'In the personal bodily existence of the individual they are represented by two other polarities, a *p'o* soul (or *anima*) and a *hun* soul (or *animus*). All during the life of the individual these two are in conflict, each striving for mastery. At death they separate and go different ways. The *anima* sinks to earth as *kuei*, a ghost-being. The *animus* rises and becomes *shên*, a revealing spirit or god. *Shên* may in time return to *Tao*.

'If the life-forces flow downward, that is, without let or hindrance into the outer world, the *anima* is victorious over the *animus*; no "spirit body" or "Golden Flower" is developed, and, at death, the ego is lost. If the life-forces are led through the "backward-flowing" process, that is, conserved, and made to "rise" instead of allowed to dissipate, the *animus* has been victorious, and the ego persists after death. It is then possessed of *shên*, the revealing spirit. A man who holds to the way of conservation all through life may reach the stage of the "Golden Flower", which then frees the ego from the conflict of the opposites, and it again becomes part of *Tao*, the undivided, Great *One*.'[1]

In this text, it will be noted, the *anima* must be controlled by the *animus* if the 'Golden Flower' which corresponds to integration in Jung's terminology, is to be developed. This is the opposite of what Jung normally means by integration. Jung, however, avoids the difficulty by pointing out that this must be so in the *East* since the *anima*, so far from being repressed, is, for Eastern people, an ever-present reality, and often more real to them than the masculine intellectual principle or *animus*. In the modern West, however, precisely the opposite is true. For Jung Western civilization is tyrannized over by the male principle of consciousness, and the female unconscious, driven underground and deprived of the effective symbolism of religion, is left to fester. Finally it will erupt in the form of mass unreason,—Nazism, of course, being the extreme but typical example of this.

What Jung means by integration, then, is the marriage of the so-called male and female portions of the psyche, the reconciliation of the conscious mind with the unconscious, both personal and collective. This is effected by the transference of the centre of gravity from the ego (the male, discriminating, and dividing principle) to what he calls the new centre of the self which thereby makes its appearance as something distinct from the old 'I'. Proust puts it rather differently: 'The permanent essence of things which is usually hidden, is set free, and our real self which often had seemed

[1] Ibid., p. 73.

dead for a long time yet was not dead altogether, awakes and comes to life as it receives the heavenly food now proffered to it.'[1]

Integration, then, would seem to mean the natural mystical experience brought under the control of the intellect. At the same time the rational principle finds itself extended by its marriage with the unconscious. Instead of being in opposition, now each nourishes the other. Evil, then, in the psyche is the separation of the rational from the instinctive, the conscious from the unconscious. Only when the two are functioning in harmony can we realize the Kingdom of God within us; for a house divided against itself cannot stand. Integration represents an advance on man's path towards his final goal. It is superior to the natural mystical experience because it absorbs it and brings it under control. This is probably what Junayd, the founder of the 'middle' school of Muslim mysticism, meant when he spoke of his ecstatic (one is tempted to say 'manic') predecessor, Abū Yazīd of Bisṭām, as having reached the first stage only on the mystic's path when he made such astonishing statements as 'I am He', and 'Glory be to me, how great is my glory', implying thereby that he was actually identical with the Deity.

Now it is obvious that if complete identity with the Deity is possible, then it would be ridiculous to say that such identity was only the beginning of the path that leads to God. When Abū Yazīd vented himself of these strange ejaculations, Junayd maintains, he was speaking in ecstasy and his words were not to be understood literally. 'Some of the utterances of Abū Yazīd,' he says, 'in their force, their profundity, and extreme significance are drawn up from an ocean to which he alone had access and which was appropriated to him alone. I saw that the utmost limit of his (spiritual) state . . . was one which few could understand from his own words when they heard of it and which few could interpret because only those who knew the (hidden) meaning of his sayings and had access to the source of his inspiration, could bear with him.'[2] These elect, however, out of their esoteric knowledge, could confidently assert that such wild and apparently blasphemous sayings were mere beginnings: 'Abū Yazīd had (indeed) spoken truly about the science of Union except that his words were only beginnings of what might be expected from one who is of the elect.'[3]

[1] See p. 57, n. 1.

[2] Abū Nasr al Sarrāj, *Kitāb al-Luma'*, ed. R. A. Nicholson, Leyden, Brill, 1914, p. 381 of the Arabic text: 'wa-kāna min kalāmi Abī Yazīda . . . li-quwwati-hi wa-ghawri-hi wa-intihā'i ma'ānī-hi mughtarafun min baḥrin qad infarada bi-hi wa-ju'ila dhālika'l-baḥru la-hu waḥda-hu. . . . thumma innī ra'aytu'l-ghāyata'l-quṣwā min ḥāli-hi . . . ḥālan qalla man yafhamu-hā 'an-hu aw yu'abbiru 'an-hā 'inda istimā'i-hā li-anna-hu lā yaḥtamilu-hu illā man 'arafa ma'nā-hu wa-adraka mustaqā-hu.'

[3] Ibid.: 'wa-qad waṣafa ashyā'a min 'ilmi'l-tawḥīdi ṣaḥīḥatan illā anna-hā bi-

Such sayings as those we have quoted from Abū Yazīd, sayings technically known as *shaṭḥīyāt* or 'overflowings', are thus considered by Junayd to be symptomatic of an elementary stage in the mystic's career only. 'These ecstatic utterances', says the author, 'seldom, if ever, occur to those who have perfected themselves since these are firmly established in their mystical doctrine. Only beginners who are nevertheless chosen to reach absolute perfection, will fall into ecstasies such as these.'[1]

The great Muhammadan mystical doctor, Ghazālī, also has occasion to refer to Abū Yazīd whose monistic utterances were so shocking to the orthodox, and he too explains them away as mystical 'drunkenness'.[2] From the cases we have analysed hitherto,—and particularly from those of Rimbaud and John Custance,—it would seem that Junayd who prided himself on the 'sobriety' of his doctrine, must have recognized the danger of these sudden 'illuminations' in which the novice saw himself as identical with God. Such ecstasies were uncontrollable and did not conform to the *maqāmāt* or 'stations' on the mystic's path. Junayd therefore explained them as misconceptions of the beginner; and in this he was probably right, at least in the case of Abū Yazīd, for the latter had so unbalanced a nature that it would be surprising if he had not manic-depressive tendencies. He was, moreover, like Rimbaud, torn between two conflicting loyalties,—his loyalty to the transcendent God of Islam and the extreme humility that went with it on the one hand, and loyalty to what appears to have been a more or less absolute monism which he seems to have imbibed from his spiritual director and which almost certainly derived from the Vedānta.[3] His wild oscillations between these two extremes would go far to explain the self-contradictoriness of his recorded sayings. Abū Yazīd's more outrageous utterances can be explained as pan-en-henic in nature and his claim to be identical with God can best be explained on the assumption that he was using the term 'God' or rather 'He' in the sense of the Vedāntin *Brahman* perhaps imperfectly understood, just as Custance seems to use the word 'God' in the sense of the collective unconscious. Both are cases of 'positive inflation' rather than 'integration'.

The achievement of integration which, according to Jung and *The Secret of the Golden Flower*, represents the union and reconciliation of the male and female principles in the psyche, would seem to explain many parts of the Upaniṣads. Thus the conjunction of the opposites resulting in

dāyātun fī-mā yuṭlabu min-hā'l-murādūna li-dhālika.'

[1] Ibid., p. 380: 'wa-aqallu mā yūjadu li-ahli'l-kamāli'l-shaṭḥu li-anna-hum mutamakkinūna fī ma'ānī-him wa-inna-mā waqa'a fī'l-shaṭḥi man kāna fī bidāyatin wa-kāna murādan bi'l-wuṣūli ilā'l-kamāli wa'l-ghāyati.'

[2] See below, p. 157.

[3] See below, p. 161.

union is clearly indicated in the following passage. 'As a man when in the embrace of a well-loved woman knows nothing, neither outside nor inside, so does this man (*puruṣa*) when in the embrace of the intelligent self know nothing within or without. That is his form in which his desire is fulfilled, in which the Self is his desire, in which he has no desire and has passed beyond sorrow.'[1]

The passage in question is a description of what happens to the soul in deep, dreamless sleep technically known as *suṣupti* or 'good sleep'. In this state the soul imagines itself to be a god or a king, and it thinks 'I am this (world), I am (the) whole'.[2] 'This is his highest world', the Upaniṣad adds.

We noticed, when we were dealing with the case of Rimbaud, that, according to the orthodox Jungian interpretation of symbols, Rimbaud seemed to be undergoing both positive and negative inflation simultaneously and that these again (with the appearance of the 'integrating' symbol of the Cross) fused into a temporary integration of personality under the control of the self ('Il s'est chargé de ma vie', &c.). Precisely the same could be said of the Upaniṣadic passage with which we are now dealing. The soul is *idam*, 'this', 'the world', and it is *sarvo*, 'all' or 'whole',—'homo etiam mundus est, sed non contracte omnia, quoniam homo. Est igitur homo μικρόκοσμος'.

As in Rimbaud's case the author of the Upaniṣad sees himself as 'dispensé de toute morale':[3] things are no longer what they seem, for 'it is a strange and lovely land beyond individuality, and incidentally also beyond good and evil, since the opposites are reconciled, and the peace that passes all understanding rules supreme'.[4] In this land 'a father becomes no father (*a-pitā*), a mother no mother, the worlds no worlds, the gods no gods, the Vedas no Vedas. There a thief becomes no thief, the murderer of an embryo no murderer of an embryo, a Caṇḍāla no Caṇḍāla,[5] a Paulkasa no Paulkasa,[6] a mendicant no mendicant, an ascetic no ascetic. (The Brahman which the

[1] *Bṛhadāraṇyaka Up.*, 4. 3. 21: 'tad yathā priyayā striyā saṁpariṣvakto na bāhyaṁ kiñcana veda nāntaram, evam evāyaṁ puruṣaḥ prājñenātmanā saṁpariṣvakto na bāhyaṁ kiñcana veda nāntaram. tad vā asya etad āpta-kāmam ātma-kāmam akāmaṁ rūpaṁ śokāntaram.'

[2] *aham evedam sarvo'smi.* In his translation of the Upaniṣads (*The Thirteen Principal Upanishads*, 2nd ed., Oxford, 1931), Hume translates 'I am this world-all' for which one would expect *aham evedaṁ sarvam asmi. Sarvo* (masc.) cannot agree with *idam* (neut.). We must then translate, 'I am this (meaning, as usual, "the world"): I am all (whole or complete).'

[3] *Œuvres Complètes*, p. 243.

[4] Custance, *Adventure into the Unconscious*, p. 4.

[5] The son of a Śūdra father and Brahman mother, that is, of a marriage that is, by Brahmanical standards, monstrous.

[6] The son of a Śūdra father and a Kṣatriya (warrior-caste) mother.

released soul becomes) is accompanied by neither good (*puṇyena*) nor evil. He (the soul) has passed beyond all the troubles of the heart'.[1]

We are no longer dealing with either Rimbaud who induced madness in himself nor with Custance who had the good or bad fortune to suffer from a genuine manic psychosis; we are dealing with the sacred books of one of the world's greatest religions. The present passage, however, is so strongly reminiscent of the phenomena we have already discussed that we cannot avoid the same conclusion in this case as well. The experience described by the Upaniṣad is undoubtedly what Jung calls 'integration' (*sarvo'smi*, 'I am all or whole'), but it also has the characteristics of mania, the megalomania ('He is as a king or a god') and the deceptive expansion against which Qushayrī warned. Finally, of course, there is the claim to have passed beyond good and evil.

The mere fact that the Upaniṣads are revered as a sacred book by hundreds of millions should not blind us to the fact that they are the efforts of relatively primitive men to discover an adequate philosophy of the universe. They are a heterogeneous collection of texts, often loosely put together, in which many conflicting ideas can be found. Sometimes they are grotesque, sometimes childish; but sometimes they show an astonishing insight into the nature of things and have, for this reason, been rightly, though some think excessively, admired. Fundamentally they are concerned with the nature of Being, not with ethics or morality.

It does, however, seem fairly clear that the early Upaniṣads, in their present state, are governed by two distinct modes of thought, primitive speculation on the nature of the universe and its 'ground', very much on the lines of the pre-Socratics in Greece, and Yogic meditation in which magical correspondences between man and the universe, the microcosm and macrocosm, play a leading part. That the result of such speculation should show a rich variety is, then, scarcely surprising; and Professor Surendranath Dasgupta does well to warn us to 'turn a deaf ear to the absolute claims of the[se] exponents (of the Upaniṣads), and ⟨to⟩ look upon the Upaniṣads not as a systematic treatise but as a repository of diverse currents of thought —the melting pot in which all later philosophic ideas were still in a state of fusion'.[2] It is, then, not surprising that passages appear in the Upaniṣads which state clearly (as does the passage we have just quoted) that from the absolute point of view good and evil have no meaning: they are opposites

[1] *Bṛhadāraṇyaka Up.*, 4. 3. 22: 'atra pitā apitā bhavati, mātā amātā, lokā alokā, devā adevā, vedā avedā; atra steno 'steno bhavati, bhrūṇa-hā abhrūṇa-hā, caṇḍālo 'caṇḍālaḥ, paulkaso 'paulkasaḥ, śramaṇo 'śramaṇas, tāpaso 'tāpaso. 'nanvāgataṁ puṇyenānanvāgataṁ pāpena; tīrṇo hi tadā sarvān śokān hṛdayasya bhavati.'

[2] S. Dasgupta, *A History of Indian Philosophy*, Cambridge, 1922, vol. i, p. 42.

(*dvandvas*) which are reconciled in the One Brahman, or rather disappear in it as being non-existent. This does not mean that the primitive Hindus were devoid of all moral sense; it means only that they had not as yet considered the relationship between Being and the Good. It is then pointless to quote the 'amoral' passages from the Upaniṣads as being parallel, for instance, to Eckhart's literally 'shocking' thesis which he propounds in his eighty-fourth[1] sermon that God is not, in his essence, good. Eckhart inherited the whole of mediaeval scholastic philosophy, and when he states that God is neither good, better, nor best, he is deliberately trying to shock his audience into reassessing what is meant by the 'goodness' of God,—a divine attribute on which he expatiates elsewhere with all the passionate lyricism that is his.

The value of the Upaniṣads, as opposed to the philosophers who were later to build systems out of those passages which suited their particular thesis best, lies precisely in their undeveloped ontology and theology, and in the fact that they do present such a bewildering variety of mystical doctrine. It is then only by trying to sort out the various forms of mysticism in other traditions that one can hope to form a just estimate of their achievement. So far we have distinguished two main forms of 'natural' mysticism, the pan-en-henic which is the mysticism of Nature, the sense of union with all creation, which is explained by Jung as a descent into the collective unconscious or as 'positive inflation'. Secondly we have discovered the phenomenon of 'integration' formulated by Jung as a result both of clinical experience and of a close study of European alchemical texts and their opposite numbers in China. This, it would appear, is as far as purely natural mysticism and 'natural' psychology can take us. And this is, precisely, where religious or theistic mysticism begins.

Jung, despite his respect for religion and its power to heal an injured soul by means of a symbolism that is, in his words, 'psychologically true', is nevertheless interested not in religion as such, but in the magic which infects and affects all the great religions to a greater or lesser extent. Thus he finds his psychological theories reflected and confirmed in alchemic, Tantric Buddhist, and Taoist texts. His sympathy with Catholicism as against Protestantism is based on the fact that the Catholic Church has made room for symbols which, according to him, have universal validity, while orthodox Protestantism has swept aside the symbols and left us with only the male, rational, and divisive 'ego' principle: it has wholly neglected the so-called female, irrational, and instinctive side of our being. Thus

[1] In the edition of F. Pfeiffer, Leipzig, Göschen, 1857: 9th sermon in M. de Gandillac, *Maître Eckhart, Traités et Sermons*, Paris, Aubier, 1942.

Catholicism is superior to Protestantism, according to Jung, because his 'archetypes' which are part and parcel of the collective unconscious appear in Catholic myth and practice far more clearly than they can do in a Protestant environment.

Probably few would deny that Catholicism has succeeded not only in maintaining itself in existence but in increasing, extending, and deepening its influence in this present century of unbelief as much by its 'magical' elements as by any truth it may claim to possess. Yet whatever there may be of 'psychological truth' in the doctrines and liturgy of the Catholic Church is, from the religious point of view, irrelevant. Thus, even if we are prepared to admit the truth of Jung's explanation of the *Hieros Gamos* in pagan religions, alchemy, and tantrism, it is doubtful whether there is any validity in his transference of this myth to the mystical nuptials of the Christian soul with Christ. The fact that neither Jung nor his disciples seem to have undertaken an analysis of any of the Christian mystics on alchemical lines may indicate that they have contented themselves with the superficial resemblance without having read sufficiently deeply in the literature concerned. It is significant too that though they have adduced all manner of evidence from paganism, Hinduism, Buddhism, and Taoism, they have left the Muslim mystics strictly out of account; for early Muslim mysticism continues the Christian variety in a strange dress and does not, apparently, lend itself to interpretation by 'depth psychology'.

It is typical of Jung's method that he should criticize the Christian doctrine of the Trinity not on the ground that it is 'psychologically untrue', but because, as a symbol of perfection, it is found to fall short of this psychological 'truth'. Integration, we are told, is always symbolized by the figure 4 (square, circle, or cross). The 'fourth' is the female, passive, irrational, dark, chaotic element which must come to light in any symbol of the 'whole'. This is what is found in alchemical texts and in the *maṇḍalas* of Tantric Hinduism and Buddhism which Jung has found so helpful in his psychological studies. In this connexion it is, perhaps, of some interest to note that the symbolism of the square is used in Christian art as the symbol of the totality of the Godhead. As Professor Wind pointed out in the Chichele Lectures in Oxford in 1955, such a symbol appears in place of the conventional halo around the head of God the Father in Raphael's *Disputa* in the Sala della Segnatura in the Vatican. The square halo, according to Wind, represents the Three Divine Persons together with the One Divine Nature, the 'fourth' being, as it should be, the totality,—and it should, I suppose, be remembered that *totalitas*, *deitas*, and *natura* are all *feminine* nouns in Latin as are θεότης and φύσις in Greek and *kullīyat*, *ilāhīyat*, and *dhāt* in Arabic. Similar Trinity-Quaternities are to be found in Manichaeanism and Zervanism[1] in which the Deity itself is added to its essential characteristics,—in this case Space (or Light), Power, and Wisdom, plus Zurvān-Time as the totality of the Godhead.

It is touching that Jung should see in the definition of the dogma of the Assumption 'the most important religious event since the Reformation'[2] since it established the 'eternal feminine', as he thinks, in the heart of the Godhead. For the first time in the history of Christianity, it might be said, the trinitarian Śiva, the eternal male, has been provided with his Śakti,—reason is united with energy, the divisive intellectual ego with the fluid unconscious,—a *Hieros Gamos* on classical alchemical lines. We shall have more to say about the mystical marriage of the soul with Christ or God in a later chapter. Here it will be sufficient to say that the human soul, the spirit in its wholeness,—whatever the 'sexual' relationship may be between the constituent parts of the *psyche*,—is and must be passive and receptive in its relationship to God: hence the mystics usually speak of the soul as feminine, and God appears in Christianity as one God in three male Persons.[3]

The symbolical significance of the dogma of the Assumption is not the deification of the 'eternal feminine', *anima*, collective unconscious, or whatever it may be, but the deification of the human soul as represented by Mary, who in common with all human beings is the daughter of the One Father, and is, in her own right, the spouse of the Holy Ghost and Mother of the Son. Through the Immaculate Conception she is sinless and therefore 'whole', an integrated personality already. Her reception of, and fertilization by, the Holy Ghost symbolizes not a step towards integration which is already hers, but that vital step beyond the purely human sphere, beyond the *imago Dei*, the image of God, to God Himself. This is the step that the purely monistic mystic can never take as we hope to show in a later chapter.

Jung takes from religion only what confirms and illustrates his psychology. Hence his interest in (and distortion of) Catholicism which, as he points out, 'demonstrates her maternal character, because she allows the

[1] See R. C. Zaehner, *Zurvan, A Zoroastrian Dilemma*, Oxford, 1955, pp. 196–231.

[2] C. G. Jung, *Answer to Job*, E.T., London, Routledge and Kegan Paul, 1954, p. 169.

[3] The argument from gender (the Holy Ghost being *feminine* in Hebrew (*ruach*) though neuter in Greek (πνεῦμα) and masculine in Latin (*spiritus*)) seems worthless. So too in German the sun is feminine and the moon masculine, whereas in ancient Persian both are masculine and appear as such in mythology. The Jungians tend to disregard the evidence of comparative religion when it fails to corroborate their own theories.

tree growing out of her matrix to develop according to its own laws':[1] or in other words, the Church will admit any amount of 'psychological truth' from any pagan or non-Christian creed in so far as these are not wholly incompatible with her own dogmas which she holds to be revealed truth.

Where Jung inevitably parts company with Christianity, whether Orthodox, Catholic, or Protestant,—as opposed to Gnosticism, Hinduism, and Taoism,—is in the matter of the nature of the Godhead and the problem of evil. Though the whole tradition of Christian mysticism recognizes the human soul as the *imago Dei* and as the tabernacle of the Holy Ghost in which the whole Trinity delights to dwell, it cannot by any means identify the immanent God with either the totality of the psyche or with any specific content of it,—not even with the 'archetype of the self'.

Jung, as a psychologist, seems to have been perhaps too deeply influenced by the alchemists with their passion for the *conjunctio oppositorum* to have any clear idea of his own of the nature of evil and of sin. Gnosticism and similar religions equated evil with matter, the dark and heavy elements (earth and water) which, according to the Jungians, represent the collective unconscious as, no doubt, they do. The 'evil' in the collective unconscious which appears as the 'archetype of the shadow',[2] the seamy side of every man, must be brought out into the open and reconciled with the positive side of the personality. The question is whether Jung does not really mean by this that sin must be transmuted into its opposite, that the considerable amount of 'libido' necessary for the commission of mortal sin should be transformed into psychologically healing and creative activity; for it is a commonplace that sin must imply a diminution, a contraction, or lesion of the whole human personality. It does, therefore, not seem to make much sense to say, for instance, that pride should be brought out into the open and reconciled with the whole of the psyche. It has to be brought out into the open, all right; but once recognized for what it is, that is, a deliberate circumscription of the whole personality to the 'ego', it must of course be eliminated altogether, since so long as it subsists at all, the shift from the ego to the new centre of the self, which Jung sees to be essential to integration, can never take place. In this context the Thomist doctrine that evil is essentially a privation seems to make sense. If we adopt Jung's premiss that integration is the final cause or good of human beings on the purely natural plane, then, obviously, the seven deadly sins are, each and all of them, a privation of some essential element in the integrated whole. Pride, by which Lucifer fell and through which he tempted Adam to his fall, is

[1] C. G. Jung, ibid., p. 172.

[2] See especially *Collected Works*, vol. xvi, pp. 238–9.

rightly regarded by Christians as the deadliest of the deadly sins, because it is most obviously a separating function: it separates man from man, and separates the conscious ego from its unconscious roots. Inevitably it leads to a split personality. Thus, to my mind at least, there can be no question of coming to terms with the evil that is within us, because it is precisely this evil that prevents the realization of the 'self' in Jung's sense of that word. To suppose that one has passed beyond good and evil is perhaps the subtlest form that pride can take; for it seems to be the transference of an essentially positive and masculine sin to the negative and feminine side of the psyche. It is so unnatural a state as to constitute madness: it is, in fact, the hall-mark of mania, and is dangerous precisely because it comes upon you as a shattering revelation of truth. It is not for nothing that both Qushayrī and Baudelaire, in their different contexts, issued so grave a warning against it, for it is to mistake the unco-ordinated collective unconscious for what Jung calls the 'self': it is to mistake the part, and the irrational and genuinely amoral part at that, for the whole.

We have seen[1] that the Muslim philosophers, and particularly Avicenna and to a lesser extent Ghazālī, insist that 'anger' and 'lust', by which they mean the aggressive and sexual instincts, are natural constituents of the human psyche and are, as such, ineradicable. Each should be used to restrain and temper the other. They are not in themselves evil but are compared respectively by Ghazālī to a wild animal and a pack-animal.[2] It is probably these two faculties that Jung has chiefly in mind when he discusses the 'shadow', since it is these qualities which principally contribute to loss of self-control, a condition, as Jung points out, when one is no longer 'oneself', when one 'forgets oneself', or is 'beside oneself';[3] and his remedy,—bringing the shadow out into the open,—is not very different from Avicenna's. The result of this bringing the shadow up into consciousness, however, is to recognize it for what it is. And what it is seems to be the aggressive and sexual instincts which, once recognized, have to be subjected to the reason or, in Jung's terminology, the conscious mind. This is not to acknowledge and accept the evil in oneself, but to redirect to rational and moral ends instinctual urges which, except in Manichaean eyes, are not in themselves evil but neutral.

The collective unconscious, like the natural mystical experience which seems to proceed from it, is neutral in itself. To quote the *Sāṁkhya-Kārikā* again, 'nothing is more generous than Nature,[4] or so I think.

[1] See above, p. 106.

[2] *Kīmiyā-yi Sa'ādat*, vol. i, p. 9. See above, p. 107.

[3] *The Integration of the Personality*, E.T., p. 20.

[4] For 'Nature' one might well substitute 'collective unconscious'.

Content that she has been seen by the soul, she never again exposes herself to him'.[1]

To identify matter, the body, and instinctive life with evil is pure Manichaeanism, the *pessima haeresium*, and does to some extent account for the extreme confusion of Jung's pandaemonium of the collective unconscious. The Zoroastrian view of evil seems far saner and should serve as a necessary corrective to the crypto-Manichaeanism of Jungian psychology. For the Zoroastrians evil is not a privation of a good as it is for orthodox Christians: it is a separate *spiritual* principle, hostile to God and to the material universe which God creates as a bastion against Ahriman, the eternal substance of evil, who is the author of death, 'the negation of life, and naked aggression, ... wrong-mindedness, stupidity, blind self-assertiveness, error'.[2]

Ahriman, then, the principle of evil, is a pure spirit, wholly and completely divorced from matter which, as God's bastion against him, is his enemy as much as is God Himself. Matter, then, for the Zoroastrians, is wholly good; and for them, presumably, the natural mystical experience which, however we choose to explain it, is felt as a communion with all life in Nature,—and *prāṇa*, the Universal Soul, Mother Nature, *élan vital*, and *libido* all seem to boil down to this,—would seem to be an unqualified good.

In this respect Christianity and Hinduism both stand midway between the conflicting dualisms of Zoroaster and Mānī. Matter, Nature, or 'the world' are rightly regarded as being a neutral substance in so far as good and evil are concerned. In so far as the collective unconscious is an identical reflection of the macrocosm (the universe) in the microcosm (man), it is a force which being 'neutral', that is, 'natural' as opposed to 'voluntary', and incapable of purposive as opposed to automatic evolutionary action, can either co-operate with good in the achievement of man's final cause which for the Jungian is integration and for the Christian 'deification' for which integration must be the first and indispensable step, or it can co-operate with evil in the frustration of this end. If I understand it correctly, 'integration' means the reduction of the three constituents of the psyche to a balanced and ordered whole of which the 'self' is the centre. The self is, as Jung himself says, the God-image,[3] and for the Christian this *imago Dei is* the immortal soul and, by the mere fact of its likeness to God, is capable of 'deification'. Obviously for as long as a man has not found the

[1] *Sāṁkhya-Kārikā*, § 61: see above, p. 99.

[2] R. C. Zaehner, *The Teachings of the Magi*, London, George Allen and Unwin, 1956, p. 55.

[3] *Answer to Job*, p. 177.

second self which is his immortal soul made 'in the image and likeness of God', he is in no position to find his divine exemplar.

Sin is what distorts and dissipates the personality, what throws it off its balance; for, theologically, sin is what deflects a man away from his final cause, therefore from integration necessarily since this must be an essential stage on man's painful journey towards God. Thus to speak of integrating the 'shadow' either into the 'individuated' psyche or into the Deity is nonsense, if by the shadow is understood evil in the sense of a privation of some good, a maiming of oneself. If, on the other hand, the shadow simply means untamed instinct, then its being brought out into the open will mean, in practice, its taming. Thus it would appear that the misunderstandings that have arisen between the Jungians and Christianity, may be little more than a matter of terminology.

This digression has taken us a long way from the consideration of the Upaniṣads and the purely natural experience that seemed to emerge from the passage we had occasion to quote from the *Bṛhadāraṇyaka* and which seemed to supply an instance of Jung's integration of the personality and the emergence of the self as the centre (as well as the circumference)[1] of the psyche. If we have been right in identifying the natural mystical experience which Huxley sampled under the influence of mescalin and which comes to many others unexpectedly and quite unsummoned, with what is technically called mania, and if both are to be explained as a direct experience of what, for lack of a more precise word, we still must call the collective unconscious, then it must follow that the next stage, the integration of the unconscious and the conscious mind in the 'self', must be a more advanced stage. Thus if, as Huxley once maintained, he could understand precisely what is meant by the Beatific Vision when still under the influence of mescalin, it would seem to follow,—assuming that by that statement he actually meant that he was really enjoying that vision,—that the Beatific Vision is a state that can be transcended. If this is really so, then it follows that the vision of God is a natural concomitant of mania, that it can be induced by drugs, and that since the vision makes nonsense of common morality, let alone of the virtues of humility and charity, then the picture of God which we derive from the teaching of Jesus of Nazareth must be false.

Let us, however, return for the moment to the Sāṁkhya conception of *puruṣa* and *prakṛti* with which we began the chapter. Certain obvious parallels between this theory and that of the Chinese *Secret of the Golden Flower* immediately suggest themselves. *Puruṣa* is by definition masculine;

[1] *The Integration of the Personality*, p. 96.

prakṛti, feminine in gender, is also feminine in nature, and here you have a rough Indian parallel to the Chinese *yang* and *yin*. Similarly just as in the *Golden Flower* the return to Tao is through *yang* or the male side only, so too in the Indian system 'liberation' consists in the isolation of the male *puruṣa* for all eternity from the female, the isolation of the soul or spirit, as perhaps it should be more properly called, from Nature. Now the Sāṁkhya system is strictly atheist, and we are therefore still left on a natural or purely psychological plane. The Sāṁkhya, however, marks an advance beyond nature mysticism in that it makes a clear distinction between Nature on the one hand and the immortal soul or spirit on the other. It holds that man's spirit is an immortal, immutable, and passionless monad, and that neither the body nor the reason, nor what Aristotle and the Muslim philosophers call the lower soul, really belong to him. He is essentially other than they, and his eternal destiny is to rid himself for ever of the whole psycho-physical apparatus. This is the reverse of integration. There is no vision of the unity of man with Nature, nor is it a case of this vision being utilized to build up the whole man. Nature, the perpetually changing and impermanent, is rejected by *puruṣa*, spirit, out of hand. All the attributes of Nature which include *buddhi* or universal intelligence and *ahaṁkāra* or the sense of being an ego, or in Jung's terminology the collective unconscious and the conscious mind, are rejected, and the spirit remains in perfect and blissful isolation in and with itself for ever and ever, since in its essence it cannot change. It is above both the conscious and the unconscious. That *buddhi*, in the Sāṁkhya system, really does mean something very like the collective unconscious in Jung's system seems to be indicated by the fact that its synonym is *mahat*, 'the great', and that it is prior to the *ahaṁkāra*, the ego principle, which is represented as deriving from it. It would, however, be more correct to describe it as the 'collective consciousness', universal awareness that precedes individual consciousness. This is what the nature mystics claim to experience: it is what Rimbaud called 'l'intelligence universelle' and Huxley 'Mind at Large'.

To put it another way: one can only speak of the collective *unconscious* from the point of view of the average modern Western man who is totally unaware of such an entity, but who nevertheless pays involuntary tribute to it in his pathetic addiction to the comic strip where the Jungian archetypes flourish uninhibitedly. If we speak from the point of view of the nature mystic or the manic, it would be far more accurate to speak of this entity as the 'collective consciousness', and this is precisely what *buddhi* means. The Sāṁkhya is not primarily concerned with any purely psychological state, it is concerned with the spirit and its release from *all* psychological states, and from all that ties it to the body and the psyche. It is, in fact, concerned with religion, even though it is an atheistical religion.

Buddhism too has always been a stumbling-block to Western religious thinkers; for Buddhism is undoubtedly a religion, and in its primitive form it is as undoubtedly atheistical, at least in the sense that we normally understand that word. But though the Buddhist scriptures lay such tremendous emphasis on the impermanence of all things, there are passages enough to show that over against this ever-changing world the Buddha saw something that did not change, over against *prakṛti* he saw *puruṣa* though he would not have formulated it thus. He calls it 'deathlessness, peace, the unchanging state of *Nirvāṇa*';[1] or more clearly he says, 'There is, monks, an unborn, not become, not made, uncompounded, and were it not, monks, for this unborn, not become, not made, uncompounded, no escape could be shown here for what is born, has become, is made, is compounded. But because there is, monks, an unborn, not become, not made, uncompounded, therefore an escape can be shown for what is born, has become, is made, is compounded.'[2]

Thus the Buddha, like the Sāṁkhya, recognizes that there is an eternal being transcending time, space, and change: and this is the beginning of religion. Moreover the Hindus, overwhelmingly, and the Buddhists when they are off their guard, speak of this eternal being as the 'self',—a term which Jung borrowed from them, but used to mean something rather different. The Sāṁkhya contents itself with noting that each individual has an immortal substrate which is totally distinct from its psychological make-up. This immortal substrate is mixed up in Nature through no fault or desire of its own, for it is itself totally impassive. Since there is no God superior to the *puruṣa*, the soul's only fruition can be to disentangle itself from what is purely temporal, to rediscover itself in its essence. This essence is, of course, quite distinct from the mere ego, the *ahaṁkāra*, which, as we have seen, is an evolute of *prakṛti* or Nature. This may be the 'second self' that Proust discovered in himself, but in that case the integration of the personality around this self, as practised by Proust and recommended by Jung, is not at all what the Sāṁkhya envisages. For in the Sāṁkhya there is certainly no integration of anything into anything else, there is only the complete withdrawal of the eternal from all that is temporal: all contact between the two orders must be completely cut off. In the Middle East a very similar doctrine was developed by Mānī, the founder of the Manichees. The problem for him was the same, how could the soul be released from matter

[1] *Suttanipāta*, 204: *apud* Conze, *Buddhist Texts through the Ages*, p. 93.

[2] *Udāna*, 80–81: ibid., p. 95.

or Nature? The Manichees, of course, went much farther and identified matter with evil, but they did also believe in a God who was supremely good and with whom ultimate union was possible. The Sāṁkhya admits no such being and therefore sees beatitude as the final isolation of the soul.

The Sāṁkhya, moreover, is the philosophic basis on which Yoga technique was originally grafted. The only major difference between the two systems is that the Yoga did acknowledge a being called the Lord (*Īśvara*), which is sometimes translated as 'God'. This is totally misleading, for the *Īśvara* of the Yoga system is simply a bigger and better *puruṣa* who helps on other *puruṣas* to liberation. '*Īśvara*', the Yoga aphorisms say, 'is a special *puruṣa* untouched by troubles, deeds, their consequences, or hopes.'[1] He is almighty and can grant liberation to whomsoever he will: he it is who is responsible for both the union and the separation of the *puruṣas* and *prakṛti*. God, in the classical Yoga, is nothing more than a *deus ex machina* invented for the purpose of explaining how the individual *puruṣas* ever became involved in *prakṛti*; and this appears to be his only function. It is perhaps the strangest conception of 'God' known to the whole of religion; for though his pre-excellence and omnipotence are admitted, there is no question of the soul drawing near to him for any other purpose than that of obtaining his aid in separating it from Nature. This is typical of the whole stream of classical Hinduism in that it attaches what seems to us a quite excessive importance to detachment as such. A similar emphasis is to be found in both the Christian and Muslim mystics, but in their case detachment from the world is the necessary corollary to exclusive attachment to God. The Sāṁkhya-Yoga will have none of this; for when the Yoga introduces the idea of the Lord which it doubtless borrowed from one of the current theistic systems, he is introduced for no other purpose than to help the soul towards isolation. Modern exponents of the *Yoga-sūtras*, moreover, normally introduce at this point the conception of the *iṣṭa-devatā*, 'the deity of your choice'. This deity may be anyone or anything at all, and fulfils no function except to provide a fixed point of meditation. When this purpose has been served, the god is discarded and the Yogin passes beyond him to the real business of mental concentration, the achievement of *kaivalyam* or 'isolation'.

The average European, if he tries to understand the Sāṁkhya-Yoga, has great difficulty in seeing why such a state of isolation should be regarded as the highest bliss; and it is significant that in a recent translation of the *Yoga-sūtras* by Messrs. Prabhavananda and Isherwood, the Sūtras are

[1] *Patañjali's Yoga-sūtras*, I. 24: 'kleśa-karma-vipākāśayair aparāmṛṣṭaḥ puruṣa-viśeṣa īśvaraḥ.'

treated as if they were a Vedāntin treatise, and not Sāṁkhya-Yogin at all. For whereas it is perfectly possible to understand that to realize oneself as the Absolute,—the good of the Vedānta,—may be productive of bliss, the complete isolation of self from all things is less obviously so. It is perhaps significant that the *Yoga-sūtras* claim that the Yoga discipline enables the disciple to obtain supernatural powers. These include not only such minor accomplishments as thought-reading, clairvoyance, clair-audition, etc., which, for all I know, may quite possibly be obtained by these means, but also such major miracles as the ability to fly or to disappear at will and, most remarkable of all, omniscience.[1] These can scarcely be anything but pure delusion, and readers of Mr. Custance's books will recognize them as such. These claims, then, indicate that the Yoga technique, like mescalin, is designed to produce praeternatural experiences akin to a manic condition. For the true Yogin, however, these are by-products and should not be allowed to deflect him from his proper goal which is isolation.

What does all this mean? Now, it would seem that the emphasis on the acquisition of praeternatural powers indicates that the Yogin is interested in achieving a manic condition akin to the experience of the nature mystics, yet not as a goal, but as a stage on the way to the true goal which is isolation. The fact that a God is introduced at an earlier stage and is then rejected as being merely a means to an end, shows that here there can be no question of a *unio mystica* as we understand it; and in fact no such claim is put forward. The goal is isolation; and isolation in the Sāṁkhya sense means the isolation of what Christians call man's immortal soul from all its purely psycho-physical adjuncts. This is the soul that has to be lost in order to be found, the 'second self' discovered by Proust, but not, as in his case, integrated with his temporal personality, but isolated from it. The Yogin's 'isolation' would then seem to be the detachment of his spirit, the highest point of the soul of the Christian mystics, from all purely physical and psychic, and therefore temporal, elements. This has been described as 'en-stasy' rather than ecstasy by Louis Gardet:[2] it is the soul contemplating itself in its essence; and in view of the fact that it has, in accomplishing the Yoga discipline, purged itself of all desire, of all that can attach it to purely created things, it must necessarily be sinless, and equally it must be devoid of positive virtue, for detachment means a total indifference to all actions, whether they be good or evil. The soul in such a state might be compared to that of a new-born child: it has reverted to original innocence in which there is neither good nor evil. 'The personality of man will be very wonderful. It will be as wonderful as the personality of a child.'

[1] *Patañjali's Yoga-sūtras*, 3. 38–49.
[2] See *Les Mardis de Dar el-Salam*, Cairo, Costa Tsoumas, 1951.

CHAPTER VII

SOME HINDU APPROACHES

'THE personality of man will be very wonderful. It will be as wonderful as the personality of a child.' In the last chapter we tried to show that this 'wonderful personality' of the child which Oscar Wilde had envisaged, meant a personality divested of all that we call sin. According to Catholic theology the souls of unbaptized infants go to what is called the 'Limbo of the Innocents'; and in this Limbo the soul enjoys the fullest natural bliss though it is deprived of the Beatific Vision of God. This seems to have been realized by Rimbaud who speaks of his own experiences as the 'ancient Hell whose doors the Son of Man opened'.[1]

We further endeavoured to show that if we accept the Sāṁkhya premisses at their own valuation and resolutely refuse to overlay them with Western theistic ideas, this would seem to be the goal of the Sāṁkhya system too. For the isolation of *puruṣa* from *prakṛti* simply means the isolation of the immortal soul from the world of change, its isolation from actions and their fruits, whether these be good or evil. This is to deny and reject any development of the personality into a richer whole which seems to be the purpose of Jung's 'individuation' or 'integration'. It is rather to revert to a state of primal innocence, and, in Freudian parlance, it would presumably be represented as a reversion to the undifferentiated state of the embryo in the womb. For the Jungians it would be the reversion to the original undifferentiated unconscious, and for Jung's disciple, Erich Neumann, it would be nothing less than 'Uroboric incest', for, according to him 'annihilation through the spirit, i.e., through the Heavenly Father, and annihilation through the unconscious, i.e., through the Earth Mother, are identical, as the study of every psychosis teaches'.[2]

These psychological interpretations, however, will not do; for the Sāṁkhya isolation of *puruṣa* refuses to fit into any of the categories. It is the very opposite of the 'annihilation' of the ego in anything at all, nor is it the integration of the ego with anything, nor is it the 'individuation' of the personality round the 'self': it is the complete isolation of the 'self' from all the products of *prakṛti*, Mother Nature, who is nothing else than the collective unconscious.

Everyone knows that Hinduism is permeated through and through with

[1] See above, p. 81.

[2] E. Neumann, *The Origins and History of Consciousness*, London, Routledge and Kegan Paul, 1954, p. 187.

magic; and it is, quite naturally, this magical element, as exhibited in the Tantras and the Yoga techniques, that has attracted the attention of the psychologists. There is, however, much more to Hinduism than this: it is not merely a system of magic: it is a religion and as such it has religious as well as psychological values. And when we say that it has religious values, we mean that it has something worth while to teach us about a changeless, eternal, Being Who sustains and indwells both the universe and the human soul. It is true that in the Sāṁkhya system which we have been discussing no such unique person exists: on the contrary we have an infinity of such persons, and these correspond to what Christians call human souls, in so far as these are considered to be immortal. *Mutatis mutandis* the *puruṣa* of the Sāṁkhya, when it enters *prakṛti*, can be likened to the Christian idea of the newly created soul as it comes to be at the time of its bodily conception. Such a soul, if I understand the doctrine correctly, will only be affected by original sin to the extent that, by the mere fact of being a *human* soul, it partakes of the specifically human defect of being separated from God as the necessary result of original sin. In other words, without a special grace, it cannot participate in the direct vision of God.

Since there is nothing in the Sāṁkhya system resembling grace, and since its aim is the isolation of the *puruṣa* from all that is transitory, it seems to follow that the natural bliss promised by the Church to the unbaptized infant is the same as the Sāṁkhya sage believes he can and will obtain when he is finally released from *prakṛti*. It is the natural bliss that inheres in a soul that is not yet touched by actual sin, nor yet, for that matter, by actual virtue, or by change or development of any kind. This, in fact, seems to be the aim of the Sāṁkhya, and indeed of the main stream of Indian religion which regards 'salvation' not as a making whole (*salvus*, *sarva*) or an 'integration', but as a separation,—a separation of the gold from the dross, the eternal from the transitory.

When we come to discuss Indian mysticism, we will no longer be speaking entirely in terms of recorded experience. The Hindu mystical classics are not autobiographical and are not the record of actual experiences undergone by given individuals. They are either mystico-magical tracts like the earlier Upaniṣads, or the exposition of mystical doctrines in verse like the later Upaniṣads and the Bhagavad-Gītā. The only relatively modern writer who calls for serious consideration is Śrī Rāmakrishna who, though in theory a non-dualist Vedāntin, was by nature a theist who, like Angelus Silesius, saw God in all things. There would be little point in discussing his famous disciple Vivekānanda here. As a religious teacher he is not in the same class as his master, and his writings exhibit an arrogance that is slightly antipathetic and tends to prejudice the reader against him. Those who are interested in the depths of foolishness of which the unconscious, operating through the natural mystical experience, is capable, are recommended to read Swami Yogananda's *Autobiography of a Yogi*.[1] One has only to compare this with Rimbaud's work to realize the truth of Baudelaire's dictum that drugs (or, in the case of Yogananda, Yoga techniques) can only raise a man's character to an infinitely higher power. Thus it is possible for Rimbaud, when in a state of what the Ṣūfīs call intoxication, to produce something totally new and totally marvellous in French poetry, while Yogananda, on first entering into *samādhi* (in this case obviously a typical natural mystical experience) writes the following *inter multa alia*:

'Dreams, wakings, states of deep *turiya* sleep,
Present, past, future, no more for me,
But ever-present, all-flowing I, I, everywhere.
Planets, stars, stardust, earth,
Volcanic bursts of doomsday cataclysms,
Creation's moulding furnace,
Glaciers of silent X-rays, burning electron floods,
Thoughts of all men, past, present, to come,
Every blade of grass, myself, mankind,
Each particle of universal dust,
Anger, greed, good, bad, salvation, lust,
I swallowed, transmuted all
Into a vast ocean of blood of my own one Being!

. . . . .

Tranquilled, unbroken thrill, eternally living, ever-new peace!
Enjoyable beyond imagination of expectancy, *samadhi*, bliss!
Not a mental chloroform
Or unconscious state without wilful return,
Samadhi but extends my conscious realm
Beyond the limits of the mortal frame
To farthest boundary of eternity
Where I, the Cosmic Sea,
Watch the little ego floating in me.' . . . etc., etc.[2]

'On me pense', as Rimbaud said. In this case 'on', presumably the personal as well as the collective unconscious, seems to be an idiot child with a smattering of Vedānta.

Rāmakrishna, however, was a serious character and was, and is, regarded by many Hindus as a saint. He, like Rimbaud and Abū Yazīd, was torn

[1] New York, Rider, 1950. [2] Ibid., p. 131.

between two doctrines, between the Vedānta which he officially professed in its extreme non-dual variety on the one hand, and an intense devotion to a personal God, usually conceived of as Kālī ('the Mother') on the other. This devotion verges on pantheism since he sees God in all things. The genuine pantheist, however, differs from the orthodox Christian only in so far as he refuses to admit the essential category of contingent being. When the pantheist says he sees a stone as God, it is more than likely that he means little more than that the stone has its own humble perfection which it derives from God: he sees the stone as God made it, and made it good. So too Rāmakrishna sees God in all men, however wicked.

'Many years ago', he is recorded as saying, 'Vaishnavacharan told me that one attains perfect Knowledge only when one sees God in man. Now I see that it is He Who is moving about in different forms, now as an honest man, now as a cheat and again as a villain. So I say, "Narayana in the form of an honest man, Narayana in the form of a swindler, Narayana in the form of a villain, Narayana in the form of a lewd person." Now the problem is how I can entertain all. I wish to feed everyone. Therefore I keep one at a time with me and entertain him.'[1]

Here we meet with something we have not met with hitherto in all our wearisome pilgrimage through 'nature mysticism', 'reversion to the unconscious', 'positive and negative inflation', 'individuation', 'integration', and all the rest. We meet with simple human goodness, a quality that none of our ecstatics (with the exception of Abū Yazīd whom I have not quoted in this connexion) have notably exhibited. 'I can entertain all. I wish to feed everyone.' Rāmakrishna's pantheism, if such it can be called, is very near Christianity, for 'inasmuch as ye have done it unto one of the least of these my brethren, ye have done it unto me'.[2] Nor is he doctrinally far removed from Christianity. Admittedly no Christian would go so far as to say 'God in the form of a cheat', for God can scarcely be said to dwell in the cheat and villain, the scribe and Pharisee, in so far as each of these is cheat, villain, scribe, and Pharisee: he dwells rather in their inmost souls despite these qualities which are in themselves merely constrictions and deformations of the personality, and this is of divine origin. Yet Rāmakrishna, who tries to put into words the feelings that well up inside him, appears at one time as a monist, and at another as a pantheist, more often as the latter. In his case the natural mystical experience which sees all things as one, and the contemplation of the Divine seem to be inextricably entangled; and this is as characteristic of the Upaniṣads themselves as it is of Rāmakrishna.

[1] *Sayings of Sri Ramakrishna*, Madras, Sri Ramakrishna Math, 1949, pp. 320–1.

[2] Matt. xxv. 40.

Here is another passage from Rāmakrishna that will illustrate our meaning:

> 'I do see the Supreme Being as the veritable Reality with my very eyes! Why then should I reason? I do actually see that it is the Absolute Who has become all things around us; it is He who appears as the finite soul and the phenomenal world! One must have an awakening of the spirit within to see this reality. As long as one is unable to see Him as the one reality, one must reason or discriminate, saying, "Not this; Not this." Of course, it would not do for one merely to say, "I have seen beyond the possibility of a doubt that it is He Who has become all! " Mere saying is not enough. By the Lord's grace the spirit must be quickened. Spiritual awakening is followed by Samadhi. In this state one forgets that one has a body; one loses all attachment to the things of the world, *i.e.*, "woman and gold"; one likes no other words than those relating to God; one is sorely troubled if called upon to listen to worldly matters. The spirit within being awakened, the next step is the realization of the Universal Spirit. It is the spirit that can realize the Spirit.'[1] 'By the spirit one goes to God.'[2]

Here Rāmakrishna's pantheistic view of Nature is shot through by the vision of God. This is no longer *simply* a pan-en-henic experience because he sees God through the veil of Nature. No pure nature mystic could say that he likes 'no other words than those relating to God': in fact they rarely mention God except as a description of their expanded selves. At the same time there can be little doubt that Rāmakrishna did see and experience something very like what Rimbaud and Jefferies did, but it obtains for him a far greater significance because he sees God manifesting himself primarily in the order of charity and grace, secondarily only in the natural order. Between Rāmakrishna, the nineteenth-century Hindu, and Angelus Silesius, the seventeenth-century convert to Catholicism, there is practically no difference.

> 'Wer selbst nicht alles ist, der ist noch zu geringe,
> Daß er dich sehen soll, mein Gott, und alle Dinge.'[3]

Both Rāmakrishna and Angelus Silesius are distinguished from the common run of pantheists by the fact that they see creation in terms of love because each conceives of the Deity as substantial Love. This is hinted at in the Bhagavad-Gītā, but is the essence of Christianity, whether mystical or otherwise.

We find things in Rāmakrishna which are so foreign to the classical Hindu tradition of *vairāgya* or 'passionlessness' that we are justified in

[1] *Sayings of Sri Ramakrishna*, p. 320.

[2] Rimbaud, *Œuvres Complètes*, p. 241.

[3] Angelus Silesius, *Cherubinischer Wandersmann*, i. 191: 'He who is not himself all, is still too small to see Thee, my God, and all things.'

concluding that they are personal to himself and *experienced* by himself. Thus

'on being asked when the enemies of man, such as lust, anger, etc., will be vanquished, the Master replied: "So long as these passions are directed towards the world and its objects, they behave like enemies. But when they are directed towards God, they become the best friends of man, for then they lead him unto God. The lust for the things of the world must be changed into the hankering for God, the anger that man feels in relation to his fellow man should be turned towards God for not revealing Himself to him. One should deal with all the passions in the same manner. These passions cannot be eradicated but can be educated." '[1]

These words seem very strange in the mouth of a Hindu, for in India the ascetic tradition by which we understand the tradition that mortifies desire in all its manifestations rather than the flesh as such, has been carried much farther than in either Christianity or Islam. Rāmakrishna, in this passage, goes against the whole tradition of *vairāgya* which can, if not properly controlled, have such deplorable results. Like Avicenna, he insists that human instincts must be transformed into positive good; he has no patience with the classical doctrine of detachment from all desires, whether good or bad. He is far nearer to Christian mysticism and to that of the Hindu theistic sects than he is to the Vedānta in that he recognizes God as the only real good and therefore the only legitimate object of desire. In this he is a thousand miles from the Sāṁkhya-Yogin ideal of self-isolation, and he is in fact deserting the very principle of the Advaita or non-dualist philosophy, the major premiss of which is that all multiplicity is illusory, and that therefore to speak of union with the Deity can only be a figure of speech. It is now time that we said something of this philosophy.

We have seen that in all the cases of the natural mystical experience we have considered, the keynote of the experience has always been one of reconciliation and of union with all things: and we have seen further that the experience sought by the Sāṁkhya-Yogins is, on the contrary, neither one of reconciliation nor of union, but, as M. Hiriyanna has said, one of disunion.[2] Theoretically the non-dualist Vedānta as expounded by Śankara and his school is the very reverse of this; for in the place of the infinite plurality of *puruṣas* or individual souls which the Sāṁkhya assumes, it puts one sole unique Absolute called Brahman, of which alone it can be said that IT IS. What the Sāṁkhya calls *prakṛti* (Nature) or *pradhāna* ('Urstoff')

[1] *Sayings of Sri Ramakrishna*, p. 141.

[2] M. Hiriyanna, *The Essentials of Indian Philosophy*, George Allen and Unwin, 1949, p. 122.

the Vedānta calls *māyā* or 'illusion'. Thus the ontological bases on which the two systems are based could scarcely be more different. Yet if they are treated as contemplative, or rather introspective, disciplines, it will be seen that in practice they amount to much the same thing.

Indeed, if the aim and purpose of meditation and concentration is to isolate the 'self'—however we understand that word—from all else, then the practical result must be that for the 'self' so liberated and isolated, all the external world as well as the body and what is merely temporal in the psyche, will cease to exist. The *Sāṁkhya-Kārikā* (§ 69) expresses this condition by saying that Nature or *prakṛti* removes herself from the perception of the soul or *puruṣa*. 'As a dancer shows herself to the audience and then stops dancing, so does Nature reveal herself to the Soul and then disappears.' Thus while Nature, in the Sāṁkhya theory, continues to exist, it is no longer cognized by the soul; and therefore, as far as the soul is concerned in its new-found isolation, it no longer exists at all. In other words, the Sāṁkhya admits that phenomena, once perceived as existing and once their existence is confirmed by repeated experiment, have a real existence apart from the perceiver. If, however, the perceiver, by training in Yoga, withdraws his senses entirely from their objects and his mind from all discursive thought, then, so far as the perceiver is concerned, nothing at all exists except himself. Whether or not the objective world continues to exist for other *puruṣas* is a matter of no concern to him at all. This is the meaning of *kaivalyam* or isolation. In practice it means emptying oneself of all content and is therefore barely distinguishable from the *śūnyatā* or 'emptiness' of the Mādhyamika Buddhists.

Stripped of its philosophical background the non-dualist Vedānta reaches precisely the same conclusion so far as experience is concerned.

The non-dualist Vedānta claims to be the true interpretation of the Vedas,—that large and heterogeneous collection of works which constitutes the Hindu sacred books. The word Vedānta means 'the end of the Veda'; and the end of the Veda consists of those cosmological and ontological treatises we know as the Upaniṣads. These, as we have had occasion to note, do not present any one consistent view of the universe, but their general teaching is one of an immanent God (if we may use the word in the context) Who pervades and controls the whole universe, *is* the whole universe, and is also the substance of the individual human soul. The following views are all represented in the Upaniṣads: (*a*) God creates the universe from His own substance and then enters into it Himself; His relation to the universe is likened to that of a spider to its web or a fire to the sparks that proceed from it: (*b*) God pervades the universe as salt pervades salt-water: (*c*) God and the universe are identical; and (*d*) God and the human soul are identical. In practice (*c*) which is pure pantheism tends to coalesce with (*d*) which is pure monism, though not necessarily so. Even Śankara who is the most uncompromising exponent of the purely monistic point of view, does not always succeed in maintaining the distinction.

The classical Upaniṣads are usually dated at from 800 to 500 B.C. The earliest of them are written in prose and are, in part, mere continuations of the elaborate sacrificial texts of the Brāhmaṇas. Like the Brāhmaṇas they are full of sympathetic magic, but they differ from these in that interest is gradually withdrawn from the cosmic significance of the sacrifice to the consideration of the cosmos itself. The earliest parts of the earliest Upaniṣads are devoted to creation myths of a very primitive kind, and they are a happy hunting-ground for psychologists for whom they represent the emergence of consciousness from the unconscious. They are, moreover, a natural continuation of the creation hymns which figure so prominently in the tenth book of the Rig-Veda. Their early speculations are materialistic: Brahman, the 'ground' of the universe, is reduced now to food (*anna*), now to breath, or again to both. In the *Chāndogya* it appears in the triple form of heat, water, and food from which all activity, including mental activity, proceeds.[1] They therefore conceive the Absolute as something material, and it is only later that it comes to be identified with 'consciousness'. At a slightly later stage, it would seem, the Brahman is identified with the individual *ātman*, a word, it should be noted, which originally referred to the body, or rather to 'the trunk of the body, as opposed to the hands and feet and other members'.[2] Originally, then, it would appear that the identification of *brahman* and *ātman* is simply the identification of the 'vital organs' of the 'microcosm' with the supposedly corresponding organs of the macrocosm. The experience that went with it cannot have materially differed from those we described in Chapter III. From such beginnings, it would seem, both pantheism and the classical monism of Śankara must have developed. The oldest passage which can bear both a pantheistic and a monistic interpretation is found in the *Śatapatha Brāhmaṇa* (10. 6. 3) and is then presumably older than the Upaniṣads themselves. It is repeated in the Chāndogya Upaniṣad which is itself perhaps the oldest but one of the extant Upaniṣads. The passage runs as follows:

'All this (world) is Brahman. Let one worship it in all quietness as *tajjalān*.' (The latter word, which has no meaning, is interpreted by the commentators as meaning 'that from which one is born, into which one is dissolved, and that in

[1] See above, p. 65.

[2] See A. B. Keith, *The Sāṁkhya System*, Calcutta, Association Press, undated, p. 5.

which one breathes and acts'. The passage then goes on to say:) 'He who consists of mind, whose body is breath (spirit or life), whose form is light, whose idea is the real, whose self (*ātman*) is space, through whom are all works, all desires, all scents, all tastes, who encompasses all this (i.e. the whole universe), who does not speak and has no care,—He is my self within the heart, smaller than a grain of rice or a barley-corn, or a mustard-seed, or a grain of millet, or the kernel of a grain of millet; this is my self within my heart, greater than the earth, greater than the atmosphere, greater than the sky, greater than these worlds. All works, all desires, all scents, all tastes belong to it: it encompasses all this (world), does not speak and has no cares. This my self within the heart is that Brahman. When I depart from hence I shall merge into it. He who believes this will never doubt.'[1]

This passage can, of course, be interpreted pantheistically or monistically, but I do not think that such passages as these,—and this is the most important,—can simply be written off as a natural mystical illumination similar to the experiences of Mr. Custance. This is not merely the identification of microcosm with macrocosm, the felt conviction that 'without and within are one': it is a tentative definition of the Godhead and its relationship to the individual. Brahman's essence is 'intellect' (*manas*), his 'body' is breath, spirit, or life (*prāṇa*), his form is light symbolizing as always awareness and consciousness, his *ātman* or bodily essence is space (*ākāśa*), the infinite ether. He is the author of all things, impassible, and silent. Such a being in the West is called God. This God is at the same time the *ātman*, the 'vitals' within the heart where He has no magnitude. This is a definition of God as both transcendent and immanent which might almost have been written by St. Thomas. St. Thomas does, in fact, write, 'God is above all things by the excellence of His nature; nevertheless, He is in all things *as causing the being of all things*.'[2] He is, moreover, present in rational creatures in a special way 'as the object of operation in the operator',[3] that is to say as the object fully known is actually present in the knower, or the beloved in the lover.

St. John of the Cross supplies a yet clearer parallel, for according to him 'the centre of the soul *is* God; and, when the soul has attained to Him according to the whole capacity of its being, and according to the force of its operation, it will have reached the last and the deep centre of the soul,

[1] *Chāndogya Up.*, 3. 14: 'sarvaṁ khalv idaṁ brahma tajjalān iti śānta upāsita. . . . manomayaḥ prāṇa-śarīro bhā-rūpaḥ satya-saṁkalpa ākāśātmā sarva-karmā sarva-kāmaḥ sarva-gandhaḥ sarva-rasaḥ sarvam idam abhyātto 'vāky anādaraḥ, eṣa ma ātmāntar hṛdaye, 'ṇīyān vrīher vā yavād vā sarṣapād vā śyāmākād vā śyāmāka-taṇḍulād vā; eṣa ma ātmāntar hṛdaye, jyāyān pṛthivyā, jyāyān antarikṣāj, jyāyān divo, jyāyān ebhyo lokebhyaḥ, sarva-karmā sarva-kāmaḥ sarva-gandhaḥ sarva-rasaḥ, sarvam idam abhyātto 'vāky anādara; eṣa ma ātmāntar hṛdaya, etad brahmaitam itaḥ pretyābhisaṁbhavitāsmīti. yasya syād addhā na vicikitsāstīti.'

[2] *Summa Theol.* I. viii. 1, resp. obj. 1.

[3] Ibid. I. viii. 3, resp.

which will be when with all its powers it loves and understands and enjoys God'.[1] This is exactly parallel to the Upaniṣad: God Who is infinite is also the point without magnitude in the very centre of the human soul. That the immanent God is beyond and different from the Jungian 'self' is made probable by the marked difference between the saint and the 'integrated' personality as described by Jung and exampled in Marcel Proust.

In this Upaniṣadic passage the speculations of earlier thinkers seem to unite with an intuitive vision of the unity of all things in their ground. Brahman is no longer identified with the process of eating and being eaten which is certainly one way of thinking of the unity of organic life, or with the process of breathing, or with both; it is regarded as the origin, end, and support of all life, as life itself, of which human life is as insignificant a part as is the life of a red corpuscle in the sum total of the human body. And already in this passage the author clearly thinks of Brahman as transcending space if not time; for it is infinitely small as well as infinitely great, and this is the only way that a more or less primitive man has of defining something that has no part in matter.

Moreover, the fact that here Brahman is identified with no material element such as food or breath, as in other Upaniṣadic passages, or with water, air, or fire, as with the pre-Socratics in Greece, shows that a genuine apprehension of some eternal and changeless Being was already in progress. Thus we come upon the conception of Brahman as the *satyasya satyam*, 'the real of the real',[2] or *ens realissimum* to put it in the language of scholastic theology. He is indescribable, and can only be referred to in negatives. 'His designation is the real of the real. The vital breaths are the real, and he is their reality.'[3] But the Upaniṣads go farther than this, for after grasping that there is a reality lying beyond all the phenomenal world, they state that this reality is the sole agent and the sole perceiver: and not only this, it is also identical with the human soul. 'That imperishable', the *Bṛhadāraṇyaka* says, 'is the seer who is not seen, the hearer who is not heard, the thinker who is not thought, the understander who is not understood. Other than it there is nothing that sees, nothing that hears, nothing that thinks, nothing that understands. Across this imperishable Being is space woven, warp and woof.'[4] Or again, 'He who dwelling in the earth, yet is other than

[1] *The Living Flame of Love*, in *The Complete Works*, E.T. by E. Allison Peers, London, Burns Oates and Washbourne, vol. iii, p. 22.

[2] *Bṛhadāraṇyaka Up.* 2. 3. 6.

[3] Ibid.: 'atha nāmadheyaṁ satyasya satyam iti. prāṇā vai satyaṁ, teṣām eṣa satyam.'

[4] Ibid. 3. 8. 11: 'adṛṣṭaṁ draṣṭṛ, aśrutaṁ śrotṛ, amataṁ mantṛ, avijñātaṁ vijñātṛ; nānyad ato 'sti draṣṭṛ, nānyad ato 'sti śrotṛ, nānyad ato 'sti mantṛ, nānyad ato 'sti vijñātṛ. etasminn u khalv akṣare, Gārgi, ākāśa otaś-ca protaś-ceti.'

the earth, whom the earth does not know, whose body the earth is, who controls the earth from within,—he is your Self, the Inner Controller, the Immortal.'[1] Similarly with the waters, fire, atmosphere, the wind, the sky, the sun, the quarters of heaven, the moon and stars, darkness, light, and the senses of man, Brahman alone indwells them and controls them: 'He who, dwelling in all things, yet is other than all things, whom all things do not know, whose body all things are, who controls all things from within,—He is your Self, the Inner Controller, the Immortal.'[2] Thus the human soul comes to be identified with the divine ground of all being, and this is the essence of Hinduism. In perhaps the most famous passage of all, which is the *locus classicus* of the non-dualist Vedānta, the Upaniṣad says: 'As bees make honey by collecting pollen from trees in different places and reduce the pollen (collected) to a unity; and as the different pollens can no longer tell the difference (or say), "I am the pollen of this tree, or I am the pollen of that tree"; so too when all these creatures reach reality, they do not know that they have reached it. Whatever they are, whether tiger, lion, wolf, boar, worm, fly, gnat, or mosquito, they all become that (the ultimate reality). That which is the subtlest of the subtle, the whole world has it as its self. That is reality. That is the self, and that art thou.'[3] 'These rivers flow, the eastern towards the West and the western towards the East; from ocean to ocean they flow. They actually become the ocean. And as they do not know which one they are, so all these creatures here, though they have come forth from Being, do not know that they have come forth from Being. Whatever they are, whether tiger, lion, wolf, boar, worm, fly, gnat, or mosquito, they all become that (the ultimate reality). That which is the subtlest of the subtle, the whole world has it as its self. That is reality. That is the self, and that art thou.'[4]

[1] Ibid. 3. 7. 3: 'yaḥ pṛthivyāṁ tiṣṭan pṛthivyā antaro, yaṁ pṛthivī na veda, yasya pṛthivī śarīraṁ, yaḥ pṛthivīm antaro yamayati, eṣa ta ātmāntaryāmy amṛtaḥ.'

[2] Ibid. 3. 7. 15: 'yaḥ sarveṣu bhūteṣu tiṣṭan, sarvebhyo bhūtebhyo 'ntaro, yaṁ sarvāṇi bhūtāni na vidur, yasya sarvāṇi bhūtāni śarīraṁ, yaḥ sarvāṇi bhūtāny antaro yamayati, eṣa ta ātmāntaryāmy amṛtaḥ.'

[3] *Chāndogya Up.* 6. 9: 'yathā, somya, madhu madhukṛto nistiṣṭanti nānātyayānāṁ vṛkṣāṇāṁ rasān samavahāram ekatāṁ rasaṁ gamayanti, te yathā tatra na vivekaṁ labhante, 'muṣyāham vṛkṣasya raso 'smy, amuṣyāham vṛkṣasya raso 'smīty, evam eva khalu, somya, imāḥ sarvāḥ prajāḥ sati saṁpadya na viduḥ sati saṁpatsyāmaha iti, ta iha vyāghro vā siṁho vā vṛko vā varāho vā kīṭo vā pataṅgo vā daṅśo vā maśako vā, yadyad bhavanti, tad ābhavanti. sa ya eṣo 'ṇimā, etad-ātmyam idaṁ sarvaṁ, tat satyaṁ, sa ātmā, tat tvam asi.'

[4] Ibid. 6. 10: 'imāḥ, somya, nadyaḥ purastāt prācyaḥ syandante, paścāt pratīcyas, tāḥ samudrāt samudram evāpiyanti, sa samudra eva bhavati; tā yathā tatra na vidur, iyam aham asmīti, evam eva khalu, somya, imāḥ sarvāḥ prajāḥ sata āgatya na viduḥ sata āgacchāmaha iti, ta iha vyāghro vā siṁho vā vṛko vā varāho vā kīṭo vā pataṅgo vā daṅśo vā maśako vā yadyad bhavanti, tad ābhavanti. sa ya eṣo 'ṇimā etad-ātmyam idaṁ sarvaṁ, tat satyaṁ, sa ātmā, tat tvam asi.'

It is noticeable that in this passage which supplies the context of the famous *tat tvam asi* or 'thou art that' formula, the identification of the individual soul with the world soul has not been carried to the lengths to which the later monists were to carry it. To judge from the similes it is not so much a question of identity as a merging of individual souls into a higher unity, of the pollen into honey and of rivers into the ocean. Such Upaniṣadic passages as these seem to form a genuine bridge between theistic mysticism as we know it in the West on the one hand and nature mysticism on the other. The idea that the transcendent God is also present at the heart of the human soul in grace is almost a commonplace of Catholic mystical theology, and it is the alleged tendency among Protestants to neglect the immanent aspect of God that Jung regards as psychologically unsound. The Hindus tend to fall into the opposite extreme, and since no clear conception of God as an absolutely perfect Being emerges from the Upaniṣads, the search for the essential unity of Brahman is as liable to lead to what Huxley calls 'downward transcendence' as to an upward transcendence of the ego in God. Alternatively it leads to solipsism which necessarily puts an end to spiritual development.

On the question of whether God is personal or impersonal it seems to me that a great deal of nonsense has been talked. Professor Farmer, in his recent book on *Revelation and Religion*, put forward the view that the apprehension of God as personal was one of the prerequisites of true religion.[1] And in this I think he is absolutely right if we are content to define a person with Boethius and St. Thomas as a *rationalis naturae individua substantia*, 'an individual substance of rational nature'.[2] Now while it is true that there are passages in the Upaniṣads according to which Brahman appears simply as *prāṇa*, 'breath', or *anna*, 'food', and although in one passage it is stated that after death there is no consciousness,[3] and that since the universal spirit or Brahman is absolutely one, there is nothing at all to perceive, this is not their general teaching; for the most commonly and most often quoted description of Brahman is that of the *Taittirīya Upaniṣad* (2. 1) where He or It is described as the real (*satya*), knowledge (*jñāna*), and the infinite (*ananta*): he dwells both in the most secret place of the heart and in the highest heaven. Thus if we accept this definition and the formula that later became current among all the Vedāntin schools,—*sac-cid-ānanda*, 'Being, Awareness or Thought, and Bliss', it is very plain that we are not here dealing with an *élan vital*, libido, or energy inhering in matter, but to all intents and purposes with a living and personal God, 'an

[1] H. H. Farmer, *Revelation and Religion*, London, Nisbet, 1954, p. 79.

[2] *Summa Theol.* xxix. 1, obj. 1.

[3] *Bṛhadāraṇyaka Up.* 2. 4. 12 = 4. 5. 13.

individual substance of rational nature'. As Being Brahman is an 'individual substance', and as 'awareness, *logos*, or reason' He is manifestly of 'a rational nature'. Moreover, as *ānanda*, 'bliss', he is also Love, for *ānanda* is the ordinary word used for sexual pleasure and the 'bliss' it denotes is primarily the bliss occasioned by the union of the sexes: and no one who is at all familiar with the writings of the Christian mystics and the image of the soul as the bride of Christ which is so constantly employed, is likely to quarrel with the parallel drawn between the physical union of the sexes and the union of the soul with God.[1]

It is remarkable that Hinduism should have independently adopted this formula which is, in essence, almost identical with the Christian idea of the Trinity; and it is even more remarkable that it should have been accepted by Śankara and his school whose monism yielded nothing to Parmenides, for the formula *sac-cid-ānanda*, 'Being-Awareness-Bliss' or 'Being-Logos-Love', does introduce that plurality into the Godhead which Śankara sought so strenuously to deny, and corresponds as closely as the utter difference between the Hindu and Christian traditions permits with the Christian idea of the Holy Trinity,—the Father as Being, the Son as Logos, and the Holy Ghost as Love. From the Western and particularly from the Protestant point of view the great defect of Hinduism is its ambivalent attitude towards evil which, like Jung, it would seek to 'sublimate' into the Divine; and this is as characteristic of Rāmakrishna as it is of the Upaniṣads. This is because Hinduism does not regard evil as being simply the privation of some good, nor does it equate it with not-being (*asat*). Even had it done so, evil would still have inhered in the Godhead since the Hindus frequently speak of Brahman as being *sad-asat*,[2] 'being and not-being', regardless of the fact that 'what is not' cannot be attributed to or predicated of anything at all since, by definition, it does not exist.

The Hinduism of the Upaniṣads then is the bridge between conscious theistic mysticism on the one hand and nature mysticism or the identification of the human soul with the whole of Nature on the other. It is now time to consider the relationship between theistic mysticism and nature mysticism; and this is bound to involve us in all sorts of difficulties since it is not a subject to which purely rational categories apply and since it involves the crucial issue of whether or not God exists.

Let us first consider what is common to all mysticism.

[1] The double sense of *ānanda* is paralleled in Julian of Norwich, *Revelations of Divine Love*, chapter 44 (London, Burns Oates, 2nd ed., p. 79): 'Truth seeth God, and Wisdom beholdeth God, and of these two cometh the third: that is, a holy marvellous delight in God; which is Love.'

[2] e.g. *Bhagavad-Gītā*, 9. 19 and 11. 37.

Now, it is generally agreed that there are two primary instincts in man, the instinct of self-preservation and the sexual instinct. The first is a wholly individual instinct and is concerned with maintaining individual life; the second, *qua* instinct rather than *qua* biological purpose, is the instinct to unite with what is other than and different from oneself. The form the union will take will, naturally, depend on the sex of the individual concerned. The crude instinct of the male is to hunt and subdue, of the female to surrender and accept. The sexual instinct is in any case inimical to the instinct of self-preservation, as anyone who has observed animals in heat will have noticed: for when an animal's sexual instinct is overwhelmingly strong, its instinct of self-preservation is reduced practically to zero. So on the psychological plane, on the one hand there is pride in being a unique person, different from all others, alone, and rejoicing in one's isolation: on the other, there is the desire, usually submerged in the unconscious, to lose the sense of individuality and to merge into a greater whole. There seem to be two motives for this; first the sense of isolation becomes unbearable, for as Aristotle correctly pointed out, man *is* a social animal, however much he may regret it. Thus there comes a point in most lives when one tires of the ceaseless responsibility of having to act and choose, and one longs for a higher power to take over the direction of one's life even if the higher power is only the army or a party organization. Further one longs for a more intimate union with one's surroundings, one has a pathetic desire to belong. The equivalent of both instincts can be found in the varieties of mystical experience and mystical theory as we shall have occasion to see.

St. Paul saw mankind as a unity in Adam: human beings, by being identical in their humanity, are one in Adam, they are one natural man. Though divided by time and space they are one human block, one body, we might almost say. They are one with Adam in sin,—and 'the wages of sin is death',—and man's body must therefore die; and they are one with him in that they are 'made in the image and likeness of God', and the image of God cannot die. Adam derives from the immortal spirit of God. 'And the Lord God formed man of the slime of the earth, and breathed into his face the breath of life, and man became a living soul.' St. Paul elaborates on the theme of Genesis (here I follow the translation of Mgr. Knox).

'Mankind begins with the Adam who became, as Scripture tells us, a living soul; it is fulfilled in the Adam who has become a life-giving spirit. It was not the principle of spiritual life that came first; natural life came first, then spiritual life; the man who came first came from earth, fashioned of dust, the man who came afterwards came from heaven, and his fashion is heavenly. The nature of that earth-born man is shared by his earthly sons, the nature of the heaven-born man, by his heavenly sons; and it remains for us, who once bore the stamp of earth, to bear the stamp of heaven. What I mean, brethren, is this; the kingdom of God cannot be enjoyed by flesh and blood; the principle of corruption cannot share a life which is incorruptible.'[1]

St. Paul, in common with the Sāṁkhya-Yoga, distinguishes between the spiritual Adam and the material Adam. 'The kingdom of God cannot be enjoyed by flesh and blood; the principle of corruption cannot share a life which is incorruptible.' In other words the temporal or psycho-physical element in man cannot share in the eternal. In Sāṁkhya terms *prakṛti* cannot share in the life of *puruṣa*; and in Vedānta terms the realm of *māyā* cannot share in the life of Brahman-Ātman; or again in Muslim terms man's 'angelic' nature is alone eternal, and in the next world his bestial and animal natures cannot be participators in eternal life. In all four traditions there is a marked dualism; even though the extreme Vedāntins may call themselves *advaita* or non-dualist. The mere postulation of *māyā*, however, shows that they are in fact as dualist as the Sāṁkhya however much they may wish to disguise it. Parmenides has said all that is essential on the subject, and even that prince of monists was forced to posit a 'way of opinion' running parallel to the way of truth which affirmed the sole existence of the One without a second. Śankara's development of the doctrine of *māyā* and *avidyā*, cosmic illusion and cosmic ignorance, leads him into precisely the same difficulty. Starting from the premiss which he derives from selected passages of the Upaniṣads, that reality is One without a second, that the individual soul is identical with that reality, and that all individual souls are therefore the same reality absolutely, he can only account for the phenomenal world by stating that it is *māyā* or 'illusion', a concept for which Upaniṣadic authority is singularly poor:[2] and once 'illusion' is admitted the simple monad is shattered.

Those who are new to Śankara's conception of *māyā* or 'illusion' seem to doubt whether he really means what he says. He does. What we call the phenomenal world he regards as illusion pure and simple, with neither more nor less objective existence than has the stuff of dreams. Since, however, the individual soul is basically the same as the Absolute Brahman, it follows that this *māyā* or 'illusion' is cosmic: it is compared to the illusions produced by a juggler, or to optical illusions as when a person mistakes a piece of rope for a snake, or mother-of-pearl for silver. In other words, what Śankara is doing is to introduce duality into his Brahman which theoretically

[1] 1 Cor. xv. 45–50.

[2] The only passage in which the doctrine of *māyā* is clearly stated is *Śvetāśvatara Up.* 4. 9–10.

is one and absolutely indivisible; for the mere fact that Brahman is capable of putting on this juggler's performance shows that there must be duality within himself; for the capacity to think and dream implies that the One produces 'illusions' which, though dependent on himself, are nevertheless distinct from himself. For illusions, as Śankara himself admits, are not pure not-being, that is, pure impossibilities or contradictions in terms like 'the son of a sterile woman'. It follows then that they have an existence apart from Brahman, though dependent on him. This is what we call contingent being, that is, being that is not *a se*, 'from itself', but *ab alio*, being derived from another. To call it illusion or cosmic ignorance, and to conceive this cosmic ignorance as being a positive power creative of illusion, as Śankara does, is little more than a distortion of words. It is excessively unhelpful, and as a guide to persons in search of beatitude it can be positively dangerous.

Mysticism is the realization of unity; and unless you have a clear idea of what that unity is, you are liable to unite with the most improbable entities. Qushayrī, when speaking on the subject of *khawāṭir* or 'intuitions',[1] states that they may come from angels, Satan, the natural man, or from God Himself. These, he says, can be recognized in the following way: an intuition from an angel will be in conformity with reason and will lead to good works; an intuition from Satan will lead to sin, while an intuition from Nature will lead one to follow one's natural propensities, particularly pride and lust (and in this context one thinks of Mr. Custance's conviction that, in a sense, he was God, and of his highly sublimated dealings with prostitutes). Furthermore, says Qushayrī, a man who eats unlawful food,—and by this, I think, he means a man who voluntarily disobeys his particular ecclesiastical discipline and therefore puts himself, according to his own lights, beyond the normal operation of grace,—such a man cannot distinguish between inspirations proceeding from God and the temptations of the Devil. And this is precisely what must be feared in any religion which does not make a clear distinction between good and evil; and such a distinction cannot logically be made by anyone who is strictly a monist, for both must be equally illusory.

In the course of this book we have tried to show that what is usually called the natural mystical experience may be nothing more than an uprush from what Jung calls the collective unconscious. However, the sense that the individual is at one with all Nature, that all is one and one is all, does not mean that all is God and God is all. It is the realization of the oneness of Nature. It is quite distinct, and necessarily so, from any state, the achieve-

[1] *Risāla*, Cairo ed., p. 43.

ment of which is dependent on the withdrawal of the senses from their objects; and this is the classic technique of the Hindus. For how can a sensation, the essence of which is to feel that one actually *is* the outside world, be identical with the result of a technique which uncompromisingly separates the immortal soul from all sensible images? The state of the nature mystic which we have called the pan-en-henic state, is the exact opposite of the *kaivalyam* or 'isolation' of the Sāṁkhya-Yoga. The characteristics of this state are described in the Bhagavad-Gītā, and the passage seems worth quoting in full:

'When a man abandons all desires which affect the mind, and by himself is contented in himself, then is he known as one whose mind is tranquil. The man whose mind is untroubled in the midst of sorrow, free from desire in the midst of pleasures, from whom passion, fear, and anger have departed, whose thoughts are steady, he is known as a sage. He who is everywhere devoid of affection, taking the pleasant and the unpleasant as they come, neither welcoming the one nor detesting the other, he is firmly set in wisdom. When he withdraws his senses from their objects as a tortoise withdraws its legs on all sides, then is he firmly set in wisdom. Objects of sense disappear for the embodied soul who ceases to feed on them, yet their savour remains behind: this too disappears for one who has seen the highest. Though a man strive (for perfection) and be never so discerning, yet his senses harass him and carry off his mind by violence. With all his senses controlled, deep in meditation, a man should sit down contemplating Me as his final end. The man whose senses are under control, is firmly set in wisdom.

'When a man dwells on the objects of sense, he will develop attachment to them. Attachment breeds desire, desire anger. Anger breeds mental confusion, mental confusion plays tricks with the memory. A memory so disturbed brings on insanity (*buddhināśa*). Insanity destroys. When a man has detached his senses from passion and hatred and subjected them to the control of the "self", then he may move among the objects of sense with his "self" controlled: thus will he achieve purity (*prasāda*). In such a state all sorrows are destroyed. When his mind is thus purified, his understanding will soon be recovered. An undisciplined man has no understanding, nor has he the power to concentrate. One who has no power to concentrate knows no peace. How should there be happiness without peace? A mind that obeys the roving senses, robs a man of wisdom, even as the wind carries away a ship at sea. So he who everywhere withdraws his senses from their objects, is firmly set in wisdom.

'In what is night for all (other) creatures the disciplined soul keeps vigil; but the time when (other) creatures are awake, is night for the sage who sees. Even as the waters flow into the sea which is ever being filled yet remains motionless and still, so do all desires flow into such a man. He attains peace, not the man who desires desire. The man who abandons all desires and lives without craving or thought of "I" or "mine" attains to peace. This is the state of Brahman: no one who has attained to it is (again) confused. He who is fixed in this state at the end of his days attains the peace (*nirvāṇa*) of Brahman.'[1]

This is typical of the Hindu way of renunciation; and in this respect the Hindu tradition is at one with all the great mystical traditions. Ascetic training is essential to the achievement of any 'higher' mystical state, though the 'lower' and incalculable states may arise, as we have seen, for no reason at all, or as a result of taking drugs, or on account of a mental disturbance. The Bhagavad-Gītā takes us a stage beyond monism in that it introduces a personal and incarnate god with whom a personal relation is possible. The Gītā itself oscillates between theism as we understand it, monism, and the Sāṁkhya-Yoga theory of *puruṣa* and *prakṛti*; but the dominant theme is that of theism.

In India theism found its most ardent defender in the twelfth-century philosopher, Rāmānuja; and his case is interesting. For, whereas we find in both Christianity and Islam a distinctly monistic tendency among mystical writers as a reaction, presumably, against a theology that tends to emphasize the transcendence of God as against His immanence, in Rāmānuja we find precisely the opposite tendency. He is concerned solely with disproving the monistic position, seeing rightly that in it lay a danger to all real religion and, necessarily, all worship. For monism leads logically no farther than the Sāṁkhya position, the isolation of the 'self' *qua* immortal soul from all that moves and has its being in space and time. Whether you call your soul an individual *puruṣa* or the Absolute *nirguṇa* or qualityless Brahman makes no difference. All you can achieve is the isolation of your essence, thereby denying yourself the presence of God, since you start off on the assumption that you are identical with the Absolute of which God can only be an aspect. The soul becomes as a house swept and garnished, ready to receive visitations of any sort, whether sublime or merely ridiculous. It is plainly not enough to subdue the passions and empty one's being of all unessentials if the essential soul is to be left at the mercy of any autonomous complex which may emerge from the unconscious. The first prerequisite in the theistic mystic is to set his will and mind firmly on God, —not merely an *iṣṭa-devatā* or 'deity of one's preference' as the classical Yoga would have it,—but God Himself, the Absolute Being Who is all goodness and truth, and on Whom all other being depends. Yet even this is not enough, for it will be found that among theistic mystics it is normally God Who makes the first advances. 'I thought that I loved Him,' Abū Yazīd of Bisṭām is reported as saying, 'but when I looked (again I saw

[1] *Bhagavad-Gītā*, 2. 55–72. For transliterated text see Appendix C, p. 228.

that) his love preceded mine.'[1] Or again, 'for thirty years I looked for God, but when I paused to think He was the seeker and I the sought'.[2] So too Qushayrī tells us how Rābi'a, when asked by a man who had committed many grievous sins whether God would accept his repentance, replied, 'Nay, rather, you will repent if he turns to you in forgiveness (first)',[3] for 'you cannot delight in God before God delights in you'.[4] Such examples could be indefinitely multiplied from the Muslim literature alone. So too God's initiative can be seen at work in the history of many of the greatest of the Christian saints, the most notable examples being perhaps St. Augustine, St. Francis of Assisi, and St. Ignatius Loyola. Conversions such as these can be explained in two ways; either there is a God Who intervenes in a spectacular way in the lives of specific people and transforms what had seemed to be quite ordinary people into persons of heroic sanctity, or this same feat is performed by some inexplicable power, what Jung calls an 'autonomous complex' which forces its way up from the unconscious and constitutes itself the centre and directing principle of the soul. The second alternative really explains nothing at all. For what do we gain by calling God the God-archetype, since it is admitted that this archetype can let loose such incalculable energy and can completely transform a life? Moreover it should be clear that the 'God-archetype' or the 'God-image',[5] as a content of the unconscious and a 'psychological fact' as opposed to a mere mental concept, presupposes the existence of a God of which it can be the image. The God of Whom the archetype is the image is, presumably, in Jung's case, the Jehovah whose inconsistencies he is at pains to point out in *Answer to Job*. This is no place to argue whether the *ens realissimun* is at the same time the *summum bonum*, an idea which Jung, in the respectable company of the Zoroastrians,[6] finds 'impossible for a reflecting consciousness',[7] since this would involve us again in a lengthy debate on the nature of evil and the enormity of sin. It is, however, perhaps worth pointing out once again that the Old Testament conception of God is a continuously developing one, leading up through Isaiah and the other prophets to the Incarnation. God appears terrible only because man is stiff-necked, stupid, and wicked,—a lesson, one would have thought, that the Old Testament makes all too clear.

[1] Farīdu'd-Dīn 'Aṭṭār, *Tadhkiratu'l-Awliyā*, ed. R. A. Nicholson, London, Luzac, 1905, vol. i, p. 170: 'pandāshtam ki man ū-rā dūst mī-dāram; chūn nigah kardam, dūstī i ū marā sābiq būd.'

[2] Ibid., p. 142: 'sī sāl khudāy-rā mī-ṭalabīdam; chūn bi-nigaristam, ū ṭālib būd va man maṭlūb.'

[3] Qushayrī, *Risāla*, p. 48, l. 8: 'lā bal law tāba 'alay-ka, la-tubta.'

[4] Ibid., p. 89, l. 16: 'i'lam anna'l-'abda lā yakādu yarḍā 'an al-ḥaqqi subḥāna-hu illā ba'da an yarḍā 'an-hu'l-ḥaqqu.'

[5] *Answer to Job*, p. 177.

[6] See R. C. Zaehner, *The Teachings of the Magi*, pp. 52–66.

[7] Jung, ibid., p. 93.

Jung, however, has illumined so much that was dark before that we would do well to reconsider some of his leading ideas as seen against the background of Christian and other theologies. According to him the God-archetype dwells deep down in the unconscious, and is liable to come to the surface in various symbolic forms. Now, this is precisely what all higher religions, in so far as they are theistic, also assert. For Christians the Holy Trinity takes up its dwelling in the highest point of the spirit, while the Muslim mystics and the Upaniṣads agree that the supreme reality dwells in the depths of the heart. This is the 'smallest of the small' of the Upaniṣads which is at the same time the greatest of the great, the God Who has His being in all of us. God, then, or the 'God-archetype' is to be found at the bottom of the collective unconscious. Between Him and the conscious mind, then, will be found Jung's various, and excessively amorphous, archetypes; the shadow or dark side of the human psyche described in religions as the Devil; the *anima* and *animus* representing the complementary sexual side of men and women; the Great Mother representing Mother Nature, the *prakṛti* of the Sāṁkhya or the *māyā* of the Vedānta. Thus when the unconscious invades consciousness, or when the conscious mind, yielding to the instinct I have broadly termed sexual, seeks to merge and lose itself in the unconscious, one of many things may happen. Either it will plunge right down to the level of the Great Mother, in which case it will see itself as being at one with Nature and, as in the case of Huxley, only inanimate things will seem to share the cosmic life with the perceiver; or it will be overcome by the shadow, the Devil, in which case the subject will be the victim of what goes by the absurdly inadequate name of depression and what is so much more adequately described by the Muslim mystics as 'contraction' or 'constriction'; alternatively it may plunge triumphantly past all these nightmare horrors and reach right down to the bottom where, religion tells us, we should find the God who makes his dwelling in our inmost depths, just as the Incarnate God chose to reside in the womb of a Jewess, 'a narrow and filthy place' as a Zoroastrian polemist observes.[1]

This, however, is not the normal way of finding God as the earliest Yogins rightly sensed; for though they had no clear idea of the nature of God, they knew that it was the business of the soul to isolate itself from *prakṛti* or Nature which, with its three qualities of goodness, passion, and darkness, its attractions and repulsions, desires and hates, is plainly the same thing as Jung's collective unconscious. Their technique would seem to be explicitly designed with a view to shutting out the unconscious and

[1] *Škand-Gumānīk Vičār*, ed. P. J. de Menasce, O.P., Fribourg, 1945, ch. 15, § 33 (p. 213).

all its works, including the 'partial autonomous complex' which appears as the 'God-archetype'. By isolating consciousness from all contact with the unconscious they sought to realize their eternal essence, the 'second self' which Proust discovered and which is so often dormant for such prolonged periods. The Muslims who had a very much clearer idea of God, did precisely the same. 'What distinguishes the Ṣūfīs from all the others I have mentioned', says the tenth-century Ṣūfī, Al-Sarrāj, 'is that they abandon what does not concern them and cut off every attachment which separates them from the object of their quest; and they have no object of quest and desire except God Most High.'[1] 'And they asked Junayd, "What is Ṣūfism?" and he replied, "That you should be with God and free from attachment."'[2] The operative words are, of course, 'with God'; for as Jung rightly points out, to empty the consciousness of all content is only to invite seven devils in from the unconscious. The possibility of God filling the vacuum can only be entertained if the soul has been wholly purged from sin; and this is, in effect, what the Bhagavad-Gītā and indeed all the major Hindu ascetical classics recommend. It is perfectly possible that the ecstasy experienced by the Yogin or Vedāntin may in some cases be a genuine experience of union with God; for his intention is, in fact, the elimination of sin, or, in psychological parlance, the suppression of the whole contents of the unconscious. Thus the mere fact that he obtains a complete stillness of soul, irrespective of whether that stillness is the peace that passeth all understanding mentioned by St. Paul, shows that the 'lower' soul of which the collective unconscious would appear to be the most substantial part, can in fact be suppressed, repressed, and eliminated for good. Mystical religion proper, then, shows that the mystical state at which the religious man aims is the reverse of the natural mystical experience: it is the cutting off of one's ties with the world, the settling in quietness in one's own immortal soul, and finally the offering of that soul up to its Maker. The first stage is that to which the monist aspires: the second lies beyond and appears only to be attainable with the active help of God Who is felt to be other than the immortal soul. That the collective unconscious of Jung is real enough I am fully prepared to believe, but that God is one of its constituents awaits more convincing proof.

[1] *Kitāb al-Luma'*, p. 11: 'wa-mā tafarradū bi-hā 'an jumlati hā'ulā'i'lladhīna dhakartu-hum . . . tarku mā lā ya'nī-him wa-qaṭ'u kulli 'ilāqatin taḥūlu bayna-hum wa-bayna maṭlūbi-him wa-maqṣūdi-him idh laysa la-hum maṭlūbun wa-lā maqṣūdun ghayra'llāhi ta'ālā.'

[2] Ibid., p. 25: 'wa-suyila'l-Junaydu . . . 'an al-taṣawwufi, fa-qāla, an takūna ma'a'llāhi ta'ālā bi-lā 'ilāqatin.' There are literally hundreds of similar definitions of Ṣūfism which it would be wearisome to quote. They may all be summed up in the two words 'God only'.

We said earlier in the chapter that man is dominated by two contrary instincts,—the instinct of self-preservation and the sexual instinct. The mystical life would appear to be conditioned by two similar instincts,—that of self-preservation being most clearly represented by the Sāṁkhya-Yogin isolation of self from all psycho-physical contact, the utter self-detachment described in the passage we quoted from the Gītā. The 'sexual' instinct manifests itself in both the natural mystical experience and in the soul's relationship to God. If our analysis of the data has been at all correct, the normal progress of the mystic from ordinary ego-consciousness to 'deification' would seem to be approximately as follows.

First comes personal integration which belongs to the realm of psychology, then isolation which must be achieved by asceticism; and this entails complete detachment from the things of this world. In the case of the monistic mystic this will be the final stage as we hope to show in the next chapter. It is, however, only at this point that God starts to operate directly: the soul is led out of its isolation and is slowly transmuted into the substance of the Deity like a log of wood which is gradually assimilated to the fire.[1] In the process the dross is utterly consumed and all that remains is pure fire. This process is what the Muslim mystics call *fanā* and *baqā*, 'annihilation' and 'abiding', the latter condition also being called *fanā 'an al-fanā*, 'annihilation beyond annihilation', in Hegelian terminology 'the negation of the negation'. This denotes the 'deification' of the soul, its complete transmutation into the divine essence when the soul, though remaining itself (according to orthodox Christian and Ṣūfī doctrine), is simply the container of Deity as a wineglass contains wine.[2]

We have seen that Jung and his school define the natural mystical experience as a reversion to a primitive state of affairs when consciousness had not yet separated itself from the unconscious. For this Erich Neumann uses the richly comic term 'uroboric incest', meaning little more than the re-entry into the undifferentiated unconscious. The sexual element at this stage seems subsidiary but is no doubt there. The subsequent stage of integration is the will of the conscious ego to survive (symbolized in mythology as the fight with the dragon), and beyond this comes the actual integration of consciousness and the unconscious in the wholeness of the unified personality. This marks the emergence of the 'self' and the subjection of the ego.

[1] Cf. Eckhart, Pfeiffer, Sermons 65 and 90; Gandillac, Sermons 6 and 11: St. John of the Cross, *The Living Flame of Love*, Stanza 2 with commentary: the *Vedāntasāra* (§§ 144–5), monistic though it claims to be, uses the simile of the transformation of a lump of metal by fire.

[2] Simile used by Ghazālī: see below, p. 158.

In the next stage, that of isolation, the 'self' which, according to all religions on the one hand and Jung on the other, is immortal, asserts itself yet further and strikes off all its transitory and perishable trappings including the ego. This is its highest material bliss according to the Sāṁkhya-Yoga and the Vedānta as expounded by Śankara. In Christian terminology it is the recovery of original innocence, the garden of Eden, Limbo; and it can scarcely be an accident that Rimbaud should use all these terms.

At this stage the soul can go no farther unless and until it realizes that if it is to commune with God, its role can only be that of the bride: it must play the woman, because, as far as its relations with God are concerned, it must be entirely passive and receptive. After all links with the world of sense and imagination have been severed, there should be no danger of the soul's being overrun by devils and/or 'autonomous complexes', for these should have been finally cut away. Hence it must recognize its essential femininity: 'If man remained always a virgin', says Eckhart, 'no fruit would proceed from him. If he is to become fruitful, he must necessarily be a woman. "Woman" is the most noble word one can apply to the soul, more noble than "virgin".'[1] Similarly Suso, in his autobiography, always speaks of himself in the feminine gender, and Ghazālī recognizes that the joys of sexual union are a foretaste of heaven.[2]

The soul, then, at this stage is comparable to a virgin who falls violently in love and desires nothing so much as to be 'ravished', 'annihilated', and 'assimilated' into the beloved. There is no point at all in blinking the fact that the raptures of the theistic mystic are closely akin to the transports of sexual union, the soul playing the part of the female and God appearing as the male. There is nothing surprising in this, for if man is made in the image of God, then it would be natural that God's love would be reflected in human love, and that the love of man for woman should reflect the love of God for the soul. The marriage service, indeed, speaks of matrimony as the symbol of the bond that unites Christ with His Church: the human relationship is the symbol of the divine, not, as the psychologists hold, the divine of the human. This is absolutely appropriate, for just as the human body knows no sensation comparable in sheer joyful intensity to that which the sexual act procures for a man and a woman in love, so must the mystical experience of the soul in the embrace of God be utterly beyond all other spiritual joys. The sexual image is, moreover, particularly apt since the man both envelops and penetrates the woman, is both within and without her,

[1] Sermon 8, Pfeiffer, p. 43: Gandillac, Sermon 2, p. 124.

[2] *Kīmiyā-yi Sa'ādat*, vol. ii, p. 553: cf. Bousquet, *Ih'ya 'Ouloûm ed-Dîn*, § 98, p. 235.

just as God Who dwells at the deepest point of the soul also envelops it and covers it with His infinite love. It is for this reason that the Virgin Mary is as perfect an image of the soul in grace and in love as it is possible to find,—Mary, enveloped and penetrated through and through by the Holy Ghost and made pregnant of the eternal Wisdom of God.

To drive home the close parallel between the sexual act and the mystical union with God may seem blasphemous today. Yet the blasphemy is not in the comparison, but in the degrading of the one act of which man is capable that makes him like God both in the intensity of his union with his partner and in the fact that by this union he is a co-creator with God. All the higher religions recognize the sexual act as something holy: hence their condemnation of adultery and fornication under all circumstances. These acts are not forbidden because they are demonstrably injurious on rational grounds; they are forbidden because they are a desecration of a holy thing, they are a misuse of what is most godlike in man.

CHAPTER VIII

MONISM *VERSUS* THEISM

IN the preceding chapters we have concentrated mainly on the phenomena of nature mysticism and have contrasted these with the opposite phenomenon of 'isolation', which appears at its clearest in the Sāṁkhya system in India which provides the philosophic basis for the Yoga technique. We further came to the tentative conclusion that the Vedānta, though philosophically poles apart from the Sāṁkhya, nevertheless amounts to much the same in actual practice. In the second place we have discussed Jung's theories of the collective unconscious and kindred concepts and hope to have shown that his findings do provide some explanation for 'natural' mystical phenomena. There remain two further questions that will have to be discussed, first whether the monistic mysticism of Śankara and his school in India can be reconciled with the theistic mysticism of Christianity, and secondly whether a purely psychological explanation is sufficient to account for the latter.

Let us take Śankara first. We have seen that Śankara bases his whole philosophy on those Upaniṣadic passages which proclaim that the individual soul is identical with the Brahman, the Absolute, World Soul, or God. This leads him on to the logical and inevitable conclusion that all diversity must be illusion, a self-deception practised on itself by the Deity for reasons which he never attempts to explain. His teaching can be most readily learnt from his commentary on the Māṇḍūkya Upaniṣad: of this Upaniṣad, the shortest of all, he says, 'This Upaniṣad, with the *kārikā* (of Gauḍapāda) embodies in itself the Quintessence of the substance of the entire philosophy of Vedānta.'[1] The Upaniṣad develops in a very short compass one of the leading Upaniṣadic ideas, that of deep, dreamless sleep as the nearest approximation in this life to ultimate beatitude. We must quote the relevant passages of the Upaniṣad because, as Śankara quite rightly says, it does contain the quintessence of the non-dualist Vedānta. The terminology will seem exceedingly strange to anyone not familiar with the main ideas of the Upaniṣads, but this must not deter us from reproducing the text of this portentous little work in translation.

'All this is Brahman', it says. 'This self (*ātman*) is Brahman. This self has four parts.

[1] Quoted on the title-page, Swāmi Nikhilānanda's edition, Mysore, Sri Ramakrishna Ashrama, 1949.

'The waking state, taking cognizance of what is outside . . . experiences what is gross; this is *vaiśvānara* (common to all men) and is the first part.

'The state of sleep, taking cognizance of what is inside oneself . . . experiences what is subtle; this is *taijasa*, composed of brilliance; it is the second part.

'When the sleeper desires nothing and sees no dream, that is deep sleep. The state of deep sleep is a unified state, a mass of wisdom (*prajñāna*), composed of bliss: it experiences bliss; its mouth (or head) is thought; it is wise; this is the third part. This is the Lord of all, the knower of all, this is the inner controller, the womb of all, the origin and end of creatures.

'The fourth state has cognizance of neither what is inside nor what is outside, nor of both together: it is not a mass of wisdom, it is not wise nor yet unwise. It is unseen; there can be no commerce with it; it is impalpable, has no characteristics, unthinkable; it cannot be designated. Its essence is its firm conviction of the oneness of itself; it causes the phenomenal world to cease; it is tranquil and mild, devoid of duality. Such do they consider this fourth to be. He is the Self; he it is who should be known.'[1]

Now it will be seen that this doctrine reverses all our normal assumptions and values: for whereas we tend to regard our waking state as more real than dream, and dream than dreamless sleep, the Māṇḍūkya Upaniṣad, in common with many of its predecessors, does precisely the reverse. The phenomenal world is regarded as having rather less reality than has a dream whereas deep, dreamless sleep is seen as the nearest approximation to the 'fourth' state which is final beatitude. What is even more strange is that deep sleep is here associated with the Lord of all, that is, with God as Creator specifically described as omniscient, the immanent controller of the universe, its source and beginning, and its end. Behind and beyond God Who is symbolized as a deep sleep, is Brahman or the Godhead in its essence which of itself cannot change or originate anything. All origination and creation is pure imagination, it is simply God's deception of Himself. This theory is fully explained in Gauḍapāda's *kārikā* or commentary on the Upaniṣad, and this must be quoted *in extenso*.

'The divine Self conceives of himself by himself through his own magic power (*māyā*); he alone is aware of differences. This is the certainty of the Vedānta. With his mind turned outward he modifies different states already existing in his consciousness which themselves are finite. So does the Lord mould (or imagine) the world. Those things which are inside and whose time is (measured by) thought and those things which are outside and are subject to past and future time are all simply imagined (or moulded). There is no other cause for differentiation. What is unmanifest inside and what is revealed outside is all simply imagination. Differentiation is only in the organs of sense. First of all the individual soul is imagined, then forms in all their variety, both external

[1] *Māṇḍūkya Up.*, §§ 2–7. For transliteration see Appendix C, p. 229.

and those belonging to the self. As is one's knowledge, so is one's memory. As a rope seen indistinctly in the darkness is imagined in the form of a snake or a water-line, so also is the Self imagined (to be other than it is). Just as the false imagination ceases when the true nature of the rope is realized, and it is seen to be a rope and nothing else, so is it with the certainty (one reaches) about the Self. The Self is imagined as vital force (*prāṇa*) and innumerable other forms. This is the magic power (*māyā*) of God (*deva*) by which He is Himself deluded.'[1] . . . 'The Self though not distinct from all these forms appears as distinct from them. He who knows this will conceive of them truly without any doubt. As dream and mirage and castles in the air are seen, so is the whole universe seen by those who are learned in the Vedānta. There is neither dissolution nor origination, neither bound nor Sādhu (one who has achieved liberation), there is none who seeks release and none who is released: this is the absolute truth. The Self is conceived of both as unreal forms and as non-duality: the forms are (conceived of) through non-duality itself: therefore is non-duality propitious (*śivā*). The manifold universe does not exist as a form of reality, nor does it exist of itself. It is neither separate nor not separate (from Brahman): this is known by those who know the truth. Sages who have conquered their passions, fear, and anger, and who are well versed in the meaning of the Vedas, see the Self to be devoid of imagination, change, or conception, as causing all phenomena to cease, and as devoid of duality. Thus knowing the Self to be such, one should fix one's mind on the non-dual. Having attained to non-duality, one should behave in the world like an insensible object. The ascetic should be indifferent to praise, refrain from prayer, public worship, and funeral ceremonies, he should be at home with all that moves and all that does not, and should accept whatever comes to him. Seeing the truth in respect of himself and of the external world, having himself become of the nature of truth, taking his pleasure in it, he will never depart from the truth.'[2]

This is the monistic position in its full rigour. The text is absolutely uncompromising and clear, and we shall therefore refrain from giving more than the barest commentary. There is only one reality,—Brahman who is identical with the individual soul. The Brahman-soul, quite pointlessly, it seems, imagines both the internal world of ideas and the external world of objective phenomena, and is deceived by his own imaginings. This condition which is the state of normal human consciousness, is usually described as the state of one 'bound'. Release (*mokṣa* or *mukti*) consists in the destruction of the illusion imposed on oneself (the Self!) by oneself and against one's own will (the will of the Self). The state of release, the so-called 'fourth' state (*turīya*) is absolutely unqualifiable, but more akin to dreamless sleep than to anything else: it is equivalent to the eighth and final stage of release in Buddhism in which one passes 'entirely beyond the stage

[1] *Kārikā*, 2. 12–19. For transliteration see Appendix C, p. 229.

[2] Ibid., §§ 30–38. For transliteration see Appendix C, p. 229.

of neither consciousness nor non-consciousness', and 'attains and abides in the stage of the cessation of perception and feeling'.[1] In such a state there is no perception of external objects nor is there any discursive thought, not because one has detached oneself from them as *puruṣa* does from *prakṛti* in the Sāṁkhya system, but because one realizes that they simply do not exist: like the Bellman's map, they are 'a perfect and absolute blank'. Once release is achieved, it is realized that since nothing exists except the One, realized as oneself, all actions, all religious ceremonies, all devotion addressed to any god, the gods, or God Himself are pure illusion and absolute nothingness. For the 'released' Vedāntin sage such words as the *unio mystica* are literally meaningless; for how can there be union when there is only One?

Let us now consider what the Muslim mystics have to say about what they regard as being the highest stage of illumination. In this connexion it is better to avoid the testimony of Ḥussayn bin Manṣūr al-Ḥallāj who is probably the best known among the early Muslim mystics to non-Orientalists thanks to the devoted labours of that outstanding scholar and humanist, Professor Louis Massignon, since Ḥallāj remains a controversial figure in Islam, and the doctrines of *ḥulūl* (the descent of God into the human soul) and *ittiḥād* (identity with God) which are rightly attributed to him, are not generally accepted except by Ṣūfīs. Let us rather consider a remarkable passage from Ghazālī, the mystical doctor of Islam who made Ṣūfism respectable and who died in A.D. 1111.

Ghazālī, along with the vast majority of Muslims and Christians, believed that man and the universe were created out of nothing. Thus so far as these can be said to have being at all, it is from God. 'The existence of whatever has existence from another is borrowed; it is not self-subsistent. When its essence is considered in itself, it is pure not-being, for the only existence it has is through its relationship to what is other than itself; and this is not real existence as you learnt in the parable (of the poor man) who borrowed a robe from a rich man. Real existence is God Most High just as real light is God Most High.'[2]

Man and the universe, then, have no existence in themselves; what

[1] *Dīgha Nikāya*, ii. 111, 156, quoted in E. J. Thomas, *The History of Buddhist Thought*, 2nd ed., London, Routledge and Kegan Paul, 1951, p. 52.

[2] Ghazālī, *Mishkātu'l-Anwār*, ed. Sabrī al-Kurdī, Cairo, 1353/1935 (*Al-jawāhir al-ghawālī*), p. 121: English translation by W. H. T. Gairdner, reprint, Lahore, 1952, p. 103: 'wa-mā la-hu'l-wujūdu min ghayri-hi, fa-wujūdu-hu musta'ārun lā qawāma la-hu bi-nafsi-hi, bal idhā'tubirat dhātu-hu min ḥaythu dhāti-hi, fa-hūwa 'adamun maḥḍun, wa-inna-mā wujūdu-hu min ḥaythu nisbati-hi ilā ghayri-hi, wa-laysa dhālika bi-wujūdin ḥaqīqīyin ka-mā 'arafta fī mithāli isti'ārati'l-thawbi wa'l-ghanīyi: fal-mawjūdu'l-ḥaqqu hūwa'llāhu ta'ālā ka-mā anna'l-nūra'l-ḥaqqa hūwa'llāhu ta'ālā.'

existence they have they derive from God. Seen *sub specie aeternitatis*, then, they can have no real existence apart from God: they can only be regarded as thoughts thought by God.

'From here', says Ghazālī who is plainly describing his own mystical experience, 'the mystics ascend from the nadir of metaphor to the zenith of truth. On completing their ascent they see with a direct vision that there is nothing in existence except God and that "all things perish save His face",[1] for they all perish at some time or other; or rather they are perishing for all eternity since they cannot be conceived of in any other way. All things except God when considered in their essence *qua* essence are pure not-being. If, however, they are considered from the aspect[2] in which existence permeates them from the primal Reality, they are seen to be existent not in their own essence, but through the aspect (or manner) which accompanies Him Who gives them existence. What has existence is simply the face of God (or God-aspect). All things have two aspects, one in respect of themselves and the other in respect of their Lord. Considered as themselves, they are non-existence, but considered under the divine aspect, they are existent. So there is nothing truly existent except God and his countenance (or aspect). Thus all things are perishing save His face for all eternity. (Mystics such as) these need not wait until the Day of the Resurrection to hear the voice of God crying, "Whose is the kingdom today?" "It is God's, the One, the Overwhelming":[3] for they never cease hearing this cry. Nor do they understand His words, "God is most great", to mean that He is greater than what is other than Himself. God forbid! for there is nothing in existence apart from Him that might share existence with Him and than which He could be greater. No one attains to the degree of co-existence or even of derived existence. There is no existence apart from Him except through the aspect of Him which accompanies it. What exists is simply His face (the God-aspect). It is impossible that He should be greater than His face. The meaning of "Most Great" is that He is too great to be described as "greater" or "most great" in a sense of relation or comparison,—He is too great for anyone other than He, be he prophet or angel, to conceive of the real nature of His greatness. For no one knows God with a real knowledge except God Himself. . . .

'The mystics, after their ascent to the heavens of Reality, agree that they saw nothing in existence except God the One. Some of them attained this state through discursive reasoning, others reached it by savouring it and experiencing it. From these all plurality entirely fell away. They were drowned in pure solitude: their reason was lost in it, and they became as if dazed in it. They no longer had the capacity to recollect aught but God, nor could they in any wise remember themselves. Nothing was left to them but God. They became drunk with a drunkenness in which their reason collapsed. One of them[4] said, "I am

[1] Qur'ān, 28. 88.

[2] There is a play on the meaning of the Arabic word *wajh*, literally 'face', secondarily 'aspect' or 'manner'.

[3] Qur'ān, 40. 16.

[4] Ḥallāj.

God (the Truth)." Another[1] said, "Glory be to me! How great is my glory", while another[2] said, "Within my robe is naught but God." But the words of lovers when in a state of drunkenness must be hidden away and not broadcast. However, when their drunkenness abates and the sovereignty of their reason is restored,—and reason is God's scale on earth,—they know that this was not actual identity, but that it resembled identity as when lovers say at the height of their passion:

> "I am he whom I desire and he whom I desire is I;
> We are two souls inhabiting one body."[3]

'For it is not impossible that a man should be confronted by a mirror and should look into it and not see the mirror at all, and that he should think that the form he saw in the mirror was the form of the mirror itself and identical with it; or that he should see wine in a glass and should think that the wine is just coloured glass. And he gets used to this (way of thinking) and becomes fixed in it, and it overwhelms him. . . .

'There is a difference between saying, "The wine *is* the wineglass", and saying, "It is as if it were the wineglass." Now, when this state prevails, it is called "naughting" (*fanā*) with reference to the person who experiences it, or the "naughting beyond naughting", for (the mystic) becomes naughted to himself and naughted to his own naughting; nor is he conscious of himself in this state, nor is he conscious of his own unconsciousness; for were he conscious of his own unconsciousness, he would be conscious of himself. This condition is metaphorically called identity with reference to the man who is immersed in it, but in the language of truth (it is called) union. Beyond these truths there are further mysteries the penetration of which is not permissible.'[4]

It will be seen that the ontological theory of the Māṇḍūkya Upaniṣad and that of Ghazālī are very similar. There is, however, this difference,—and it is a very considerable one,—in the case of the Upaniṣad the initial dogma is 'The Self is Brahman', that is to say that the individual soul is actually identical with God, whereas the Muslim starts with the dogma that God alone is Absolute Being and that all things perish except His face. For the Muslim man only exists at all in so far as he is given existence by God: for the Hindu he is God and through God all things eternally, and it is only through self-deception practised involuntarily on himself by the man-God that he fails to recognize his true nature which is absolute oneness. On the premisses of the Māṇḍūkya Upaniṣad there can be no humility or sense of awe in the face of an Absolute Being who alone really exists and is distinct from man: there can be no sense of nullity or of unworthiness. There can be unity, but there can be neither union nor communion. Thus

[1] Abū Yazīd of Bisṭām, see below, pp. 161–3.

[2] Abū Sa'īd bin Abī'l-Khayr.

[3] Attributed to Ḥallāj.

[4] *Mishkāt al-Anwār*, text pp. 121–3: translation, pp. 103–8. For transliterated text see Appendix C, pp. 230–1.

the Vedāntin sees himself as the Absolute, one without a second, while the Muslim sees himself as he exists essentially apart from God as pure nothingness. So Abū Sa'īd bin Abī'l-Khayr, a Persian mystic of the tenth and eleventh centuries, spoke of himself after he thought that he had attained self-extinction in God, not as 'I', since *qua* Abū Sa'īd he no longer existed, but as 'They', the honorific plural referring to God.[1]

Anyone who reads the above-quoted passage from the *Mishkāt al-Anwār* will be struck by the inconsistency between Ghazālī's ontology which in this passage is monist, on the one hand, and his defence of Ḥallāj and Abū Yazīd *against* a purely monist interpretation of their doctrine on the other. Ghazālī, apparently himself writing under the influence of what he calls 'drunkenness' (*sukr*) in the case of Abū Yazīd and Ḥallāj, denies existence of any kind to created things: they have neither 'co-existence' nor even 'derived existence'. He therefore flatly denies such a thing as contingent or 'borrowed' being which he had admitted earlier in the passage quoted. Yet he later criticizes his two notable predecessors for having expressed precisely these views in ecstasy, because in ecstasy the mystic is conscious of God only, all consciousness of self having been obliterated. This, Ghazālī says, must be a false view: it is like the illusion created by a transparent wineglass filled with wine which an ignorant person might suppose to be identical with the wine. Hence it is wrong (and heretical) to speak of any identity of the soul with God.[2]

Ghazālī's position, when in a state of 'sobriety', seems to be that of Junayd, the very apostle of 'sobriety', whom he seems to have followed more or less slavishly: God alone exists in reality; man's temporal existence is literally nothing apart from God, and on achieving mystical illumination his 'borrowed' existence falls from him, he is annihilated or 'naughted' and God alone remains. Whether Junayd and Ghazālī really believed this,—for it is equivalent to denying one's own existence, which is absurd,—we cannot say. It was, however, the only way that they could justify mystical experience in Islam at all. If one were to remain orthodox, one could scarcely speak of union with God because that would be *shirk*, to associate others with God, and this is an unforgivable sin; nor could one speak of identity, for that would be the crassest blasphemy. The only way out, then,

[1] Al-Munawwar, *Asrār al-Tawḥīd fī maqāmāt al-shaykh Abū Sa'īd*, ed. Z. Safā, Teheran, 1953, p. 15 (in Persian).

[2] The Christian position is much less clear on this point since it is quite orthodox to speak of God as 'the deepest centre of the soul' (see above, p. 137). *Absolute* identity which Eckhart on occasions preached was among the propositions condemned by Pope John XXII (condemned propositions X to XIII, see Gandillac, pp. 264–5); but both Nicolas of Cusa and Angelus Silesius reached a position very near to this, and neither of these was condemned.

was to deny existence of any sort to anything at all except God. This could be represented as the height of orthodoxy since the orthodox themselves who admitted the derived existence of created things, could in their turn be accused of *shirk* in that they allowed anything to 'partake' of being which belongs absolutely and exclusively to God. That Ghazālī was not satisfied with this position is demonstrated by the last sentence of the passage we have quoted: 'Beyond these truths there are further mysteries the penetration of which is not permissible.' This can only mean that if he gave voice to these 'mysteries', he would fall foul of the orthodox and risk the fate of Ḥallāj who was mutilated and then crucified for the greater glory of God.[1] Elsewhere Ghazālī frankly admits that whatever is said of the highest stages of mystical experience will appear as rank infidelity (*kufr*), and this must be taken as evidence that he privately accepted the Ḥallājian doctrines of *ḥulūl* and *ittiḥād*. In the *Kīmiyā-yi Sa'ādat* he writes: 'Beyond this (the mystic) enjoys "stations" and "states" with God Most High which are difficult to describe. Indeed some speak of them as "isolation" or "identity", and some speak of a divine indwelling of the soul. Anyone who is not firmly grounded in this science and is visited by such an ecstasy, cannot give a full description of what he experiences. Whatever he says sounds like plain infidelity.'[2]

Ghazālī's 'overt' position is, however, clear enough, and it seems to be this. In ecstasy the mystic is completely overcome by the presence of God: he is paradoxically both in a state of ineffable bliss and is at the same time 'unconscious' (or so he expresses it), so completely is he filled with God's eternal Being. On emerging from the ecstasy, however, he realizes that what had seemed to be the complete obliteration of the lesser in the infinitely Great, the finite in the Infinite, was only partially true at least in so far as the human soul had in fact survived the encounter.

It must be admitted that, for comparative purposes, Muslim mysticism is a source of confusion, particularly if we are interested in studying the difference between the purely monistic position of the Māṇḍūkya Upaniṣad and the positions taken up by the Christian mystics (from whom neither Eckhart nor Angelus Silesius can be excluded). The reason is that Muslim mysticism is entirely derivative. Its beginnings are unmistakably borrowed

[1] The full story of the martyrdom of Ḥallāj will be found in Louis Massignon's monumental work, *Al-Hallaj, Martyr mystique de l'Islam*, 2 vols., Paris, Geuthner, 1922.

[2] *Kīmiyā*, vol. ii, p. 745: 'va varāyi īn maqāmāt va aḥvāl bāshad vay-rā bā ḥaqq i ta'ālā kih az ān 'ibārat dushvār tavān kard: tā gurūhī 'ibārat az ān ba-yagānagī va ittiḥād kunand, va gurūhī ba-ḥulūl kunand, va har kirā qadam andar 'ilm rāsikh na-bāshad va ān ḥāl ū-rā paydā āyad, tamāmī-yi ān ma'nī 'ibārat na-tavān kard, va harchih gūyad ṣarīḥ kufr namāyad.'

from Christianity with its overriding emphasis on love as being the very nature of God and therefore the only certainly successful way of approaching Him.[1] With Abū Yazīd in the ninth century we find Indian monism invading the Muslim mystical world, and Abū Yazīd is, for this reason, as interesting as Rimbaud in that he is torn between the classical Ṣūfī technique of love and the Hindu monistic dogma that the soul is in fact identical with God. The present author hopes to devote a full-scale study to him at a later date. Here we must confine ourselves to the concrete evidence which goes a long way to prove that it is through him that monistic Vedāntin ideas break into Ṣūfism. This is relevant to our subject, for if Abū Yazīd was indeed directly influenced by Vedāntin ideas, he can no longer be summoned as a witness to the universality of strictly monistic mysticism since his monism would then be purely derivative. The evidence, such as it is, is therefore of importance, and we must briefly examine it.

Abū Yazīd's *shaṭḥīyāt* or 'overflowings in ecstasy' are preserved by Abū Naṣr al-Sarrāj in his 'Book of Illuminations' (*Kitāb al-Luma'*),[2] the earliest systematic treatise on Ṣūfism that has come down to us. The first significant fact that Sarrāj has to tell us is that Abū Yazīd's *ustādh* or 'master' was Abū 'Alī al-Sindī,[3] a native of Sind, then, who would be likely to be either a convert from Hinduism himself or the son of a convert. That this was so is indicated by what Abū Yazīd is reported to have said about their relationship. 'I kept company with Abū 'Alī al-Sindī', he says, 'and I used to instruct him in the correct performance of his religious duties, while he used to teach me in exchange (the doctrine of) union and (esoteric) truths.'[4] This means that Abū Yazīd was teaching Abū 'Alī the outward observances of Islam, with which he can therefore hardly have been familiar, in exchange for a secret monistic doctrine which Abū 'Alī can only have acquired in his native Sind. From this we may conclude that he was actually a convert himself since no born Muslim would need to be instructed in the *farḍ* which means the observances that are incumbent on all Muslims. If then Abū 'Alī was born a Hindu, what were the doctrines he taught his friend and pupil Abū Yazīd?

To ascertain this we must consider the sayings attributed to Abū Yazīd by Sarrāj and others, and see whether they correspond to any known Indian system.

Three of these sayings are important and must be quoted. The first is as

[1] See Margaret Smith, *Studies in Early Mysticism in the Near and Middle East*, London, The Sheldon Press, 1931, *passim*.

[2] Ed. R. A. Nicholson, Leyden, Brill and London, Luzac, 1914.

[3] Sarrāj, p. 325: cf. pp. 177 and 334.

[4] Ibid., p. 177: 'ṣaḥibtu Abā 'Alīyi'l-Sindīyi, fa-kuntu ulaqqinu-hu mā yuqīma bi-hi farḍa-hu, wa-kāna yu'allimu-nī'l-tawḥīda wa'l-ḥaqā'iqa ṣarfan.'

follows: 'Once He lifted me up and placed me in His presence and said to me, "O Abū Yazīd, verily My creatures long to see thee." And I said, "Adorn me with Thy unity and clothe me in Thine I-ness and raise me up to Thy One-ness so that when Thy creatures see me, they will say, 'We have seen Thee'. And Thou art that and I am not there (at all)." '[1] As Ghazālī says, we must not expect a great deal of sense from the sayings of mystics in a state of 'drunkenness'. There is one phrase here, however, which is so astonishing that even so great an Arabist as Nicholson mistranslated it,[2] not because of the difficulty of the Arabic (for it is amazingly simple) but because the phrase appeared so extraordinary in the context that he saw no alternative but to paraphrase. The phrase is, of course, 'Thou art that' and it is identical with the phrase in the Chāndogya Upaniṣad which we have quoted above.[3] In the context of the Upaniṣad it is the climax of a series of similes emphasizing the fundamental identity of the human soul with the Brahman. In Abū Yazīd it is utterly incongruous and only seems explicable on the assumption that Abū Yazīd had picked it up from his Sindī master.[4]

The second saying is less striking, but we quote it both because it is not irrelevant and because it is typical of the style of this extraordinary man. 'As soon as I attained to His unity', he exclaims, 'I became a bird whose body was of Oneness and whose wings were of everlastingness; and I continued to fly in the air of suchness for ten years until I reached an atmosphere a hundred million times as large: and I continued to fly until I reached the field of eternity without beginning, and in it I saw the tree of Oneness . . . and I looked and saw that all of it was deceit (*khud'a*).'[5] Here the Arabic word *khud'a*, 'fraud, deception', looks like a literal translation of the Sanskrit *māyā*, 'illusion, trick, artifice, deceit, deception, fraud, jugglery, sorcery, witchcraft'. The idea of the world as 'deceit' or 'illusion' is, of course, typically Vedāntin, but foreign to Islam.

[1] Sarrāj, p. 382: 'rafa'a-nī marratan fa-aqāma-nī bayna yaday-hi wa-qāla lī, yā'bā Yazīda, inna khalqī yuḥibbūna an yaraw-ka, fa-qultu, zayyin-nī bi-waḥdānīyati-ka wa-albis-nī anānīyata-ka wa-'rfa'-nī ilā aḥadīyati-ka ḥattā idhā ra'ā-nī khalqu-ka, qālū, ra'aynā-ka, fa-takūnu anta dhāka wa-lā akūnu anā hunāka.'

[2] He translates the last part of the sentence as, 'and that only Thou mayst be there, not I'.

[3] See above, p. 139.

[4] This example by itself would not necessarily be convincing. A similar phrase is to be found in a mediaeval English mystical treatise, the anonymous *Epistle of Privy Council*: 'That that I am, Lord, I offer unto thee; for thou it art.' See *The Cloud of Unknowing*, ed. Justin McCann, revised ed., London, Burns Oates, 1952, pp. 104 and 109.

[5] Sarrāj, op. cit., p. 384: 'awwala mā ṣirtu ilā waḥdānīyati-hi, fa-ṣirtu ṭayran jismu-hu min al-aḥadīyati wa-janāḥā-hu min al-daymūmīyati, fa-lam azal aṭīru fī hawā'i'l-kayfīyati 'ashra sinīna ḥattā ṣirtu ilā hawā'in mithli dhālika māyata alfi alfi marratin fa-lam azal aṭīru ilā an ṣirtu fī maydāni'l-azalīyati, fa-ra'aytu fī-hā shajarata'l-aḥadīyati, . . . fa-naẓartu fa-'alimtu anna hādhā kullu-hu khud'atun.'

The third saying does not occur in Sarrāj, but is found in an anonymous text recently published by Abdulrahman Badawi.[1] Unfortunately no certain date can be assigned to this text, but it claims to be based on the reports of Abū Yazīd's earliest and most intimate disciples. It reads as follows: 'I sloughed off my "self" as a snake sloughs off its skin: then I looked into myself, and behold! I was He.'[2] Now this simile combined with the formula 'I am He' is found almost in the form used by Abū Yazīd in the Bṛhadāraṇyaka Upaniṣad 4. 4. 7 and 4. 4. 12. § 7 reads:

'As the slough of a snake lies on an ant-hill, dead, cast off, even so lies this body. But the incorporeal, immortal spirit is Brahman indeed, is light indeed.[3]

And in § 12 we have:

'If a person knew the Self (*ātman*)
With the thought, "I am He",
With what desire, for love of what
Would he cling to the body?'[4]

Add to this that Abū Yazīd's famous saying *ṣubḥānī*, 'Glory be to me',[5] is exactly paralleled in the late *Sannyāsa Upaniṣad* where we find *mahyam eva namo*, 'homage be to me'.[6] In the Upaniṣad the phrase comes perfectly naturally and indicates the identity of *Brahman* and *ātman*, but coming from the lips of a Muslim it sounds outrageous, and must have sounded even more so in the days of Abū Yazīd when such utterances were as yet unheard of.

Thus it seems fairly clear that Abū Yazīd's monism is directly derived from an Indian source. It unbalanced his whole outlook, for, being of simple peasant stock, he was utterly confused by the different doctrines which were supposed to explain his experiences. If half of what Farīd al-Dīn 'Attār records of him in his 'Memoirs of the Saints' (*Tadhkiratu'l-Awliyā*) is true, it seems clear that, despite his undoubted lack of balance,

[1] *Shaṭḥāt al-Ṣūfīya*, Part I, *Abū Yazīd al-Bisṭāmī*, Cairo, 1949.

[2] Badawi, op. cit., p. 77: 'insalakhtu min nafsī ka-mā tansalikhu'l-ḥiyyatu min jildihā, thumma naẓartu ilā nafsī, fa-idhā anā hūwa.' This saying is also preserved by Al-Bīrūnī (b. A.D. 973); for text, see E. Sachau, *Alberuni's India*, London, Trübner, 1887, p. 43; translation, id., London, Trübner, 1888, vol. i, p. 88. For the second *nafsī* Bīrūnī reads *dhātī*. Bīrūnī is an exceptionally good source, and the saying is likely to be authentic. 'Aṭṭār quotes the saying but changes the final phrase (quoted below, p. 196, n. 2).

[3] 'tad yathāhi-nirlvayanī valmīke mṛtā pratyastā śayīta, evam evedaṁ śarīraṁ śete. athāyam aśarīro 'mṛtaḥ prāṇo brahmaiva teja eva.'

[4] 'ātmānaṁ ced vijānīyād, ayam asmīti, puruṣaḥ, / kim icchan, kasya kāmāya śarīram anusaṁjvaret?'

[5] First recorded by Sarrāj, op. cit., p. 390. After him the phrase is quoted by almost all mystical treatises.

[6] F. Otto Schrader, *The Minor Upaniṣads*, Madras, Adyar Library, 1912, vol. i, p. 257.

he had real holiness. One has the impression that he picked up the Vedāntin adages with enthusiasm and introduced them into the wild flights of his fancy without fully understanding either them or the shocked reaction they were bound to produce on a Muslim audience.

This seems clear if we compare Abū Yazīd when not directly influenced by the Vedānta, Ghazālī, and even some early Upaniṣadic passages on the one hand with the fully monist position of the Māṇḍūkya Upaniṣad, Gauḍapāda, and Śankara on the other. We pointed out in another chapter[1] that the most ancient texts in the Upaniṣads (not excluding the *tat tvam asi* passage, as I am inclined to think) do not necessarily go farther than to identify the essence or 'deepest centre of the soul', to quote St. John of the Cross, with the infinite Brahman which is the ground of the whole universe of time and space. The *Māṇḍūkya* and Śankara rationalize this into a rigid monism which equates *mokṣa* or 'liberation' with the realization of oneself as the sole existing reality. This is quite different from the doctrine enunciated in the so-called *Śāndilya-vidyā* quoted above[2] which concedes only the identity of the 'point without magnitude' in the heart of man with Him who pervades the whole universe, 'who consists of mind, whose body is spirit, whose form is light, whose idea is the real, and whose bodily essence (*ātman*) is space'. For Śāndilya both the world and the individual exist; but God or Brahman is what gives them existence and He is therefore necessarily present in both. They are separate entities of which He is the identical ground. The *Māṇḍūkya* goes much farther, for it denies reality of any kind either to the external universe or to the universe of thought within the individual mind. There is nothing in existence at all except the One which is a 'perfect and absolute blank'. 'Liberation' means the realization that, apart from one's own immortal 'self', nothing exists at all. Brahman is no longer the identical substrate of all things since that would contradict the monist position, nor *is* it all things, for there cannot be plurality in the One; for the One just is itself and all else is pure illusion. This is, as we have already pointed out, the Sāṁkhya position *in practice*; in the West it would be called solipsism. It does much credit to the heart of the ultra-monist Vedāntins that they have always been ready to help others towards liberation; it does very little credit to their head, for what logic can there possibly be in seeking to free from illusion a person who, from the point of the would-be liberator, is, by definition, illusory? Moreover it is contrary to the quite logical advice of Gauḍapāda that one 'should behave in the world like an insensible object'.

Absolute monism will then take the ascetic or mystic as far as the stage

[1] See above, pp. 136–40. [2] See above, pp. 136–7.

of isolation (the end of the Yogin's path according to Patañjali), but this is really the end of only the *via purgativa*, the necessary first step before the 'self' in Jung's sense can enter into direct relations with God whose existence the monist is in any case forced to deny. Hence it is possible for the Vedāntin to speak of reaching a final state of bliss than which, he considers, there can be none higher. Such an idea is unthinkable to the theistic mystic for whom the riches of God, being infinite, are inexhaustible. Abū Yazīd, excited and confused as he was by Vedāntin ideas, understood this instinctively. 'Yaḥyā Mu'ādh wrote a letter to Abū Yazīd', 'Aṭṭār informs us, 'saying, "What have you to say about a person who drinks a cup of wine and becomes drunk for all eternity both in time gone by and in time to come?" Abū Yazīd replied, "I do not know; but this I know, that there is a man here who drinks oceans of eternity in a single day and night and cries out, 'Is there yet more?'" '.[1]

Monism, in practice, means the isolation of the soul from all that is other than itself. It affected Islamic mysticism through Abū Yazīd and Ḥallāj although neither succumbed to the doctrine entirely. It was left to Junayd of Baghdad, who was an elder contemporary of Ḥallāj (ninth and tenth centuries A.D.), to formulate the classical Ṣūfī doctrine of the eternal human soul which inheres in God before creation and which is based on the famous Qur'ānic passage of the *mīthāq*, God's covenant with the children of men before they were ever created. Junayd's basic doctrine resembles the Sāṁkhya and also the non-dualist Vedānta in that he regards the task of the mystic to be the annihilation of his temporal being in the 'idea' of him that is eternally in God. In a remarkable passage he thus describes the state of *fanā*, the 'naughting' or annihilation of the soul in God:

'He gave Himself to me; yet through myself was He hidden from me, for I was indeed my own worst enemy. Woe to me because of myself. He beguiled me and deluded me through my own self away from Him. My presence was the reason of my absence (from Him); and my delight consisted in my contemplation (of Him) to the utmost of my ability. . . . He annihilated me in creating me even as, in the beginning, He created me when I was not. Nor had I any effect on Him since He is beyond effects; nor could I predicate anything about Him, for to Him alone does predication belong. Did He not obliterate all trace of me by His own attribute? And obliterated as I was, all knowledge departed from me

[1] 'Aṭṭār, *Tadhkiratu'l-Awliyā*, vol. i, p. 143: 'Yaḥyā Mu'ādh . . . nāma-ī navisht bah Bāyazīd, guft, chi-gū'ī dar kasī kih qadaḥī sharāb khward va mast i azal va abad shud? Bāyazīd javāb dād kih man ān na-dānam, ān dānam kih īnjā mard hast kih dar shabānrūzī daryāhā' i azal va abad dar mī-kashad va na'reh i hal min mazīdin mī-zanad.' The same story occurs in Hujwīrī's *Kashf al-Maḥjūb*, p. 187 in Nicholson's translation (London, Luzac, 1936).

on account of His (excessive) nearness. He is the Originator, and He it is Who brings us back to Himself. . . . For "when thy Lord took from the children of Adam, from their loins, their posterity and made them testify as to themselves: 'Am I not your Lord?' and they said: 'Yea we testify',"[1] God declared that He spoke to them when they did not yet exist except in so far as He gave them existence; for He gave existence to His creation (in the beginning) in a manner that was different to His granting of existence to individual souls, in a manner that He alone knows, a manner that none but He can find out. He was the source of their existence, encompassing them, calling them to witness in the beginning when they were not,—calling them to witness when still their eternal life was utterly negated, a state in which they were from all pre-eternity. And this is His existence as Lord, His divine awareness which is proper to Him alone. Therefore did we say that when He gave existence to Man (before Man ever was), providing him with what He desired for him according to His will in its most exalted form in which none can share, this act of bestowing existence was without doubt the most perfect and the most efficacious. This existence is better, more victorious, more truly triumphant, overwhelming, and overpowering than anything to which He manifests Himself, so that the creature's individuality is completely obliterated and his (creaturely) existence passes away. No human attribute or existence can be compared to Him.'[2]

The Qur'ānic passage quoted here is a favourite one with the Ṣūfīs and was borrowed from a Christian tradition. It is God's covenant with Adam before he was ever created,—a covenant which He makes with the pre-existent souls when they are still in God and have no independent existence. The obliteration of their humanity and individuality denotes the annihilation of all the purely physical and psychical components and their return to their original state in God. 'Trust in God', Junayd says elsewhere, 'is that you should be God's, even as, before you ever were, you were God's.'[3] Asked what he understood by union the same Master replied, 'That God's servant should be before God the Glorious like a (lifeless) body over which the different modes of His ordaining flow in accordance with the ordinances of His power, in the depths of His unity: (such a man) will thus be naughted to self and to the claims of creatures and to any response he may make to the realities of God's existence and His unicity; in the reality of nearness to Him all sensation and movement will be lost when he faces God the Glorious and what He demands of him; and what He demands

[1] Qur'ān, 7. 171 (the *mīthāq* verse).

[2] From the *Kitāb al-Fanā* which is part of the *Rasā'il* of Junayd published by Ali Abdel Kader in *The Islamic Quarterly*, vol. i, no. 2, 1954, pp. 71–89 (Arabic text of our translation pp. 79–80). The Arabic is extremely obscure and our translation differs from Abdel Kader's in many places. For transliterated text see Appendix C, p. 231.

[3] 'Aṭṭār, op. cit., vol. ii, p. 31: 'tavakkul ān ast kih khudāy-rā bāshī chunānki pīsh az īn kih na-būdī khudāy-rā būdī.'

is that he should return at last to his first state, and be as he was before he was.'[1]

The idea that the human soul pre-exists its birth in time for all eternity in God is common to Hinduism, Islam, and Christianity. There is, however, a difficulty which can only be overcome either by adopting an absolutely rigorous monism or by stipulating plurality in the Godhead itself; for if you start on the premiss that God is a pure monad Who, as pure Being, can admit of no being beside Him, then it follows that the human soul, which in practice means 'I, myself',—because I can have no direct experience of other people who are all part of the objective world so far as I am concerned,—must be God, the sole, eternal, and unique Absolute. By 'I' we must, of course, understand what Proust called the 'second self', the immortal concealed behind the mortal. If, however, as even the Vedānta admits, there is differentiation in the Godhead itself, if, beside Being, there is also thought (*cit*) and bliss (*ānanda*), then there must be something that can be thought and something that can be enjoyed. Thus all religions are forced to admit plurality inherent in the One, for God could neither create nor imagine anything other than Himself had he not the potentiality of plurality in Himself. This second aspect of the Deity may be called *νοῦς* or *λόγος*, as in Philo, St. John, and the neo-Platonists, *amr*, 'the divine command or word', as in Islam, or *māyā*, 'creative illusion', as in Hinduism. In all cases it is the creative principle inherent in the One through which it is possible for it to create (or imagine) by proxy, and by which it thereby ceases to be One in the absolute sense of that absolutely extraordinary word. God, according to all religions, is infinite: yet I have never been able to follow the argument that nothing finite can issue from the infinite. Rather, one would have thought, the Infinite must be infinitely divisible, just as any monad is infinitely fractionable. Pre-existent souls, then, so far from being the totality of God, as monists would have us believe, would be better expressed as $\frac{1}{\infty}$ of ∞, which is 1, totalities in themselves, but as nothing compared to the Infinite.

There does, however, remain the assertion, so frequently made and so rarely argued, that the mystics of all countries and all times see themselves, when in a state of ecstasy, as being identical with the Absolute. How valid

[1] Qushayrī, *Risāla*, pp. 135–6: 'fa-qāla an yakūna'l-'abdu shabaḥan bayna yaday'l-lāhi subḥāna-hu tajrī 'alay-hi taṣārīfu tadbīri-hi fī majārī aḥkāmi qudrati-hi fī lujaji biḥāri tawḥīdi-hi bi'l-fanā'i 'an nafsi-hi wa-'an da'wati'l-khalqi la-hu wa-'an istijābati-hi bi-ḥaqā'iqi wujūdi-hi wa-waḥdānīyati-hi fī ḥaqīqati qurbi-hi bi-dhihābi ḥissi-hi wa-ḥarakati-hi li-qiyāmi'l-ḥaqqi subḥāna-hu la-hu fī-mā arāda min-hu, wa-hūwa an yarji'a ākhiran al-'abdu ilā awwali-hi fa-yakūna ka-mā kāna qabla an yakūna.'

is this argument? We have seen that Ghazālī discounts the utterances of his more extreme colleagues as being incorrect descriptions of an ineffable experience. We have also seen that Mr. Custance, once he emerges from his manic states, becomes conscious of an appalling blasphemy for ever having entertained the idea that he was in some sense identical with God. Further, we have seen that, on analysis, there appear to be at least three distinct mystical states which cannot be identical,—the pan-en-henic where all creaturely existence is experienced as one and one as all; the state of pure isolation of what we may now call the uncreated soul or spirit from all that is other than itself; and thirdly the simultaneous loss of the purely human personality, the 'ego', and the absorption of the uncreate spirit, the 'self', into the essence of God, in Whom both the individual personality and the whole objective world are or seem to be entirely obliterated. These three types seem to emerge clearly enough,—the pan-en-henic, the isolation of the 'self', and the return of the 'self' to God. In Christian terms the first might be regarded as the reversion of the individual soul to a state of original innocence, the oneness that the human race enjoyed in Adam who is the whole Man and therefore undifferentiated psychologically: his ego has not yet broken loose from the unconscious, and his total personality as Man, standing, as a rational being, midway between God and the brute creation, participates in both. The second state is the isolation of the individual spirit from the soul or psyche and body, from the whole psycho-physical complex which is the mortal part of man; while the third represents the return of the spirit to its immortal and infinite ground, which is God. Christians believe that beyond this there is a fourth stage called the Beatific Vision when matter in the shape of the body will share in the general deification, when 'corruptible will put on incorruptible' and the whole man will be transformed in God, and God will be 'all in all'.[1]

Into none of these categories does the pure monist naturally fit. Given his premisses and assuming that he follows a Yoga technique of renunciation of all that is mortal and perishable, it would be natural to class him with the adepts of the Sāṁkhya-Yoga, for he is intent on realizing his own soul, or to put it into the terminology we have been using in this chapter, he is intent on realizing his immortal spirit in detachment from his mortal frame. This is his bliss, and he is quite convinced that it is the supreme bliss; but so long as he sticks to his monistic view of life and feels that his philosophy is confirmed by his experience, then I do not think that his bliss can be identical with that experienced and described by the Christian and Muslim mystics (in so far as these remain theist) whose

[1] 1 Cor. xv. 28.

bliss consists rather in the total surrender of the whole personality to a God who is at the same time Love.

It is, of course, not true to say that Hindus in general had no clear idea of God as other than the human soul, for such views clearly emerge from the main teaching of the Bhagavad-Gītā, in Rāmānuja who bitterly attacks the monists, in Madhva, Caitanya, and many of the later philosophers. Yet monism has, ever since Śankara, been woven 'warp and woof' into the fabric of Hinduism and seems, almost instinctively, to be regarded as the highest type of religion of which its own purely theistic cults are merely tolerated aberrations. Thus Śankara can say,

> 'the entire realm of duality including the object and the act of devotion is illusory, and the attributeless, non-dual *Ātman* alone is Reality. The word "*upanāśrita*" in the text, meaning the one betaking himself to devotion, signifies him who has recourse to devotional exercises as means to the attainment of liberation and who further thinks that he is a devotee and Brahman is his object of worship. This *Jīva* or the embodied being further thinks that through devotional practices he, at present related to the evolved Brahman (Personal God), would attain to the ultimate Brahman after the dissolution of the body. . . . Such a *Jīva*, that is, the aspirant betaking itself to devotion, inasmuch as it knows only a partial aspect of Brahman, is called of narrow or poor intellect by those who regard Brahman as eternal and unchanging.'[1]

In another passage Śankara says,

> 'this discipline', that is, the discipline of worship, 'as well as the various (sacrificial and moral) works are prescribed by scripture for the aspirant of low and average intellect out of compassion, so that they also, following the correct disciplines, may attain to the superior knowledge. That this discipline is not for those who possess the right understanding, i.e., are not already endowed with the Knowledge of *Ātman* which is One and without a second, is supported by such scriptural passages as "That which cannot be known by the mind, but by which, they say, the mind is able to think, that alone know to be Brahman, and not that which people here adore." '[2]

Thus Śankara maintains that the highest Brahman, the One without a second, can only be attained by *sannyāsins*, men who renounce everything

[1] In this and the following quotations I follow Swāmi Nikhilānanda's slightly abbreviated paraphrase of Śankara's commentary on Gauḍapāda's *Kārikā*, first because it represents Śankara as interpreted by his present-day followers, and secondly because in direct translation the Sanskrit commentaries sound intolerably cumbersome. The Sanskrit text is available in the Ahmadabad Sanskrit series, and there is a good translation by Manilal N. Dvidevi, Theosophical Publication Fund, Bombay, 1894. Nikhilānanda's paraphrase does not, of course, do any violence to Śankara's thought. The present quotation is from Śankara's commentary to Gauḍapāda's *Kārikā*, 3. 1.

[2] Ibid.: 3. 16.

but their Selves, refuse to take part in religious ceremonies or to accept the grace of any God, and who abandon all works, whether good or evil.[1] 'By ceasing to do good to one's friends or evil to one's enemies (the *sannyāsin*) attains to the eternal Brahman by the *yoga* of meditation.'[2]

Now just as Rāmānuja and the other theistic philosophers in India attack Śankara and his followers for their extreme monism and for precisely this type of conduct which is its logical sequel, so did Ruysbroeck and Suso attack the Beghards in the European Middle Ages, for the latter held similar views and indulged in a similar quietism, believing themselves to be perfect and incapable of sin. In his *Spiritual Espousals* Ruysbroeck attacks those who seek to find perfect tranquillity in themselves. This passage is extraordinarily relevant to our theme and must be extensively quoted.

'Now observe', Ruysbroeck writes, 'that whenever man is empty and undistracted in his senses by images, and free and unoccupied in his highest powers, he attains rest by purely natural means. And all men can find and possess this rest in themselves by their mere nature, without the grace of God, if they are able to empty themselves of sensual images and of all action.'[3] Though he had obviously never heard of Vedāntin monism and could never have done so, Ruysbroeck seems not only to know exactly what this state of 'oneness without a second' is, but he describes it so accurately that one cannot but conclude that he is writing from actual experience. 'Whenever man is empty and undistracted in his senses by images, and free and unoccupied in his highest powers', such a man, we might continue, achieves the highest Brahman: for herein, precisely, lies the essence of the non-dualist Vedānta.

However, as Ruysbroeck rightly saw, such an emptying of the human person can only be the beginning of the mystical life for those who have experienced the grace of a personal God; for according to Christianity God is Love, and the Muslim mystics, particularly in Persia, were later to make this idea their own. It is present too in the tenth and thirteenth chapters of the Bhagavad-Gītā and in all the devotional, as opposed to the philosophical, writing of the Hindus. Just as Śankara despises his fellow-countrymen who continue to worship 'illusory' gods for being on a lower level than himself, so does Ruysbroeck fulminate against contemporary European quietists. There are two states of tranquillity, Ruysbroeck maintains, two types of *śānti*,—the rest one takes in one's self, purged as it has

[1] See *Māṇḍūkya Up.*, *Kārikā*, 2. 35.

[2] *Nārada Upaniṣad*, Schrader, p. 145: 'priyeṣu sveṣu sukṛtam apriyeṣu ca duṣkṛtam / visṛjya dhyāna-yogena brahmāpyeti sanātanam.'

[3] Blessed Jan van Ruysbroeck, *The Spiritual Espousals*, tr. Eric Colledge, London, Faber and Faber, 1952, pp. 166–7.

been of all affections and desires, and the rest in God when the living flame kindled by the fire of God is reunited with the divine fire. Thus Ruysbroeck has no patience with those who are content to rest in the self or Self,—and it can make no difference whether we spell this word with a capital letter or not since, in Sanskrit, there are no capital letters,—for this state, blissful though it undoubtedly is, is not union with God. It is the eternal spirit of the individual man contemplating itself in itself, as it issued from the mind of God but, because of original sin, separated from God, though otherwise sinless.

These men, says Ruysbroeck, 'are, as it seems to them, occupied in the contemplation of God, and they believe themselves to be the holiest men alive. Yet they live in opposition and dissimilarity to God and all saints and all good men. . . .

'Through the natural rest which they feel and have in themselves in emptiness, they maintain that they are free, and united with God without mean, and that they are advanced beyond all the exercises of Holy Church, and beyond the commandments of God, and beyond the law, and beyond all the virtuous works which one can in any way practise.' Here one calls to mind Śankara's contempt for those who perform the duties laid down by their religion and his preference for the perfect Yogin's withdrawal from all works. 'For', Ruysbroeck goes on to say, 'this emptiness seems to them to be so great that no-one ought to hinder them with the performance of any work, however good it be, for their emptiness is of greater excellence than are all virtues. And therefore they remain in mere passivity without the performance of any work directed up towards God or down towards man, just like the instrument which is itself passive and awaits the time when its owner wishes to work.'[1] Such men are indeed suspended between heaven and earth, isolated from man and Nature because they have severed all attachments, and isolated from God because the oneness of isolation is their end and goal, and because a conviction that they are the Absolute constitutes the toughest possible barrier between them and a possible irruption of grace: they 'maintain that they cannot advance, for they have achieved a life of unity and emptiness beyond which one cannot advance and in which there is no exercise'.[2]

It will be remembered that Christ said, 'No man cometh to the Father, but by me'.[3] It is, of course, possible to take this saying in an absolutely literal sense and thereby to dismiss all non-Christian religions as being merely false. It is, however, legitimate and certainly more charitable to

[1] Ibid., pp. 170–1.
[2] Ibid., p. 173.
[3] John xiv. 6.

interpret this saying, so far as it applies to mysticism, to mean that unless one approaches the Father through the Son and as a son with the trust and helplessness of a child, there is very little chance of finding Him,—none at all, it would appear, if you insist either that you are identical with the Father or that the Father is an illusion. Hence a sharp distinction must be drawn between those forms of religion in which love or charity plays a predominant part and those in which it does not. In Christian mysticism love is all-important, and it must be so, since God Himself is defined as Love. In Islam too, because the Muslims inherited more than they knew from the Christians, it assumes ever-increasing importance despite the predominantly terrifying picture of God we find in the Qur'ān. In Hinduism this religion of love breaks through in the Gītā and in the cults of both Viṣṇu and Śiva, and, of course, in the worship of Rāma and Krishna as incarnations of Viṣṇu. 'I am the origin of all,' says Krishna in the Bhagavad-Gītā, 'from me all things evolve. Thinking thus do wise men, immersed in love (*bhāva*), worship Me. Thinking of Me, devoting their lives to Me, enlightening each other, and speaking of Me always, they are contented and rejoice. To these worshippers of Mine, always controlled, I give a steady mind by which they may approach Me, for I loved them first.'[1] This and very much else that is similar will be found in Hindu literature, yet always the shadow of a self-satisfied monism stalks behind it.

And in monism there can be no love,—there is ecstasy and trance and deep peace, what Ruysbroeck calls 'rest', but there cannot be the ecstasy of union nor the loss of self in God which is the goal of Christian, Muslim, and all theistic mysticism.

'And therefore', says Ruysbroeck, 'all those men are deceived whose intention it is to sink themselves in natural rest, and who do not seek God with desire nor find Him in delectable love. For the rest which they possess consists in an emptying of themselves, to which they are inclined by nature and by habit. And in this natural rest men cannot find God. But it brings man indeed into an emptiness which heathens and Jews are able to find, and all men, however evil they may be, if they live in their sins with untroubled conscience, and are able to empty themselves of all images and all action. In this emptiness rest is sufficient and great, and it is in itself no sin, for it is in all men by nature, if they knew how to make themselves empty.'[2]

All mystics, including Ruysbroeck, agree that no progress in the inner

[1] *BhagG.* 10. 8–10: 'ahaṁ sarvasya prabhavo, mattaḥ sarvaṁ pravartate; / iti matvā bhajante māṁ budhā bhāva-samanvitāḥ. / mac-cittā mad-gata-prāṇā bodhayantaḥ parasparam, / kathayantaśca māṁ nityaṁ tuṣyantica ramantica. / teṣāṁ satata-yuktānāṁ bhajatāṁ prīti-pūrvakam / dadāmi buddhi-yogaṁ taṁ yena mām upayānti te.'

[2] Op. cit., p. 167.

life is possible without detachment from all things worldly, from all that comes to be and passes away, and above all from the individual ego or self. They are agreed that the 'second self', as Proust calls it, must be discovered and brought out into the open. The temptation is that with the finding of this second self the aspirant after spiritual perfection should think that he has reached his goal and that the 'second self', the *ātman* of the Vedānta, is God. It is very significant that Ruysbroeck uses the words 'emptiness' and 'unity' to describe this state. The first is, of course, the word used to describe ultimate bliss as conceived of by the Mādhyamika Buddhists, and the second is the keyword of the Vedānta. A Buddhist work speaks of this 'emptiness' in the following terms:

> 'The Yogins who abide in the vision of emptiness do not at all apprehend the skandhas, elements and sense-fields as if they were something in themselves; in consequence they do not enter upon discursive ideas with these as objects, make no discriminations, by inclination to the ideas of I and mine do not give rise to a host of defilements which have the false view of individuality for its root, do not perform any actions, and, in consequence, do not experience the transmigration which consists in birth, old age and death. It is thus, when one resorts to emptiness, characterized as blissful and as the appeasing of all discursive ideas, that all the discursive ideas, which are a net of thought-construction, disappear. When discursive ideas have disappeared, discrimination comes to rest, and with it all karma and defilement, and all kinds of rebirth. Hence one calls emptiness Nirvana, as it brings to rest (nirvriti) all discursive ideas.'[1]

In this context let us repeat what Ruysbroeck said on the subject though he had no experience of either Buddhists or Yogins. 'In this emptiness rest is sufficient and great, and it is itself no sin, for it is in all men by nature, if they know how to make themselves empty.' But delectable though this state obviously is, it is not the Beatific Vision, nor is it in any sense a union with God; it is only the purification of the vessel which can, if it will, be filled with God. Emptiness is the prelude to Holiness. To rest in this emptiness is dangerous for this is a 'house swept and garnished', and though it is possible that God may enter in if the furniture is fair, it is equally likely that the proverbial seven devils will rush in if either the remaining furniture is foul or if there is no furniture at all; for 'when men wish to exercise and possess this rest without the works of virtue, then they fall into spiritual pride, and into a self-complacency from which they seldom recover. And at such times they believe themselves to have and to be that which they never achieve'.[2]

[1] From Candrakīrti, *Prasannapadā*, quoted by E. Conze, *Buddhist Texts through the Ages*, pp. 168–9.

[2] Op. cit., pp. 167–8.

'When a man possesses this rest in emptiness, and when the impulse of love seems to him to be a hindrance, so in resting he remains within himself, and lives contrary to the first manner which unites man with God; and this is a beginning of all spiritual error.'[1]

It must be noted that Ruysbroeck, who was himself a mystic so extreme in his claims on behalf of the essential union of the soul with God that he was suspect of heresy, saw in this monistic quietism the greatest threat to all religion. For though he was convinced,—and he appears to be speaking from experience,—that the state of complete tranquillity in emptiness was only a stepping-stone on the way to God, and not an essential one at that, he saw that those who held the opposite view could scarcely be convinced of their error, if error it is. 'For according to their way of thinking, they possess everything that they might pray or yearn for. And thus they are poor in spirit, for they are without desire, and they have forsaken everything, and live without any choice of their own, for it seems to them that they have passed beyond everything into an emptiness where they possess that for the sake of which all the exercises of Holy Church are ordained and set. And thus, according to them, no one is able to give to them or to take from them, not even God Himself; for it appears to them that they have advanced beyond all exercises and all virtues. And they have attained, they think, to a perfect passivity in which they are finished with all virtues. And they say that greater labour is needed to be finished with virtue in passivity than to attain to virtue.' And 'according to their way of thinking they are exalted above all the orders of saints and of angels and above every reward which one can in any way deserve. And therefore they say that they can never increase in virtue, that they can never deserve a greater reward, and also that they can never sin again'.[2]

'I hope that few such men will be found, but such as are, they are the evillest and most harmful men that live, and it is hard for them to be converted. And sometimes they are possessed by the devil, and then they are so able in his service that one cannot well win them over by argument.'[3]

Words could scarcely be stronger than these; and they demonstrate beyond all reasonable doubt the abyss that separates the theistic mystic from the monist.

[1] *The Spiritual Espousals*, p. 168. [2] Ibid., p. 171. [3] Ibid., p. 172.

CHAPTER IX

THEISM *VERSUS* MONISM

WE have seen that Ruysbroeck attacked the monistic quietists on the grounds that they were merely finding rest in an emptiness within themselves without reference to God, that they considered themselves beyond good and evil and beyond all moral laws, and thirdly that they were convinced that they had achieved the ultimate perfection beyond which it is impossible to go.

On the other side we find Śankara and the Indian monists insisting with equal vigour that when the individual soul realizes itself as the Absolute, this is a stage beyond which it cannot go. It should, however, be borne in mind that in India Śankara is quite as well known as the author of devotional hymns of considerable beauty to both the great gods Śiva and Viṣṇu as he is as the systematizer of the *advaita* or non-dualist Vedānta. Śankara admits the usefulness of works in general for those who have not attained *mokṣa* or liberation from the bonds of purely ephemeral life. They can be a help to the worshipper, and the *Yoga-Sūtras* of Patañjali recommend devotion to Īśvara, the Lord, as one of the steps on the way to liberation. Thus there is nothing inconsistent in Śankara's composing hymns to either Viṣṇu or Śiva if, as he knew from experience, these were aids towards liberation, distracting, as they did, the attention of the worshipper from his own ego. To be more precise, there is no inconsistency in writing hymns for the purpose of giving the mind a subject on which to concentrate, but there seems to be an inconsistency in writing hymns for other people who, in the strictly monistic view, are illusory. The Vedāntin seeks to avoid this dilemma by stating that individual souls are all, in reality, Brahman. Once they realize this fact they are absolutely and completely identical with all other 'liberated' souls, for 'What thou art, that am I'.[1] This raises a serious difficulty, for it implies that in X who is a liberated soul, Brahman shines in his absolute oneness, whereas in Y who is still bound, He is the subject of the illusion of duality. Thus, given the existence of other souls apart from one's own it is impossible for one (or Brahman) ever to achieve total liberation since the bound souls always limit one by their ignorance. The Vedāntin would presumably counter this argument by saying that by realizing himself as the one reality X at the same time realizes the one reality in all people, a reality of which they themselves are ignorant. This will mean that X is

[1] *Kauṣītakī Upaniṣad*, I. 6: 'yas tvam asi so 'ham asmi.'

identical with Y and that what Y conceives himself to be is illusory; in other words X *is* the real Y while what Y takes to be himself does not exist at all.[1] In practice, of course, it has never been demonstrated that any given soul has ever achieved 'identity' with any other. Such a relationship would imply not only identity of essence (X = Brahman = Y), but also the identity of all the 'illusory adjuncts' (*upādhis*) in *māyā* seen and experienced by the apparently distinct but actually identical X and Y. This is not possible unless X and Y are both omniscient and their respective omnisciences can be shown not only to be identical but to correspond to observed fact. Until monists can prove that such identity is possible, they would do better to adhere to a strictly solipsist position. In any case if Śankara had been told of the experiences of Christian and Muslim mystics he would merely have seen in them a laudable exercise in devotion to an imaginary being carried to extreme and incomprehensible lengths, for in Christian mysticism he would have seen merely a variant of what he himself knew in India as *bhakti*, the devotion rendered to personal gods, conceived of in human form, and often as incarnations of the supreme spirit. Thus modern writers like M. Schuon will tell us that Christianity is predominantly 'bhāktic' or devotional, not 'jñānic', 'gnostic', that is concerned with *knowledge* of the Deity. This is to misunderstand Christianity completely and to use the Sanskrit word *jñāna* as if it meant some universal metaphysical truth, a meaning that it will not sustain. *Jñāna* like *gnōsis* derives from the Indo-European root √*gno-*, 'to know' (gnosco, *γι-γνω-σκω*, know, znat', etc.): it means, according to derivation, 'knowledge' or 'science'. To speak of the 'way of knowledge' as contrasted with the 'way of devotion' is misleading. The terms *jñāna* and *gnosis* are in fact conventionally (and arrogantly) used by the adherents of different metaphysical theories to designate their own particular theory which claims, like its rivals, to lead to 'liberation' or, in the case of the Gnostics, to the understanding of a particular metaphysical 'truth'. That these theories are distinct from one another shows that the word, despite its etymology, does not mean 'knowledge' as that word is commonly understood in the English tongue: it means simply 'a strongly held opinion' or 'conviction'. It means what the Greeks, with their customary accuracy, called a 'dogma'. To call such opinions 'knowledge' is to assert one's own infallibility, which is either fatuous or a sign of acute mania. 'Knowledge' of God, to the Christian contemplative too, means primarily assent to the Christian dogma that God is Absolute Being, Omniscient Wisdom, and Indefectible Love: it is the necessary assumption

[1] This is the position argued by Śankara in his *Ātmabodha* or '(Book of) Self-Knowledge'.

which makes the love of God not only possible but supremely worthwhile. It would be foolish, however, to blink the fact that such an assumption which is the reverse of obvious, has no claim to validity except in so far as it was revealed in the teaching and Person of Jesus Christ, Who, according to the Christian scriptures, claimed to be God. 'Knowledge' in this context means what it means for the followers of other religions,—'knowledge' (whether true or false) gained from the 'dogmas' or firmly held opinions of individuals as these have been defined or modified by the believers in the credentials of the individual concerned. There are as many *jñānas* as there are religions, sects, and sub-sects. To use the word to mean the one metaphysical truth that is alleged to be basic to all 'true' (!) religion, as M. Schuon does, is simply to confuse further a subject that is already quite sufficiently confused.

In Christian mysticism the dogma of the love of God is put to the test. It is claimed that to know God is to love Him and to love Him to the exclusion of all else. To know the *ens realissimum* which is at the same time the *summum bonum* must necessarily mean to love it. There is not and cannot be any conflict. It is only when there is a possibility that the *summum bonum* may be separated from the *ens realissimum*, when Being is regarded as being beyond the Good, that the possibility of every sort of distortion and 'error' creeps in. That Ruysbroeck should castigate in such violent terms those who rested 'in emptiness' and who thought that 'they had passed beyond everything' and possessed 'that for the sake of which all the exercises of Holy Church are ordained', is only explicable if he felt with great urgency that this belief led to a spiritual and mystical atrophy. In the case of Śankara it is possible that I have misunderstood what he himself says in his commentary on the Māṇḍūkya Upaniṣad and Gauḍapāda's *kārikā*, and that his rigorously Parmenidean position should not be unduly stressed, and that he should be judged as much on his hymns as on his commentaries. I would then quote a hymn of his and I think it is a typical one. To avoid any possible misrepresentation of him we will reproduce the hymn in full.

'Day and night, evening and morning, winter and spring ever return; Time sports and life passes away; yet the breath of hope brings no release. Worship Govinda, worship Govinda, worship Govinda, deluded man. When Time is finished and rolled up, rules of grammar cannot avail you.

'With fire in front of him and the sun on his back, knees tucked up to his chin at night, beggar's bread in the palm of his hand, his dwelling beneath a tree, even (to such a religious mendicant) the toils of hope bring no release. Worship Govinda, etc.

'So long as a man can pile up wealth, so long will he be surrounded by his own people and so long will he be loved; after that he will live in a decrepit body, and no one asks him how he fares at home. Worship Govinda, etc.

'(Then there is the mendicant) with matted hair, or bald, or with hair close shaved, variously clad in saffron robes; seeing he sees not, deluded, and thinking only of his belly, clad in various robes. Worship Govinda, etc.

'Yet if a man study the Bhagavad-Gītā a little or drink only a drop or two of the Ganges waters or worship Krishna only once, how should death pay attention to him? Worship Govinda, etc.

'(Then consider) a body decayed, grey-haired, bald, teeth gone, and face fallen in. The old man takes his stick to walk,—yet the complex of hope brings him no release. Worship Govinda, etc.

'(See) the child clinging to his games, the youth in love with his mistress, the old man immersed in thought, none of them holds fast to the highest Brahman. Worship Govinda, etc.

'O Krishna, in this phenomenal world so hard to traverse and so much to be pitied, ward off from us rebirth and re-death, ward off yet another sojourn in a mother's womb. Worship Govinda, etc.

'Night succeeds day and day night, come the half-months, months, half-years, and years,—yet enduring hope brings no release. Worship Govinda, etc.

'When youth's vigour is gone, what is ever-changing passion? When the water is dried up, what good is the pool? When wealth is spent, who will wait upon you? When reality is known, what becomes of the phenomenal world? Worship Govinda, etc.

'You see a woman's heavy breasts and navel, all a show put on by delusion and *māyā*. Think of it repeatedly as a mere compound of flesh and fat. Worship Govinda, etc.

'Who are you? who am I? whence have I come? who is my mother, who my father? Think of all this as having no substance, leave it all as the stuff of dreams. Worship Govinda, etc.

'Chant (religious) songs more than a thousand times, think always of the form of Viṣṇu, meditate in the company of good men, give your property to the afflicted. Worship Govinda, etc.

'So long as the soul dwells in the body, so long does one's family ask after one's health. When life has gone and the body is no more, even a wife will fear the corpse. Worship Govinda, etc.

'For pleasure we enjoy the delights of love, then disease takes hold of our body. And if indeed on earth death is a refuge,—yet the pursuit of evil brings no release. Worship Govinda, etc.

'Adorn yourself with rags for the road, make your path the renunciation of good and evil. (Say), "I am not, nor you, nor yet this world": then for what should you grieve? Worship Govinda, etc.

'Though you perform pilgrimages to the Ganges, keep your vows and give alms, all this without "knowledge" (is worthless); and no release can be obtained in a hundred births. Worship Govinda, etc.'[1]

This is a typical example of Śankara's hymns. The message is this: despise the world, for it is transitory; worship God, and do good works. All this, however, is only for the spiritually immature and can, of itself, lead nowhere. This is made quite clear in the last two stanzas where it is said that release from transmigratory existence can only come through *jñāna*, 'knowledge' of the 'truth' of the non-dualist Vedānta, that is the *ātma-bodha*, the 'knowledge of the self', and not through good deeds or through any act of devotion. For Śankara worship is simply a means of concentrating the mind and is much inferior to Yoga technique from this point of view. Further, half the value of the hymn would seem to lie in the repetition of the refrain (*bhaja govindaṁ, bhaja govindaṁ, bhaja govindaṁ, mūḍhamate*). This is a well-known technique for inducing a state of self-hypnosis and was practised both by the Hesychasts and the early Ṣūfīs. As we have seen, Tennyson produced the same result by repeating his own name.[2] Self-hypnosis, moreover, would appear to be a milestone on the way to 'self-realization'.

In this context it is as well to remember that Hinduism has some very strange ideas about the nature of belief, although these notions fit in very nicely with Jung's psychology. Apart from Brahman which is the sole reality and identical with the human soul, the other deities are merely more or less adequate representations of that reality; they are *iṣṭa-devatāḥ*, 'gods from among whom one may choose' whichever is most suitable to one's temperament. There is not, then, in monistic thought at least, any idea that the god can himself have any value, he is far from being what Professor Farmer calls 'axiologically other; that is to say, as being in Himself the realized perfection of all value, including in this both all true human values (of which He is the source) and also certain values which, transcending all possible human values, constitute the unapproachable and ineffable divine glory'.[3] So it is that the Hindu seems to find nothing incongruous to Deity in the shifts and pranks of Krishna who is regarded as an incarnation of the supreme being, for 'whatever idea a person is shown, that he sees, that he enjoys, and that he becomes: possessed of that idea he realizes it'.[4] Or again 'a person becomes of the same nature as his thought',[5] and 'whatever idea

[1] See Swāmi Nikhilānanda, *Self-Knowledge*, Madras, Sri Ramakrishna Math, 1947, pp. 287–97. For transliterated text see Appendix C, pp. 232–3.

[2] See above, p. 36.

[3] H. H. Farmer, *Revelation and Religion*, London, Nisbet, 1954, p. 78.

[4] *Māṇḍūkya Up.*, *Kārikā*, 2. 29: 'yaṁ bhāvaṁ darśayed yasya, taṁ bhāvaṁ sa tu paśyati, / taṁ cāvati, sa bhūtvā, 'sau tad-grahaḥ samupaiti tam.'

[5] *Maitreya Up.*, Schrader, p. 110: 'yac-cittas tanmayo bhavati.'

you have in mind when you quit the body at death, that idea you will realize'.[1] It has frequently been said that man makes his gods in his own image. In post-Upaniṣadic Hinduism this would seem to be literally true, except that the gods themselves are freely acknowledged to be phantasms by at least those who had realized their unity with the absolute Brahman. Presumably the reason why the advanced monist who has outgrown these 'childish things' tolerates these practices, is because he sees that they are able to produce that other sort of natural mysticism which we have called pan-en-henism and which produces a unifying experience in which the sense of individuality is lost and merged in a blissful sense of the unity of all Nature. This, though the very opposite of the Vedāntin ideal in which the individual realizes himself as the One without a second and therefore cuts himself off from all that is not himself, is nevertheless akin to that ideal in so far as it is unitary, though its unity is, by monistic standards, necessarily inferior since it is a unity in multiplicity. Similarly, as Ruysbroeck saw, the absolute unity of a 'released' soul in repose is superficially akin to the unity that the soul of the mystic finds in God: yet between the two there seems to be all the difference in the world.

In this context it is instructive to compare the use of the reflexive pronoun in Sanskrit and Arabic. In Sanskrit we have *ātman* meaning either the individual self or the Highest Self. The word, however, is a reflexive pronoun and in the early texts is used of the trunk of the body as distinct from the head, arms, and legs. Later it comes to be used simply as a reflexive pronoun or to mean the human self and then, by transference, the 'Self' or real nature of ultimate reality. In Arabic the word *nafs* (the original meaning of which was probably 'breath', cf. *nafas*) is also used of the human self, but in Islamic mysticism it is this 'self' that is the enemy which must at all costs be slain if union with God is to be obtained. 'Whoso would attain to absolute trust in God,' we read, 'let him dig a grave for his self and bury it therein',[2] or again 'the man who fears (God) is he who fears his own self more than he fears Satan',[3] for 'God draws' His elect to Himself and 'tears them away from their selves (and any part they may think they have) in their actions, and establishes them in Himself'.[4] Shiblī, a disciple of Junayd, expressed this total loss of 'self' in the following words: 'Had I been with

[1] *Nārada Up.*, ibid., p. 178: 'yaṁ yaṁ vâpi smaran bhāvaṁ tyajaty ante kalevaram, / taṁ tam eva samāpnoti.'

[2] Sarrāj, *Kitāb al-Luma'*, p. 53: 'man arāda an yaqūma bi-ḥaqqi'l-tawakkuli, falyaḥfira li-nafsi-hi qabran wa-yadfina-hā fī-hi.'

[3] Ibid., p. 61: 'al-khā'ifu 'indī man yakhāfu min nafsi-hi akthara mim-mā yakhāfu min al-shayṭāni.'

[4] Ibid., p. 355: 'man yakūnu min-hum arfa'a, jadhaba-humu'l-ḥaqqu wa-maḥā-hum 'an nufūsi-him fī ḥarakāti-him wa-athbata-hum 'inda nafsi-hi.'

God, I would have lost Him; but (as it is) I am obliterated in Him, that is to say, there is nothing of "me" left, nor is there anything (that occurs) through me or (proceeds) from me, for all is from Him and through Him and His.'[1]

Now if we take 'self' in the Jungian sense as the centre of the integrated personality which both preserves the delicate balance between the conscious ego and the unconscious, the 'self' which Jung says is both the centre of the personality and its circumference, it is clear that the aim of the Ṣūfī and the monistic *sannyāsin* are radically different. In the one case you see a person thirsting for annihilation in the Beloved as the moth seeks extinction in the candle, in the other you see a person divesting himself of every possible quality in order to dwell in a blissful emptiness,—described by Śankara, in accordance with Upaniṣadic authority, as Awareness and Bliss. In the one case you have a ray of light returning to its source, or the drop of water dissolving in wine; in the other you have the drop of water imagining itself to be the ocean because it has no experience of the ocean nor can it adequately conceive what the word means. The paradox seems to be that the Vedānta of Śankara is based on certain passages of the Upaniṣads which take up a rigidly monist position and these passages themselves develop from the pantheistic conception of the universe which sees the unity of being as rooted in Brahman, but does not yet demand that that unity should be an absolute monad. Losing sight completely of a whole series of Upaniṣadic myths which describe the procession of the universe from God as from a material cause, a system develops which, by insisting overmuch on the absolute unity of being and the absolute reality of the human soul, is forced to identify the two completely, thereby excluding God as an ontological impossibility.

It is true that Vedāntin monism superficially resembles some of the more extreme utterances of the German mystics of the fourteenth century, and it is no accident that writers on the Vedānta so frequently quote Eckhart as an independent witness to the truth of their message. In particular our attention is rightly drawn to the distinction which Eckhart makes between the triune God and the Godhead and to the fact that he sometimes refers to the latter as the Nothing.[2] The distinction between God and the Godhead

[1] Ibid.: 'law kuntu anā maʿa-hu, fātanī; wa-lākinnī maḥwun fī-mā hūwa, yaʿnī laysa minnī shay'un wa-lā bī shay'un wa-lā 'annī shay'un, wa'l-kullu min-hu wa-bi-hi wa-la-hu.'

[2] The description of God as 'Nothing' is not peculiar to Eckhart. The *Cloud of Unknowing* speaks of God as 'this nought'. 'For I tell thee truly that I had rather be so nowhere bodily, wrestling with that blind nought, than to be so great a lord that I might when I would be everywhere bodily, merrily playing with all this aught as a lord with his own' (ed. McCann, p. 91: cf. the Postscript 'Of that mystic saying "Nothing and nothing make nothing"' reproduced on

has been compared to the distinction made by Śankara between the *para-brahman* or supreme Brahman and the *apara-brahman* or lower Brahman who is the agent through whose ignorance (*avidyā*) or self-deception (*māyā*) this (illusory) world is created. There can be little doubt, however, that Eckhart was out to shock and that he succeeded. What he never did, however, except when speaking in deliberate hyperbole and even in his most imaginative moments when he saw himself as having passed beyond God into the unfathomable abyss of the Godhead, was to deny the existence of what was other than the Godhead with which he, during these moments, felt himself to be identified. One may argue with Otto[1] that this phenomenal world is only unreal,—a mirage, as Śankara says,—from the point of view of the absolute monistic 'truth'. It is a mirage imagined by Brahman itself and therefore the only existing cosmic mirage. Since Brahman is one, the mirage too can only be one, that is, the world as it is, and not otherwise. This is in fact a point on which Śankara attacks the Buddhists who denied any basis at all to the phenomenal world and were content to make the goal of human striving a complete and absolute blank (*śūnyatā*, 'emptiness'). But there is not only a difference in tone between Eckhart and Śankara, which Otto himself fully brought out; there is obviously a fundamental difference in the experiences which must have formed the basis of the two men's writing. For whereas Śankara sees 'liberation' only as a complete and utter dissociation from all that is other than the eternal 'self', Eckhart does not experience it as liberation at all. Like all genuine mystics he must start as a *mukta*, a released man, if he is to get anywhere at all. Release from the temporal is only the beginning of the plunge into the eternal: so it is not possible for Eckhart to reach his goal because the depths of God (or the Godhead as he prefers to call Him) are forever unfathomable, and however far the deification of man may go, it can never reach the end. Thus, though he may say with Majnūn, the mad lover of Laylā, 'I am Laylā', or with Abū Yazīd 'I am Thou',[2] however close the identification may be, he knows that there are and always will be deeper and darker places to be plumbed. For when the soul reaches the essence of the Godhead itself beyond the Trinity, Eckhart tells us, 'It sinks ever deeper into the abyss of the Godhead so that it never comes to the bottom (*niemer grunt envindet*).'[3] Again he says, 'When first the soul breaks forth, it does not perceive God *qua* God:

p. 217 there). As the *Cloud* explains, 'nowhere bodily is everywhere ghostly', and this seems to mean little more than that spirit is not perceptible to the bodily senses. Eckhart's description of God as 'Nothing' was not among the condemned propositions and Suso develops the idea after him.

[1] R. Otto, *Mysticism East and West* (E.T.), London, Macmillan, 1932, p. 154.

[2] Sarrāj, *Kitāb al-Luma'*, p. 360; cf. Nicholson's digest, p. 95.

[3] Ed. Pfeiffer, p. 501.

it delves (*gründet*) and searches ever farther and grasps God in His unity (*einunge*) and in His solitude (*einoede*); it grasps Him in His desolation (*wüestunge*) and in His ground. Still it is not satisfied, but seeks rather for what is in the Godhead and in the essence (*eigentuome*) of His proper nature.'[1]

Śankara, on the other hand, can state quite simply that reality is 'One without a second' and that 'thou art that' reality: it is only a question of realizing this. Once the illusory adjuncts are disposed of by the practice of Yoga, then there is complete self-realization and absolute peace and rest. The goal has been achieved and there cannot be any further progress; this is the *paramā gatiḥ*, the final state beyond which it is impossible to go. Readers of the *Waste Land* will remember that the Sanskrit for 'peace' or 'rest' is *śāntiḥ*. This word is formed from the root *śam-* which means 'to grow calm, to stop or desist' and by extension 'to kill'. Similarly the participle *śānta* means 'calm, stopped' or 'dead'. This state of rest which is akin to death is regarded as the highest state. But when we turn to the Muslims we find that such a state is condemned out of hand. 'Knowledge is the reverse of ignorance,' says Ghazālī, 'and ignorance is a necessary concomitant of darkness, and darkness belongs to (the state of) rest, and rest is near to non-existence.'[2] This association of rest with darkness is reminiscent of the whole Upaniṣadic concept of sleep and the theory that deep, dreamless sleep is the nearest approach to final beatitude, the so-called *turīya* or 'fourth state'. For Ghazālī it represents a spiritual death.

Now no one will deny that dreamless sleep, so far as it can be described as a state at all, is a blissful state in that all worry and all irritating desire is laid to rest; it is the nearest thing to death,—to non-existence, as Ghazālī pointed out. This seems to be borne out by the sequence in the Bṛhadāraṇyaka Upaniṣad, 4. 3. 7–4. 4. 2, where the progression of the soul from the waking state (called 'being in this world') through dream and dreamless sleep to death is described. Finally at the time of death

'when this self becomes feeble and as it were confused, then do these breaths gather round him. He collects these particles of brilliance together and goes down into the heart. When the person in the eye departs back (to the sun which is its source), then does he cease to see forms. "He is becoming one", they say; "he does not see". "He is becoming one", they say; "he does not smell". "He is becoming one", they say; "he does not taste". "He is becoming one", they

[1] Ibid., p. 266: Gandillac, p. 167. For further examples illustrating this point see Otto, op. cit. (E.T.), pp. 185–7.

[2] Ghazālī, *Risālat al-Ladunnīya*, *apud* Ṣabrī, *Al-Jawāhir al-Ghawālī*, Cairo, 1353/1935, p. 22: 'wa-dhālika anna'l-'ilma ḍiddu'l-jahli, wa'l-jahla min lawāzimi'l-ẓulmati, wa'l-ẓulmata min ḥayzi'l-sukūni, wa'l-sukūna qarībun min al-'adami.'

say; "he does not speak". "He is becoming one", they say; "he does not hear". "He is becoming one", they say; "he does not think". "He is becoming one", they say; "he does not feel". "He is becoming one", they say: "he does not know". The tip of his heart begins to shine. Lighted by this brilliance the self departs, either by the eye, or by the head, or by other parts of the body. As he goes out the spirit follows him. As the spirit goes out all the breaths follow it. He becomes conscious. What has consciousness follows after him.'[1]

Thus death, like dreamless sleep, is regarded as a state in which a person 'becomes one'; it is, one might think, the unity brought about by the cessation of all activity and therefore of all multiplicity, the unity, in other words, of complete unconsciousness. Such an opinion, however, is belied by the text itself and the sequel shows that this is not the Upaniṣad's interpretation of what happens at death. 'The man who is without desire, devoid of desire, whose desires have been fulfilled, whose desire is the Self,—his vital breaths do not depart. Being Brahman, he reaches Brahman.'[2] This could be interpreted on strictly monistic lines, but the sequel shows that the *Bṛhadāraṇyaka* has not yet reached this position, it is still pantheistic or pan-en-henic. 'He who has found and become aware of his self and entered into this impenetrable abode, he is the maker of all, the maker of the whole world, he is the whole world.'[3] This passage can be fitted into two of the three categories of mysticism which we have analysed. It certainly is not the mysticism of 'isolation', the separation of spirit from matter, of the eternal from the temporal. It is, however, pantheistic or pan-en-henic in that it says that the soul *is* the universe. It could also be interpreted as a case of genuine theistic mysticism in which the soul feels itself to be identical with God. The objection to such an interpretation, however, is that no theistic mystic could claim that his union with God is so close that he can lay claim to attributes like the power to create which are specifically divine. It is this and the fact that, for as long as they remain orthodox in

[1] *Bṛhadāraṇyaka Up.*, 4. 4. 1–2: 'sa yatrāyam ātmā 'balyaṁ nyetya saṁmoham iva nyeti, athainam ete prāṇā abhisamāyanti; sa etās tejo-mātrāḥ samabhyādadāno hṛdayam evānvavakrāmati; sa yatraiṣa cākṣuṣaḥ puruṣaḥ parāṅ paryāvartate, 'thārūpa-jño bhavati. / ekībhavati, na paśyatīty āhuḥ. ekībhavati, na jighratīty āhuḥ. ekībhavati, na rasayata ity āhuḥ. ekībhavati, na vadatīty āhuḥ. ekībhavati, na śṛnotīty āhuḥ. ekībhavati, na manuta ity āhuḥ. ekībhavati, na spṛśatīty āhuḥ. ekībhavati, na vijānātīty āhuḥ. tasya haitasya hṛdayasyāgraṁ pradyotate; tena pradyotenaiṣa ātmā niṣkrāmati cakṣuṣto vā mūrdhno vā 'nyebhyo vā śarīra-deśebhyaḥ. tam utkrāmantaṁ prāṇo 'nūtkrāmati; prāṇam anūtkrāmantaṁ sarve prāṇā anūtkrāmanti. savijñāno bhavati; savijñānam evānvavakrāmati.'

[2] Ibid., 4. 4. 6: 'yo 'kāmo niṣkāma āptakāma ātma-kāmo, na tasya prāṇā utkrāmanti. brahmaiva san, brahmāpy eti.'

[3] Ibid., 4. 4. 13: 'yasyānuvittaḥ pratibuddha ātmā, asmin saṁdehye gahane praviṣṭaḥ, / sa viśva-kṛt, sa hi sarvasya kartā tasya, lokaḥ sa u loka eva.'

both Christianity and Islam, mystics do not lay claim to any praeternatural powers or arrogate to themselves the divine attributes of omnipotence and omniscience, that distinguishes them from purely paranoiac cases, among whom we must unfortunately reckon some of the later Ṣūfīs, and notably Abū Sa'īd bin Abī'l-Khayr whom Nicholson has introduced to European readers.[1] On the other hand the *Bṛhadāraṇyaka* passage seems to sum up in a nutshell some of Mr. Custance's more extraordinary sensations when in a state of mania.

Let us quote again from his writings. 'I feel so close to God,' he writes, 'so inspired by His Spirit that in a sense I am God. I see the future, plan the Universe, save mankind; I am utterly and completely immortal; I am even male and female. The whole Universe, animate and inanimate, past, present, and future, is within me. All nature and life, all spirits, are co-operating and connected with me; all things are possible. I am in a sense identical with all spirits from God to Satan. I reconcile Good and Evil and create light, darkness, worlds, universes.'[2] In short he feels himself to be both the creator of the world and the world itself; he comprises all eternity and all space.

This state is characteristic of acute mania, and there seems to be no way of avoiding the conclusion that what the *Bṛhadāraṇyaka* is describing in the passage quoted is this pan-en-henic experience with the added phenomenon that the adept sees himself not only as the All but also as the Creator. This is no longer speculation; it is felt experience, the experience of an abnormally expanded consciousness which is indistinguishable from the experiences we attempted to analyse in the first three chapters and from the experience of Mr. Custance when in a state of mania. If these words occurred elsewhere than in the Upaniṣads, there is little doubt that they would be classed as a typical example of extreme megalomania. Such ultra-pantheistic passages as these which are in such marked contrast to the rigid monism of the *Māṇḍūkya* can, however, be fitted into that extraordinary philosophy by equating the pantheistic vision with *māyā*.

Since the individual soul is identical not only with the 'higher' (undifferentiated) Brahman but also with the 'lower' (differentiated and creative) Brahman which evolves *māyā* (the world), the world will be seen as being one's self inside one's self because it is imagined by one's self as a dream; and it has absolutely no existence apart from the dreamer. So it is perfectly correct to describe oneself as the 'creator of the world'. This state of mind we have seen to be identical with the pan-en-henic experience. It is,

[1] R. A. Nicholson, *Studies in Islamic Mysticism*, Cambridge, 1921.

[2] See above, p. 91.

however, only a partial realization of the ultimate reality of the monists, for we are still in the realm of multiplicity, and Brahman still has characteristics. Identification with the *saguṇa Brahman*, 'the Brahman with qualities', only has been reached. The ultimate truth is that described in the *Māṇḍūkya* where the *nirguṇa Brahman*, 'the Brahman without qualities', is reached and in which there is no duality whatsoever.

The process seems to be approximately as follows: first the sage is visited by the pan-en-henic experience in which he sees no difference between 'within and without' and in which the outside world seems to be inside him. This experience he compares to dream experience and therefore concludes that the phenomenal world is really nothing more than a dream dreamt by himself. The only difference is that the phenomenal world remains persistently the same dream whereas the dreams of sleep are ever-changing. In trance, however, both the waking and the sleeping dream disappear and the subject is left conscious only of himself in his inmost essence. This essence he identifies with Brahman, the ground of the universe, because, in his pan-en-henic experience, he has 'realized' that the world is his own creation in that it is he who has imagined it, and that this creation is therefore illusory. Scripture, however, teaches that Brahman is the ground, the 'inner controller', and creator of the universe: the pan-en-henic experience, on the other hand, shows that 'I' am the creator of the universe. From this it follows logically that I am Brahman. Having discovered this, the only further step necessary is to practise Yoga with a view to detaching oneself from all the temporal and spatial things that one has imagined. Then one will realize onself, not, as the poor Sāṁkhya-Yogins and Marcel Proust thought, as one among many *puruṣas*, but as the sole existing reality. Beyond this, of course, it is impossible to go.

The passage we have quoted from the *Bṛhadāraṇyaka* represents, of course, only one of many views expressed in the Upaniṣads; and it seems to be based on a praeternatural experience akin to acute mania. This marks the Upaniṣads off clearly from early Greek speculative thought; for whereas their search for a first cause of the phenomenal world is paralleled in the speculations of the pre-Socratics, the monistic and pantheistic formulas can scarcely have been arrived at except as a result of praeternatural experience. Thus, whereas such phrases as 'He is the whole world' are as terse a formulation of the pan-en-henic experience as is likely to be found anywhere, 'Thou art that' and 'I am Brahman' express with equal concision the realization of the human soul as the Absolute or what it takes to be the Absolute. The two combine in the philosophy of Śankara and bear a distinct but deceptive resemblance to the more advanced speculations of

Christian and Muslim mystics. One main difference between the latter and the former is that while Brahman is conceived of as being beyond good and evil, the Christian God at least is, by definition, goodness itself since, according to St. Thomas, Good and Being are interchangeable terms. This is of course the salient practical difference between the two types of mysticism. Thus, while there are passages in the Upaniṣads which indicate clearly that good and evil are only relative terms since the Absolute is unaffected by them, this is never the case with the Christian and Muslim mystics so long as they remain orthodox. Eckhart's ambivalence on this point brought down on him the Papal condemnation. The clearest example of this amoralism we find in the Kauṣītakī Upaniṣad where we find the god Indra, speaking as the Absolute, boasting of the violent deeds attributed to him in the Rig-Veda; he says:

'Understand me as I am. This indeed I deem to be what is most useful to man,—to understand me. I slew the three-headed son of Tvaṣṭṛ; I delivered the Avāṅmukhas, ascetics, to the hyenas. Transgressing many compacts I transfixed the people of Prahlāda in the sky, the Paulomas in the atmosphere, the Kālakāńśyas on earth. Yet not one single hair of mine was injured. So with one who knows me, his world is injured by no deed whatsoever, not by the murder of his father, not by the murder of his mother, not by theft, not by the slaughter of an embryo. Whatever evil he does, he does not blanch.'[1]

Many theistic mystics have come across this mood and have issued the most vigorous warnings against it. We have already seen what Ruysbroeck has to say on the subject. Ghazālī, in a different context, is in agreement with him: he is speaking of persons who claim to be Ṣūfīs but whose conduct belies their claim:

'They claim', he says, 'that they have reached such a state of intimacy with God that they are absolved from the duty of prayer and that the drinking of wine, disobedience, and the living off state property become lawful to them. There is no doubt at all that such persons should be killed even though there may be a difference of opinion about their eternal punishment in Hell. The killing of one such person is more meritorious than the slaughter of a hundred infidels, since the harm they do to religion is greater; for they open up a door to licence which cannot be closed.'[2]

[1] *Kauṣītakī Up.*, 3. 1: 'mām eva vijānīhy. etad evāhaṁ manuṣyāya hitatamaṁ manye yan māṁ vijānīyāt. tri-śīrṣaṇaṁ tvāṣṭram ahanam. avāṅmukhān yatīn sālā-vṛkebhyaḥ prāyaccham. bahvīḥ saṁdhā atikramya divi prahlādīn atṛṇam aham, antarikṣe paulomān, pṛthivyāṁ kālakāśyāṅs. tasya me tatra na loma ca nāmīyate. sa yo māṁ vijānīyān, nāsya kena ca karmaṇā loko mīyate, na mātṛ-vadhena, na pitṛ-vadhena, na steyena, na bhrūṇa-hatyayā. nāsya pāpaṁ cana cakṛṣo mukhān nīlaṁ vettīti.'

[2] Ghazālī, *Fayṣal al-Tafriqa bayn al-Islām wa'l-Zandaqa*, *apud* Ṣabrī, *Jawāhir al-Ghawālī*, p. 94: 'wa-min jinsi dhālika

Junayd, too, who lived nearly two centuries before Ghazālī, was acutely aware of this amoral tendency which was already beginning to find favour among Ṣūfīs and which resulted in a complete quietism and moral laxness. He was asked to comment on the following thesis: 'Those who have a (direct) knowledge of God reach a state in which they leave behind them good works and the fear of God.' Junayd left his interlocutor in no doubt at all about his opinion. 'This is the doctrine', he said, 'proclaimed by those who teach "the falling away of works". In my opinion it is a monstrous doctrine. A fornicator or thief is better off than people who talk like that.'[1]

Ruysbroeck too saw that it was possible for false mystics to exist and that through them all mysticism might fall into discredit: his language is very nearly as strong as that of Ghazālī. 'These men', he says, 'all live in error and the greatest evil, and they are therefore to be shunned as is the fiend of hell. But if you have well understood the teaching which I have already expounded to you in various fashions, you will know well that they are deceived, for they live contrary to God and to righteousness and to all His saints. And they are all the forerunners of Antichrist, making ready his way that leads to every unbelief; for they wish to be free of the commandments of God and of virtue, and to be empty and united with God without love and charity.'[2]

This is the crux: for if we accept such isolated Upaniṣadic passages as 'He does not become greater by good action nor inferior by bad action'[3] and understand thereby that Brahman is beyond good and evil and necessarily indifferent to them, then we must say that Brahman, in so far as he is the first principle and therefore God, cannot be described as good: he is not the sum of all conceivable perfections as the Christian God is, he has no moral qualities whatever; and least of all can he be described as love since love implies duality, and what is 'One without a second' can neither love nor be loved.

It would then appear that there is more truth in the Hindu maxim that what we imagine, that we become, than is entirely comfortable. It seems

mā yadda'ī-hi ba'ḍu man yadda'ī'l-taṣawwufa, anna-hu qad balagha ḥālatan bayna-hu wa-bayna'llāhi ta'ālā, asqaṭat 'an-hu'l-ṣalāta wa-ḥalla la-hu shurbu'l-khamri wa'l-ma'āṣī wa-aklu māli'l-sulṭāni. fa-hādhā mim-man lā shakka fī wujūbi qatli-hi wa-in kāna fī'l-ḥukmi bi-khulūdi-hi fī'l-nāri naẓarun. wa-qatlu mithli hādhā afḍalu min qatli mā'ati kāfirin idh ḍararu-hu fī'l-dīni a'ẓamu, wa-yanfatiḥu bi-hi bābun min al-ibāḥati lā yansaddu.'

[1] Abū Abdulrahmān al-Sulamī, *Ṭabaqāt al-Ṣūfīya*, ed. Sudayba, Cairo, 1372/1953, p. 159: 'ahlu'l-ma'rifati bi'llāhi yaṣilūna ilā tarki'l-ḥarakāti min bābi'l-birri wa'l-taqwā ilā'llāhi ta'ālā. fa-qāla'l-Junaydu: inna hādhā qawlu qawmin takallamū bi-isqāṭi'l-a'māli, wa-hādhihi 'indī aẓīmatun; wa'lladhī yasriqu wa-yaznī aḥsanu ḥālan min alladhī yaqūlu hādhā.'

[2] *The Spiritual Espousals*, p. 173.

[3] *Bṛhadāraṇyaka Up.*, 4. 4. 22: 'sa na sādhunā karmaṇā bhūyān, no evāsādhunā kanīyān.'

that a convinced monist can only have a purely monistic experience, for any theistic experience would have to be written off by him as ultimately illusory, since personal gods are little more than convenient fictions. The case of Ruysbroeck, however, shows that the reverse is not true; for Ruysbroeck speaks so clearly of this 'natural rest in emptiness' which, as he himself says, is no sin that it can only be assumed that he had experienced it. What then of the combined experience of the All as oneself and oneself as the Absolute One? This is very nearly what Mr. Custance experienced and what seems to be the import of the passage from the Bṛhadāraṇyaka Upaniṣad with which we have just dealt. We have tried to show that this does not seem to tally with the experience of Christian mystics; but if we insist that it does, then it is plain that God is only another word for the spirit which animates all Nature, the power 'more subtle than electricity' of which Richard Jefferies speaks in which the concepts of good and evil have no meaning.

When we turn to the theistic mystics the picture is quite different: for according to them the end of man is not to participate in God in the mode of 'an insensible object' as Gauḍapāda would have it, or as an animal, but in the mode that is specific to the mystic as a human person, as 'an individual substance of rational nature', and as the image of God Himself. His 'deification' means the realization of God's idea of him as he existed for all eternity in His mind. This doctrine is as clear in Christianity as it is in Ṣūfism. The human soul is eternal in that it dwells in God as an eternal idea. St. Thomas Aquinas develops this theme in common with the mystics:

'God', writes the Angelic Doctor, 'is the first exemplary cause of all things. In proof whereof we must consider that if for the production of anything an exemplar is necessary, it is in order that the effect may receive a determinate form. For an artificer produces a determinate form in matter by reason of the exemplar before him, whether it be the exemplar beheld externally, or the exemplar interiorly conceived in the mind. Now it is manifest that things made by nature receive determinate forms. This determination of forms must be reduced to the divine wisdom as its first principle, for divine wisdom devised the order of the universe residing in the distinction of things. And therefore we must say that in the divine wisdom are the models of all things, which we have called *ideas*—*i.e.*, exemplary forms existing in the divine mind. And although these ideas are multiplied by their relations to things, nevertheless, they are not really distinct from the divine essence, inasmuch as the likeness of that essence can be shared diversely by different things. In this manner, therefore, God Himself is the first exemplar of all things.'[1]

The mystic, then, as Junayd saw, is engaged in realizing himself as his

[1] *Summa Theologica*, Q. 44, Art. 3 (tr. Anton C. Pegis).

own final cause; he is realizing himself as an idea inhering in the essence of God. Man must 'become what he is' as Jung has said; but once he has entered the created world his being will necessarily be different from the eternal being he has as an idea of God.

'They have been in Him as their eternal exemplar', Suso writes, and that exemplar 'is His eternal essence, in the sense in which it is communicated to the creatures, in order that they may participate in it. Note, however, that all creatures exist eternally as God in God, and are not distinguished in Him essentially, except in the sense already mentioned. They are the same life, essence and power, so far as they are in God, and are the same One and nothing less. But after the issuing forth, through which they receive their own being, every creature has its own special separate essence, its own form, which gives it its natural being, because form gives essence, separate and divided, both from the Divine essence and from all others. Thus, the natural form of the stone causes it to have its own being, for the stone is not God, and God is not the stone, although the stone and all creatures are what they are through Him. And in this issuing forth all creatures have attained their God, for when the creature finds itself to be a creature, it acknowledges its Creator and God.'[1]

And, Suso continues, 'the being of the creatures in God is not that of a creature, but the creatureliness of every creature is nobler for it, and more useful, than the being it has in God. For what advantage has a stone or a man or any creature in its status as a creature, from the fact that it has been eternally in God?'

Thus Suso, though a disciple of Eckhart, goes farther than both his master and Junayd, and maintains that man as he actually exists in this world has, at least humanly speaking, a greater dignity and a greater worth than he has as a pre-existent idea in God. This is not to devalue man in his eternal being in God, but to give to man as a *creature* of God a dignity on his own account which as an idea of God's he lacked. It is merely to state that in this respect the Heavenly Father in whose image man is made, does not differ from human fathers on earth; for what father ever valued his preconceived notion of what his son might be like more than the son who is actually born to him?

So too, Suso might claim, to be a created being is nobler than to inhere eternally in God; and this can only mean that the creature that emerges from the Divine Wisdom is endowed with a worth of its own which is freely bestowed on it by God and which makes it what it is. The newly created soul in grace is of value simply because, though issuing from God, it is distinct from Him in that it has a created freedom either to

[1] Henry Suso, *Little Book of Truth*, ch. iii, tr. J. M. Clark, London, Faber and Faber, 1953, p. 180.

return to Him and reunite with Him in that particular mode of love which only the creature can feel for its Creator and which in God and *qua* God it could never have enjoyed; alternatively it is free to rest in its own derived existence unaware that this existence is from God. This is what Adam did, and this is original sin. Therefore, since we inherit original sin, it is inaccurate to say that natural man, as he is in original sin, wilfully rejects God. Through Adam's sin and through his absurd egotism, through his desire to be like God without participation in Him, man is born in ignorance of the very existence of God. In the dreamless sleep of the embryo, as the psychologists have told us, there is a blissful unconsciousness, a physical union with the mother, a native innocence to which the individual in his 'manic', 'mystical', 'inspired', or merely lunatic moments aspires to return: for we are all one in Adam, and this oneness we, at rare moments or under the influence of drugs, can and do feel. Yet every human being repeats the sin of Adam in that he separates himself from his fellows as Adam separated himself from God. The instinct that makes the child say 'I' at a certain stage of his development is the inherited self-assertion of the First Man who made the supreme mistake of seeking eternal happiness in himself, in his *ātman*, rather than in God. So it is that in every discipline that calls itself mystical, the first step must be the taming, or rather the destruction, of the sense of individuality: only then can one say, 'I am Brahman', 'I am this all', thereby identifying oneself with undifferentiated Man or farther back still with undifferentiated Nature. And 'in this emptiness rest is sufficient and great, and it is in itself no sin, for it is in all men by nature, if they know how to make themselves empty'.

Assuming, as we are still encouraged to do, that man developed physically from the higher apes, we must interpret the creation of Adam as an original infusion of the divine essence into what had previously been an anthropoid ape. Adam, then, would represent the union of the orders of nature and grace, the order of coming to be and passing away which is created from nothing by God, and the infused spirit of God. Adam, after he sinned, brought bodily death into the world, but did not and could not destroy his soul, because the soul was infused into him from God and was therefore itself divine. Though Adam may have repented, he was no longer able to take the supreme step of offering himself back completely and entirely to God, because he had lost contact with his source and could no longer find it again. Thus, tradition has it, at death his soul departed to Limbo where, like all disinterested Yogins who have sought to separate their immortal souls from all that is transient and ungodlike, yet who cannot acknowledge God, it enjoyed the highest natural bliss, the soul's contemplation of itself as it issued from the hand of God and of all created things as they are in the sight of God. This natural bliss it could, and its successors often do, mistake for the final bliss of heaven where God is enjoyed in His entirety, His essence, and His eternity.

The proof, it seems to me, that I am not talking pure nonsense is in the complete difference of approach which separates the theistic from the monistic mystic. The latter achieves liberation entirely by his own efforts since there is no God apart from himself to help him or with Whom he can be united. In the case of the theistic mystic, on the other hand, it is always God who takes the first step, and it is God Who works in the soul and makes it fit for union. 'I sought for God for thirty years,' says our old friend Abū Yazīd, 'I thought it was I who desired Him, but no, it was He who desired me.'[1]

St. John of the Cross likened the soul in search of God to a log of wood which is consumed by fire in which the fire only is operative.

> 'The soul that is in a state of transformation of love may be said to be, in its ordinary habit, like to the log of wood that is continually assailed by the fire; and the acts of this soul are the flame that arises from the fire of love: the more intense is the fire of union, the more vehemently does its flame issue forth. In the which flame the acts of the will are united and rise upward, being carried away and absorbed in the flame of the Holy Spirit, even as the angel rose upward to God in the flame of the sacrifice of Manue. In this state, therefore, the soul can perform no acts, but it is the Holy Spirit that moves it to perform them; wherefore all its acts are Divine, since it is impelled and moved to them by God. Hence it seems to the soul that whensoever this flame breaks forth, causing it to love with the Divine temper and sweetness, it is granting it eternal life, since it raises it to the operation of God in God.'[2]

Such language is typical of all Christian mystics: in all cases they feel that there is very little that soul can itself do, for it is God Himself Who works in them and makes them fit for union. On the other side, as Mr. Custance tells us, it is equally true that in manic states it is possible to have experiences in which one thinks that one is God, creator and planner of the universe, and that this feeling is accompanied by an overwhelming conviction that this is no mere illusion. Thus it would appear that one can never be absolutely certain what the source of any given praeternatural experience is: the mere fact that it is overwhelmingly strong does not of itself prove that it is from God. On the contrary a strong case could be made

[1] Badawī, *Shaṭḥāt al-Ṣūfīya*, vol. i, p. 69: 'ṭalabtu'llāha thalāthīna sannatan, fa-idhā anā ẓanantu annī aradtu-hu, fa-idhā hūwa arāda-nī.'

[2] *The Living Flame of Love*, tr. E. Allison Peers, London, Burns Oates and Washbourne, 1953, pp. 18–19.

out that the experiences of the saints in ecstasy are really no different from the manic states described by Mr. Custance, and that both derive from the collective unconscious.

We have already said that when the mystic claims attributes that are necessarily divine and demonstrably not human,—such as omnipotence and omniscience,—it is fairly clear that he is not enjoying union with God, but rather some sort of natural mystical experience. Apart from this important consideration it would seem that the mystic who is genuinely inspired by the divine love, will show this to the world by the holiness of his life and by an abiding humility in face of the immense favours bestowed which always he will see to be God's doing, not his own. Only such criteria can enable us to distinguish between the genuine state of union with God and the 'natural' or rather 'praeternatural' phenomena we have been discussing.

I have tried to show that both manic states and the self-isolation of the Sāṁkhya-Yoga can be theologically interpreted, in their very different ways, as a return to the state of original innocence and that this is very much how Jung interprets the collective unconscious, namely a consciousness that precedes individuality and which may therefore be regarded as either prenatal or as that consciousness which is generically present in man. In the words of one of Jung's younger disciples,

'the "collective" refers to a level of psychic contents that is deeper than, prior to, and more fundamental than the individual personality . . . in the sense that as something generically present in *man*, it is collectively held by all men. Most essentially what Jung intends to convey by his concept is not that the unconscious is held in common as a collective inheritance, but rather that the unconscious contains materials which are held collectively by all men *because* they have a psychic reality which is *prior to personal experience*.'[1]

That Jung admits the God-archetype as being the most powerful constituent in the collective unconscious, and the one which can develop into the most formidable 'autonomous complex', does not, of course, mean that God exists only in the collective unconscious and is therefore only a *psychological* as opposed to an ontological reality. As St. Thomas, Suso and many others have said, God is our eternal exemplar; and, being the ground of the human soul, it follows that, according to Christian dogma, this exemplar must be the heart and centre of the human psyche. The 'God-archetype' is a perfectly correct way of describing the 'image of God' which is in all of us, for it was in this image that Adam was created. This archetype

[1] Ira Progoff, *Jung's Psychology and its Social Meaning*, London, Routledge and Kegan Paul, 1953, pp. 53–54.

can never appear perfectly in a mere human being since it must be distorted by original sin. No true image is likely to be reflected by a rusty mirror, as the Ṣūfīs never tire of pointing out. The purpose of asceticism is to polish the mirror so that the reflection or image of God may perfectly emerge. So far non-theistic mysticism may take us: it can polish the mirror by the practice of total detachment from created things in order that the reflection of the One Reality may be seen. The real mystical experience in which God takes over from His own image, begins only when the rust and the dirt have been removed. The dirt and the rust are called *upādhis* or 'illusory adjuncts' in the Vedānta system; but whereas the Vedānta leaves off when the mirror is clean, it is only at this point that the *via mystica* proper of the Christian begins. Moreover, the mirrors, which are our souls, are more often than not distorting mirrors, and they are bound to be so if the doctrine of original sin is both meaningful and true: and such distortions are liable to be taken for the truth by anyone who has not had actual experience of the truth. Thus the God-archetype is liable to appear in mythology, as in the visions of neurotics, in an often absurdly distorted form. All the mythological archetypes are, as Jung would say, psychologically true, but they do not correctly represent the truth because, one and all, they are distorted in the imperfect mirror of fallen man. Thus it is that the experience of so-called mystics, though they always reflect the truth of the oneness of Being, reflect it falsely, for even a perfect mirror cannot exactly reproduce the reality. A reflection of the sun remains a reflection and can never be the sun.

According to an obscure sect in South-West Persia called the *Ahl i Ḥaqq* the sun, or his representative, periodically becomes incarnate on earth. This again is psychologically true; for the true nature of God can only be made comprehensible to man if it is presented in human form. All the major religions that are not atheistical hold that God in His essence is ultimately incomprehensible to the intellect: nor could He or can He be even partially comprehended unless He condescends to manifest Himself in human form. And if He does this, then this Man-God must be what Jung calls psychologically true as well as morally true. If it is true that God is Love, pure Being, and pure Goodness, it follows that the God-Man, besides exhibiting all the moral virtues in their most perfect form, must also make a complete sacrifice of his purely human 'self' to God, for as man he must pay back the existence he has been lent by Him. The mythological saviour gods of antiquity and the great incarnate gods of India are all unsatisfactory from the mystical point of view; for the essence of theistic mysticism is expressed in the two key words of the Ṣūfīs,—*fanā* and *baqā*, the 'destruction' of the individual soul to God and its 'survival' in God and as God. 'For when a man is thus taken out of himself, so that he neither knows anything about himself, nor about anything else, and above all, is made calm in the ground of the eternal Nothing, then he is really lost to himself'[1] and dead to himself.

Thus, even if there were no historical truth in the Christian myth, it is at least an enactment on earth of what all theistic mystics claim to experience. Christ, however, both as God and as Man, is exempt from sin; he was what the Indians would call a *jīvanmukta*, 'one liberated while still alive'; that is to say, He is the second Adam, free from sin, and therefore always in a state of beatitude, the Image of God, unwarped and unsoiled. His life and His death reflect faithfully the very life of God,—a life that is a perpetual giving, and giving again. Christ's morality is no longer a morality of negatives; it is no longer 'Thou shalt not kill', but 'Love thine enemy'; no longer 'Thou shalt not steal', but 'give your coat as well as your cloak': it is the morality of 'Be ye perfect even as your Father in heaven is perfect', and of 'Love one another' even as the Persons of the Holy Trinity love one another.

Christ was Man as well as God; and as Man there was no other end possible for Him except death on the Cross; for by the Cross was symbolized the essential relationship between the creature and its Creator. The creature has no existence of its own: all it has, it has from God; and only by restoring its borrowed existence to its rightful Owner, knowing that by so doing it will be no more, can the proper relationship between Creator and creature be restored. Christ's sacrifice, the total sacrifice of what has being only on loan to Being itself, is the perfect exemplar of the sacrifice that all men must make if they wish to share in the life of God, and not merely to enjoy the contemplation of their own soul. And, as in the mystical experience of those who believe in God, there is no *fanā* without *baqā*, no immolation without survival, so was it necessary for Christ both to die on the four-cornered Cross which symbolizes wholeness and to rise again from the dead, immortal as Man and eternal in His Godhead. It was necessary for the corruptible to put on the incorruptible so that man might fully share in the life of God.

At the same time it was necessary that Christ should be God as well as Man, not only that the sacrifice should have infinite value as theology teaches us, but that God Himself might be seen as He is, as a perpetual giving of Himself: and it was necessary too in order that we might understand this at least about God, that His creation is not, as some Hindus would have us

[1] Suso, *The Little Book of Truth*, p. 198.

believe, a 'sport' or a dream; it is something to which He is wholly committed, and for which He assumes a human body and lets that body suffer the death of the Cross to show mankind that though He is and always will be misunderstood, He understands that our finite minds find the whole thing infinitely puzzling, and that there is no way of convincing us that all will be made well, as Julian of Norwich puts it, except by Himself taking on death and suffering that He may be one with us in all things. 'Greater love hath no man than that he should lay down his life for his friends.' So God dies on the Cross so that we may live eternally in Him; and by the Cross He symbolizes the very life of the Godhead, the Son dying always to the Father and living always and eternally in the Holy Ghost, 'the Lord and Giver of life'.

Similarly, just as Christ's death and resurrection are a physical enactment of the spiritual reality of the mystical experience, and beyond it of the Beatific Vision, so is the mystical experience itself the image of the life of God in His Trinity.

'For out of this same unity the Everlasting Word is evermore born of the Father, and through this birth the Father acknowledges the Son and in the Son all things. And the Son acknowledges the Father and in the Father all things, for They are one single nature. And out of this mutual contemplation of the Father and the Son in Their eternal illumination, there flows an eternal satisfaction, an unfathomable love, and that is the Holy Spirit. And through the Holy Spirit and the everlasting wisdom, God inclines Himself in discretion towards each one of His creatures, and gives to each one and enkindles him in love according to his excellence and according to the state in which he is and is chosen through his virtues and the eternal providence of God.'[1]

It seems strange that a Muslim mystic, no less a one than Abū Yazīd of Bisṭām, despite the influences that had been at work on him, saw that where there is love, there must there be trinity as well as unity. 'I looked and saw', he is reported as saying, 'that Lover, Love, and Beloved are all one, for in the world of union all must be One.'[2] The same instinct prompted another Ṣūfī to say when asked about the divine Unity, 'Union, He Who unites, and He Who is united,—and that is three'.[3] This, then, is the life in which man is called to share,—*sat, cit, ānanda*,—Being, Awareness, and Bliss,—

[1] Ruysbroeck, *The Spiritual Espousals*, p. 136.

[2] Farīdu'd-Dīn 'Aṭṭār, *Tadhkiratu'l-Awliyā*, vol. i, p. 160: 'nigah kardam, 'āshiq va ma'shūq va 'ishq yakī dīdam kih dar 'ālam i tawḥīd hameh yakī tavān būd.' The attribution to Abū Yazīd is probably not genuine.

[3] Qushayrī, *Risāla*, p. 136, l. 30: 'tawḥīdun wa-muwaḥḥidun wa-muwaḥḥadun, hādhihi thalāthatun.' So too for Abraham Abulafia, the thirteenth-century Jewish mystic, the Master 'is called *Sekhel*, *Maskil* and *Muskal*, that is the *Knowledge*, the *Knower* and the *Known*, all at the same time, since all three are one in Him'. See Gershom G. Scholem, *Major Trends in Jewish Mysticism*, London, Thames and Hudson, 1955, p. 141.

the Father, the Word, and the Spirit of Love,—the life of the three Persons of the Holy Trinity which must be Three as well as One since love is a sheer impossibility if there is neither lover nor beloved, just as knowledge is a sheer impossibility if there is neither knower nor known.

'You shall know that the heavenly Father, as He is a living depth, has gone operatively with all that lives in Him into His Son, as into the everlasting wisdom which is He; and this same wisdom, and all that lives in it, is operatively returned again into the Father, that is into the same depths whence it proceeds. And from this meeting springs the third Person, between the Father and the Son, that is the Holy Ghost, the love of Them both, Who is one with both of Them in the same nature. And the Holy Ghost embraces and transfuses, operatively and in delectation, the Father and the Son and all that lives in Them, with so great riches and joy that concerning this all creatures must evermore be silent. For the incomprehensible miracle that lies in this love everlastingly exceeds the comprehension of all creatures. But in the spirit, above himself and one with the Spirit of God, man understands and savours this wonder without wonderment, and tastes and sees without measure as God does, the riches which are God, in the unity of the living depths where man possesses Him according to the manner of His uncreated being.'[1]

[1] Ruysbroeck, *The Spiritual Espousals*, p. 189.

CHAPTER X

CONCLUSION

In the course of this book we have tried to investigate the truth of the assertion that 'mysticism' is an unvarying phenomenon observable throughout the entire world and at all ages, and that it may (and does) make its appearance in all and any religious system. This thesis is commonly supported by 'indifferentists', those generous but loose-minded persons who would have us believe that all religions are equally true and that proselytism of any sort is therefore wrong, and that the Spirit of God manifests itself in different guises throughout the length and breadth of this wide world, adapting itself to the different conditions of men and exhibiting the One Truth here in Jesus Christ, there in Krishna or in the Buddha, or again in Lao Tzu or Muhammad. This view may be dictated by greatness of heart: it has, however, all too frequently been associated with a distaste for constructive thought exhibiting itself in theology, and for dogmatism of any kind, and it has too often sprung from an intellectual laziness which would content itself with comfortable half-truths rather than come to grips with the hard facts which so persistently and unkindly break into the fine-spun web of good intentions. It is only when the facts have been grasped and the differences analysed that there can be any hope of discerning a divine purpose behind the always antagonistic and sometimes warring creeds. The function of the student of comparative religion must be to analyse the facts and point out the differences; only then will he be in a position to see whether or not it is possible to discern sufficient common ground between the different manifestations of religion to justify him in attempting to discover whether a divine plan is discernible or whether the whole of creation and man's sojourn on earth are nothing more than a joke, the *līlā* or sport of the deity as some Hindus would maintain.

In this book our investigations have led to the tentative conclusion that what goes by the name of mysticism, so far from being an identical expression of the selfsame Universal Spirit, falls into three distinct categories. Under the general heading of mysticism we have not included those experiences that are sometimes associated with it,—clairvoyance, clair-audition, telepathy, thought-reading, levitation, bi-location, and the rest: we have confined ourselves to praeternatural experiences in which sense perception and discursive thought are transcended in an immediate apperception of a unity or union which is apprehended as lying beyond and transcending the multiplicity of the world as we know it. Because these experiences are recorded at all times and from all parts of the world, it is fatally easy to assume that because they are, one and all, praeternatural, that is, not explicable in the present state of our knowledge, and because the keynote of all of them is 'union', they must necessarily be the same. It is not realized often enough that once these experiences are assumed to be identical and of identical provenance, the conclusion that the transports of the saint and the ecstasies of the manic are identical cannot be escaped. If this were really so, and if these praeternatural experiences were what religion is principally concerned with, then the only sensible course to adopt would be that which Rimbaud followed: we should all attempt to induce in ourselves an attack of acute mania; and this is in fact the solution that Mr. Huxley seems to propound in *The Doors of Perception*.

That 'nature mysticism' exists and is widely attested is not open to serious doubt. How the experience is to be explained is quite another matter. To identify it with the experience of Christian or Muslim saints, however, is hardly admissible, as I hope to have shown, however inadequately, in the course of this work. In this connexion it is significant that though Mr. Custance christened his familiar spirit Tyche-Teresa in recognition of the supposed fact that the Saint of Avila's experiences were comparable to, or even identical with, his own, he never quotes from her works though the words of Plotinus come readily enough to his lips.

Though it is easy enough to dismiss the experiences of the nature mystic as mere hallucination, this is really begging the question; for, in all cases of this experience, the impression of *reality* they leave behind is quite overwhelming. In every case,—whether the experience comes unheralded or whether it is produced by drugs or Yoga techniques,—the result is the same;—the person who has had the experience feels that he has gone through something of tremendous significance beside which the ordinary world of sense perception and discursive thought is almost the shadow of a shade. Huxley expresses this with the German word *Istigkeit*, and he has thereby fully caught the mood. The experience seems overpoweringly *real*; its authority obtrudes itself and will not be denied. It is this quality in it, I believe, which makes those who have been the subject of such a visitation assume that this must be identical with what the mystical saints have experienced. The Ṣūfīs reply to their critics by saying that their criticism is about as valid as that of a teetotaller who vainly tries to understand the pleasures of drunkenness without ever having tasted wine. It will not help him to know that wine is the fermented juice of the grape or what its chemical constituents are: until he has actually drunk deeply, he will never understand the exhilaration of the drinker. Similarly no child who has not reached the age of adolescence can understand what pleasure there can possibly be in the sexual act which seems to him revolting. So with the nature mystics,—it is extremely difficult for the purely rational man to understand in what the excitement and the joy consist, or why it should be that the sensation of losing one's individuality should be so intensely prized. No comparison is adequate: the nearest, perhaps, as Huxley saw, is an intense absorption in music or painting, or in dancing, for all these can be used as aids to produce such a condition, and the Ṣūfīs introduced song and dance, and the contemplation of beautiful boys, very early as aids to the attainment of praeternatural states. Yet even so, they can serve only as the faintest adumbrations, they can scarcely claim even to approximate to the real thing.

Ṣūfism is, in this respect, perhaps more instructive than either Christian or Indian mysticism. The distinction that Qushayrī drew between *basṭ*, or the sense of one's personality expanding indefinitely, and actual communion with God, is rarely met with again, and the opposition of the conservatives to the use of song and dance as stimulants broke down all too soon, because, as Ṣūfism degenerated, the achievement of ecstasy as such became the Ṣūfī's goal regardless of whether such ecstasies proceeded from the hand of God or not. The later Ṣūfīs came to assume that all ecstasy was divine, and thereby put a ready weapon into the hands of the orthodox: for whereas sanctity is its own argument, mania is not, and no genuinely religious person is likely to be impressed by one who claims either to be in direct communion with God or actually to be identical with Him, if his conduct is, in fact, sub-human. Thus the confusion that is popularly made between nature mysticism and the mysticism of the Christian saints can only discredit the latter. By making the confusion one is forced into the position that God is simply another term for Nature; and it is an observable fact that in Nature there is neither morality nor charity nor even common decency. God, then, is reduced to the sum-total of natural impulses in which the terms 'good' and 'evil' have no meaning. Such a god is sub-human, a god fit for animals, not for rational creatures; and to experience such a god has rightly been termed 'downward transcendence' by Mr. Huxley.

In *The Doors of Perception* Huxley uses the following admirable phrase: 'I was seeing what Adam had seen on the morning of his creation—the miracle, moment by moment, of naked existence.' However one interprets the legend of the first man in Genesis, I think that Huxley has hit upon a fruitful idea. If we accept the theory of the evolution of man's body from that of the higher apes, we are still faced with the insuperable problem of how man developed both an aesthetic and a moral sense of which there is no sign at all in all the brute creation, unless this were somehow infused into him by a power that was itself possessed of these two qualities in a superlative degree. How was it possible for the Adam of Mr. Huxley to see beauty of such intense meaningfulness in what is to the mere animal only a hunting-ground for food? It is, then, not far-fetched, if we accept the hypothesis of a first man at all, whatever his purely bodily origin may have been, to suppose that Adam did see something very much like what Mr. Huxley saw,—Nature seen for the first time *as it is* by the first creature who was capable of discerning beauty, and simultaneously felt intensely as the very substance from which his animal being had been drawn. This vision was in fact not beyond, but prior to, good and evil, for Adam, having no neighbours, had no duties towards them, while in Nature he experienced the beauty of God's handiwork which could only make him love God the more. Adam's innocence was the innocence of a child, and it was only on reaching man's estate that, like the heroes of the psychological romances of all schools of psychology, he was assailed by the original Oedipus complex, the desire to set up house for himself and to do away with his Father. That is original sin.

According to the Judaeo-Christian legend Adam's body was formed 'from the slime of the earth' (Gen. ii. 7) and his spirit was infused into him by God. According to a Zoroastrian catechism God (Ohrmazd) is man's father and the earth is his mother.[1] If we accept this story for the purposes of our present argument in place of the similar account of Genesis ii, the Oedipus complex is even more clear. If Adam's experience of Nature was that of the nature mystic, then original sin will appear as the prototype and archetype of the Oedipus complex itself: Adam rejects the heavenly Father in favour of Mother Nature, the Earth. He returns to Nature not as he was when still an animal, but as a man who sees all the beauty of Nature which she has nevertheless not of herself but of God. His contemplation of the 'miracle, moment by moment, of naked existence' was God's gift to him at the moment he emerged from ape-hood into manhood: He showed Nature to him as in His own eyes He had made it, and it was 'very good'. Adam's sin, seen in this context, was to reject God, the Father, in favour of Nature, his 'mother', from whom his body derived, regardless of the fact that the beauty he saw in her could never have been any more apparent to him than it was to the apes, had God not given him the gift of discerning beauty in her. Original sin, then, is to mistake the lesser good for goodness

[1] R. C. Zaehner, *The Teachings of the Magi*, p. 21.

itself, to mistake created beauty for the uncreate Godhead. It is, as Jung rightly points out, a recession to childhood and beyond, for by falling in love with Mother Nature Adam would have thereby refused to accept the moral and social duties that marriage and the propagation of children brought with them. Had he not rejected God, he would have seen that the moral law, 'natural law' as the theologians call it, is the same divine law operating in human affairs as are the laws of Nature in the purely natural order. The *ṛta* of the Vedic poets and the *dharma* of their successors express precisely this: it is the divine law as expressed in Nature as the orderly procession of cause and effect, and in moral human behaviour it is the 'natural law' as applicable to man which, were it not for original sin, he would see to be as inevitable as is the operation of the laws of Nature in the physical world. Sin brings its own punishment as inevitably as the heating of water to a given temperature produces steam; and this idea is perfectly expressed in the Indian doctrine of *karma*,—actions, always and everywhere, produce their good and evil fruits in the agent.

I am painfully aware that all the explanations I have offered for the natural mystical experience have been inadequate: we are always reduced to similes, and can only hope that the similes throw some light on the nature of the problem. But the problem is there and must be faced: and it is the problem of praeternatural experiences which take account of neither good nor evil. If my halting explanations seem childish, then I can only hope that qualified theologians will produce something more convincing. The problem, however, seemed worth stating.

Secondly a word must be said in conclusion about the validity of Jung's researches and the effect they are likely to have on religion. It will not, I hope, be unfair to say that Jung does not know himself where he stands theologically since he is not concerned with the God of any theology but with the God-archetype as he finds it in his patients; and this archetype appears in protean and ambivalent forms. I have pointed out in another chapter that Jung's attitude towards evil seems to be fundamentally Manichaean. The 'dark, feminine', instinctive side of human nature is what we have inherited from the animals; it is neither good nor evil, but has, as Jung has demonstrated, great potentialities for both. That it must be integrated into the total psyche, few will deny; but to equate it with moral evil or with the Devil, and then to assert that evil as such has to be integrated into the whole psyche, shows a certain confusion of thought. Because the Manichees did precisely this, because they identified matter with concupiscence[1] and asserted that this, rather than pride, was the root

[1] The Greek ὕλη appears in the Middle Persian Manichaean texts as *āz*, 'concupiscence'.

of all evil, they were condemned by the Church as the *pessima haeresium*. What Jung appears to mean is that the material, instinctive, and non-rational side of our nature must be given its proper place in the integrated psyche. Ghazālī somewhere likens the relationship between the rational soul and the twin faculties of lust and anger to a man, his pack-animal, and his dog, the proper place of the two latter being that of an obedient servant. So too the Hindus speak of 'taming' the passions (*dam-*, *dānta*). This relationship which, in Islam, goes back to Plato's *Republic* seems as good a way of describing the integrated personality as any. Beyond integration, however, there is again separation, the separation of the immortal soul from all its mortal trappings, of *yang* from *yin*, of *puruṣa* from *prakṛti*. This would normally take place in the second half of life when the instincts lose much of their force and the isolation of the spirit seems less 'unnatural'. This is what is prescribed by the Sāṁkhya-Yoga: it is the natural preparation of the soul for life after death. Given the immortality of the soul, it is little more than a reasonable precaution, for it can be readily believed that a discarnate existence for which one is unprepared can be as profoundly disquieting as that described by Mr. Huxley in *Time must have a Stop*.

However, if there is a God, and if it is true that our relations with Him will be very much more intimate after death, then 'it is not enough to know only that He exists, but one must know His nature and His will'.[1] This is even more important for the mystic than it is for the ordinary man, for the mystic is in fact the man who has a foretaste in this life of life after death; and just as the experiences of those who have taken mescalin have, to a certain extent, varied according to their beliefs, so will the experiences of persons who tame their senses and discipline their minds with a view to reaching a higher reality.

Indian religion is right in describing the object of religious disciplines as being *mokṣa* or liberation. By this they mean liberation from what St. Paul calls 'the flesh', that is, the life of blind instinct, the animal in man. Beyond this they also seek liberation from the third of Avicenna's three components of the lower soul, 'imagination' or distracting thought. As their final goal the Sāṁkhya-Yogins seek their own immortal soul in its nakedness and isolation. Having no clear idea of God, they cannot seek union with Him, nor do they claim to.

The Vedāntins are in a different case. The Upaniṣads teach that Brahman is both the source of all things and that He includes all things. Greater than all the universe, he is yet the fine point without magnitude which is the

[1] *Škand-Gumānīk Vičār*, ed. Menasce, Fribourg, 1945, p. 117 (ch. 10, § 37).

deep centre of the human heart. In so far as they teach this, they are fully at one with the mystical teaching of the Catholic Church. However, they also teach that Brahman *is* the universe and that he *is* the human soul. Rāmānuja and his followers interpret this as being a metaphor and as meaning that the universe and human souls are what he calls the 'body' of God whereas God or Brahman remains distinct from them though they are wholly dependent on Him. Here again there is full agreement between Rāmānuja and Catholic mystical tradition. Whether Rāmānuja or Śankara more accurately represents the general trend of Upaniṣadic teaching must be left to the Hindus to decide. It is, however, fair to point out that the concept of *māyā*, the cosmic illusion, is only adumbrated and never formulated in the classical Upaniṣads themselves. Śankara and his followers, by establishing complete identity between the human soul and the Absolute, do in fact accept the Sāṁkhya-Yoga view *in practice*, for self-realization means for them, no less than for the Sāṁkhya-Yogin, the isolation of the immortal soul from all that is not itself. As we have tried to point out in another chapter there is much in the Vedānta philosophy which fits in with what Mr. Custance says when in a manic state, particularly the claim that the 'released' individual must make to be identical with the creator (of an imaginary universe). Precisely these views were attacked by Ruysbroeck who rightly saw that all people who firmly held them, must think that they had reached the highest possible mystical state, what the Hindus call the *paramā gatiḥ*, whereas they had only reached the stage of self-isolation, of rest and 'emptiness' within themselves. Believing this to be union with God, they were prevented from taking any further step because they believed there was no further step to take. This, for Ruysbroeck, as for any Christian, was manifestly absurd, for how, as Abū Yazīd once said,[1] could one ever come to the end of the Godhead?

Here, then, are two distinct and mutually opposed types of mysticism, —the monist and the theistic. This is not a question of Christianity and Islam *versus* Hinduism and Buddhism: it is an unbridgeable gulf between all those who see God as incomparably greater than oneself, though He is, at the same time, the root and ground of one's being, and those who maintain that soul and God are one and the same and that all else is pure illusion. For them Christian mysticism is simply *bhakti* or devotion to a personal god carried to ludicrous extremes, whereas for the theist the monist's idea of 'liberation' is simply the realization of his immortal soul in separation from God, and is only, as Junayd pointed out, a stage in the path of the beginner. He is still in the bondage of original sin.

[1] See above, p. 165.

Hinduism has its theists as well as its monists; and the Bhagavad-Gītā as well as Rāmānuja stand nearer to St. John of the Cross than they do to Śankara. This is a quarrel that cuts clean across the conventional distinctions of creeds. In each of the great religions there have been upholders of both doctrines. Even Christianity has not completely avoided the monistic extreme even though it makes nonsense of its basic doctrine that God is Love. Meister Eckhart, for instance, at times adopted a fully monistic position, and Angelus Silesius could well be interpreted monistically though a literal interpretation of the *Cherubinischer Wandersmann*, taken out of the context of his other work, is scarcely permissible since mystics, when writing in verse, allow themselves, like all poets, the boldest figures of speech.

Nevertheless, the Christian mystical tradition is, on the whole, strongly opposed to monism for the reasons already stated. The same is true of Indian theists; and the fact that the two traditions have existed in India side by side seems to be sufficient refutation of the theory, which is a half-truth only, that sectarian dogma necessarily modifies the actual nature of the mystic's experience. Rāmānuja's quarrel with Śankara is as fundamental as Ruysbroeck's with the Beghards. For neither was this a question of different paths leading to one goal; it was the goal itself that was in question. The fact that there has never been an official orthodoxy in India makes the struggle there the more interesting, for the mystical current could not thus be diverted, if diversion it is, into any one theological channel. The mystic was (and is) free to follow the most rigid monism or some type of theism. Hence the interest of Rāmakrishna who, though a professed non-dualist Vedāntin, nevertheless is at his best and most convincing when he worships God as the 'Mother' as Julian of Norwich had done in Europe in very different circumstances. Rāmakrishna succeeded in breaking through the monistic shell because his nature was naturally expansive and his whole attitude to life was one of love. His case shows that the grace of God is withheld from no one, whatever his inherited theology, provided he is animated by charity. This could not be, if what Christians affirm is not true, namely, that God is Love.

Similarly, although the strictly orthodox among the Muslims maintained that it is not legitimate to speak of the love of God because love implies kinship and God is unlike His creation in every respect, the Ṣūfīs nevertheless made love the foundation of their relationship with God and finished up (in Junayd and Ghazālī) by reaching a position that approaches very closely to that of St. John of the Cross. All this goes to show that where there is genuine love, there will God be: and not only will He be there, He will make His presence deeply felt. Christian mysticism and Muslim mysticism at its best are not, whatever they may be, the mere upsurge of the God-archetype from the unconscious. They are what they claim to be, an intimate communion of the human soul with its Maker; and since God is holy and absolute goodness, the mystic, so far as he is united with God, will be absolutely free from sin. He will not be either above or beyond good and evil, but evil will not be able to touch him, since in God who is perfect there is no possibility of evil, the essence of imperfection.

In the words of Suso, 'In so far as man remains in himself, he can fall into sin, as Saint John says: "If we say that we have no sin, we deceive ourselves, and the truth is not in us." But in so far as he does not remain in himself, he does not commit sin, as Saint John says in his *Epistle*, that the man who is born of God does not sin, nor err, for the Divine seed remains in him.'[1] This doctrine must be true for any soul that is actually 'deified' in God, as St. John of the Cross would say. No living man, however, can presume that the union he enjoys with God can be so perfect that a lapse is no longer possible. This is precisely what Ruysbroeck accused the Beghards of doing. By mistaking a monistic 'possession of their own souls' for identification with the Deity, they considered that whatever they did or did not do must be perfect because divine. This Junayd called *isqāṭ al-aʿmāl*, 'the falling away of works', and condemned it in the strongest possible terms. Ghazālī went farther still and, being an orthodox Muslim at least in so far as conforming to the religious law was concerned, he considered the slaughter of such heretics to be a pious work. Such passions are not raised in humane men except when they see a gross perversion of what they hold to be the truth. Thus it seems that theists and monists cannot ever agree; for the former see in the latter's final state only the isolation of the soul in 'natural rest', while the latter regard the transports of the former as an early stage on the way to isolation, the stage of *bhakti* which, for the monist, means paying homage to a deity which one has oneself imagined. This is, perhaps, because in India the available deities as represented in legend could not satisfy the religious mind as being undistorted images of the one true God.

Ruysbroeck attacked the monists of his time on the grounds that the mysticism they practised was devoid of love: hence they could not possibly get beyond their 'self' in the Jungian sense, their *ātman*. Because they were able to find within themselves 'sufficient rest', they thought they had reached the highest bliss attainable by man. In actual fact, Ruysbroeck maintained, they were shutting themselves off from God; and this is bound to happen to the mystic whose religion only offers him an inadequate image of God.

[1] *The Little Book of Truth*, p. 196.

In Christ, Christianity claims, God manifested Himself perfectly. Not only is the moral stature of Christ infinitely superior to that of the deities of the Hindu pantheon, but His life, death, and resurrection represent in the body what the mystic must experience in the soul. Even if we interpret the story of the resurrection in purely Jungian terms,—the death of the 'ego' and the birth of the 'self' in the resurrected Christ,—even so the 'self' must then ascend to the Father as Christ ascended into heaven and 'sitteth at the right hand of God, the Father, Almighty'. The Christian 'myth' is the complete antithesis to the monistic type of 'religion', for it is no more possible for Christ to exist apart from the Father and the Holy Ghost than it is for natural man to rid himself of his intellect and will. Hence the Son of Man, having crucified the 'ego' on the Cross, ascends into heaven where He is eternally united with the Father through the force of attraction which is the Holy Ghost Who is substantial love and substantial joy. Thus, paradoxically enough, the doctrine of the Trinity, so far from being a stumbling-block in the mystic's way to being 'oned' with God, is his most effective aid; for even Eckhart is always returning to it, monist though he appears to be. God cannot *be* love, as St. John the Evangelist teaches, if He is not at the same time Three, for love is an impossibility if there is neither lover nor beloved. True, the procession of the Holy Ghost comes logically after the Father and the Son because without these Two the Third Who is love cannot exist or operate; but the Holy Ghost is none the less the centre and essence of the Godhead; He is what makes God God, for whereas man, God's image, can never become identical with what he thinks, in God the divine Thought, because it can only be perfect, is always swept back into the divine Being by the irresistible power of the Holy Ghost Who, being the Living Flame of Love, eternally welds the divine substance into an indissoluble unity in which Being is Thought through the miracle of the Spirit of Love through Whom the other Two have distinct being in one thrice holy substance. *Sat, Cit, Ānanda*: Being, Thought, and Joy, this is how the Vedāntins define Brahman, and the definition is, from the Christian point of view, absolutely correct; for despite Śankara's interpretation of the doctrine, such a God is no Parmenidean monad. He is a *living* God endlessly rejoicing in Himself; and His joy in Himself and His love of His Son Whom He eternally conceives in Himself is the crown and perfection of His Godhead. And as God is in Himself, so does He operate in the human soul when it attains to the Beatific Vision; for as Christ was conceived in Mary's womb, so is He conceived in the receptive soul which thereby enters into the full life of the Trinity where it shares in the eternal outpouring of the Holy Ghost rejoicing for ever in His Being and his Thought.

APPENDIX A

SOME RECENT MESCALIN EXPERIMENTS

THE following account by Mrs. Rosalind Heywood was published in the *Manchester Guardian* on 29 May 1954.

'. . . My claim to comment on these adventurous proposals is that I too have acted as a guinea-pig for scientists investigating mescalin and have shared Mr. Huxley's revelation, though in another form. The drug caused him to see our normal world transfigured and made profoundly more significant. It pitchforked me into an inner world, overwhelming and different in kind from that mediated to us by our senses. Are we all, I wonder, quite ready for that? Choirs of Seraphs might lull some babies to sleep. Being flung into the Bay of Biscay might teach them to swim. But others would find these things a strain.

Mescalin, it will be remembered, induces a temporary condition of schizophrenia, but it cannot be predicted what form this will take for any particular person. From Mr. Huxley's account he was not driven "in". He perceived the exterior world of sensory perception, blissfully transfigured. And this good fortune, he feels confident, will be shared by nearly all takers of the drug. "Only", he says, "to those who have recently had jaundice or who suffer from periodical depression or chronic anxiety" does mescalin bring a taste of hell or purgatory. But his confidence does not seem entirely confirmed by the experience of guinea-pigs in this country.

Of these, one man of high scientific competence had visions of geometrical shapes, but later on he fell into a state of unqualified, uncontrollable mental distress. A psychiatrist alternated between extreme distress and intense bliss. Another man had exterior hallucinations of tropical forests, parrots and all, outside his London window, and of Eastern beauties on his drawing-room chairs. A linguistic analyst had no interesting experiences. Nor did a lady who had spent two years in a Buddhist convent. A painter shared Mr. Huxley's vision of our normal outer world, pulsating and transfigured. Another man, as famous for his kindly temperament as for his great learning, might have expected immediate transport to the Elysian Fields. But this did not happen. Certain exterior objects became for him things of vivid, colourful beauty, but his inner experiences were slight, though at one moment he did remark with philosophical equanimity, "I should judge myself now to be in the infernal rather than the celestial regions."

To answer the investigator's questions while under the drug is exceedingly difficult, for words *must* mislead when used to describe conditions for which they were not designed. This guinea-pig, for instance, was asked to describe the patterns by which she was surrounded. The following is an extract from a tape-recording:

Guinea-pig. There are so many patterns. In fact there are all the patterns in the world. . . . Anything I say about them will be so misleading that it is almost better to say nothing.

Investigator. Why misleading?

Guinea-pig. Because if I said they were solid you would think I meant they were solid. . . . I can't "see" them. . . . It is the awareness of pattern you see. You can't say it is visual or auditory. . . . It is the *awareness* of pattern. . . . Now you are trying to make me divide them up into one or another and you can't do that. . . . *No,* you can't say a great mass of pattern. It is PATTERN.

Later, I seemed to wander farther into a hinterland of essence.

Investigator. Which was the most pleasant of the images you have just seen?

Guinea-pig. The pure light at the top of the mountain. But that is a nonsensical way to describe it, because of course it was not at the top of the mountain but inside. But to say inside is nonsense too. Well, central, then, will that do? . . . You have got to be very very careful because if you get yourself caught up in all those relationships you will be exploded. . . . Oh! It is *circular!* It is like all the Gods in the world!

Investigator. What was circular?

Guinea-pig. I don't know. . . . It's a God shooting his arrows, millions and millions of him shooting his arrows. . . dancing!' . . . *Now* I see the point of the Hindu sculptures. . . .

Investigator. Are these Hindu deities you are seeing now?

Guinea-pig. If you like to say Hindu deities in an effort to formulate what I am seeing now, yes. But you cannot say these are Hindu deities. You can only say Hindu deities are these. It is *quite* different. . . . *Now* I see the point of designs and patterns . . . modern art . . . the non-objective pictures. . . . Then they *did* see those things! They are just expressing the dance . . . more and more and more . . . upside down and everyway about. . . .

Those extracts may perhaps give a feeble hint of the blissful experiences. Others were terrible. I seemed to be caught like a wasp in the sordid brown treacle of a man's anger. I saw a wild black figure chopping off heads, because it was so funny to see them fall. Worst of all, I came upon the "lost", squatting, grey-veiled, among grey rocks, "at the bottom", unable to communicate, alone beyond despair. I longed passionately to arouse and comfort them, but knew myself unworthy. None less, I seemed aware, than the High Gods could do that, by sinking themselves in sacrifice even lower than the lost, to become the objects of their pity and compassion.

But, even when blissful, the cosmic, interweaving, impersonal, inevitable, indifferent, relentless, eternal "beingness" of the inner world in the end grew overwhelming. I do not feel I could have survived much longer, without the protective covering of my own little ego, but for the appearance of a celestial female figure. She did not seem to be linked with any particular religion. I described her as "coming out of the gold, clothed in soft blues and purples, infinitely benign and compassionate . . . like a pearl coming into a world of diamond. . . ". She was gay with a gaiety no scherzo can even hint at and she laughed at me and said, "You were being shown the universe before the principle of communication, which is love, has been injected into it. Now you see the next job."

When I remember her now, I can take an extreme laughing delight in all natural things, a sparrow, a leaf of celery, an apple, a child's smile.

But does such a sense of rescue come to all who take the drug? Supposing in my case the Celestial Figure had not appeared. Supposing one had not been made aware that the High Gods could save the lost. Might not the universe manifest itself to some not very tough guinea-pigs in a guise too overwhelming for them to face? Is *everyone* ready for a dose of "Mind at Large"?'

The following is an account of his experiences under mescalin by Mr. Raymond Mortimer published in *The Sunday Times* on 14 August 1955.

'The increase in visual perceptiveness did prove staggering. I did not respond more vigorously to paintings or to the patterns on materials; but colour took on a prodigious intensity, and form appeared more three-dimensional. The room looked like a rich Impressionist picture, so sensitive was I to the gradations in tonal value and reflected colour. Otherwise the vision was the reverse of Impressionist: the outlines were very sharply defined. The leaves in a vase seemed made of metal, so did the hair of the persons in the room; and their heads and the folds in their clothes were sculptural, as if seen in a stereoscope. I was reminded of certain Mannerist pictures of the sixteenth century.

My vision, I must emphasize, was not distorted: I saw only what was there, but I saw it with unprecedented acuteness. Mr. Huxley, following Bergson and Broad, suggests that normally the brain and nervous system make us selective in our vision, blinding us to much that is visible when it offers no information of practical value. The work of some (but not most) great painters proves that they have overcome this partial blindness: and I felt that I had been lent the eyes of a great painter, seeing colour like Renoir or Monet, and form like Michelangelo or Bronzino. This was an unforgettable experience, and I believe moreover that it has left me able to use my eyes better than before.

Another effect was at least equally extraordinary. Thought and memory remained; emotion entirely vanished. I remembered without pleasure or pain; I looked forward without desire or fear. I was shown photographs of Italian architecture: I listened to Chopin on a gramophone; I repeated lines from a favourite poem: though I recognized the excellences of these works, I was entirely unmoved by any of them. I thought without the faintest affection of the persons to whom I am most attached; I could muster no resentment against persons who had treated me badly.

Whereas Mr. Huxley felt that he had blessedly escaped from self, I remained highly conscious of self, losing merely my emotional responses (except to colour and form). I was acutely interested in the experience I was undergoing, and in nothing else. My personal opinions and beliefs remained unchanged.

Complete emotional detachment might be expected to make one think more clearly and thus to modify one's opinions. It did nothing of the sort. Though my thoughts about Hitler, for instance, were not coloured by any of my usual disgust, my intellect calmly condemned him. I *knew*, but I did not *feel*, the difference between right and wrong, or between love and hate. . . . In my experience it did not diminish self-control, remove inhibitions, or increase suggestibility. My mind had become neither less individual nor weaker, but emotionally I had ceased to be a person.

Mescalin, it is said, produces some of the same symptoms as schizophrenia. According to Mr. Huxley it brings to most people the heavenly part of that disease—and "hell and purgatory only to those who have had a recent case of jaundice or who suffer from periodical depressions or chronic anxiety". To the best of my knowledge I am free from all of these, yet the drug eventually produced the most horrifying experience I have ever known. The dose had certainly been too strong for me: I suffered from recurrent nausea and often felt on the point of passing out. This hampered my delight in the revelation of visual beauty, and was presumably responsible for the misery that followed.

Some five hours after taking the mescalin the inability to feel suddenly became alarming in the extreme. Had the drug merely paralysed my emotions, I wondered, or had it perhaps destroyed them for ever? Life without them would be unendurable. Then I decided that this terror was itself an emotion, and that its appearance meant that I was emerging from the influence of the drug. This reasoning brought momentary relief, but I now began to suffer a generalized apprehension amounting to panic. I was not frightened of pain or death; I was frightened only of continuing to exist in my present unmotivated anguish. Though my brain was lucid, I was suffering the torments caused by some forms of madness. A sleeping-pill at last brought a merciful unconsciousness.'

APPENDIX B

THE AUTHOR'S EXPERIENCE WITH MESCALIN

AT my own request I was the subject of an experiment with mescalin on 3 December 1955. Dr. J. R. Smythies of the Psychological Laboratory, Cambridge, administered the drug and supervised my reactions. He was assisted by Mr. E. Osborn of the Society for Psychical Research. Also present were Dr. A. C. Allison, Student of Christ Church, and Mr. Alan Tyson, Fellow of All Souls, who is a student of psychology. The experiment took place in my own rooms in All Souls College, Oxford.

0·4 gram of mescalin was administered at 11.40 a.m. on 3 December. This was accompanied by ½ tablet of dramamine to prevent possible nausea. Before the drug took effect Dr. Smythies questioned me on previous hypnagogic experiences. I told him that, when dozing or before falling asleep, I frequently saw faces forming in front of me. These faces are usually dimly lit against a black ground: they form, stay for a few seconds, and then disappear. As one face disappears, another slowly takes its place and disappears in its turn, and so on. The faces are usually of one type (old or middle-aged women, less frequently men, practically never young men or women, never children). These faces are never familiar. Another phenomenon which occurs to me when dozing or before going to sleep is that I appear to be reading a book. I see the print clearly and distinguish the words, but the words rarely seem to have any particular significance. The books I appear to be reading are never books with which I am familiar, but frequently deal with whatever subject I have been reading during the day.

At 11.50 I was shown various objects and my reactions to them were noted. This was recorded on a tape-recorder, but the conversation is not sufficiently interesting to be reported in full. Three reproductions of Italian renaissance pictures, one of which I was later to see when under the influence of the drug, were shown to me. The one I was to look at later was a detail of the 'Adoration of the Magi' by Gentile da Fabriano (the original of which is in the Uffizi at Florence).

I explained that in this picture I was principally attracted by the richness of the colouring and the delicacy and sumptuousness of the draperies. I also looked at the best of my Persian rugs,—a Feraghan of extraordinarily rich design with a basic colouring of deep, glowing russets,—and said that I hoped to have a chance of examining it when the drug had 'taken', since it appeared that the one phenomenon common to most mescalin-takers was a pronounced heightening of the sense of colour. I also asked if I might listen to Berlioz's *Te Deum*, almost my favourite work in all music, 'which puts me into a manic state anyway'. The investigators then showed me a Persian cigarette box of very ordinary workmanship which I happen to possess, a wineglass which, when held up to the light, shows a deep crimson, and, as a totally neutral object, an ink pot. I further expressed a desire to see the dust-jacket of the Nixa recording of Berlioz's *Symphonie Funèbre et Triomphale.* This is divided into four unequal rectangles, two brilliantly green, one brilliantly red, and one black. In the red rectangle is reproduced a distorted version of Michelangelo's 'David' as far as the navel; in the much smaller black rectangle is the head of a Bellini Madonna. The 'David', as reproduced, I described as 'interesting in a sinister kind of way'. I was also asked to look at a small cut-glass decanter and a group of flowers which I had purchased for the occasion.

At 12.55 no reaction had taken place except light-headedness. I was asked to look intently at an electric light bulb to test me for the after-image. As I gazed at the bulb, it seemed to grow brighter and to expand a little.[1] On shutting my eyes the after-image behaved on more or less conventional lines,—starting as green in the centre of my visual field, it ascended, appeared to explode, became red in the middle and green outside. It changed colour so often, exploded into a dim bluish pattern and reformed again so often that I could not describe these metamorphoses quickly enough. The image that remains most clearly in my memory is that of a slowly mounting fiery ball which reminded me of an atomic explosion. I thought it sinister and described it as 'horrid'. I disliked the experience and said that what displeased me most was 'the fact that one's losing control of oneself'. My conscious resistance to the drug was, indeed, very strong, and this may account for the fact that it took so long to operate.

At this point it should perhaps be stated that as the day approached on which I was to take the drug, I had become increasingly uneasy. I dreamt about it three nights running and, quite irrationally, feared either that it might be fatal, or that it might make me permanently mad. These fears (which Mr. Raymond Mortimer experienced when under the influence of the drug) were not wholly serious and did not occur at any point once the drug had begun to work. It is true that it occurred to me at a later stage, when I had a pronounced sensation of cold in my extremities and in my genitals, that I might quite possibly die; but, in the curious state of mind I was then in and which I shall attempt to describe, I considered this of no possible interest to anyone, least of all to myself. It seemed to me to be wholly God's affair what happened to me, and I was very firmly convinced that He was merciful.

Shortly after the after-image experiment I asked Mr. Tyson to take the investigators in turn down to lunch. He took Mr. Osborn and left Dr. Smythies with me. I was still suffering from nothing worse than light-headedness and, accompanied by Dr. Smythies, I took a stroll in the great quadrangle to see whether the twin towers and the Radcliffe Camera were much as before: they were. I then took Dr. Smythies into the buttery for lunch and, according to those present, behaved in a perfectly normal manner. I did not myself eat nor did I feel any inclination to do so. We then proceeded to the coffee room where I had a little very weak coffee. I then suggested that, since the drug was taking

[1] I have repeated this experiment subsequently and found that the impression of increased brightness repeated itself, and I even fancied the bulb grew a little larger.

so long to act, we might go for a stroll through Christ Church Meadow, finally debouching into Christ Church where I had successively been a scholar, senior scholar, and research lecturer. I was particularly anxious to do this as I hoped the drug would be beginning to work as we reached Christ Church and I wished to see what (if anything) happened to Tom Tower when seen under the influence of mescalin. I wished to do this because when I first saw it at the age of eighteen, it made a quite overwhelming impression on me. This impression I have never wholly lost.

We left All Souls at about 1.30 p.m., crossed the High without difficulty and walked down towards Magdalen. I was still feeling light-headed and felt that I was having some difficulty in controlling my legs. I pointed out objects of architectural interest and enlightened my guests (I still thought of them as guests rather than as medical supervisors) as to the state of the controversy about the Oxford inner relief roads. We turned into the Meadow at Rose Lane, and proceeded down the Broad Walk. In the High I had a curious sensation in my body which reminded me of what Mr. Custance describes as a 'tingling at the base of the spine' which, according to him, usually precedes a bout of mania. It was rather like that. In the Broad Walk this sensation occurred, but more strongly. It felt as if something warm were surging up the body. The sensation occurred again and again until the climax of the experiment was reached, and in all cases after a period of quiescence. I did not like it at all.

From the Broad Walk we turned right and reached Merton Street. I now felt that the drug was about to 'take': something was going to happen, but not just yet, I thought. As I wanted 'things to happen' when I entered Tom Quad, I steered my guests into Merton Chapel because I felt sure that the drug needed a little time yet in which to act. The Chapel was looking the same as usual: I looked at the very beautiful east window, but was more conscious of the damp and dank which do so much to mar that noble edifice. I was also feeling rather giddy.

From Merton we proceeded to Christ Church through Canterbury Gate and Peckwater Quad. On emerging into Tom Quad, the moment I had been eagerly anticipating, nothing happened at all. Tom Tower stood there as he always has done, looking precisely the same. I was rather disappointed that my guests did not admire him more. We walked along the east side of the quad and entered the Cathedral. I had no special interest in the Cathedral, but since it is certainly the most beautiful mediaeval ecclesiastical interior in Oxford, I thought my guests ought to be given the opportunity of seeing it, since as a 'subject' I must, so far, have been a disappointment.

On entering the Cathedral things began to happen. I stood at the west end of the nave under the organ-loft and looked down into the choir. The choir terminates in a rose window above, below which is an arcade; below this again are two small Norman windows. The rose window and the lower windows contain very respectable nineteenth-century stained glass. As I looked, the rose window seemed to expand and contract rhythmically, its pattern continually changing meanwhile. The effect was interesting certainly, but seemed to me less beautiful than its normal state. After a short while I found this growing and shrinking annoying, and proceeded down the northern aisle. As I walked up it I noticed that the Burne-Jones window in front was also behaving in a curious manner. The window did not seem distinctly visible; it was as if there were thin veils of gossamer between me and it. On coming closer I was struck by the left-hand figure, a young man in profile with hand upraised. His head and hand moved slightly in the direction in which he was looking, but he could not get any farther because, it seemed to me, he was imprisoned in the glass. The patterns made by the actual pieces of glass were meanwhile leading a life independent of the life of the figures depicted on them. Like the pattern of the rose window they were perpetually on the move, forming and reforming, and not remaining still for a moment. It was rather like looking at figures through rippling water, but it was a kind of water that prevented the figures from doing what they wanted to do, hard though they tried to do it. Meanwhile the haloes of the four figures seemed to glow with an intenser lustre. This was, however, not so, for the other colours had all faded into various degrees of white and whitish grey. On returning to the Cathedral later the haloes seemed to be precisely as they were before, whereas all the rest had changed completely: under the influence of the drug they were drained of all positive colour.

Leaving the Burne-Jones I went to look at some mediaeval glass in the Latin Chapel, but this refused to have anything to do with the drug, and remained obstinately itself. I then wished to look at the window at the west end of the north aisle since it contained vivid yellows and greens which I thought might seem more intense now that the drug had started to work. The window, however, looked, if anything, more drab than usual and I passed on back to the west end of the nave. There I took up my position again.

The rose window was still behaving in the same unusual way, expanding and contracting in a rhythmical manner. By now I found this irritating and transferred my attention to the centre of the choir's fan-vaulting. This I saw with absolute clarity; the pattern was simple and every detail was clearly etched. The stone seemed to be slightly more yellowish in the centre of my vision, though there was no change in the colourings of the surrounding pendants. I was astonished to find when I returned to the Cathedral that the pattern I had seen so clearly was not in fact the pattern as it actually is on the vault. What I had seen was very much simpler and less intricate. Though the pattern itself stayed absolutely still, everything else was in perpetual motion. At one time the whole choir would gently roll like a ship, sometimes in time with the organ (which was playing) and sometimes following a rhythm all its own. The roof of the choir, too, would expand and contract; and the pendants performed what seemed to be a ritual dance of their own, sometimes multiplying themselves, and sometimes coalescing. Meanwhile the rose window continued to expand and contract and interfered gravely with the figures being executed by the rolling choir as a whole and with the individual motions of the fan-vaulting. I was delighted with the choir's performance and distinctly annoyed by the rival performance put on by the rose window. It did not seem to me interesting or beautiful in itself and merely interfered with the grave dance of the stone-work. Whenever I transferred my glance to the top of the vault the same pattern appeared with absolute clarity and the dancing pendants fell rhythmically into place, pursuing their concerted life beneath it.

It was strange that though the choir was undergoing these delicate metamorphoses, the rest of the Cathedral remained motionless, including the arch that separated the choir from the transept which acted as a frame to the scene that was taking place beyond. One of the investigators then asked me to look at one of the nearer pillars in the nave. It remained absolutely motionless. I respected it for that.

At this point I wished to emerge into Tom Quad to see whether Tom Tower was still behaving in a normal way. He was. We then proceeded to the grand staircase since I was very interested to know whether the fan-tracery there was behaving in the same way as the fan-vaulting in the Cathedral. I was surprised to see that it remained absolutely motionless, but seemed very much lower and less impressive than usual. This disappointed me as I thought my visitors would carry away a very poor opinion of Oxford architecture.

We then returned to the Cathedral and I looked at the Burne-Jones window at the west end of the south aisle. This behaved in precisely the same way as its companion at the other end of the Cathedral,—the same forming and reforming of patterns, the same impression that the figures were trying to fight themselves free of the glass, the same reduction of all colours to shades of white and whitish grey, the same persistent glowing of the reds.

I would have liked to have stayed in this magical Cathedral a little longer, but the investigators considered that it was time to return to All Souls. Both Tom Quad and Peckwater looked much as usual, though, when I returned to them the next day, they looked grander and more impressive than they had under the influence of the drug. By this time I had no difficulty at all in walking but had a curious sensation that my body was under perfect control, which seemed odd, for I was certainly, I thought, in no position to control it. The body seemed momentarily to be leading an autonomous life of its own,—and very well it managed it,—whereas 'I' was becoming increasingly confused and unsure of myself. On reaching the High, I felt very grateful for the presence of my companions; for, though there was not overmuch traffic, I was not absolutely certain that what I saw was actually there.

* * * * *

On returning to my rooms I sat down, feeling rather tired. The time was now 2.45, and the investigators tried to elicit a more or less clear account of my experiences in the Cathedral.

'In the Cathedral', I replied, 'I started looking at the rose window which at first seemed to be fairly clear and then it faded. . . . I'm sorry, things are coming a bit odd. . . . I don't seem to be able to remember, I can't express myself any more. . . . I'm not feeling very . . . er . . . sensible at the moment.'

I was then asked about things around me and how they were behaving. I was feeling rather exhausted and had some difficulty in replying.

'They're going up and down rather,' I said, '. . . very misty . . . the bookcase pattern forms and reforms. I wish it'd stay where it was. Dr. Allison is recognizable, I'm glad to say . . . (sigh). I'm sorry to look at you like this . . . (another sigh). Things are just *queer*. They don't stay in the same place very long, but they don't change very much.' In actual fact, though Dr. Allison's face was much the same, his right ear had expanded quite considerably, but I somehow felt it would be impolite to draw attention to this.

I was then asked to look at the Gentile da Fabriano 'Adoration of the Magi'. At first it looked 'precisely as it was before', and for some time remained so. 'Nothing seems to happen', I remarked in a bored voice; then 'the second Magi (*sic*) moved his hand quite a lot then. He's bringing up the . . . no. (Testily) Come on, come on, come on (encouraging the Magus). He's trying to get up . . . doesn't make it. Trying to take his crown off . . . (deep breathing). . . . On the whole it stays very like the picture it really is. He's out of focus, the middle one; he has moved. . . . He was much more up this way a little while ago. . . . He's bending down a bit.'

Investigator. 'Any more solid, would you say?'

R. C. Z. 'More solid? I should say a little . . . yes . . . yes. It's not the same picture and yet it isn't, you know (*sic*) . . . (sighs). . . . Colour, I suppose, a little intenser. Not much.' The reason why the picture wasn't the same was, I think, that though nothing was now moving, parts of it were expanding and others contracting almost imperceptibly.

I was looking at the picture by daylight, and the investigators now shone a lamp on it. At this the picture appeared to come to life. It was the second Magus again who started it. He again moved his outstretched hand slightly forward and seemed to be trying hard to take his crown off. I half hoped that he would take it off, but since he didn't, I realized that *of course* he couldn't because he couldn't get out of the picture any more than the figures in the Cathedral could get out of their glass. But whereas I felt sympathetic to the figures in the Cathedral, the poor Magus' predicament seemed to me wildly amusing. In any case I now broke into uncontrollable laughter which was to last, on and off, for over an hour. The occasion for this excessive hilarity was, I suppose, the Magus; but this did not seem wholly clear to me at the time.

'What do you find so funny, Professor Zaehner?' an investigator asked:

R. C. Z. (ecstatically). 'Nothing.' This was true: everything had suddenly become so totally funny that to single out one thing rather than another would not at all have conveyed this experience of total funniness. I could only continue to laugh till I cried. The situation was not made one bit better by the behaviour of the Magi. The eldest, who is represented as kneeling and about to kiss the Infant Jesus' feet, seemed to advance while the Child attempted to push him back. And now it became clear that the Magus was not going to kiss the Child's feet: he was trying to bite them and the Child would not let him. Perhaps because, as I explained to the investigators before the experiment began, I had always admired this picture for the beauty and richness of its colouring, not for its religious content, I was not shocked by the thought of the Magus biting the feet of the Infant Jesus. I simply did not connect this grotesque scene with the actual subject of the picture. Even in my manic state I made a clear distinction between the world of 'funniness' and objects or pictures which seemed to me genuinely sacred. This will appear in the sequel.

When this initial laughing fit had subsided I looked round and complained:

R. C. Z. 'You all look so serious.'

Investigator. 'We can't enjoy it to the same extent you can.'

R. C. Z. (convulsed). 'No, I suppose you can't.' (Further gusts of uncontrollable laughter.)

Attempts were made to interest me in other pictures, but without success. 'I don't mind what I do', I said, but really meant that I just wanted to laugh on in peace, 'laughing at nothing' as I described it. Efforts to interest me in books were equally vain until it became clear that the investigators wished to test whether I was still able to read correctly. This seemed worth trying. Things were still moving about in an inconsequential way though the majority of them stood still. It would be interesting to see what words were doing on the printed page. Finally I was induced to start reading the opening passage of Proust's *Du Côté de chez Swann.* The words and lines were, indeed, up to the oddest tricks; they seemed to be in a state of perpetual flux and it required a great effort to find the right line and to stick to it once found. I read, or rather chanted, the first paragraph more or less correctly. It came out like this:

' "Longtemps je me suis couché de bonne heure. Parfois, à peine ma bougie éteinte, mes yeux se fermaient si vite que je n'avais pas le temps de me dire: Je m'endors."—I wish to say that I am not doing anything of the kind.—"Et une demi-heure après, la pensée qu'il était temps de chercher le sommeil m'éveillait."—That can't be right.—"Je voulais poser le volume . . ." come on, volume (pronounced as French), where do you want to be posé-ed?' The lines and words were now inextricably mixed up, which accounts for the last remark. ' " . . . que je croyais avoir encore dans les mains et souffler la lumière." This is one of the stupid things I read in my dreams.' (More laughter.)

Investigator. 'You do that in your dreams, do you?'

R. C. Z. (astonished at his naïveté). Don't be silly. It's the sort of thing I *read* in my dreams. I wish Proust was half as funny as that. . . . I'd give. . . . Take him away.' (Much laughter throughout.)

Investigator. 'Would you like another book?'

R. C. Z. 'No, they're all the same.'

Investigator. 'All rather stupid?'

R. C. Z. 'It doesn't seem to make much difference, the words change round anyhow.'

I then asked Dr. Allison what the book was which made his wife laugh so much when she was my pupil (she had been). He could not tell me, so I dismissed the matter with a favourable comment on his wife: 'She was a good girl.' Silence for a few moments, then:

R. C. Z. 'I wish everyone wasn't being so unfriendly.'

Investigator. 'Do we seem unfriendly?'

R. C. Z. (loudly and emphatically). 'Frightfully.' (Prolonged and uproarious laughter.)

More books were pressed on me and immediately rejected. 'Take it away, it's psycho-analysis.' Finally I was offered the first volume of *The Golden Bough.* Opening at p. 17 I saw the words 'Diana & Virbius' which I read as 'Diana and Virbio', a conjunction that struck me as being quite excruciatingly funny.

I read the paragraph starting 'Among the ancient Celts of Gaul . . .' more or less correctly, but with great difficulty because the words were behaving in an even more unruly manner than they had in Proust. Finally I could make nothing of it, but at last the word 'ancestors' seemed to stand still.

R. C. Z. 'The ancestors are settling down now. They're, they're, they're staying in the same place for one moment. Nice of them. Jolly nice of them. (Uncontrollable laughter.) This is the silliest test I have ever had to go through. You all take it so seriously. (Laughter.) Really you shouldn't be so serious. It's Diana, you see. (More uncontrollable laughter.) Here, wait a minute. (This addressed to the book.) "She did not reign alone in her grove at Nemi. Two lesser divinities shared her forest sanctuary. One was Egeria, the nymph of the clear water which, bubbling from the basaltic rocks, used to fall in graceful cascades into the mills of the modern village of Nemi mentioned by Ovid." Oh, that's clever of him. (Squeaks of delight.) This is quite an interesting book. What is it? Oh, *The Golden Bough.* Very funny. (More uncontrollable laughter.) One of the great comic classics.'

However, Diana appeared to have served her purpose: 'We've *had* her, let's go on to something different.' Turning the pages I was much distressed by the fact that Sir James Frazer's paragraphs were so long. 'Why doesn't he split his paragraphs?' I testily enquired. 'They're all over the place. . . . It's all wrong. I was brought up as an undergraduate not to do such a thing. Wicked.' I then started to read on p. 272:

' "The reader will observe"—I hope he jolly well will too (more uncontrollable laughter)—"how exactly the Japs . . . Javanese . . . try to make rain from the antithesis of Indian observations." ' I then read a sentence more or less correctly, but was once again defeated by the mobility of the print. When the book seemed to settle down for a bit, I was slightly annoyed: 'They're moving again now, it's much funnier.' The following sentence, 'It is the old fallacy that the effect resembles its cause', brought on a wild paroxysm of mirth. This struck me as being really exceptionally funny. The idea that there actually still were people who believed in causes and effects, seemed to me grotesque: how could people be so silly? 'Oh, this is stupid', I exclaimed. 'Oh, the man's playing the fool.'

The quotations from Sir James Frazer, it will have been observed, went a little wrong. This was because I was no longer master of the mobile print, I could no longer distinguish the right line, and the resultant nonsense seemed to me far more satisfying than what was actually written although that too, heaven knows, was funny enough.

I now asked Tyson for a glass of water since the quite immoderate amount of laughing I had been doing, had made me very thirsty. On Tyson's return:

R. C. Z. 'I was about to tell you my great thoughts about it. I'll think twice about that because . . .'

Tyson. 'What were they?'

R. C. Z. 'No, no, it's all right. I'll tell you when they come again.' In actual fact I did not disclose the 'great thought' because even then it seemed trite and amounted only to 'Everything is much funnier than it seems'.

Throughout this manic period I had been suffering from a feeling of cold in my extremities and also in my genitals. The cold feeling seemed to be creeping up my legs. It was slightly unpleasant, but in no way alarming.

Investigator. 'This is very like the record of the laughing policeman, do you know it?'

R. C. Z. 'Is it funny?'

Investigator. 'Very funny indeed.'

R. C. Z. 'Bet it isn't.' (Giggles, long pause.) 'Where's Charles?'[1]

Tyson. 'I expect he's in his rooms.'

R. C. Z. 'Let him stay there. You should ask him to be on time. Two seconds ago I'd have been pleased to see Charles. If he hasn't got the civility to turn up when he is wanted' (remainder incomprehensible owing to hysterical laughter).

Investigator. 'How does the water taste?'

R. C. Z. 'Rather like water, I'm afraid. I'm just rather dehydrated. . . . Is that the right word? . . . Hydration taking place . . . oh dear . . .' (giggles).

Investigator. 'How are the feet?'

R. C. Z. 'Oh, as cold as ever.' (Sighs.)

Investigator. 'Do you have any other sensations?'

R. C. Z. 'No . . . only laughter, if you call that a sensation. (Laughter.) Cold feet, certainly. Jolly cold feet. . . . Oh dear! They're crooked too.'

Investigator. 'They're crooked?'

R. C. Z. 'Not more than usual, I don't think.'

Investigator. 'You're holding them crooked.'

R. C. Z. 'It doesn't seem to make much difference which way you hold them if they're crooked when you start.' (Uncontrollable laughter.)

At this stage the investigator tried to interest me in a Persian carpet which lies in front of the fireplace. The design is a medallion on a rich crimson ground.

R. C. Z. 'It's just the old rose window all over again, isn't it?'

Investigator. 'It's not quite the same as the rose window: it's nearer for one thing.'

R. C. Z. (emphatically). 'It's *just* the same. Just a dull old thing sitting in the middle of a spider's web.'

I was again asked to look at it.

R. C. Z. 'I don't want to look at the thing.'

Asked to look at the books, I said:

'Don't want to look at the books: why should I want to look at the books?'

Investigator. 'Describe what's going on there.'

R. C. Z. 'Why should anything go on there? Just a lot of books.'

[1] Charles Monteith, Fellow of All Souls.

On being asked to note any peculiarity of colour or shape I replied wearily: 'I don't think anything like that's going to happen. I'm quite prepared for these things to happen, but I don't think they do much.'

Investigator. 'When you say it's just like the rose window, you mean it's behaving like it?'

R. C. Z. 'No, it just shows it's shoddy stuff.'

Investigator. 'Why, this isn't shoddy stuff, is it?'

R. C. Z. 'I *know*, I paid for it.' (Uncontrollable laughter.) 'I know that wasn't funny, but it seemed so to me.'

Tyson then showed me E. M. Forster's *Hill of Devi.* I had met Mr. Forster the previous year and liked him very much, and Tyson reminded me of the fact. After attempts at polite and more or less sane conversation on the subject of Mr. Forster's health, I concluded in an aggressive tone: 'He's a *very nice man.*' Turning to the frontispiece, a portrait of the Indian Prince under whom Mr. Forster served, I observed sagely, 'He knew about chaps, this one. . . . Nice silly man.'

The time was now 3.30.

I was now shown a reproduction of Michelangelo's 'Holy Family'.

R. C. Z. 'Now I suppose I'm meant to make intelligent comments on this.'

Investigator. 'Is there any movement there?'

R. C. Z. 'No. . . . I can't think why you expect things to move.' (Uncontrollable laughter.) 'Except that I do.'

Investigator. 'Do you?'

R. C. Z. 'Of course I don't, I mean unless they happen to be moving, you wouldn't expect them to, would you?'

I heard Allison say something like, 'There's quite a lot of method in this madness'.

R. C. Z. 'Don't whisper behind the scenes, it's rude. (Sighs) . . . Ah! . . . (sighs deeply) . . . I've got to go on looking at this, have I? I *knew* they'd try and make me look at these ruddy things. Why *should* I look at these things? . . . Silly. Oh, I'm sorry . . . (laughter). . . . Native manners overcome drug . . .' (more laughter).

More pictures were shown me but with little effect until I asked to look at reproductions of Raphael's 'Deposition.' I fetched the book myself since no one else could find it. I had no difficulty in moving about. Running through the details I had no desire to laugh.

R. C. Z. 'All much too serious. . . . This is because it's a really serious picture.' This was the first time I had stopped laughing since looking at the Gentile da Fabriano. The reason was that Raphael is to me an essentially religious and 'numinous' painter. I was still in a world of nonsensical fantasy, and I realized that Raphael could not fit in there,—not for me at any rate. The original of the picture is in the Borghese Gallery in Rome and I had not long ago looked at the picture with the present Warden of All Souls. The investigators asked me to describe where the original was. I could not remember the name of the Borghese Gallery nor could I describe where it was.

R. C. Z. 'Can't remember where it was . . . (sighs). . . . How can I describe it? How can you describe anything when you can't remember what they're called?. . . Ring up the Warden, he knows. . . . Precious little response to that one . . . (laughter) . . . (peremptorily): Ring him up. . . . I suppose I'll have to ring him up myself. . . . What? (loud and annoyed) . . . I'll go and see the Warden when he wants to see me, and I don't think that'll be till tomorrow afternoon. (Uncontrollable laughter.) No. Oh, I've got to look at this, haven't I? I know you keep trying to make things happen, but they don't *want* to happen. . . . That's where you're all wrong. . . .' This remark, mad though it was, reflected one of my basic convictions, namely, that it is wrong to try to make others behave in a way that is not natural to them. In my manic state, 'things' had come to life and should therefore be treated with the respect due to living organisms. I was not quite mad enough not to realize that they were not really alive: even so, I really did think it wrong to interfere with them if they (like myself) happened to want to rest.

At this point I suddenly wanted to have a look at the dust-jacket of the *Symphonie Funèbre et Triomphale*:

R. C. Z. 'Oh, let's have a look at that silly old creature we talked about before we took the drug. (Laughter) . . . Oh, the *Symphonie Funèbre et Triomphale*, but *not* the *Symphonie Funèbre et Triomphale* but the dust-jacket of the *Symphonie Funèbre et Triomphale* . . . (triumphantly) and if that's not clear, I don't know what is. (More laughter) . . . See if he's going to dance around. (Looking at the dust-jacket) Just shows him up, you see, stupid old thing. Just nothing there at all, you see. No good, can't get away with it, can't get away with it. Just tripe, like everything else.'

Investigator. 'End of art.'

I was now handed the Phaidon Press edition of Berenson's *Italian Painters of the Renaissance*. I opened it at p. 114 where there is a colour reproduction of a praying figure from Piero della Francesca's 'Nativity' in the National Gallery.

R. C. Z. 'This bloke I really do think has got something, or at least I used to.'

Investigator. 'Do you enjoy looking at that?'

R. C. Z. 'I wish you'ld leave me alone. . . . You keep interrupting.'

Still, as far as I remember, looking at the same picture, I said:

R. C. Z. 'Let's have a look at her . . . (sighs). . . . 'If you want to know what I feel about that, it's a holy thing not to be looked at when you're drugged.'

A book of reproductions of Picasso drawings was now produced and opened at an abstract black and white design.[1] The design at once sprang to life and the pattern moved about and changed continually:

Investigator. 'What do you think this particular thing shows?'

R. C. Z. (defiantly). 'Shows *what*?'

Investigator. 'Well . . . can you recognize anything in it?'

R. C. Z. 'Well, if it would stay still for a minute I might . . . extraordinary. . . . No, why should I recognize anything? It was all right when it was moving, but now it's stopped still, it's just silly. (Turns pages and comes to rest on pp. 106–7)

[1] *L'Œuvre gravé de Picasso*, La Guilde du Livre, Lausanne, 1955, p. 137.

... Ah, those chaps are coming up.... Slightly indecent. No ... no. ... (Turns more pages and comes to rest at p. 47) ... Really people shouldn't twist themselves up so. (Laughs, then sighs. Turns to p. 78.) There's the good old collective unconscious looking out.' (General laughter.)

Investigator. 'What do you think of this?' (I think we had now moved to p. 104.)

R. C. Z. 'Oh, that girl, she's got all the right things. Even she's bloody dull. That's the trouble with Jung, he doesn't realize how dull his collective unconscious is . . . (laughs). . . . Well, I'm sorry you can't interest me in anything. (To the picture) Oh don't make mouths at me, don't be silly. . . . Yes. . . . Oh, this is the sort of thing that goes on when I fall asleep. Just this sort of racket exactly. Yes, they fit into a pattern. Do be one face and not another. I know you're doing your best, I know you're doing your best. . . . Come on; well, you want to be a Red Indian, do you? All right, all right, I'm not stopping you. All right. Yes, you're settling down. Yes, yes. Very nice Red Indian you are too. That's right. Now you can go away . . . (picture fades slightly). . . . Better . . . um. . . . Settling down, settling down. . . . (testily) Come on. (Same image emerges) We've had you before. It's no good, no good. No. She's back again. I'm afraid it's because there's a picture at the bottom of it and not just nothing at all. (Looking at picture on opposite page) Ah, this bloke's interesting, he doesn't seem to have got a nose. Doesn't seem to fit together much. . . . (bored) Oh, it's a Picasso, that's why. (General laughter.) . . . If you give me a picture of absolutely nothing at all, I might be able to make something of it.' (Uncontrollable laughter.)

The investigators now tried me on the Rorschach test.

R. C. Z. 'Oh, why were you so interested in that bottle of ink before lunch, anyhow?'

Investigator. 'Just a neutral object.'

R. C. Z. (decidedly). '*Very* neutral, I should think.'

The drug was now beginning to wear off, I think. Looking back on it, my reasoning (if such it can be called) seems to have been rather like this. Ever since the drug had started to work things depicted seemed to be trying to escape from the material in which they were depicted. They were trying to come to life, but never quite succeeded. However much the material might move, the figure imprisoned in it could never get free. The more definite the figure was, the less able was it to escape; yet if it was not at all definite, no recognizable figure emerged. The only solution appeared to be a confrontation with 'a picture of absolutely nothing at all'. Yet when confronted with the inky mess known as a Rorschach, I became totally uninterested. I was not able or willing to impose an image on to it, since basically I wanted the actual figures represented to come to life and behave as they wanted to behave. I did not want to impose figures of my own, hence I found myself incapable of visualizing anything at all.

As the Rorschach was being prepared, Mr. Stuart Hampshire came in.

R. C. Z. (hearing someone come in). 'Who's that? Charles? Oh, Stuart, hallo, old boy.' Here follows a cascade of really manic laughter. The reason for this was, I think, that Hampshire had come in and was behaving as he ordinarily does.

This was immensely reassuring since I was perfectly well aware that the rest of them were not behaving naturally at all. They were investigating my reactions and trying (oh, so obviously) to humour a lunatic. Hence the uncontrolled joy with which I greeted Hampshire.

R. C. Z. 'Stuart, don't let them take you in.' This needs some explanation. There had been some question of Hampshire's taking the drug since the reactions of philosophers were likely to be of interest. I wished to tell Hampshire that he really need not waste his time since all the drug did was to reduce everything to the level of pure farce:

R. C. Z. 'Everything is very funny indeed.' (More uncontrollable laughter.)

S. N. H. 'How long has this been lasting?'

R. C. Z. 'Oh, quite a time. Ever since the Cathedral stopped going round . . . (peremptorily to Tyson who had already supplied, on request, endless glasses of water) Alan, water. . . . If you laugh as much as that and sweat as much as I do, you need an awful lot of water . . . (uncontrollable laughter). Physiological fact.'

Tyson now returned with a glass of water. The room seemed to be getting awfully full of people and it brought the cabin scene of the Marx Brothers' film 'A Night at the Opera' vividly to my mind:

R. C. Z. 'Ah, this is getting like a Marx Brothers' film . . . (general laughter). . . . Endless glasses of water . . .' (uncontrollable laughter).

The Rorschach was now handed to me:

Investigator. 'That's a Rorschach.'

R. C. Z. 'You've been working all out for me, have you? Now what's supposed to happen to this?'

Investigator. 'This is a . . . ink blot.'

R. C. Z. 'Ink blot . . . there seem to me a great many ink blots. Would you mind getting me some blotting paper?'

Investigator. 'It's just a bit damp in the middle.'

R. C. Z. 'It looks jolly wet to me.'

Investigator. 'A very, very small damp bit in the middle.'

R. C. Z. 'It's wet, not just damp.'

Investigator. 'No, just damp.'

R. C. Z. 'It looks *very* wet to me. What do you expect to happen to the silly thing for heaven's sake? . . . Well, if you'ld only let me get some control of myself instead of drugging an honest chap . . . (laughter). . . . There, here am I. . . . This is supposed to be a serious test . . . (more laughter). . . . No . . . oh, dear. Oh, gosh, my feet are so cold . . . oh dear . . . I wish there wasn't this tomb-like silence around one every time one opens one's mouth. . . .' (Laughter.)

S. N. H. 'There's a feeling you ought to say some great things from time to time.'

This was the sort of remark that made sense to me. At least Hampshire was not trying to make me do all kinds of things I didn't want to do: he wasn't continually thrusting pictures into my hands and talking about those idiotic Rorschachs. This explains the following remark:

R. C. Z. 'Stuart's about the only person who talks a word of sense in this room.'

Here I once again burst into uncontrollable laughter, walked up and down the room (quite steadily) laughing and laughing and laughing. Observing the Feraghan rug hanging on the wall, I noticed delightedly that it was precisely the same as ever. That would teach these silly investigators, I thought, not to try and play tricks with my property. The investigators had by now become identified with the drug and I resented both the drug and the investigators. I fear I was very trying to them.

Since I was now incapable of doing anything but laugh, Hampshire took his leave with an encouraging smile (it was his own smile, and that pleased me quite extraordinarily and somehow proved that here was one man at least who didn't try to make people and things do what they didn't want to do).

N.B. The tape-recording comes to an end at this point which was, I suppose, the climax of my manic phase.

Efforts were now made to induce me to listen to music. This produced the usual negative reaction. I sat down again, apathetically refusing to be interested in anything. I was asked to close my eyes and to try to visualize something I liked. I could think of nothing whatever I liked. The investigators then suggested a glass of water, large quantities of which I had been drinking. Try as I might I could visualize absolutely nothing. The investigators now no longer seemed to want to interest me in things. Their tactics were wise, for I finally suggested myself that Berlioz's *Te Deum* be played on the gramophone. I was still very conscious of the cold in my feet which had now spread to the hands, genitals, and lower abdomen, and which seemed to be creeping up my legs. This I found vaguely disquieting, thought it might be dangerous, but didn't mind if it was.

I wasn't sure about the *Te Deum*. Perhaps it would be boring like everything else. Yet the moment the music went on, I was completely absorbed. It is a magnificently noisy work, and the moment it started, I knew I just wanted to lie limply in my chair and let the music in, choirs, brass, tympani, and all. The 'phenomena' had not stopped. Things, and particularly the lines on the fireplace, refused to stand still, my feet and hands were still as cold as ever, and at one stage my left hand looked half its normal size. These were now no more than irritating distractions. I closed my eyes, but patterns,—though very inoffensive and indeterminate ones,—continued to form. On opening them again the lines on the fireplace were up to their old tricks. As the *Te Deum* came near to its end, however, things settled down and I found I felt very exhausted but wide awake. Otherwise I felt absolutely all right and declined Dr. Smythies's kind offer of a sleeping pill.

Berlioz's *Te Deum* has, for me, religious as well as musical significance; and the fact that I asked for it to be played showed that at that stage I felt the manic phase had passed sufficiently for me to think about religious things. In the manic stage Raphael had stopped the laughter and the praying figure of Piero della Francesca had elicited the sane remark 'It's a holy thing not to be looked at when you're drugged'. Berlioz seemed to bridge the two worlds. Before the experiment I had said that his *Te Deum* 'puts me into a manic state anyway'. A friend of mine who came in just before the work began, agreed that that was the effect it had on him. To me it was quite different; it brought me back to the real world, slowly and surely, without violent transition. My only regret was that I should still be distracted from the music, the full strength and beauty of which I felt I was missing.

During the performance of the first side of the *Te Deum* I became increasingly conscious of the cold in my feet and hands. I thought that if this cold should reach my heart, I would probably die. This thought did not worry me at all, and I felt strongly that this was God's concern, not mine, and that He would certainly be merciful.

* * * * *

I would not presume to draw any conclusions from so trivial an experience. It was interesting and it certainly seemed hilariously funny. All along, however, I felt that the experience was in a sense 'anti-religious', I mean, not conformable with religious experience or in the same category. In Huxley's terminology 'self-transcendence' of a sort did take place, but transcendence into a world of farcical meaninglessness. All things were one in the sense that they were all, at the height of my manic state, equally funny: the quality of 'funniness' and incongruity had swallowed up all others. I was never frightened, and as, under the influence of Berlioz, I slowly returned to sanity, my normal religious consciousness, which was never completely swamped, returned in full vigour. There was no longer any reason why I should be afraid.

I would not wish to take the drug again, but purely on moral grounds. I should be most interested to know whether the drug taken elsewhere and in a different and less friendly environment would produce different effects; but the more the experience fades into the past, the clearer does it seem to me that, in principle, artificial interference with consciousness is, except for valid medical reasons, wrong.

As far as I am concerned, mescalin was quite unable to reproduce the 'natural mystical experience' I have described elsewhere. I half hoped it would. However, once the drug started working and I was plunged into a universe of farce, I realized that this was not to be. The two experiences were so totally different that I refused, during the experiment, to be tempted by Rimbaud. He too, like Raphael, was too 'serious'.

The fact that I am an assiduous reader of *Alice through the Looking-Glass* is probably not irrelevant to the nature of my experience.

APPENDIX C

TRANSLITERATED PASSAGES

1. For English translation see Chapter V, pp. 85–86.

Al-Qushayrī, *Risāla*, pp. 32–33. Transliteration of the Arabic text:

wa-humā ḥālatāni ba'da'l-taraqqī'l-'abdi 'an ḥālati'l-khawfi wa'l-rajā'i; fa'l-qabḍu li'l-'ārifi bi-manzilati'l-khawfi li'l-musta'nifi, wa'l-basṭu li'l-'ārifi bi-manzilati'l-rajā'i li'l-musta'nifi. wa-min al-faṣli bayna'l-qabḍi wa'l-khawfi wa'l-basṭi wa'l-rajā'i anna'l-khawfa inna-mā yakūnu min shayy'in fī'l-mustaqbili, immā an yukhāfa fawtu maḥbūbin aw hujūmu maḥdhūrin, wa-ka-dhālika'l-rajā'u inna-mā yakūnu bi-ta'mīli maḥbūbin fī'l-mustaqbili aw bi taṭallu'i zawāli maḥdhūrin wa-kifāyati makrūhin fī'l-musta'nifi. wa-ammā'l-qabḍu, fa-li-ma'nan ḥāṣilin fī'l-waqti, wa-ka-dhālika'l-basṭu. fa-ṣāḥibu'l-khawfi wa'l-rajā'i ta'allaqa qalbu-hu fī ḥālatay-hi bi-ājili-hi, wa-ṣāḥibu'l-qabḍi wa'l-basṭi ukhidha waqtu-hu bi-wāridin ghalaba 'alay-hi fī 'ājili-hi. thumma tatafāwatu nu'ūtu-hum fī'l-qabḍi wa'l-basṭi 'alā ḥasbi tafāwuti-him fī aḥwāli-him; fa-min wāridin yūjibu qabḍan, wa-lākin yabqā masāghun li'l-ashyā'i'l-ukhari li-anna-hu ghayru mustawfin, wa-min maqbūḍin lā masāgha li-ghayri wāridi-hi fī-hi li-anna-hu ma'khūdhun 'an-hu bi'l-kullīyati bi-wāridi-hi, ka-mā qāla ba'ḍu-hum,—anā radmun, ay lā masāgha fīya. wa-ka-dhālika'l-mabsūṭu qad yakūnu fī-hi basṭun yasa'u'l-khalqa, fa-lā yastawḥishu min akthari'l-ashyā'i, wa-yakūnu mabsūṭan lā yu'aththiru fī-hi shayy'un bi-ḥālin min al-aḥwāli. . . . wa-min adnā mūjibāti'l-qabḍi an yarida 'alā qalbi-hi wāridun mūjibu-hu ishāratun ilā 'itābin wa-ramzun bi-istiḥqāqi ta'dībin, fa-yaḥṣulu fī'l-qalbi lā maḥālata qabḍun: wa-qad yakūnu mūjiba ba'ḍi'l-wāridāti ishāratun ilā taqrībin aw iqbālin bi-naw'i luṭfin wa tarḥībin, fa-yaḥṣula li'l-qalbi basṭun. . . . wa-qad yakūnu qabḍun yashkulu 'alā ṣāḥibi-hi sababu-hu, yajidu fī qalbi-hi qabḍan lā yadrī mūjiba-hu wa-lā sababa-hu; fa-sabīlu ṣāḥibi hādhā'l-qabḍi'l-taslīmu ḥattā yamḍī dhālika'l-waqtu, li-anna-hu, law takallafa nafya-hu aw 'staqbala'l-waqta qabla hujūmi-hi 'alay-hi bi-ikhtiyāri-hi, zāda fī qabḍi-hi wa-la'alla-hu yu'addu dhālika min-hu sū'a adabin, wa-idhā 'staslama li-ḥukmi'l-waqti fa-'an qarībin yazūlu'l-qabḍu. . . . wa-qad yakūnu basṭun yaridu baghtatan wa-yuṣādifu ṣāḥiba-hu faltatan lā ya'rifu la-hu sababan, yahuzzu ṣāḥiba-hu wa-yastafizzu-hu; fa-sabīlu ṣāḥibi-hi'l-sukūnu wa-murā'ātu'l-adabi, fa-inna fī hādhā'l-waqti la-hu khaṭaran 'aẓīman fal-yaḥdhara ṣāḥibu-hu makran khafīyan, ka-dhā qāla ba'ḍu-hum,—futiḥa 'alayya bābun min al-basṭi, fa-zalaltu zallatan, fa-ḥujibtu 'an maqāmī. wa-li-hādhā qālū,—qif 'alā'l-bisāṭi, wa-iyyāka wa'l-inbisāṭa. wa-qad 'adda ahlu'l-taḥqīqi ḥālatay'l-qabḍi wa'l-basṭi min jumlati mā 'sta'ādhū min-hu li-anna-humā bi'l-iḍāfati ilā mā fawqa-humā min istiḥlāki'l-'abdi wa-indirāji-hi fī'l-ḥaqīqati faqrun wa-ḍarrun.

2. For English translation see Chapter VII, pp. 145–6.

Bhagavad-Gītā, 2. 55–72, transliterated text:

prajahāti yadā kāmān sarvān, Pārtha, manogatān,
ātmany evātmanā tuṣṭaḥ sthita-prajñas tadocyate.

duḥkheṣv anudvigna-manāḥ, sukheṣu vigata-spṛhaḥ,
vīta-rāga-bhaya-krodhaḥ sthita-dhīr munir ucyate.

yaḥ sarvatrānabhisnehas, tat-tat prāpya śubhāśubhaṁ,
nābhinandati na dveṣṭi, tasya prajñā pratiṣṭhitā.

yadā saṁharate cāyaṁ kūrmo 'ṅgānīva sarvaśaḥ
indriyāṇīndriyārthebhyas, tasya prajñā pratiṣṭhitā.

viṣayā vinivartante nirāhārasya dehinaḥ
rasa-varjaṁ; raso 'py asya paraṁ dṛṣṭvā nivartate.

yatato hy api, Kaunteya, puruṣasya vipaścitaḥ
indriyāṇi pramāthīni haranti prasabhaṁ manaḥ.

tāni sarvāni saṁyamya, yukta āsīta mat-paraḥ;
vaśe hi yasyendriyāṇi, tasya prajñā pratiṣṭhitā.

dhyāyato viṣayān puṁsaḥ sangas teṣūpajāyate,
sangāt saṁjāyate kāmaḥ, kāmāt krodho 'bhijāyate.

krodhād bhavati saṁmohaḥ, saṁmohāt smṛti-vibhramaḥ,
smṛti-bhraṁśād buddhi-nāśo, buddhi-nāśāt praṇaśyati.

rāga-dveṣa-viyuktais tu viṣayān indriyaiś caran
ātma-vaśyair vidheyātmā prasādam adhigacchati.

prasāde sarva-duḥkhānām hānir asyopajāyate;
prasanna-cetaso hy āśu buddhiḥ paryavatiṣṭhate.

nāsti buddhir ayuktasya, na cāyuktasya bhāvanā,
na cābhāvayataḥ śāntir; aśāntasya kutaḥ sukham?

indriyāṇāṁ hi caratāṁ yan mano 'nuvidhīyate,
tad asya harati prajñāṁ vāyur nāvam ivāmbhasi.

tasmād yasya, mahābāho, nigṛhītāni sarvaśaḥ
indriyāṇīndriyārthebhyas, tasya prajñā pratiṣṭhitā.

yā niśā sarva-bhūtānāṁ, tasyāṁ jāgarti saṁyamī;
yasyāṁ jāgrati bhūtāni, sā niśā paśyato muneḥ.

āpūryamānam acala-pratiṣṭhaṁ samudram āpaḥ praviśanti yadvat,
tadvat kāmā yaṁ praviśanti sarve, sa śāntim āpnoti, na kāma-kāmī.

vihāya kāmān yaḥ sarvān pumāṁś carati niḥspṛhaḥ,
nirmamo, nirahaṁkāraḥ, sa śāntim adhigacchati.

eṣā brāhmī sthitiḥ, Pārtha, naināṁ prāpya vimuhyati;
sthitvā 'syām anta-kāle 'pi brahma-nirvāṇam ṛcchati.

3. For English translation see Chapter VIII, pp. 153–4.

Māṇḍūkya Upaniṣad, §§ 2–7:

(2) sarvaṁ hy etad brahmāyam ātmā brahma. so 'yam ātmā catuṣpāt.

(3) jāgarita-sthāno bahiṣ-prajñaḥ . . . sthūla-bhug, vaiśvānaraḥ, prathamaḥ pādaḥ.

(4) svapna-sthāno 'ntaḥ-prajñaḥ . . . pravivikta-bhuk, taijaso, dvitīyaḥ pādaḥ.

(5) yatra supto na kaṁcana kāmaṁ kāmayate, na kaṁcana svapnaṁ paśyati, tat suṣuptam. suṣupta-sthānam ekībhūtaḥ prajñāna-ghana evānandamayo hy ānanda-bhuk, ceto-mukhaḥ, prājñas, tṛtīyaḥ pādaḥ.

(6) eṣa sarveśvara, eṣa sarva-jña, eṣo 'ntaryāmy, eṣa yoniḥ sarvasya, prabhavāpyayau hi bhūtānām.

(7) nāntaḥ-prajñaṁ, na bahiṣ-prajñaṁ, nobhayataḥ-prajñaṁ, na prajñāna-ghanaṁ, na prajñaṁ, nāprajñam. adṛṣṭam, avyavahāryam, agrāhyam, alakṣaṇam, acintyam, avyapadeśyam, ekātma-pratyaya-sāraṁ, prapancopaśamaṁ, śāntaṁ, śivam, advaitaṁ, caturthaṁ manyante. sa ātmā, sa vijñeyaḥ.

4. For English translation see Chapter VIII, pp. 154–5.

Gauḍapāda's *Kārikā*, 2. 12–19:

(12) kalpayaty ātmanātmānam ātmā devaḥ sva-māyayā
sa eva budhyate bhedān iti vedānta-niścayaḥ.

(13) vikaroty aparāṅ bhāvān antaś citte vyavasthitān
niyatāṅś-ca bahiścitta evaṁ kalpayate prabhuḥ.

(14) citta-kālā hi ye 'ntas tu dvaya-kālāś-ca ye bahiḥ
kalpitā eva te sarve: viśeṣo nānya-hetukaḥ.

(15) avyaktā eva ye 'ntas tu sphuṭā eva ca ye bahiḥ
kalpitā eva te sarve: viśeṣas tv indriyāntare.

(16) jīvaṁ kalpayate pūrvaṁ tato bhāvāṅ pṛthag-vidhān
bāhyān ādhyātmikāṅścaiva: yathā-vidyas tathā-smṛtiḥ.

(17) aniścitā yathā rajjur andhakāre vikalpitā
sarpa-dhārādibhir bhāvais tadvad ātmā vikalpitaḥ.

(18) niścitāyām yathā rajjvāṁ vikalpo vinivartate
rajjur eveti cādvaitaṁ tadvad ātma-viniścayaḥ.

(19) prāṇādibhir anantaiśca bhāvair etair vikalpitaḥ
māyaiṣā tasya devasya yayā saṁmohitaḥ svayam.

5. For English translation see Chapter VIII, p. 155.

Ibid., 30–38:

(30) etair eṣo 'pṛthag-bhāvaiḥ, pṛthag eveti lakṣitaḥ:
evaṁ yo veda, tattvena kalpayet so 'viśaṅkitaḥ.

(31) svapna-māye yathā dṛṣṭe, gandharva-nagaraṁ yathā,
tathā viśvam idaṁ dṛṣṭaṁ vedānteṣu vicakṣaṇaiḥ.

(32) na virodho na cotpattir, na baddho na ca sādhakaḥ,
na mumukṣur na vai mukta ity eṣā paramārthatā.

(33) bhāvair asadbhir evāyam advayena ca kalpitaḥ,
bhāvā apy advayenaiva, tasmād advayatā śivā.

(34) nātma-bhāvena nānedaṁ na svenāpi kathaṁcana,
na pṛthag nāpṛthak kiṁcid iti tattva-vido viduḥ.
(35) vīta-rāga-bhaya-krodhair munibhir veda-pāra-gaiḥ
nirvikalpo hy ayam dṛṣṭaḥ prapancopaśamo 'dvayaḥ.
(36) tasmād evaṁ viditvainam advaite yojayet smṛtim,
advaitaṁ samanuprāpya jaḍaval lokam ācaret.
(37) nistutir nirnamaskāro niḥsvadhākāra eva ca
calācala-niketaś-ca yatir yadṛcchiko bhavet.
(38) tattvam ādhyātmikaṁ dṛṣṭvā, tattvaṁ dṛṣṭvā tu bāhyataḥ,
tattvībhūtas tad-ārāmas tattvād apracyuto bhavet.

6. For English translation see Chapter VIII, pp. 157–8.

Ghazālī, *Mishkāt al-Anwār*, ed. Ṣabrī, Cairo, 1353/1935, pp. 121–3:

min hāhunā yataraqqā'l-'ārifūna min haḍīḍi'l-majāzi ilā dhurwati'l-ḥaqīqati, wa'stakmalū ma'ārija-hum, fa-ra'aw bi'l-mushāhadati'l-'ayānīyati an laysa fī'l-wujūdi illā'llāhu wa-anna kulla shay'in hālikun illā wajha-hu li-anna-hu yaṣīru hālikan fī waqtin min al-awqāti, bal hūwa hālikun azalan wa-abadan, idh lā yutaṣawwaru illā ka-dhālika, fa-inna kulla shay'in siwā-hu idhā "tubirat dhātu-hu min ḥaythu dhāti-hi, fa-hūwa 'adamun maḥḍun, wa-idhā "tubira min al-wajhi'lladhī yasrī ilay-hi'l-wujūdu min al-awwali'l-ḥaqqi, ru'iya mawjūdan, lā fī dhāti-hi, bal min al-wajhi'lladhī yalī mūjida-hu, fa-yakūnu'l-mawjūdu wajha'llāhi faqaṭ. wa-li-kulli shay'in wajhāni, wajhun ilā nafsi-hi, wa-wajhun ilā rabbi-hi. fa-hūwa bi-i'tibāri wajhi nafsi-hi 'adamun, wa-bi-i'tibāri wajhi-'llāhi wujūdun, fa-idhan lā mawjūda illā'llāha wa-wajha-hu, fa-idhan kullu shay'in hālikun illā wajha-hu azalan wa-abadan. wa-lam yaftaqir hā'ulā'i ilā qiyāmi'l-qiyāmati li-yastami'ū nidā'a'l-bārī, 'li-man al-mulku'l-yawma, li'llāhi'l-wāḥidi'l-qahhāri'. bal hādhā'l-nidā'u lā yufāriqu sam'a-hum abadan, wa-lam yafhamū min ma'nā qawli-hi 'Allāhu akbaru' anna-hu akbaru min ghayri-hi, ḥāsha li'llāhi, idh laysa fī'l-wujūdi ma'a-hu ghayru-hu ḥattā yakūna hūwa akbara min-hu, bal laysa li-ghayri-hi rutbatu'l-ma'īyati, bal rutbatu'l-taba'īyati, bal laysa li-ghayri-hi wujūdun illā min al-wajhi'lladhī yalī-hi, fa'l-mawjūdu wajhu-hu faqaṭ; wa-muḥālun an yakūna akbara min wajhi-hi, bal ma'nā-hu akbaru min an yuqāla la-hu akbaru bi-ma'nā'l-iḍāfati wa'l-muqāyasati wa-akbaru min an yudrika ghayru-hu kunha kibriyā'i-hi, nabīyan kāna aw malakan, bal lā ya'rifu'llāha kunha ma'rifati-hi illā hūwa. . . .

al-'ārifūna ba'da'l-'urūji ilā samā'i'l-ḥaqīqati 'ttafaqū 'alā anna-hum lam yaraw fī'l-wujūdi illā'l-wāḥida'l-ḥaqqa, lākinna min-hum man kāna la-hu hādhihi-'l-ḥālatu 'irfānan 'ilmīyan, wa-min-hum man ṣāra la-hu dhawqan wa-ḥālan, wa'ntafat 'an-humi'l-kathratu bi'l-kullīyati, wa'staghraqū bi'l-fardānīyati-'l-maḥḍati, wa'stahwat fī-hā 'uqūlu-hum, fa-ṣārū ka'l-mabhūtīna fī-hi, wa-lam yabqa fī-him muttasa'un li-dhikri ghayri'llāhi wa-lā li-dhikri anfusi-him ayḍan, fa-lam yabqa 'inda-hum illā'llāha, fa-sakirū sukran, waqa'a dūna-hu sulṭānu 'uqūli-him; fa-qāla ba'ḍu-hum 'anā'l-ḥaqqu', wa-qāla'l-ākharu 'subḥānī, mā a'ẓama sha'nī', wa-qāla'l-ākharu 'mā fī'l-jubbati illā'llāha'. wa-kalāmu'l-'ushshāqi fī ḥāli'l-sukri yuṭwā wa-lā yuḥkī, fa-lammā khaffa 'an-hum sukru-hum wa-ruddū ilā sulṭāni'l-'aqli'lladhī hūwa mīzānu'llāhi fī arḍi-hi, 'arafū anna dhālika lam yakun ḥaqīqata'l-ittiḥādi, bal yushbihu'l-ittiḥāda mithlu qawli'l-'āshiqi fī ḥāli farṭi'l-'ishqi:

anā man ahwā wa-man ahwā anā;
naḥnu rūḥāni ḥalalnā badanā.

fa-lā yab'udu an yafja'a'l-insānu mir'ātan fa-yanẓura fī-hā wa-lam yara'l-mir'āta qaṭṭu, fa-yaẓunna anna'l-ṣūrata'llatī ra'ā-hā fī'l-mir'āti hīya ṣūratu'l-mir'āti muttaḥidatun bi-hā, wa-yarā'l-khamra fī'l-zajāji fa-yaẓunna anna'l-khamrata lawnu'l-zajāji, fa-idhā ṣāra dhālika 'inda-hu ma'lūfan wa-rasakha fī-hi qadamu-hu 'staghraqa-hu. . . .

wa farqun bayna an yuqāla'l-khamru qadaḥun wa-bayna an yuqāla ka-anna-hu qadaḥun. wa-hādhihi'l-ḥālatu idhā ghalabat summiyat bi'l-iḍāfati ilā ṣāḥibi'l-ḥāli fanā'an, bal fanā'a'l-fanā'i li-anna-hu faniya 'an nafsi-hi wa-faniya 'an fanā'i-hi. fa-inna-hu laysa yash'uru bi-nafsi-hi fī tilka'l-ḥāli, wa-lā bi-'adami shu'ūri-hi bi-nafsi-hi, wa-law sha'ara bi-'adami shu'ūri-hi bi-nafsi-hi, la-kāna qad sha'ara bi-nafsi-hi: wa-tusammā hādhihi'l-ḥālu bi'l-iḍāfati ilā'l-mustaghriqi fī-hā bi-lisāni'l-majāzi ittiḥādan, wa-bi-lisāni'l-ḥaqīqati tawḥīdan, wa-warā'a hādhihi'l-ḥaqā'iqi ayḍan asrārun lā yajūzu'l-khawḍu fī-hā.

7. For English translation see Chapter VIII, pp. 165–6.

Junayd, *Kitāb al-Fanā*, *Islamic Quarterly*, vol. i, no. 2, 1954, pp. 79–80:
wahaba-nī-hi, thumma 'statara bī 'annī, fa-anā aḍarru'l-ashyā'i 'alayya. al-waylu lī minnī. akāda-nī wa-'an-hu bī khada'a-nī. kāna ḥuḍūrī sababa faqdī, wa-kānat mut'atī bi-mushāhidatī kamāla jahdī. . . . afnā-nī bi-inshā'ī ka-mā anshā-nī badyan fī ḥāli fanā'ī; fa-lam ūthir 'alay-hi li-birā'ati-hi min al-āthāri, wa-lam ukhbir 'an-hu idh kāna mutawalliyan li'l-ikhbāri. a laysa qad maḥā rasmī bi-ṣifati-hi? wa-bi-imtiḥā'ī fāta 'ilmī fī qurbi-hi; fa-hūwa'l-mubdi'u ka-mā hūwa'l-mu'īdu. . . . 'wa-idhā akhadha rabbu-ka min banī Ādama' ilā qawli-hi 'shahidnā', fa-qad akhbara-ka 'azza wa-jalla anna-hu khāṭaba-hum wa-hum ghayru mawjūdīna illā bi-wujūdi-hi la-hum, idh kāna wājidan li'l-khalīqati bi-ghayri ma'nā wujūdi-hi li-anfusi-hā, bi'l-ma'nā'lladhī lā ya'lamu-hu ghayru-hu, wa-lā yajidu-hu siwā-hu. fa-qad kāna wājidan muḥīṭan shāhidan 'alay-him badyan fī ḥāli fanā'i-him 'an baqā'i-himi'lladhīna kānū fī'l-azali li'l-azali. fa-dhālika hūwa'l-wujūdu'l-rabbānī wa'l-idrāku'l-ilāhī'lladhī lā yanbaghī illā la-hu jalla wa-'azza. wa-li-dhālika qulnā inna-hu idhā kāna wājidan li'l-'abdi yujrī 'alay-hi murāda-hu min haythu yashā'u bi-ṣifati-hi'l-muta'ālīyati'llatī lā yushāriku fī-hā, kāna dhālika'l-wujūdu atamma'l-wujūdi wa-amḍā-hu lā maḥālata, wa-hūwa awlā wa-aghlabu wa-aḥaqqu bi'l-ghalbati wa'l-qahri wa-ṣiḥḥati'l-istīlā'i 'alā mā yabdū 'alay-hi, ḥattā yumḥā rasmu-hu 'āmmatan wa-yadhhaba wujūdu-hu, idh lā ṣifata basharīyata wa-wujūda laysa yaqūmu bi-hi.

8. For English translation see Chapter IX, pp. 177–9.

Swāmi Nikhilānanda, *Self-Knowledge*, Madras, Sri Ramakrishna Math, 1947, pp. 287–97: Sanskrit text of Śankara's 'Hymn of Renunciation':

dina-yāminyau sāyaṁ prātaś śaśira-vasantau punar āyātaḥ,
kālaḥ krīḍati, gacchaty āyus; tad api na muñcaty āśā-vāyuḥ.
bhaja Govindaṁ, bhaja Govindaṁ, bhaja Govindaṁ, mūḍhamate;
saṁprāpte sannihite kāle nahi nahi rakṣati ḍḍakṛñkarane.

agre vahniḥ, pṛṣṭhe bhānū, rātrau cubuka-samarpita-jānuḥ,
kara-tala-bhikṣas taru-tala-vāsas, tad api na muñcaty āśā-pāśaḥ.
bhaja Govindaṁ, etc.

yāvad vittopārjana-śaktas, tāvan nija-parivāro raktaḥ;
paścāj jīvati jarjara-dehe, vārtām ko'pi na pṛcchati gehe.
bhaja Govindaṁ, etc.

jaṭilo muṇḍī luñcita-keśaḥ kāṣāyāmbara-bahukṛta-veṣaḥ,
paśyann api ca na paśyati mūḍho udara-nimitto bahukṛta-veṣaḥ.
bhaja Govindaṁ, etc.

bhagavad-gītā kiñcid adhītā, gaṅgā-jala-lava-kaṇikā pītā,
sakṛd api yasya murāri-samarcā, tasya yamaḥ kiṁ kurute carcām?
bhaja Govindaṁ, etc.

aṅgaṁ galitaṁ palitaṁ muṇḍaṁ daśana-vihīnaṁ jātaṁ tuṇḍam;
vṛddho yāti gṛhītvā daṇḍaṁ, tad api na muñcaty āśā-piṇḍam.
bhaja Govindaṁ, etc.

bālas tāvat krīḍā-saktaḥ, tarunas tāvat taruṇī-raktaḥ,
vṛddhas tāvac cintā-magnaḥ, pare brahmani ko'pi na lagnaḥ.
bhaja Govindaṁ, etc.

punar api jananaṁ, punar api maraṇaṁ, punar api jananī-jaṭhare śayanam;
iha saṁsāre bahu-dustāre kṛpayāpāre pāhi, murāre.
bhaja Govindaṁ, etc.

punar api rajanī, punar api divasaḥ, punar api pakṣaḥ, punar api māsaḥ,
punar apy ayanaṁ, punar api varṣaṁ, tad api na muñcaty āśā-marṣam.
bhaja Govindaṁ, etc.

vayasi gate kaḥ kāma-vikāraś, śuṣke nīre kaḥ kāsāraḥ?
kṣīne vitte kaḥ parivāro, jñāte tattve kas saṁsāraḥ?
bhaja Govindaṁ, etc.

nārī-stana-bhara-nābhī-deśaṁ dṛṣṭvā māyā-mohāveśam,
etan māṅsa-vasādi-vikāraṁ manasi vicintaya vāraṁ vāram,
bhaja Govindaṁ, etc.

kas tvaṁ, ko 'haṁ, kuta āyātaḥ, ko me jananī, ko me tātaḥ?
iti paribhāvaya sarvam asāraṁ, viśvaṁ tyaktvā svapna-vicāram.
bhaja Govindaṁ, etc.

geyaṁ gītānām asahasraṁ, dhyeyaṁ śrī-pati-rūpam ajasram,
neyaṁ saj-jana-saṅge cittaṁ, deyaṁ dīna-janāya ca vittam.
bhaja Govindaṁ, etc.

yāvaj jīvo nivasati dehe, tāvat pṛcchati kuśalaṁ gehe;
gatavati vāyau dehāpāye bhāryā bibhyati tasmin kāye.
bhaja Govindaṁ, etc.

sukhataḥ kriyate rāmā-bhogaḥ, paścād dhanta śarīre rogaḥ;
yady api loke maraṇaṁ śaraṇaṁ, tad api na muñcati pāpācaraṇam.
bhaja Govindaṁ, etc.

rathyā-karpaṭa-viracita-kanthaḥ puṇyāpuṇya-vivarjita-panthaḥ,
nāhaṁ, na tvaṁ, nāyaṁ lokas; tad api kim arthaṁ kriyate śokaḥ.
bhaja Govindaṁ, etc.

kurute gangā-sāgara-gamanaṁ, vrata-paripālanam, athavā dānam;
jñāna-vihīne sarvam anena muktir na bhavati janma-śatena.
bhaja Govindaṁ, etc.

[redacted]

INDEX